For Whose Protection?

For Whose Protection?

Reproductive Hazards and
Exclusionary Policies in
the United States and Britain

Sally J. Kenney

Ann Arbor

THE UNIVERSITY OF MICHIGAN PRESS

Copyright © by the University of Michigan 1992
All rights reserved
Published in the United States of America by
The University of Michigan Press
Manufactured in the United States of America

1995   1994   1993   1992   4   3   2   1

Library of Congress Cataloging-in-Publication Data

Kenney, Sally Jane.
    For whose protection? : reproductive hazards and exclusionary
policies in the United States and Britain / Sally J. Kenney.
        p.   cm.
    Includes bibliographical references and index.
    ISBN 0-472-10235-4 (alk. paper). — ISBN 0-472-08176-4 (pbk. :
alk. paper)
    1. Sex discrimination in employment—Law and legislation—United
States.   2. Pregnant women—Employment—Law and legislation—United
States.   3. Sex discrimination in employment—Law and legislation—
Great Britain.   4. Pregnant women—Employment—Law and legislation—
Great Britain.   I. Title.
K1772.K46   1992
344.41'014133—dc20
[344.10414133]   92-28363
                                                                    CIP

For Norman

Acknowledgments

I would first like to acknowledge the number of people who helped me gain access to information such as Sheila McKechnie, and the staff at the ASTMS office in Bishops Stortford, and Dave Gee of the G&M in Esher. Thanks, too, to the many other trade union health and safety representatives who gave generously of their time. My gratitude extends also to the few employers or employers' groups who agreed to interviews: representatives from Ford, Fissons, the Lead Industries Association, and the Confederation of British Industry. To the faculty at the Socio-Legal Center in Wolfson, thanks to Peter Manning for help in formulating the structure of the dissertation and for his encouragement, and Keith Hawkins and Paul Fenn for their efforts, unfortunately unsuccessful, to obtain access to Health and Safety Executive documents concerning lead. Thanks to all the staff at the Health and Safety Executive and Equal Opportunities Commission, particularly Richard Collins, Alice Leonard, and Christine Jackson, for their frank comments. The others are best left unnamed. Thanks, too, to John Manos, editor of the *Health and Safety Information Bulletin*, and Michael Rubenstein, editor of the *Equal Opportunities Review*, for helping me gain access to information about employers in Britain.

Special thanks to Ed Cooke, former counsel for the House Education and Labor Committee, for help obtaining information from the Equal Employment Opportunity Commission, and for his unfailing belief in the importance of the issue and my project. My thanks to Donna Lenhoff of the Women's Legal Defense Fund for her time and for sharing materials about the 1980 EEOC guidelines. My admiration and gratitude extend to Joan Bertin of the ACLU Women's Rights Project, who, more than any other person, has kept this issue alive and provides legal advice to women excluded from jobs. Thanks for the inspiration, for the example you set, for your legal and political advice, for your encouragement and sense of humor, and for your generosity in sharing materials. Thank you, too, for your helpful comments on chapter 6.

For financial assistance, my gratitude extends to Princeton University, as well as the Department of Law at the Northeast London Polytechnic for employing me and sharing its scarce library, photocopying, and computing facilities. Thanks, too, to Anne Bottomley.

I am indebted to all those who read and commented on my manuscript: to Laurie Gibson, for reading and commenting on chapters 1 through 6, to Elizabeth Vallance of Queen Mary College for reading a draft of chapter 1 and for her support and encouragement, to G. R. Boynton for his comments on the Introduction, and to Mary Hilderbrand and Lonnie Carlisle for support in a dissertation group, for listening to presentations and for reading drafts.

Thanks to Barbara Harrisson, Sue Barlow, and other fellow members of the London Women and Work Hazards Group for their information, support, and dedication to the issue.

For help in selecting my topic and formulating my thesis, thanks to Stan Katz. Thanks to both Stan Katz and Kay Warren for support and encouragement above and beyond the call of duty. Without their efforts, the dissertation would not have been defended, nor would it have evolved into a book. Special thanks to Kay Warren for her dedication to fostering a strong intellectual environment for Women's Studies at Princeton University. I would also like to acknowledge Walter Murphy, who supervised the dissertation, and Jennifer Hochschild, who served on my committee.

Many people contributed to turning the dissertation into a book, foremost of course is LeAnn Fields at the University of Michigan Press, the editor of one's dreams. LeAnn is blessed not only with a wonderful sense of humor, but also with the ability to offer very carefully crafted praise that secures maximum effect. Christina Milton did a magnificent job of copyediting; for her skill, patience, and understanding, I am most grateful. Thanks to Berenice Carroll for reading the manuscript and for her detailed suggestions, support, and encouragement. Thanks to Jeff Cox and Linda Kerber for their gentle, yet astute, efforts to improve the historical chapter. Thanks to Chris McCrudden and Michael Rubenstein for their thoughtful comments on chapter 3.

To Martha Chamallas, I would like to offer my thanks for many things, first and foremost for her careful reading of the entire manuscript and detailed comments, but also for mentoring me as a legal scholar and for offering direction in reading and thinking in both sex discrimination doctrine and feminist legal thought. I owe her, Margery Wolf, Florence Babb, and Susan Birrell, and the Program in Women's Studies at the University of Iowa, thanks for a working computer, research assistants, and for a supportive feminist intellectual environment. Thanks, too, to Donna Bailey for help with editing. Thanks to Mary Tabor for research assistance. To Nancy Reincke, thanks for superb editing, proofreading, foraging in the law library (not the normal stomping ground for English doctoral students), humor, and support. Thanks to the Feminist Theory reading group for intellectual stimulation and much merriment, and also to our work group: Susan Lawrence, Phyllis Rooney, Teresa Mangum, and Geeta Patel, for their support.

My heartfelt thanks to my friends and family for listening to me drone on for years about this project and for belief in its importance, even before

International Union, UAW v. Johnson Controls.[1] Without the love and support of Midge Quant and Mary Harper, the dissertation would never have been written. Special thanks to Linda Kenney and Jack Kaplan for their support and encouragement and payment of exorbitant phone bills. Thanks, too, to my mom, Ruth Kenney-Randolph, for her enthusiasm for the project and for financial support that included buying me a computer so I could work at home. To Norman S. J. Foster, thanks for reading many drafts, for daring to criticize regardless of the response, for proofreading, late night printing and suggestions, for computer wizardry, for an even temper, for enthusiasm, and for your unwavering belief that it really was going to be a book one day.

Finally, to Jacky Page, Barbara Christman, Betty Riggs, Donna Martin, Lola Rymer, Mary Tucker, Rita Zuniga, Carole Doerr, Sylvia Hayes, Theresa Wright, Virginia Green, Pat Grant, Gloyce Qualls, Queen Elizabeth Foster, Opal Whitehair, Linda Matheny, Denise Cline, Mary Carpenter, Carolyn Lowe, Joyce Richardson, Linda Moore, Deborah Nicely, Linda Huggins, Lois Sweetman, Linda Burdick, Elsie Nason, Mary Estelle Schmitt, Shirley Jean Mackey, Mary Craig, Anna May Penny, Donald Penny, and all the women and men who stand up for their right to safe work and right to control their own reproductive choices, thanks for the inspiration.

1. International Union, United Automobile, Aerospace and Agricultural Implement Workers of America, UAW, et al. v. Johnson Controls, Inc., 111 S.Ct 1196 (1991).

Contents

Introduction

This book is about employers who exclude women, whose infertility is not medically documented, from allegedly hazardous work because they might become pregnant and what happened when those women charged their employers with unlawful sex discrimination in British and U.S. courts and tribunals. The responses of judges, trade unionists, workers, employers, scientists, feminists, and policymakers to such policies vary enormously. I define exclusionary policies as those that exclude all nonsterilized, premenopausal women from allegedly hazardous work. Just as those who oppose abortion call themselves pro life and have won a measure of acceptance for that term, employers and commentators usually prefer the term *fetal protection policies*, however partial their protection of future generations and however removed from an actual fetus. The nomenclature is important. Calling exclusionary policies fetal protection policies renders women invisible—mere vessels that may contain a fetus. Once women are mere vessels, we can conceive of the woman as separate from the fetus, capable of behaving in ways that endanger it, rather than seeing the fetus as part of the woman. Fetal protection policies seek to protect potential fetuses rather than women. The term *protective* suggests a benign and laudable policy, yet one that is also paternalistic. Potential fetuses cannot protect themselves, so employers must intervene on their behalf.

The term *exclusionary policy* places the emphasis on the women whom employers seek to remove or bar from jobs. It connotes discrimination. Women workers have always known that protection is at best a mixed blessing. Chapter 1 recounts the history of protective labor legislation in both Britain and the United States and demonstrates how women fought to eliminate the disadvantages that ensued from such laws. The history makes clear that protective legislation is often motivated by a desire to eliminate competition or to exert control over women as well as a desire to improve their working conditions. I prefer the term *exclusionary policies* precisely because I do not see such policies as protecting the unborn but as discriminating against women.

To say that exclusionary policies are discriminatory is not to take the position that employers are motivated by a sinister desire to discriminate against women, to relegate them to low-paid jobs (which are often equally hazardous), or to keep them in the home, although some evidence supports such a proposition. My claim is that the policies reflect gendered thinking.[1] Employers and judges often see a woman's childbearing role as superseding her role as a breadwinner. They interpret scientific evidence differently when it is about women rather than men, and they adopt a different posture toward risks resulting from women's exposure to hazards. They respond to the risk of tort liability resulting from women's exposure but not the same or even greater risk stemming from men's exposure. Finally, supporters of exclusionary policies accept the proposition that if women are different from men, employers can treat them less favorably by excluding them from jobs. When men's reproductive health is threatened, employers ignore the risk, inform their workers (who may choose to assume that risk), or shut down production altogether. Excluding men is unthinkable.

Exploring judges' rulings on exclusionary policies exposes the inadequacy of the concept of equality upon which our ideas about discrimination rest. Although the differences in outcomes of cases in Britain and the United States are significant (particularly after the Supreme Court's decision in *UAW v. Johnson Controls*[2]) and reflect differences between the two countries' legal and political institutions, the similarities between judges' handling of the cases are instructive. Judges in both countries expressed similar difficulties in applying sex discrimination law to cases of exclusionary policies. They are hard cases—the kind of cases one puts on law school exams. Some judges see these cases as hard because the differential treatment of women stems from "real," that is, biological, differences between men and women rather than from stereotypes about men's and women's different social roles. As such, some judges have found exclusionary policies to be reasonable and interpreted sex discrimination law to permit them.

Feminists find cases on exclusionary policies hard because exposing the discriminatory aspects of the case requires a sophistication in both science and law. The political choices one makes in taking sides in the scientific and legal debates on this issue do not lend themselves easily to picket signs, sound bites, or one-page memos. The policies seemingly force feminists to choose between advocating either special or equal treatment. Special treatment may lead to barring women from more than 20 million jobs in the United States alone. Equal treatment may fail to accommodate legitimate fears about damaging both men's and women's reproductive capacities. Feminists in both

---

1. See Carol Smart's discussion of the law as gendered rather than sexist or male in "The Woman in Legal Discourse," Women's Studies Paper Series, University of Utrecht, May 16, 1991.

2. International Union, United Automobile, Aerospace and Agricultural Implement Workers of America, UAW v. Johnson Controls, Inc., 111 S.Ct. 1196 (1991).

countries must deal with how to accommodate men's and women's different reproductive capacities and the consequences of treating them differently even if they do not articulate the debate in terms of special versus equal treatment. Thus, examining cases on exclusionary policies helps bring debates over equality and protective legislation into sharper focus. How does the dominant vision of equality encompass the issue of biological differences? How have judges and employers interpreted discrimination law to deal with this matter? What alternative vision of equality can feminists offer? Embedded in this debate are competing views about who should control women's bodies and competing visions of how to reconcile women's roles as childbearers and breadwinners.

This book leads those interested in exclusionary policies through the mine field by focusing on legal cases. The Supreme Court's landmark decision in *UAW v. Johnson Controls*, declaring exclusionary policies to be unlawful sex discrimination, put the question of the discriminatory impact of policies on reproductive hazards back on the public policy agenda after more than ten years of forced hibernation. Policymakers may be interested in my arguments that exclusionary policies discriminate against both men and women, are not scientifically justified, and are unsound as a matter of public policy.

Exploring the public policy debate raised by litigation over exclusionary policies is but one small part of this book. I use one area of law to explore and illuminate important institutional differences between the legal and political systems in Britain and the United States. Specialists in British politics or in comparative law may find the analysis of the different legal systems, feminist movements, sex discrimination law, and health and safety policy-making interesting. By comparing and contrasting litigation on exclusionary policies in both countries, the book provides a concrete example of the significance of political and legal differences. When considering broader institutional effects, I try to illuminate the significance of the characteristics of well-placed individuals, be they judges, members of tribunals, officials at the enforcement agencies, litigators, or plaintiffs. Their talents, vision, prejudices, and limitations are important variables in explaining the outcomes, as are the institutional variables.

While the book has all the strengths of a case study, it also has similar limitations. The sample of cases is small. Although it provides an example of the differences between U.S. and British judges, feminist groups, and health and safety policy-making processes and confirms and illustrates what others have shown, this case study does not, in and of itself, prove or disprove general statements about political institutions, judges, feminist movements, or legal systems.

I compare cases on exclusionary policies in the United States and Britain because the British sex discrimination law was modeled on U.S. law and the closeness of the laws provides an ideal case to show systemic differences, but the comparison is valuable independent of the academic enterprise of comparing political and legal institutions. Looking at similarities in judges and members of tribunals' reasoning on these cases exposes the gendered nature of law and widespread problems with the prevailing liberal conception of equality.[3] The book uses cases on exclusionary policies as a way of critiquing and exploring competing conceptions of discrimination. At the heart of these disputes are disagreements about sexual differences, the nature of oppression, the objectivity and neutrality of law, and the vision of equality.

Those interested in discrimination law or theories of equality may find the consolidation and synthesis of information about litigation on exclusionary policies and the application of legal theory to this question useful. I believe the larger contribution is bringing feminist theory to bear on legal analysis by taking a small set of cases and analyzing legal opinions; the results of such analyses may alter how we, and, I hope, judges and policymakers as well, conceptualize discrimination.

Feminist theory brings an understanding and critique of the sex/gender dichotomy to an analysis of exclusionary policies. Second, it explores how differences are socially constructed and readily translate into disadvantage, how differentiation leads to hierarchy. Third, the basis of feminist theory is women's experience. Feminist ethics have offered a critique of philosophy's penchant for treating social and moral questions in the abstract. The abstract framing of questions often conceals important conceptual choices with real political consequences. Instead, feminist theorists invite us to consider important questions by placing them in the contexts of real women's lives. Fourth, feminists have a clear answer to the question of who should control women's bodies, an answer infrequently reflected in social practice. Finally, feminist methodology encourages women whose lives are affected by policies to develop their own critique and agenda for change. Scholars and legislators must listen to women. This approach extends to the proposition that white women do not speak for women of color nor middle-class women for working-class women. I shall deal with each point briefly in turn.

Feminists drew a distinction between sex and gender for a political purpose: to show that the roles society assigns to women are socially constructed. They do not flow naturally and inevitably from biology, but are chosen and created. The category of sex encompasses fixed, largely immutable biological differences that are given, true, and indisputable facts. Gender includes the characteristics that society ascribes to each biological sex— for example, nurturing, aggression, or intuition. By exploring cultural variations in the set of characteristics ascribed to the sexes as well as how these

---

3. For an explanation of the distinction between a concept and a conception see Ronald Dworkin, *Taking Rights Seriously* (Cambridge: Harvard University Press, 1977).

changed over time and vary across race and class, feminists demonstrated that the rhetoric of biological difference was deployed to make any given societal arrangement seem natural and, therefore, unchangeable and right, even ordained by God.[4]

The sex/gender dichotomy was useful in showing the variability of gender—gender characteristics were not caused by sex differences but, instead, were mapped onto them. As feminists investigated the variability of gender they also discovered the variability of sex. Not only did society's definition of what it was to be masculine or feminine and what was appropriate work for men and women change over time and vary across cultures, but the understanding of what constituted sex differences varied as well. Greek philosophers argued that the male contributed the entire embryo and the female was just an incubator and that women suffered from the malady of the wandering womb.[5] Scientists once thought that the placenta was a nonpermeable membrane that protected the fetus from all toxic elements. Theologians argued that male and female fetuses received a soul at different times. In the nineteenth century, physicians believed that if girls used their brains it diverted energy from their reproductive organs, necessary for procreation.[6]

As feminists began to show the variability of gender and to deny that gender flowed naturally from sex, the radical or postmodern critique questioned the very dichotomy of sex and gender. It began to seem more plausible to believe that our understanding of biological difference reflects our cultural notions of male and female and the values attached to each. The body is a text of culture.[7] Even if one took a middle position between empiricism and postmodernism, that is, between believing there are objective, knowable sex differences that are not a mere reflection of values and believing that biological differences are mere social constructs, one would have to admit that cultural bias infects our choice of where to look for answers to scientific questions, influences what questions are important, and determines the language and metaphors we use to describe scientific findings.[8] The culture's shaping of the questions and sense of where to look for answers dramatically

4. Janet Sayrs, *Biological Politics: Feminist and Anti-Feminist Perspectives* (London: Tavistock, 1982).

5. See Carol Delaney, "The Meaning of Patriarchy and the Virgin Birth Debate," *Man* 21 (September 1986): 508.

6. See Ruth Hubbard, "The Political Nature of 'Human Nature,'" in *Theoretical Perspectives on Sexual Difference*, ed. by Deborah L. Rhode (New Haven: Yale University Press, 1990), 63–73; see also other essays in that volume, and Sayrs, 8–22.

7. Susan R. Bordo, "The Body and the Reproduction of Femininity: A Feminist Appropriation of Foucault," in *Gender/Body/Knowledge: Feminist Reconstructions of Being and Knowing*, ed. by Alison Jaggar and Susan R. Bordo (New Brunswick, N.J.: Rutgers University Press, 1989), 15.

8. Emily Martin, "The Egg and the Sperm: How Science Has Constructed a Romance Based on Stereotypical Male-Female Roles," *Signs* 16 (1991): 485–501.

affects the production of scientific knowledge. For example, despite our belief that scientists have now proven that both men and women contribute to reproduction—women the eggs, men the sperm—thus overturning the ideas of the ancient Greeks, nearly all scientific studies of reproductive hazards continue to study only women's exposure.[9] Not surprisingly, the result is that evidence shows that pregnant women's exposure to some substances poses a risk to the fetus, while little evidence shows how men's exposure to toxic substances might adversely affect their offspring.

Scientists have most recently debunked what has been labeled "the macho sperm theory." The way scientists conceptualized reproduction was that only the fittest, strongest, perfect sperm streaked through to fertilize the passive egg. The possibility that the "most competent" sperm may be damaged was unthinkable. Now scientists believe that the egg chemically "beckons" sperm to it, calling into question the passive egg–active sperm model.[10] Scientists now believe that the egg and sperm are mutually active partners.[11] As Dr. Davis from the National Academy of Sciences quipped, "You don't have to be Sigmund Freud to figure out there are cultural factors to say why we have paid so much attention to the female and so little to the male."[12] These scientific understandings in turn shape the development of employment policies.

If what constitutes scientific truth is constantly changing and reflects the views of the investigator or cultural norms, then the dichotomy between sex and gender breaks down. There are no longer undisputed truths of sex differences distinct from culturally constructed views about gender differences. Both feminists and antifeminists now attack the notion of the dichotomy, although feminists recognize its usefulness. The antifeminist argues that what is wrong with the dichotomy is that gender distinctions are the direct result of fixed differences between the sexes, appropriately recognized by society. There is no dichotomy because it is all sex. Feminists, after creating the category of gender to argue that differences between men and women are cultural constructs, are moving toward the position that it is all gender—there is no discoverable truth of sexual difference separate from society's values.[13]

---

9. Devra Lee Davis, "Fathers and Fetuses," *New York Times*, January 1, 1991.

10. "Chemical May Draw Sperm to Egg," *New York Times*, April 2, 1991.

11. Martin, 494.

12. Sandra Blakeslee, "Research on Birth Defects Turns to Flaws in Sperm," *New York Times*, January 1, 1991.

13. These arguments are one small piece of a larger debate within feminist theory about epistemology. See Mary E. Hawkesworth, "Knowers, Knowing, Known: Feminist Theory and Claims of Truth," *Signs* 14 (1989): 533–57, and her discussion of Sandra Harding and Merill Hintikka, eds., *Discovering Reality: Feminist Perspectives on Epistemology, Metaphysics, Methodology and Philosophy of Science* (Dordrecht, Holland: Reidel, 1983); Sandra Harding, *The Science Question in Feminism* (Ithaca, N.Y.: Cornell University Press, 1986); Nancy Hartsock, *Money, Sex and Power: Towards a Feminist Historical Materialism* (New York: Longman, 1983);

Chapters 3 and 4 show how one's views about the sex/gender dichotomy and the nature of sex differences affects one's view about whether discrimination has occurred. Calling into question this dichotomy enhances our understanding of discrimination. Deconstructing and critiquing how judges and policymakers understand it is an important part of feminist legal thought, relevant to cases on exclusionary policies. Chapters 3 and 4 demonstrate how discrimination law rests on a dichotomy between sex and gender so that it is not discrimination if employers act on the basis of "real," that is, biological, sex differences.

As well as offering insight into the sex and gender dichotomy, feminist theory, particularly the work of feminist legal scholars, provides a critique of how difference is created and how it translates into disadvantage. Feminists face a dilemma. They must use the category of women as an organizing tool to fight women's oppression. In scholarship, focusing on women's differences from men has been an important tool for questioning prevailing theories of psychological development or the notion of the Renaissance or what constitutes politics. Feminists have shown how middle-class white men are the norm and women and other "others" are silenced, marginalized, and excluded when they fail to conform to that norm. Emphasizing difference risks valorizing the characteristics of the oppressed while reinforcing and perpetuating socially constructed differences, thereby legitimating our own subordination. Furthermore, by emphasizing women's differences from men, we risk falling into essentialism, creating a category of "woman" that deemphasizes differences among women and establishes white, middle-class, heterosexual women as the norm and silences other women.

What to do about what Harvard legal scholar Martha Minow calls the "dilemma of difference" has plagued feminists at least since the nineteenth century.

> Focusing on differences poses the risk of recreating them. Especially when used by decision makers who award benefits and distribute burdens, traits of difference can carry meanings uncontrolled and unwelcomed by those to whom they are assigned. Yet denying those differences undermines the value they may have to those who cherish them as part of their own identity.[14]

Both British and U.S. feminists faced the dilemma in confronting the question of protective labor legislation for women in the nineteenth and twentieth centuries. British and U.S. feminists face the problem again today in con-

---

Alison Jaggar, *Feminist Politics and Human Nature* (Totowa, N.J.: Rowman and Allanheld, 1983).

14. Martha Minow, "Justice Engendered," *Harvard Law Review* 101 (1987): 12. See discussion on pp. 72–73, in this volume.

sidering policies for pregnancy, childbirth, and parenting. Comparing British and U.S. feminists to each other and over time sheds light on what U.S. feminists have called the special versus equal treatment debate. Feminists have different strategies for dealing with this dilemma. British, and even European, feminists do not try to resolve the dilemma the same way, nor is either group monolithic.

In both Britain and the United States, feminists have used litigation as a point around which to rally, to educate, to set the agenda, and to debate. Cases on exclusionary policies, like cases on pregnancy discrimination, provide an opportunity for critiquing and challenging prevailing limited notions of equality and the acceptance of treating those who are different less favorably. It also provides an opportunity for comparing and contrasting different feminist approaches to the same problem. Feminists, like disability rights activists, have questioned why it is just, reasonable, and lawful to penalize people for varying from a socially constructed norm that privileges the characteristics and experiences of one group of people. Why is conforming to the characteristics of the dominant group the only way to obtain the benefits of society? Should gays and lesbians have to show that they are just like "normal" heterosexual couples to avoid criminal sanctions for their conduct? Feminists have questioned why being different than men—for example in physically bearing children—is a justification for being second-class workers. Why should difference translate to disadvantage?

The third contribution of feminist theory that is useful for understanding cases on exclusionary policies is placing abstract moral questions in the context of women's lives. By abstracting moral or legal questions from the particulars of a case, it is easier to make unexamined political choices in that process of abstraction or framing the questions. For example, political scientist Rosalind Petchesky shows how, by abstracting, we have posed the woman and fetus as moral agents with competing rights and interests.[15] To do so we must symbolically take the fetus out of the woman's body and see the two as separate. In fact, we can only have this icon or symbol of a disembodied fetus, a symbol that has been so powerful in the pro life movement, if we are thinking of pregnant women as empty space.

Legal cases, too, abstract legal questions from the complex facts of a case. This method of framing a legal question often precludes raising other political questions and obscures the realm of choice in constructing the question. For example, in cases on exclusionary policies, judges may ask: Should employers protect potential life? When framed in this way, it is hard to answer in the negative. Yet if we look at the question in the concrete, by looking at

---

15. Rosalind Petchesky, "Fetal Images: The Power of Visual Culture in the Politics of Reproduction," *Feminist Studies* 13 (Summer 1987): 263–92.

what sorts of employers have implemented exclusionary policies, what their employment histories reveal about their commitment to both equality and health and safety, and how they implemented their policies, their efforts seem less noble. The way employers have gone about pursuing a laudable goal triggers suspicion and brings all such policies into disrepute. Chapters 5, 6, and 7 scrutinize the details of the policies by going beyond the legal opinions.

Fourth, feminist theory takes a position on the question of who should control women's bodies. Connected to the symbolic removal of the fetus from women's bodies in the debate over abortion are prosecuting and incarcerating pregnant women who abuse alcohol or illegal drugs.[16] Many people are alarmed by the idea of pregnant women using drugs, as they are alarmed at the idea of pregnant women working with hazardous substances. Feminists, however, reject the idea of using criminal law to solve the problem of substance abuse during pregnancy and worry about the way in which police and prosecutors would selectively enforce the law.[17] Similarly, feminists reject the idea that employers can be trusted to protect the reproductive capacities of all employees. They doubt that so-called fetal protection policies will actually protect workers from risks rather than merely exclude women and leave men without protection. Who, as a group, has the better track record of looking after the health of fetuses? Mothers or chemical companies? Women or employers? Should employers leave some choices to women, choices it continues to leave to men? Or should the state permit employers to exclude women, regardless of their parenting choices, while leaving men at risk?

Finally, feminist theory requires that we listen to women whose lives are affected by policies. What do women workers say about exclusionary policies? What do men workers, whose reproductive health is also at risk, say? What sort of policies would women workers develop if they had power? Why have working women challenged, rather than applauded, exclusionary policies?

Feminist theory clarifies the issues raised by litigation over exclusionary policies, explains the perplexing variation in responses to exclusionary policies, and exposes what is wrong with policies that strike so many as reasonable. Analyzing these cases highlights important political and legal differences in institutions and social movements in Britain and the United States. Exploring the similarities in judges' reasoning in these cases and similarities in the development of doctrines on sex discrimination law, these cases provide an opportunity for rethinking the concept of discrimination embedded in the law and contributing to a feminist re-vision of equality.

---

16. Janet Gallagher, "Prenatal Invasions and Interventions: What's Wrong with Fetal Rights," *Harvard Women's Law Journal* 10 (Spring 1987): 9–58.

17. See Sherrill Cohen and Nadine Taub, eds., *Reproductive Laws for the 1990s* (Clifton, N.J.: Humana Press, 1988).

CHAPTER 1

The Historical Context for Exclusionary Policies

The history of exclusionary policies and protective legislation shows how beliefs about the biological basis of sex differences have been used to justify public policies that treat men and women differently, and usually treat women less favorably than men. Our understanding of the facts of biological difference, their translation into practice, their magnification of gender differences, and their role in the perpetuation of the subordination of women vary dramatically over time and cultures as well as between races and classes of the same society at any one time. Static, transhistorical, universal theories about women's oppression have largely given way to studies exploring variations in how oppression operated and how women resisted. Similarly, understanding the oppression of women as resulting from conscious and intentional acts, creating the image of a transhistorical conspiracy—characteristic of early radical feminist scholarship—has been modified by an expanded notion of power. Power lies both in the ability to determine how sex differences are conceived, as well as the ability to have that conception reflected in public policies. As Susan Bordo notes, drawing on Foucault,

> we must first abandon the idea of power as something possessed by one group and leveled against another, and we must think instead of the network of practices, institutions, and technologies that sustain positions of dominance and subordination within a particular domain . . . . we need an analytics adequate to describe a power whose central mechanisms are not repressive, but *constitutive*.[1]

Analyzing exclusionary policies and protective legislation reveals how gender gets mapped onto biological difference, and how constituting women as vessels for reproduction operates to women's disadvantage.

Our understanding of the science of reproduction, and particularly reproductive hazards in the workplace, reflects societal norms about gender

---

1. Susan R. Bordo, "The Body and the Reproduction of Femininity: A Feminist Appropriation of Foucault," in *Gender/Body/Knowledge: Feminist Reconstructions of Being and Knowing*, ed. by Alison Jaggar and Susan R. Bordo (New Brunswick, N.J.: Rutgers University Press, 1989), 15.

roles. Our values and ways of thinking about social practices shape where we look for information, how we conceptualize the reproductive process, and how we conceive of biological differences. Yet we often treat scientific findings as objective, universal truths rather than as cultural products. Scientific "findings" become the building blocks for social practice as if they were unshakable foundations on which to base public policy. Scientific evidence can be used to challenge conventional understandings or to reinforce them or both. This study focuses on how judges, policymakers, and employers interpret and employ these "objective" facts to reinforce social practices that may be under threat or changing.

The history of reproductive hazards shows how scientific and conventional understandings of sex differences translate into public policies. Recounting the dramatic story of thalidomide as well as examining the incidence of sterility and other reproductive effects from workplace exposures demonstrates how scientific information may be transposed by the media, is filtered into public consciousness, and is embedded in public policy. The media's reporting of accidents and risks is often not a measured one, particularly if it has anything to do with women and reproduction. Instead, certain risks or incidents receive sensationalistic coverage while other, equally serious or even more serious, threats are ignored. Yet our understanding of the evidence shapes not only what research gets done but also the direction of public policy and our acceptance of workplace practices.

The historical context for exclusionary policies encompasses more than the stories about reproductive hazards in the late twentieth century—it includes the history of protective legislation in Britain and the United States in the last 150 years. Protective legislation is the general term for laws passed in the late nineteenth and early twentieth centuries to prohibit women from holding certain jobs, to restrict the number of hours they could work, and to regulate the conditions of their employment.[2] That we refer to this disparate body of legislation by a single term and call it protective shows that its opponents lost an important rhetorical battle. The legislation often failed to protect men and women workers most at risk, and many viewed the protection as a thin guise for discrimination. The application of the term *protective* gets stretched to the limit when it is used to describe bans on women working in certain industries altogether, or bans on married women's employment. Bowing to convention, I will use the term *protective legislation* to encompass all restrictions, yet I question both the motives of its proponents and the asserted beneficial effects of such laws.

Not surprisingly, many commentators who have analyzed exclusionary policies in the late twentieth century, particularly in the United States, saw

---

2. See Olive Banks, *Faces of Feminism: A Study of Feminism as a Social Movement* (Oxford: Martin Robertson, 1981).

parallels between protective legislation and exclusionary policies. Feminists not only quickly saw the threat to women's employment opportunities, but they noticed that the proponents' professed motive of concern for women often coexisted with a desire to remove women from competition and an (often unconscious) acceptance of asserted biological and social differences just as it had in the past. As feminist legal scholar Barbara Babcock noted, the persistence of the debate over protective laws suggests that "it [the controversy] has always been based in large part on conflicting ideologies about sex roles and the family."[3] The sincere goals of middle-class reformers to improve working conditions for women (and all workers) meshed easily with other, less laudable goals. A variety of motivations converged, and, in both eras, each side questioned the other's motives; the slurs and accusations are remarkably similar.

The partial and limited nature of both protective legislation and exclusionary policies made feminists suspicious. Men needed protection too, and the state rarely extended the restrictions to men. The laws only covered certain industries, often leaving the most exploited workers without any protection. Many job categories dominated by women, particularly those deemed essential however dangerous, remained unregulated. Feminists were not only suspicious of the selective nature of the application of protective and exclusionary policies across different employment sectors, but were quick to notice that support for protective or exclusionary policies did not translate into support for other public policies that ostensibly served the same goals of enhancing maternal and fetal health, such as prenatal care and parental leave.

The effects of protective legislation, like those of exclusionary policies, were hotly contested. Critics claimed they cost women jobs, reduced wages, and further segregated the market. Feminists worried that reinforcing the perceptions of significant differences in men's and women's roles in reproduction, as well as accepting men's and women's different responsibilities for housework and child care, further reinforced different and unequal gender roles in other domains. Acknowledging difference soon led to penalizing difference as difference became disadvantage.

For both sets of policies, women became an undifferentiated group, defined by their biological capacity regardless of their reproductive choices. The role women played in childrearing became naturalized: women's biological characteristics were used as the justification for different social roles. Reproduction became what women were for, their biological destiny. Woman equals mother. Women's health became a public concern that justified state control of their working conditions and their bodies. Women maintained little, if any, say over what public policy options they considered optimal. (Legisla-

---

3. Barbara Allen Babcock et al., *Sex Discrimination and the Law: Causes and Remedies* (Boston: Little, Brown and Company, 1975), 246.

tures passed protective laws before women had the vote.) Feminists commented that treating all women as frail because some have been weakened by childbirth is like treating all men as disabled because some are disabled veterans.[4]

The varied voices of working-class women have been infrequently heard in the debates over protective legislation and exclusionary policies. Their position on protective legislation was overlooked as middle-class reformers debated middle-class feminists. Furthermore, by focusing on women's special needs and debating whether women should work at all and, if so, in what sorts of jobs, attention was diverted from what needed to be changed about the workplace. It is always easier to remove some workers than to make the workplace safe for everyone. Dividing workers reduces their ability to assert common interests.

Examining the variety of feminist responses to protective legislation in the past informs our understanding of current exclusionary policies. The history of protective legislation shows how feminists have sought to accommodate difference, yet resist the danger that recognizing difference will be to women's disadvantage and lead inevitably to discrimination. Which groups have embraced the goal of formal legal equality and for what ends? Exploring the history provides a basis for understanding how feminists in Britain and the United States have responded to exclusionary policies. In addition, the history provides an understanding of how perspectives on the facts of biological difference are marshaled in support of employment policies.

Why compare the history of reproductive hazards and protective legislation in the United States with the history in Britain? The history reveals that the battles took place in different arenas. A comparison highlights the significance of where the battles took place—in courts, in legislatures, or in the executive branch—which reflect differences in the two political systems and political cultures. It also indicates where the battles over exclusionary policies might take place in the future. Knowing in which arena the debates may take place makes it easier to predict the outcome or at least what factors will be most important.

Furthermore, a comparative approach enlarges our understanding of how public policies incorporate perceptions of sex differences and illuminates how some feminists came to believe that public policies should recognize and accommodate biological differences. British feminists were more receptive to recognizing difference while their U.S. counterparts have been gridlocked in a special treatment versus equal treatment debate. Both groups must respond to the same set of issues. A comparative analysis broadens our own debate by suggesting alternative approaches to the same problem.

---

4. William H. Chafe, *The American Woman: Her Changing Social, Economic, and Political Roles, 1920–1970* (London: Oxford University Press, 1972), 126.

Defining Reproductive Hazards

The term *reproductive hazard* encompasses many different effects. It is important to recognize that both men and women can be injured and that the damage can occur before conception as well as during pregnancy. A *mutagen* irreparably changes the DNA of the chromosomes of either parent. These mutations are then passed on to future generations. A *teratogen* causes damage to the developing embryo (first eight weeks of pregnancy) or fetus (from eight weeks to birth). A teratogen could be *embryotoxic* or *fetotoxic* without otherwise affecting the mother in any adverse way. Scientists have explored, for example, whether aspirin is teratogenic. Aspirin has beneficial effects for the mother, but researchers wondered whether it adversely affected a developing fetus. A *gametotoxin* damages germ cells (eggs and sperm) before fertilization. Sperm may actually be more easily damaged than eggs. A woman has all of her eggs at birth, but a man produces sperm continuously and dividing cells are more susceptible to harm. On the other hand, damage to eggs is irreversible, but because the eggs are nestled in a woman's abdomen, her body protects the eggs more than a man's body protects sperm.

Teratogens may so interfere with the developing embryo or fetus that they cause a miscarriage (*abortifacient*). Substances may cause impotence or irregular periods or reduce sexual desire. A substance is *carcinogenic* if it causes the growth of tumors that may lead to cancer. Some substances, such as diethylstilbestrol, may not be carcinogenic to a woman, but may lead to an increased susceptibility to cancer in her offspring.

Clearly, reproductive hazards encompass more than substances that damage a developing fetus or cause miscarriages. Yet we often think of reproductive hazards only in those terms. When the issue of reproductive hazards is raised, most people first think of VDTs. To my knowledge, there is no evidence that VDTs damage a developing fetus, and only some disputed evidence that VDT operators have a higher rate of miscarriage. Other substances, such as radiation, lead, benzene, or vinyl chloride, have a proven record of causing a wide variety of reproductive hazards. If our goal is to produce healthy offspring, we must be concerned about substances that render men infertile, produce mutations in germ cells, or are associated with men's exposure as well as women's exposure. For example, some evidence suggests that men's exposure to lead causes changes in their sperm cells and decreases their sexual desire. Yet when dealing with lead, employers tend to focus solely on the effects lead might have on a developing fetus. Evidence suggests that pregnant women exposed to anesthetic gases have a higher rate of miscarriage than other women, but this is also the case for the partners of exposed men. Clearly, excluding one sex, or all pregnant women, is not going to solve the problem. Radiation has the potential to cause mutations in the germ cells of both men and women, to render both sexes infertile, or to interfere with a developing fetus. We know very little about the reproductive hazards of most substances and less still about the degree of risk associated with different levels of exposure. But, certainly, there is no scientific basis for assuming women are more vulnerable than men, or that most substances are likely to have only teratogenic effects.

Scientists continue to look for evidence of reproductive hazards by studying only women. A recent study of the semiconductor industry looked for evidence of an elevated rate of miscarriage among women workers. Investigators did not question the partners of exposed men or search for other types of reproductive hazards. It is not surprising, then, that what little evidence does exist focuses on the risks of women's exposure.

Two factors shape the way we think about reproductive hazards: the thalidomide tragedy and the growing awareness of occupational cancer. The German firm Chemie Grunenthal developed thalidomide and marketed it internationally in 1958 as a drug to alleviate morning sickness in pregnant women. Drugs, which people ingest voluntarily, unlike substances people encounter in the workplace, must undergo an extensive battery of tests to establish their safety before companies may sell them in either Britain or the United States. When the company tested thalidomide, it did not produce malformations in rats, but it did produce malformations in the offspring of rabbits in later tests.[5] Because thalidomide only produced malformations in certain species, and because not all women who took thalidomide during pregnancy gave birth to malformed children, only after thalidomide caused thousands of malformed children to be born did governmental agencies in both countries make tests for drugs even more stringent. The company withdrew thalidomide from the market in 1961.

The children who were born deformed shared a characteristic deformity: truncated or missing arms and legs and other organ and facial defects. This striking, repeated deformity made it possible to identify the cause.[6] The British Royal Commission on Civil Liability reported in 1978 that 8,000 to 10,000 children worldwide were born deformed as a result of exposure to thalidomide. Although the drug company never formally admitted liability, it did pay £20 million compensation in Britain to settle claims out of court.[7]

The thalidomide tragedy raised people's awareness of the possibility that drugs and other substances could interfere with the development of a fetus

---

5. The thalidomide tragedy cast severe doubts on the adequacy of animal tests for identifying substances that may pose serious dangers to humans. See A. C. Fletcher, *Reproductive Hazards of Work* (Manchester: Equal Opportunities Commission, 1985), 28.

6. D. H. M. Woollam, "Principles of Teratogenesis: Mode of Action of Thalidomide," *Proceedings of the Royal Society of Medicine* 58 (July 1965): 498.

7. *Report of the Royal Commission on Civil Liability and Compensation for Personal Injury*, Cmnd 7054 (London: HMSO, 1978), 300.

without adversely affecting the mother and without affecting the children of all the pregnant women who took it. It called into question the relevance of animal data for humans and made more uncertain the question of which animals were most likely to replicate human responses. It also made people more uneasy about scientific or governmental stamps of approval for drugs and undermined public confidence in scientists' ability to predict effects and the government's ability to safeguard the population against them. The thalidomide experience showed that, even in the strongest of cases, it is difficult to prove causation of malformations in court. Finally, it transformed the field of teratology and expanded scientific interest in testing for terato-genic effects. As one authority commented, "In mammalian teratology the time scale can really be divided into two eras, 'before thalidomide' and 'after thalidomide.'"[8]

The growing concern about reproductive hazards in the workplace comes when the population is not only more aware than it had been of the vul-nerability of the fetus, but also as public awareness of its vulnerability to occupational cancer is greatly heightened. Cancer is not only the leading cause of death in Britain, it is also the disease most feared by the population.[9] The incidence of cancer is rising,[10] and its marked variation according to social class, occupation, country, and life-style suggests that it is related to particular substances rather than random events. In the 1970s, evidence was accumulating about the link between smoking and lung cancer, between food additives and other kinds of cancer, and the high incidence of bladder cancer in rubber workers highlighted workers' susceptibility. The public is starting to recognize that substances that may have no immediate unhealthy side effects may lead to cancer after long periods of exposure. We are now more receptive to the idea of a link between occupational exposures and poor health.

A few sensational cases taken up by the media have generated what little awareness there is of reproductive hazards. In 1977, a study revealed that at least eleven workers in California exposed during production of the pesticide Dibromochloropropane (DBCP) had become sterile. After a study done in 1961 had shown DBCP to produce testicular atrophy and sterility in animals, additional studies throughout the early 1970s raised questions about the safety of DBCP.[11] Male workers had known for some time that none of their wives had conceived, but only after the 1977 study did the government ban DBCP

---

8. Woollam, 498.

9. Lesley Doyal et al., *Cancer in Britain: the Politics of Prevention* (London: Pluto, 1983), 1.

10. Ibid., 11. Between 1951 and 1975 the crude cancer death rate in males in Britain increased by 1 percent per year.

11. See Nancy Miller Chenier, *Reproductive Hazards of Work: Men, Women and the Fertility Gamble* (Ottawa: Canadian Advisory Council on the Status of Women, 1982), 16–18.

and the company shut down production. Some of the workers have recovered their fertility, although their offspring have a higher rate of birth defects.[12]

The DBCP incident highlights several significant points about reproductive hazards in the workplace. First, workers were guinea pigs; the government banned DBCP only after people were injured, despite animal studies indicating a risk. Second, although nearly all scientific studies focus on reproductive injuries to women, DBCP impaired men's capacity to reproduce. Third, injuries to men's reproductive capacities may be harder to uncover than women's, if men are embarrassed to discuss reproductive matters with co-workers. In another British case, a doctor linked pesticides to impotence in farm workers, labeled "the Derbyshire Droop," after four out of five farm workers independently complained to him.[13]

The Scandinavian countries, whose system of collecting and recording health statistics is superior to the United States's and Britain's, began to raise questions about workers exposed to solvents and anaesthetic gases. Yet in both Britain and the United States, this information rarely seeps into the public consciousness beyond the scientific community. In a rare exception, concern about the health of workers manufacturing the synthetic hormone DES (diethylstilbestrol) as well as discoveries of gynecomastia (enlargement of the breasts in men) in manufacturers of the contraceptive pill captured the media's attention. In Britain, Thames television produced a network program on the subject. Prior to *UAW v. Johnson Controls* and the awareness of the potential reproductive hazards of lead, the leading issue was the suggestion that women who work with video display terminals have an elevated risk of miscarriage.[14]

From time to time, such blitzes in the media have raised awareness of the potential of reproductive hazards. The publicity surrounding American Cyanamid's policy in 1978, however, awakened international concern for the potential discriminatory effects of exclusionary policies. American Cyanamid gave women at its plant in Willow Island, West Virginia, the option of having their doctors sterilize them or losing high-paying blue-collar jobs that exposed them to lead. Under its "fetal protection policy," Cyanamid refused to hire any woman who did not have proof of surgical sterilization.[15] The Occupational Safety and Health Administration publicized its efforts to stop Cyanamid's

---

12. See Fletcher, 81–82.

13. Ibid., 80, citing M. L. E. Espir et al., "Impotence in Farm Workers Using Toxic chemicals," *British Medical Journal* 1 (1970): 423–25.

14. See Marilyn K. Goldhaber, Michael R. Polen, and Robert A. Hiatt, "The Risk of Miscarriage and Birth Defects Among Women Who Use Video Display Terminals During Pregnancy," *American Journal of Industrial Medicine* 13 (1988): 695–706. Epidemiologists, however, vigorously disagree about the evidence on VDTs and miscarriage.

15. U.S. Congress, Office of Technology Assessment, *Reproductive Health Hazards in the Workplace* (Washington, D.C.: U.S. Government Printing Office, 1985); Oil, Chemical and Atomic Workers, International Union v. American Cyanamid Company, 741 F.2d 444 (D.C. Cir. 1984).

policy, the *New York Times* and *Wall Street Journal* ran stories,[16] several law journals analyzed its legality, and even members of the European Parliament discussed the case when considering a European Community standard for occupational exposure to lead. As one commentator observed: "Willow Island [the location of the Cyanamid plant] thus became a symbol of a new and very bitter phase in the struggle between workers and corporations over the question of occupational health and safety."[17]

Prior to *UAW v. Johnson Controls*, the most common associations with the phrase "reproductive hazards" were VDTs and Cyanamid. Yet if the short history of reproductive hazards shows anything, it is that such workplace disasters have frequently injured men. It is men who became sterile after exposure to DBCP, grew breasts while manufacturing the pill, and became impotent in Derbyshire after working with pesticides. A recent study of companies in Massachusetts whose workers were exposed to four known or strongly suspected reproductive hazards examined companies' awareness of the hazards and their employment policies.[18] All four substances represented hazards to men's and women's reproductive capacities. The study showed that only 40 percent of the companies acknowledged that the substances might be reproductive hazards.

The study also revealed that nearly 20 percent of the companies excluded certain classes of workers from working with reproductive hazards. "With one exception, all restrictions and transfers applied to women only—even when scientific evidence supports potential reproductive risk to both sexes."[19] Neither the scientific evidence nor the history of reproductive hazards leads logically to such an outcome. If reproductive hazards affect men and women and if history shows that the occupational disasters often have involved male workers, why do employers choose to restrict only women? How did the issue of reproductive hazards, an issue that affects men and women, become narrowed to an issue that affects only women and an issue primarily about VDTs? A place to look for the answer is how employers, trade unions, and legislators came to exclude women from certain forms of employment in the past.

16. "Company and Union in Dispute as Women Undergo Sterilization," *New York Times*, January 4, 1979; "Four Women Assert Jobs Were Linked to Sterilization," *New York Times*, January 5, 1979; "The Women at Cyanamid," *New York Times*, January 7, 1979; Philip Shabecoff, "Job Threats to Workers' Fertility Emerging as Civil Liberties Issue," *New York Times*, January 15, 1979; Brenton R. Schlender, "Sterilization is Main Issue in OSHA Suits," *Wall Street Journal*, December 9, 1980; Gail Bronson, "Bitter Reaction: Issue of Fetal Damage Stirs Women Workers at Chemical Plants," *Wall Street Journal*, February 9, 1979.

17. Ronald Bayer, "Women, Work, and Reproductive Hazards: The Costs of Fetal Protection," *Hastings Center Report* 12 (October 1982): 14.

18. Maureen Paul, Cynthia Daniels, and Robert Rosofsky, "Corporate Response to Reproductive Hazards in the Workplace: Results of the Family, Work, and Health Survey," *American Journal of Industrial Medicine* 16 (1989): 267–80. The substances were lead, radiation, glycol ethers, and mercury. For each, the evidence of reproductive hazards is more compelling than for VDTs.

19. Ibid., 267.

Protective Legislation in Britain

British laws that sought to protect women by regulating their conditions of employment or barring them from certain jobs altogether followed concern with the working conditions of children—a statutory link that continues today. Women's health is often valued not exclusively for its own sake, but because it affects the health of children. The industrialization and urbanization of nineteenth-century Britain produced a variety of social ills. Reformers' concern for public health led them to modernize and restructure local government and to seek to regulate industry. As Parliament became more democratic, middle-class reformers gained access to parliamentary committees and royal commissions. They first used these vehicles to scrutinize the working conditions of children and, later, of women.[20]

When the Regulation of Chimney Sweepers Act of 1788 and the Health and Morals of Apprentices Act of 1802 restricted the employment of children, the demand for women workers, an alternative source of cheap labor, increased. Short-Time Committees, whose goal was a ten-hour day for all workers, campaigned for legislation to limit the number of hours women could work in factories. Some of these Short-Time Committees also supported a ban on married women working when their husbands were employed and campaigned for a family wage.[21] In 1832, medical witnesses before the Select Committee on the Labour of Children in Factories commented on the harmful moral and physical effects of factory work on women. The new factory inspectors echoed their concern. The catalyst for change, however, was the first report of the Committee on the Employment of Women and Children in Mines and Collieries in 1842. It so shocked the public that it created a climate conducive to the passage of legislation forbidding women's employment underground in mines and restricting the hours they could work in factories.

Factories and mines neither employed the largest numbers of women nor were the most exploitative workplaces women encountered, yet they captured the reformers' attention. Most employed women in the mid-nineteenth century worked in jobs that were an extension of their domestic responsibilities rather than in factories or mines.[22] Those who were employed in factories were concentrated in the textile industry. In fact, women outnumbered men in all sectors of the textile industry except woolens for most of the nineteenth

20. Susan Atkins and Brenda Hoggett, *Women and the Law* (Oxford: Basil Blackwell, 1984), 12.

21. Sheila Lewenhak, *Women and Trade Unions* (New York: St. Martin's, 1977), 54; B. L. Hutchins and A. Harrison, *A History of Factory Legislation*, 3d ed. (London: P. S. King and Son, 1926), 65.

22. Pat Thane, "Late Victorian Women," in *Later Victorian Britain, 1867–1900*, ed. T. R. Gourvish and Alan O'Day, 175–208 (London: Macmillan, 1988), 188; Sally Alexander, *Women's Work in Nineteenth-Century London: A Study of the Years 1820–50* (London: Journeyman Press, 1983), 20–22.

century.[23] It is not surprising, then, that the Factory Act of 1844, the first law limiting the number of hours women could work in factories, regulated the textile industry, restricting working hours to twelve per day.[24]

Assessing the motives of both the advocates and opponents of protective legislation is difficult. Protective legislation took many forms and each type garnered a different coalition of support. Support and opposition varied over time, across regions, and with different types of workplaces. The term *protective legislation* itself is too broad a category. For example, some working-class women may have supported hours restrictions in particular factories when they knew they would not lose their jobs and production would have to shut down for men as well, but may have actively resisted attempts to ban women from working in factories altogether or to ban married women. Working women did not respond to all restrictions in the same way or as a group; they frequently disagreed. Recounting the history of these disagreements, however, is difficult because working-class women's voices have been muted by historians (when they have been recorded at all). Middle-class reformers who wrote books, factory inspector's reports, pamphlets, and parliamentary commission reports left more documentation of their views.

Both advocates and opponents of protective legislation impugned each other's motives. Both sides vigorously disagreed about the effects of the legislation. Each side had its own self-reported motives; each side made insulting accusations about the other side's motivations. Clearly, there is some truth in all the charges. Those who favored protective legislation claimed that their opponents were middle-class women who were merely extrapolating from their own experience of being denied employment opportunity[25]— feminists who saw working women as needing the opportunity to work in every occupation rather than recognizing that what they really needed was protection from exploitation. They were charged with being detached from the lives of real working-class women, particularly those in unskilled occupations.[26] Supporters of the restrictions further charged the other side with favoring formal legal equality for its own sake[27]—having "fallen into the blank and unfruitful individualism that has blighted the women's movement of the middle class"[28]—rather than because it improved the conditions of

---

23. Norbert Soldon, *Women in British Trade Unions, 1874–1976* (Totowa, N.J.: Rowman and Littlefields, 1978), 2.

24. W. B. Creighton, *Working Women and the Law* (New York: Mansell, 1979), 21–22.

25. Hutchins and Harrison, 183–84.

26. Of course, women could not express their views at the ballot box. Hutchins and Harrison pleaded that this should not be a reason for opposing restrictions (199).

27. "For the most part the Open Door Council appealed to middle-class women. The protective legislation it opposed, described earlier, was generally not as oppressive to working-class women as their middle-class sisters believed. It was preposterous to expect the TUC to turn back the clock in the name of some sort of ideological consistency" (Soldon, 126).

28. Hutchins and Harrison, 198.

women's lives. Finally, opponents of protective legislation were charged with being the stooges of industry. The argument went as follows: once employers lost the important symbolic battle over whether the state could interfere in the employment contract, industry needed a more persuasive argument to counter the restrictions than their continued desire for unfettered exploitation. They used middle-class feminists to champion the rhetoric of equality when, in fact, employers wanted freedom to exploit women workers.[29] Some trade unionists went further than claiming middle-class women were the unwitting pawns of industry and claimed that opponents of protective legislation such as Millicent Fawcett were shareholders in factories acting on their class interests.

Few of the supporters of protective legislation squarely addressed the issue of working-class women's opposition. Maybe they thought such women to be so desperate that they would sacrifice their long-term needs and well being for short-term gains. They needed jobs so badly that they would work under any conditions for meager pay.

If supporters of protective legislation had deep suspicions of their opponents' motives, they also had very strong opinions about both the need for protective legislation as well as the effects of such legislation. The supporters of the first laws argued that both men and women workers benefited from restrictions on women.[30] Unions also hoped that protective legislation might be the wedge for legislation to improve the working conditions of all workers.[31] Hutchins and Harrison accused those seeking a ten-hour day of "hiding behind women's petticoats,"[32] claiming men were using women's special needs as a way of obtaining benefits for themselves. Once won, the restrictions on women could be extended to men. In factories that relied heavily on women's labor, if employers were forced to reduce the number of hours women and children worked, reformers and trade unionists foresaw that employers would have to shut down early. Men would then also reap the benefits of shorter hours. Progressive employers who had already reduced the hours of women and children sought to prevent less-scrupulous employers from having a competitive advantage.[33] Furthermore, using legislation to secure better working conditions for women helped the cause of using the state to negotiate better conditions for workers, tearing down the opposition to state intervention in labor relations. Angela Coyle saw the legislation as an important concession— "the legal recognition of a *socially* defined working day (as opposed to one defined by capital)"—and as an important stage in the development of state intervention in the exchange struck between capital and labor.[34]

---

29. Lewenhak, 74.
30. Hutchins and Harrison, 49.
31. Soldon, 14.
32. Hutchins and Harrison, 65.
33. Creighton, 24.
34. Angela Coyle, "The Protection Racket?" *Feminist Review* 4 (1980): 5.

There were additional reasons for singling out women. Employers usually paid women less than men. The claim was that women were less able to do the job because they were physically weaker, but usually it was just that women were willing to work for less and had little hope of getting more.[35] Fewer women were members of trade unions that could negotiate improved working conditions on their behalf and, therefore, women workers arguably needed legal protection. Trade union lore suggests that women were more difficult to organize and so needed legislation to protect them.[36] Women did organize, and they organized against the odds of heavy family responsibilities and the intense hostility and discrimination of many trade unions. But they were concentrated in domestic work or smaller workplaces, which made it difficult for them to organize.

Supporters of protective legislation saw little need to distinguish between different groups of women. Those women who did not bear children or were not responsible for child care or housework benefited or suffered from the restrictions as well. The needs of the "exceptional" woman were outweighed by the needs of her "weaker" sisters.

Those who opposed protective legislation characterized the other side's motives very differently. First, they saw protective legislation as a thin guise for eliminating competition. Even Hutchins and Harrison, strong supporters of restrictions, recognized this motive.[37] Working men feared being undercut by women workers whom employers paid a lower wage.[38]

> The continuing pressure for shorter hours of work was one aspect of the policy of reducing competition from women for work. After the 1833 Factory Act was passed, considerably restricting the use of child labour in cotton factories, women replaced children. So, similarly, it was hoped that a restriction on women's hours of work would cause employers to replace women with men. It was true that men trade unionists hoped in the long run to reduce the length of the working-day for themselves, but the immediate battle was for work.[39]

Rather than asserting their joint class interest in improved working conditions, working-class men sought to exclude, rather than organize, prospective competition or to demand equal pay for women. As early as 1808, fledgling unions barred women from organized trades, and they repeatedly called for excluding women in times of high unemployment.[40]

---

35. Lewenhak, 51.

36. Alice Kessler-Harris, "Where are the Organized Women Workers?" *Feminist Studies* 3 (Fall 1975): 92–110.

37. Hutchins and Harrison, 49.

38. Creighton, 24–26.

39. Lewenhak, 53–54.

40. Lindsay Mackie and Polly Pattullo, *Women at Work* (London: Tavistock, 1977), 161.

Those who opposed protective legislation charged the other side with seeking the continued subordination of women. Opponents mustered considerable evidence that working-class men and middle-class reformers saw women's place as in the home. If women worked, their employment should be an extension of their domestic duties. This view explains the reformers' preoccupation with factory work and coal mining. Women factory workers and miners were "out of place" because their work was not an extension of women's domestic duties in the same way that working in a laundry was. Reformers also saw women's employment as interfering with their domestic and familial responsibilities and as threatening to male authority in the family. The demise of male authority in the home meant the demise of the family, and ultimately, then, of society.

> Lord Shaftesbury, whose Mines Act of 1842 forbade women and children under ten years of age to go down mines, said: 'Domestic life and domestic discipline must soon be at an end; society will consist of individuals no longer grouped in families; so early is the separation of husband and wife.'[41]

Not only was women's employment a potential threat to male power in the home, but some middle-class reformers feared women would be morally compromised by the potential for dangerous interactions in the working world. Some male trade unionists advocated protective legislation for women as part of a broader campaign for workers' rights or to eliminate competition, but most ultimately endorsed the middle-class reformers' patriarchal concerns with women's morality or male authority. In 1877, trade unionist Henry Broadhurst declared to the Trades Union Congress, only three years old: "It was the duty of men and husbands to bring about a condition of things where their wives should be in their proper sphere at home instead of being dragged into competition of livelihood with the great and strong men of the world."[42] Many expressed the view that men needed jobs more than women, although many women were the sole support or essential contributors to their families.

Those favoring protective legislation also worried that women would abandon their "double duty" in the home if they worked. Working-class men expressed their fears of women's economic independence through the following jingle.

> Mary had a little loom, and unto it did go,
> And every Sunday afternoon, you should have seen the show,

---

41. Mackie and Pattullo, 140–41.
42. Soldon, 19; Thane, 202. Thane suggests Broadhurst's comments may not have represented the views of the majority of male trade unionists.

With veil, kid gloves and gaiters, too, she goes out on the mash,
She fairly knocks the men out now, because she gets the cash.[43]

Opponents of protective legislation were also suspicious about its promised benefits. They were quick to point out that the legislation was always partial; the 1844 Factories Act did not remove women from factory work altogether. The laws ignored jobs in which women were concentrated—agricultural and domestic work and sweatshops—and thus failed to prevent the exploitation of most women workers.

Removal of women from the heavy labour and grim conditions of underground work in the mines thirty years earlier was advanced as one of the beneficial effects of protective legislation for women. But public interest in relieving women of heavy work had stopped there. They still worked at chain-making and in the brick fields.[44]

When women workers were covered, employers could apply for an exemption. Furthermore, the laws were never adequately enforced.

The call for extending the benefits to men and treating all workers the same never came. Men negotiated directly with their employers for conditions better than those mandated by the state. Unions often preferred collective bargaining to legislation. Thus, protective legislation only marginally helped in the fight for restricting hours for men and improving working conditions for all.

Whatever benefits women gained from protection, opponents argued, were outweighed by the discriminatory effects of the laws. Opponents claimed that protective legislation had the harmful effect of leading to excluding women from work.[45] Either the restrictions themselves explicitly excluded women or employers failed to hire workers who could not work overtime, had to have breaks, or could not work at night. Protective legislation reduced women's wages and helped segregate the job market still further. The nexus between protection and discrimination was a subject of debate from the beginning.

Opponents also bemoaned the long-term effects of reinforcing biological and social differences between the sexes rather than pushing for changes in the division of labor in the home. They criticized those who advocated restrictions on the basis of women's double day rather than campaigning for men to do

---

43. Lewenhak, 92.

44. Ibid., 73.

45. "The League's fears appeared justified when, in 1882, in the case of the Black Country metal unions and then in 1885, through the Coal Mines Regulation Act in the case of the Miners' Federation of Great Britain, attempts were made to use legislation to exclude women from working" (Lewenhak, 74).

their share. The fear was that recognizing and seeking to accommodate this imbalance in the home merely reinforced it and gave it legitimacy. Feminists criticized those advocating protective legislation for failing to see that the legislation quickly worked to women's disadvantage. The effect of reinforcing women's difference from men in their employment situation and household responsibilities is that it became easier to regard women as marginal workers who could be banned from work in times of high unemployment. Treating women differently also had a more symbolic effect. It was no coincidence that legislation restricting employment applied to both women and children. Both were seen as less fully human, less able to secure their rights, and more vulnerable to exploitation.

Historians have considered the different motivations and analyzed the effects of the legislation. The impetus for protective legislation, however, varied within groups, over time, and when applied to different workplaces. In a case study of the passage of the Mines Regulation Act of 1842, Jane Humphries skillfully examined the interplay of various motivations in a particular workplace at a particular time in history.[46] She refuted the claim that, as workers, men generally favored protective legislation to eliminate competition, and, as heads of households, they favored it in order to exert more control over women. In the mines, jobs were segregated by sex. Women mainly transported coal, and girls and boys competed only against each other. Like some factories then, the mines operated on a team or family system where all worked together and the father collected the wages for his family. Under this system, men and women did not compete with each other. The system reinforced rather than challenged patriarchal control of men over their wives and children. Thus, banning women from work in the mines threatened the ability of the family unit to survive economically, unless mine owners paid men a family wage or women got jobs elsewhere.

While Humphries's findings cast doubt on the patriarchal motives of working-class miners who supported protective legislation, her findings about the comments of the middle-class commissioners who investigated women's work in the mines are revealing. Instead of focusing on the dangers of women working through the late stages of pregnancy and even sometimes giving birth in the mines, or the conditions of work that left a male miner spent at forty and a woman old at thirty, or the high risk of a fatal accident that all miners faced, reformers were preoccupied with the immorality of women's work in the mines and with working-class women's sexuality.

The Victorians' golden rule that it was better to be preoccupied than occupied with sex is demonstrated in the 1842 Report which reveals the

---

46. Jane Humphries, "Protective Legislation, the Capitalist State, and Working Class Men: The Case of the 1842 Mines Regulation Act," *Feminist Review* 7 (Spring 1981): 1–33.

commissioners, sub-commissioners and bourgeois witnesses as obsessed with the '*morals*' of collier women. 'Morals' meant sexual behaviour. Drunkenness, immodesty and profanity were also relevant but only because they were seen as symptomatic of promiscuity.[47]

It was this outrage against bourgeois sexuality and concern over the disintegration of the family as an institution that shocked the public and secured quick passage of the act following publication of the report in 1842.[48] Factory inspectors were shocked by women's vulgar language and that men and women worked together in the darkness.

One Factory Commissioner wrote: They are to be found alike vulgar in manner and obscene language: but who can feel surprised at their debased condition when they are known to be constantly associated, and associated only, with men and boys, living and labouring in a state of disgusting nakedness and brutality.[49]

Not only were reformers concerned about women's independence, immorality, and exploitation, but in the mines women were "out of place." Hutchins and Harrison's account is instructive: "It has often been told how from an early age they were employed in dragging trucks of coal to which they were harnessed by a chain and girdle, going on all-fours, in conditions of dirt, heat, and indecency which are scarcely printable" (82). Women on all fours appears scandalous in the mines but acceptable if they are scrubbing someone else's floors. Perhaps the rhetorical force of an underground location, like hell, made it worse. Why was it acceptable for men to be treated like beasts of burden, hauling carts filled with coal, but not women? Surely agricultural work was as dirty and physically exhausting for women?

If morality and concern about the family motivated middle-class reformers, Humphries provides no clear answer about what motivated male miners. She rules out a fear of competition and a desire for more control over women but unearths no other reason for their support. Her findings do not contradict the finding that such motives were at work in other industries, drove other groups, and led to the passage of other legislation. Humphries's case study documents how class affected one's position on protective legislation. In this case, working-class men and women shared an interest in opposing the removal of women from the mines, while those who ran the mines presumably benefited from women's cheap labor. Middle-class reformers who purported to champion the cause of women's health also expressed a desire to

---

47. Ibid., 25.
48. Lewenhak, 54.
49. Gail Braybon, *Women Workers in the First World War* (London: Croom Helm, 1981), 20.

impose their ideology about women's proper roles and proper sexual behavior on the working class.

Women actively voiced their views on protective legislation. Some middle-class women opposed protective legislation, some trade unionists supported it. In the latter part of the nineteenth century, the Women's Rights Opposition Movement opposed protective legislation. This movement had begun in the 1850s and later merged into a campaign for women's social and political emancipation.[50] Emma Paterson, founder of the Women's Protective and Provident League (later the Women's Trade Union League), took her opposition to protective legislation to the trade union movement.[51] She believed that such laws served only to restrict women's employment, arguing that women workers should be unionized instead.[52] Suffrage leader Millicent Fawcett opposed protective legislation; her husband put the case against it to Parliament in the 1870s. Suffrage societies organized protests on restrictions on particular industries.[53] Under new leadership, however, the Trade Union League began to support protective legislation and, despite opposition from groups of women workers, women trade unionists increasingly supported it. After World War I, this position was not only held by women trade unionists but also became Labour Party policy.[54] Although groups of working-class women have always opposed protective legislation,[55] particularly when it led to their exclusion from work, for most of the twentieth century the official trade union position favored it.

The class dynamics were reversed in the early twentieth century. Middle-class reformers sought protective legislation in the nineteenth century and were faced with some opposition from employed women. In the early twentieth century, middle-class feminists such as the National Union of Societies for Equal Citizenship (NUSEC) and the Women's Freedom League fought protective legislation.[56] The Open Door Council fought "to secure that women shall be free to work and protected on the same terms as men."[57] It fought legislation banning women from exposure to lead paint. The Open Door Council and the NUSEC led a fight against a new Factories Bill in 1927, but in the same year at an annual conference their opposition to protective legislation was overturned when Eleanor Rathbone replaced Millicent Fawcett

50. Creighton, 25.

51. Hutchins and Harrison, 187–89.

52. Banks, 105–8; Lewenhak, 69–73.

53. Ray Strachey, *The Cause: A Short History of the Women's Movement in Great Britain* (London: Bell and Sons, 1928), 234–37.

54. Banks, 108.

55. Lewenhak, 40–42; Strachey, 236–37.

56. Banks, 169.

57. Blanche Weisen Cook, ed., *Chrystal Eastman: On Woman and Revolution* (London: Oxford University Press, 1978), 214.

as president. Feminist members of the conference, including Fawcett, resigned in favor of the social reformers.[58] By the end of the decade, equal rights feminists were no longer dominant in the movement and their campaigns against protective legislation dwindled.[59]

Opposition to protective legislation also died out within the trade union movement. The Labour Party officially supported protective legislation for women. The demise of opposition coincided with the incorporation of the National Federation of Women Workers and the Women's Trade Union League into the TUC in 1921.[60] Working women not only lost their autonomy within the TUC, but they lost some of their most articulate advocates, such as Emma Paterson. It was harder for them to push their claims without a separate organization, and their sections were downgraded and their power eroded in reorganizations.[61] Groups of women workers at the grass roots, however, such as women printers, continued to protest the restrictions on women working.[62] Working women overwhelmingly preferred factory work to domestic service and protested being forced to return.[63] But what was a heated controversy within both feminist and trade union organizations changed to a consensus behind protective legislation in Britain as middle-class women changed their focus to other issues and working-class opposition was defeated within the Trade Union Women's Conference.[64]

The discriminatory impact of protective legislation led the International Labour Organization (ILO) to rethink its support for banning women from working nights—a position that was continually debated within the organization. As legal bans on the employment of married women in the public service and in industry became widespread in the early 1900s,[65] the dire consequences that flowed from women's reduced employment opportunities, forcing them to conceal their marriages and pregnancies in industry, prompted the ILO to modify its position on protective legislation for women. Recognizing the discriminatory effects of emphasizing women's differences as well as the reality that many women had to work, the ILO's literature and campaigns began to play down women's biological differences from men and, instead, emphasized women's ability to do the same job. Because it came to believe preventing women from working evenings and nights led employers to discriminate against them, in the 1930s the ILO no longer supported blanket

---

58. Eastman labeled the groups equalitarians or pure-Feminists and humanitarians or social reformers (228–29).

59. Banks, 170–73.

60. Lewenhak, 175.

61. Ibid., 189.

62. Ibid., 212.

63. Braybon, 26; Thane, 188.

64. Strachey, 245.

65. Braybon, 94, 169.

exclusions.[66] The British TUC opposed the change in the ILO's policy,[67] although the Women's Advisory Committee within the TUC stopped its opposition to the ILO in 1936, concluding that the restraints on night work were detrimental to women's right to work.[68] Their views carried little weight within the TUC as a whole. Despite the mixed motives of those who called for protective legislation and the vocal opposition of some, for the most part women and trade unions in Britain have supported it for at least fifty years.

In the second half of the nineteenth century, the British Parliament limited the number of hours women could work in factories and banned them from working underground in coal mines.[69] In the early twentieth century, Parliament banned women from working at night. The increased demand for labor during the two world wars, however, forced the Minister of Labour to grant a series of exemptions.[70] The Factories Act of 1961 restricting women's employment consolidated earlier statutes: the Young Persons and Children Act of 1920 and the Hours of Employment (Conventions) Act of 1936. In 1979, restrictions covered 17 percent of the female workforce.[71] The most significant effect of the arrangement was to prohibit women from working evenings and nights or overtime in factories unless the Health and Safety Executive had granted their employer an exemption. These restrictions limited women's earning potential. In 1980, the average weekly overtime pay received by men was £15.20 per week while women earned an average of £2.50 overtime per week.[72] Other protective legislation limited the number of hours women could work in certain industries, set different weight-lifting limits for men and women, required that women (but not men) take breaks after fixed periods, prohibited women from working in certain hazardous environments, prohibited women from cleaning moving machinery, and restricted women's ability to return to work immediately after childbirth.

Trade unionists quickly recognized the requirement that employers seek exemptions from the ban on working at night was a mere formality. In 1979,

---

66. Soldon, 127. See Carol Riegelman Lubin and Anne Winslow, *Social Justice for Women: The International Labor Organization and Women* (Durham, N.C.: Duke University Press, 1990), 28–32, 39–40.

67. Lewenhak, 212.

68. Ibid., 234.

69. Miners completed the cycle of excluding women in the 1950s, convincing the Coal Board to exclude women from screening coal at the pithead (Lewenhak, 258).

70. Braybon, 184–86. Braybon describes how, after the war, in the press, women moved from being the saviors of the country, by working, to being ruthless self-seekers depriving men of their livelihood.

71. Equal Opportunities Commission, *Health and Safety Legislation: Should We Distinguish Between Men and Women?* (Manchester: Equal Opportunities Commission, 1979), 23.

72. Helen Dingwall, "Protective Legislation for Women: A Case of Legal Discrimination?" (B. Sc. diss., University of Bath School of Humanities and Social Sciences, 1983), 35.

the Equal Opportunities Commission recognized the shift toward automatic granting of exemptions.

> Furthermore, with the alteration in public attitudes to women's work, and the greater demand for shiftwork by employers or women themselves, the Health and Safety Executive's attitude to the restrictions seems to have changed somewhat, over the past few years. The enormous increase in the number of women authorized to work at night is evidence of this. (In the past five years the numbers have more than doubled.) So is the fact that Exemption Orders, once applied for, are now very rarely refused.[73]

In the 1970s, both the British Parliament and the European Community evaded the issue of protective legislation in their legislative initiatives promoting equality for women. The EC's Equal Treatment Directive of 1976 ordered all member states to end discrimination against women and "to put into effect the principle of equal treatment for men and women as regards access to employment, including promotion, and to vocational training and as regards working conditions."[74] The directive defined equal treatment as meaning "that there shall be no discrimination whatsoever on grounds of sex either directly or indirectly." Except for provisions on pregnancy and maternity, the EC's Council of Ministers saw protective legislation for women as contrary to the principle of equal treatment contained in the directive; but rather than forbid such legislative enactments, the directive ordered member states to continue to review such statutes to insure that the concern for protection that inspired them was still well founded.

Seeking to harmonize its national laws with impending European directives and responding to groups within Britain, the British Parliament passed the Sex Discrimination Act of 1975.[75] During the debates over the Equal Pay Act of 1970, Barbara Castle, Secretary of State for Employment, had been under pressure to abolish protective legislation in return for support for equal pay. While recognizing "there are a number of absurd anomalies" in the law and "the need for these restrictions is disappearing fast," she argued "it would be quite wrong to make the introduction of this legislation conditional on the blanket removal of the hours restrictions."[76] Instead, she wanted them treated separately. The Conservatives wanted the removal of the protective legislation as a quid pro quo for bringing in equal pay. It was thus employers who

---

73. EOC, *Health and Safety Legislation*, 26. The exemptions remained in effect until passage of the Sex Discrimination Act of 1986.

74. 76/207/EEC.

75. Creighton, 31–33; see also chap. 3.

76. *Parliamentary Debates* (Commons), 5th ser. vol. 795 (1970), col. 922.

marshaled the rhetoric of formal legal equality in advocating the removal of restrictions on who could work when.

The standing committee that considered the bill voted to abolish protective legislation. During the second reading of the bill on the floor of the House, however, the Government sought to overturn the committee's decision. Wanting neither to rescind protective legislation altogether nor lose the opportunity of passing the Sex Discrimination Bill, the Government proposed that the newly created Equal Opportunities Commission review the need for protective laws. John Fraser argued that this review was "not just to reverse a Government defeat in Committee," urging the House "not to be too hasty and to think carefully before sweeping away all these provisions without any thought."[77] Michael Alison argued that protective legislation ran contrary to the aim of the Bill—to provide equal opportunities for women—and that protective legislation effectively barred women from lucrative manual trades. While Jo Richardson (Labour spokeswoman on Women) scoffed at the suggestion "it was entering the promised land to work on an assembly line in the electronics industry," she argued that women should have the choice. Although she felt that much of the legislation was outmoded and had voted for its repeal in committee, Richardson agreed to the Government's compromise of having all protective legislation reviewed by the Equal Opportunities Commission.[78] Thus, as is often the case in politics, the legislature delayed action by appointing a committee to look into the matter, and Parliament passed the Sex Discrimination Act.

Neither business nor trade unions have significantly changed their positions on protective legislation for fifty years, although the Government's action in 1986 made the debate, at least for the duration of that Government, moot. The Confederation of British Industry (CBI), an organization of British companies comparable to the U.S. Chamber of Commerce and National Association of Manufacturers combined, wanted to get rid of protective legislation because it interfered with management's freedom to manage. Although not a great campaigner for women's rights, the CBI pushed for formal legal equality on a number of fronts. The CBI argued that women should be able to choose whether or not they want to work. (The Institute of Personnel Management also argued that women should decide for themselves.)[79] Second, since employed women generally work only thirty-eight hours per week anyway (less than the statutory minimum), removing restrictions would not excessively take them away from their families. Third, since only 26 percent of employed married women are between twenty and thirty-nine, the years when they are most likely to have small children, it was unfair to base restrictions on the fear that this minority might overwork. Fourth, the requirement for equal

---

77. *Parliamentary Debates* (Commons), 5th ser. vol. 893 (1975), cols. 1580–83.

78. Ibid., col. 1587.

79. Mackie and Pattullo, 142–43.

pay and other statutory safeguards eliminated the danger of exploiting women during high unemployment. Fifth, despite the ability to get exemptions, section VI of the Factories Act (which limited hours of work) *did* restrict employers' ability to employ people during the evenings and at night. Sixth, part VI of the act was far too rigid and complex and brought the entire act into disrepute. The CBI, thus, not only took the position of advocating equality for women, but differentiated between the interests and social responsibilities of different groups of women rather than lumping them together as a group.[80]

The Trades Union Congress (TUC), an organization of British unions comparable to the AFL-CIO in the United States, supported the retention of protective legislation for several reasons. The TUC claimed that it wanted to end discriminatory treatment for women by extending benefits of protective legislation to men—leveling up, not down. Perhaps adherence to the negotiating principle that one never gives anything up without receiving something in return explains the TUC's defense of protective legislation. The TUC argued that winning formal equality or an equality of exploitation did not justify relinquishing existing protection. Furthermore, the TUC maintained that, in fact, protective laws did not keep women out of jobs. Employers could easily get exemptions and, furthermore, men's and women's jobs were already segregated for a variety of reasons that had nothing to do with protective legislation. Thus, removal of protective legislation would not end job segregation.

Whether protective legislation caused discrimination against women formed a central point of disagreement. The main focus was the prohibition on working evenings and nights (called shifts). The TUC argued that medical evidence proved that working evening and night shifts was bad for everyone; but it further argued that men and women had different social roles: women, whether employed or not, had the major responsibility for childrearing and housework. Given this difference, working nights was especially harmful to women who cared for small children and did housework all day and might be tempted to work evenings or nights and damage their health. Thus, while the TUC was simultaneously arguing for an end to a legal recognition of difference (by demanding a leveling up, not down) it was also arguing that women needed special protection by virtue of their different social roles.

The TUC did not argue that single women or women who did not take care of children—those who did not fit the societal stereotype of wife and mother—should be able to work at night. The law recognized no distinctions among women. In the parliamentary debates, Jeff Rooker recognized that not only was there widespread abuse of the protective legislation but also that it unfairly restricted women who did not have families and who did not need this alleged protection from overwork.[81] The restriction on women also failed to

---

80. Creighton, 32.
81. *Parliamentary Debates* (Commons), 5th ser. vol. 893 (1975), col. 1586.

protect men who had primary responsibility for child care. This issue aside, the TUC saw the Confederation of British Industry's argument for freedom of choice as a sham and feared employers would require more women to work at night.

Feminist Angela Coyle took issue with the TUC's justification, but not its position. She criticized the TUC's emphasis on differences between men and women.

> The problem with the current legislation is that it does not genuinely "protect" women but rather operates paternalistically to reinforce women's condition of inequality. Protective legislation must be argued for on the basis of different criteria. That is to say, it is *not* because of their domestic commitments that women need such legislation, but because it is a *progressive* demand. Rather than seeing the issue as the "backwardness" of women, as Barbara Castle did in 1969, when as Secretary of State for Employment, she asked "Is there any need for these restrictions?" and as the EOC asks in 1979, "Should we distinguish between men and women," the point that has to be made is that nobody should have to work either shift work or nights.[82]

Coyle also criticized the TUC for not challenging the division of labor within the family.

The Equal Opportunities Commission (EOC) took evidence from many individuals and groups and issued its findings in *Health and Safety Legislation: Should We Distinguish Between Men and Women?* The report, which came four years after the passage of the Sex Discrimination Act, endorsed many of the CBI's arguments for abolishing protective legislation and urged readers to recall "in reaching conclusions and making recommendations, it is important to state that equal opportunity must be our first consideration."[83] Although the EOC reviewed the entire range of restrictions, its main focus was evening and night shifts. The EOC had commissioned the Office of Population and Census Studies to survey attitudes toward working shifts and had also examined the medical evidence.

> Our most important finding is that the hours of work legislation constitutes a barrier—often an artificial one—to equal pay and job opportunities for women. So long as this legislation remains as it is at present, women as workers will be disadvantaged. Therefore we cannot accept the retention of the legislation in its present form, because discrimination will continue to arise out of it.[84]

---

82. Coyle, 10.
83. EOC, *Health and Safety Legislation*, 92.
84. Ibid.

The EOC rejected the TUC's proposal to extend limits on working evenings and nights to men as ineffective and too costly to industry. If the ban were extended to men, the EOC argued, the same economic considerations that justified exemptions for women working nights would justify granting exemptions for men, leading only to more bureaucracy. Leaving largely unquestioned the need for industry to operate during the evening and night, the EOC concluded that medical evidence did not support the claim that working shifts is hazardous to health. It further asserted that most women preferred to have the choice whether to work evenings and nights and left virtually untouched whether women should work in the mines. (The EOC did recommend that the laws be reformed so that women engineers and those who spend only part of their time underground not be excluded.)

The EOC's focus on evening and night shifts as the most important aspect of protective legislation accurately reflected the emphasis of the debate about protective legislation in Britain. The report did, however, discuss whether there should be separate standards for men and women working with hazardous substances. The EOC recommended equal standards where "reasonably practicable" but neglected to define that phrase. Where equal standards were not practical, the EOC urged employers to define "women of reproductive capacity" narrowly. The EOC thus called for a change in what it reported the Health and Safety Executive's (HSE) position to be: favoring the exclusion of all women aged fifteen to fifty-five from hazardous work environments regardless of their marital status or method of contraception. The EOC preferred a narrower definition of "women of reproductive capacity" than the HSE's, and recommended defining women of reproductive capacity as those women not taking active steps to avoid pregnancy. The EOC argued that women, like men, should be able to judge the risk for themselves. As to other protective laws setting different weight-lifting limits and requiring meal and rest breaks, the EOC proposed having a single provision applicable to both sexes. The EOC's report thus favored treating men and women the same whenever "practicable" rather than having separate standards for men and women.

Two of the three TUC members of the EOC dissented from the recommendations that the legal restrictions on night work and shift work be abolished: "These two Commissioners consider that these recommendations are not the right way to deal with equality between men and women. Instead, the provisions currently applying to women should cover men."[85] Ethel Chipchase, the third TUC member, reportedly came to believe that the restrictions led to discrimination, and did not join the dissent. This was rumored to have caused serious repercussions for her within the TUC. Mackie and Pattullo argued that "official TUC policy, however, does not necessarily represent the opinions of the grass roots of the union movement. There is debate

---

85. Ibid., 126.

between men and women and between women and women as to the merits of protective legislation."[86] Feminist trade unionists have a difficult course to navigate when their own positions are at odds with TUC policy. The official TUC policy favors continued restrictions, but there continued to be complaints within the National Women's Advisory Committee and elsewhere.[87]

The EOC had no power to implement its recommendations because enforcement and rule-making responsibility rests with the Health and Safety Commission. Both the Health and Safety Commission (HSC) and the EOC are tripartite bodies, made up of representatives from the CBI, the TUC, and civil servants. The commissions direct the work of the agencies, the Health and Safety Executive and the Equal Opportunities Commission. (The name Equal Opportunities Commission can refer confusingly to both the supervisory body of commissioners and to the agency. I use EOC to refer to the agency and commission to refer to the directive body that heads the agency.) After the EOC made its recommendations on protective legislation, it was up to the HSC to implement them, if it so chose. Although the HSC and the EOC have a duty to consult each other on these matters, either body could make its recommendations separately if the two were not in agreement. The 1974 Health and Safety at Work Act grants the Health and Safety Commission power to recommend guidance notes, codes of practice, standards, and regulations for health and safety at work.[88] It is thus the HSC, and to a lesser extent the minister (Secretary of State for Employment), and not Parliament that initiates changes in current regulations.

From 1979 to 1986, the TUC representatives on the Health and Safety Commission, who opposed the repeal of protective legislation, vetoed any proposals to change regulations. The Health and Safety Commission's function is to recommend changes in the law to the Secretary of State for Employment, but the secretary could act on his or her own initiative and lay proposals before Parliament. Parliament does not debate these statutory instruments, nor does it vote on them like other legislation. Ministers simply announce them as finished products that carry the force of law. Although the TUC's position on protective legislation on the Health and Safety Commission had been uncompromising, the secretary could have taken the initiative to introduce his own proposals to abolish protective legislation. The secretary did not do this,[89] and, from 1979 until the Government introduced legislation in 1986, the TUC

---

86. Mackie and Pattullo, 143.

87. Lewenhak, 287–88.

88. For a fuller discussion of the Health and Safety Executive's power to propose changes in the law and Parliament's weak oversight powers, see Charles D. Drake and Frank B. Wright, *Law of Health and Safety at Work: The New Approach* (London: Sweet and Maxwell, 1983), 110–16.

89. Feminists and trade unionists feared that the secretary would repeal the law through statutory instrument (Roger Bibbings, Health and Safety Officer, Trades Union Congress, interview with author, London, November 13, 1985).

managed to keep the Health and Safety Executive from acting on the Equal Opportunities Commission's recommendations.

Contrary to the situation in the United States, the only feminist group in Britain that campaigned on the issue of protective legislation in the last twenty-five years called for its retention. Feminists joined business and labor in debating protective legislation. In the nineteenth and early twentieth centuries, some working-class women and middle-class feminists inside and outside the trade union movement campaigned against restrictive laws. Those groups died out and few, if any, feminist groups in the mid-twentieth century have actively opposed protective legislation in Britain.[90] While there was a distinctively feminist voice among both working-class and middle-class women in the late nineteenth and early twentieth centuries, those voices have been muted or silenced completely for most of the twentieth century.

British feminist groups divide broadly into three camps. Radical feminists campaign mainly on violence against women, form a counterculture, and engage in a politics of protest rather than a politics of reform. They are most active in promoting women's centers, running battered women's shelters and peace camps, and promoting a separatist women's culture. Socialist feminists campaign within trade unions, the Labour Party, and the Left generally, and express their concerns in the context of class politics. By far the largest group in Britain, unlike in the United States, they dominate the few interest groups organized solely around women's and feminist issues and are the most articulate and most reported in the media. Liberal feminists seek formal legal equality and reform, rather than radical change, and focus on rights of citizenship and employment. They are often professional women who are less interested in challenging race, class, and gender hierarchies simultaneously and are less concerned with questions of sexuality. Unlike their counterparts in the United States, British liberal feminists have not organized in large numbers and there is no real forum for liberal academic and professional women to exert their influence.[91]

The EOC most often takes a liberal feminist position, although some radical and socialist feminists have worked within or exerted pressure on the agency. The origins, structure, and appointment process for the commission and its chair assure such a result. The agency has been a reform agency, largely set apart from the feminist movement (chap. 3 considers the agency at

---

90. Categorizing women is problematic. I do not mean to imply that the categories working-class women, feminists, or middle-class women are mutually exclusive.

91. Joyce Gelb, "Social Movement 'Success': A Comparative Analysis of Feminism in the United States and the United Kingdom," in *The Women's Movements of the United States and Western Europe: Consciousness, Political Opportunity and Public Policy*, ed. by Mary Fainsod Katzenstein and Carol McClurg Mueller (Philadelphia: Temple University Press, 1987), 267–89. For other sources, see chap. 3.

greater length). The agency's stand against protective legislation and for formal legal equality incurred the wrath of the organized feminist movement.

The National Council for Civil Liberties (NCCL), previously one of the most active organizations on women's rights, is likely to ally itself with trade union interests and the Left generally; most women in this group would consider themselves socialist feminists. The NCCL's U.S. counterpart, the American Civil Liberties Union, is more likely to adopt wholeheartedly the language of individual rights and formal legal equality, while the NCCL is concerned about collective rights and is acutely conscious of class issues. It is not surprising, then, that the Women's Rights Unit of the British NCCL advocated the trade union position on protective legislation while, in the United States, the ACLU Women's Rights Project vigorously opposes any special treatment.

When the Labour Party took office in 1974, the NCCL wrote to Roy Jenkins, the new Home Secretary, asking for assurance that the Government would not repeal the laws on protective legislation. In 1975, the NCCL Women's Rights Unit published a pamphlet entitled "Women Factory Workers: The Case Against Repealing the Protective Laws." Although it recognized that the social climate had changed and that it was no longer seen as immoral for women to work nights, its main argument against repeal was that women still had two jobs. They had primary responsibility for housework and child care as well as holding down a paid job. The NCCL argued further that working shifts was bad for both men's and women's health and was socially disruptive. Assuming most people only work nights because it pays better, the NCCL argued that ways should be found to protect all workers and limit work at night to those workplaces, such as hospitals, where it was essential. The NCCL tried to turn the freedom of choice argument on its head, maintaining that if protective legislation were abolished, more women would be pushed into working nights to keep their jobs. It argued that abolishing protective legislation would not insure equal pay for women because employers had been busily segregating the workplace since 1970 when the Equal Pay Act was passed (it did not take effect until 1975). Thus, protective legislation gave women the freedom to choose to work during the day.

In 1979, the NCCL Women's Rights Unit published *The Shift Work Swindle* that criticized the Equal Opportunities Commission's proposals for reforming the law on protective legislation. Its main criticism was that the recommendations reflected a false concept of equal opportunity between the sexes, saying "equality is blindly pursued by the EOC, for its own sake, without regard to the relative impact on men and women of equal provisions under the law."[92] The NCCL's goal was to remove the need for special legal protection.

---

92. Jean Coussins, *The Shift Work Swindle: Or How the EOC's Proposals to Repeal Protective Legislation Would Really Affect Women Workers* (London: National Council for Civil Liberties Rights for Women Unit, 1979), 9.

In an ideal society no legislation that limited hours of employment by reference to sex would be necessary, other than the provision for maternity leave. Women are not inherently weaker or less capable of working long hours or anti-social hours. We wish to work towards a society where individuals can choose freely the job which suits them best, unfettered by distinctions of sex.[93]

Furthermore, it argued that equal vulnerability to exploitation was a false equality. Agreeing with the TUC that there should be a leveling up, not down, the NCCL denied the EOC's claim that women were being excluded from jobs because of the protective legislation and denied that repeal would "open up the gates of opportunity and higher pay to women in general."[94] Not only did it assert that the EOC lacked hard evidence for this claim, but it pointed out that the EOC seemed more worried about employers' need for flexibility than women's health and employment.

The NCCL also disputed the EOC's conclusions from its survey on women's attitudes toward working shifts. While the EOC interpreted the survey as proving that some women wanted such work, the NCCL criticized the EOC's inability to separate choice from need and further faulted its evidence of public support for the repeal of the laws. Drawing on the NCCL's own information from talking to workers, it claimed that working shifts was unhealthy for all employees. The NCCL said that the EOC's report was an example of "the EOC['s] excelling itself in discussing a question which affects many people's everyday lives as if it were a neatly compartmentalized issue."[95] Not content merely to keep the current provisions of the protective legislation, the NCCL advocated extending some of the provisions to men. It suggested, whenever possible, that workers be able to choose whether to do work during the evening or night rather than being required to do so by employers. The NCCL recommended that before the HSE granted exemptions, it poll workers to determine their preferences. Moreover, the NCCL called for better transportation and facilities for those working nights and for parental rights.

Feminists within the trade union movement joined the criticism of the EOC's report. Sheila McKechnie, then Health and Safety Officer for the Association of Scientific, Technical, and Managerial Staff (ASTMS), disputed that protective legislation led to discrimination, arguing that the EOC had presented no evidence for its position. She put the burden on the EOC to prove discrimination before the protection is removed.[96]

---

93. Ibid., 16.
94. Ibid., 10.
95. Ibid., 14.
96. ASTMS Comments on EOC Report, May 11, 1983, 3, on file at ASTMS office in Bishops Stortford.

Other feminist analysts criticized the report but were troubled by protective legislation. Feminist academic Jeanne Gregory commented, "If the report's attack on patriarchy is half-hearted and ineffectual, its attack on capitalism is almost non-existent."[97] She further criticized the report for not examining other countries' alterations in their protective legislation, such as that in the United States or Norway and Sweden, where restrictions on night work for both sexes appear to have been introduced without ruinous consequence.[98] Other feminist scholars have been critical of protective legislation. Helen Dingwall rejected the need for protective laws while Angela Coyle argued for their retention but modification: "As a piece of legislation it is very hard to defend. It represents a conglomeration of reactionary and paternalistic interests, and even on its own terms, it has never worked properly."[99] Jo Richardson, the feminist MP, has also spoken out against it. These feminists' concerns are not reflected in either the TUC's or NCCL's position.

In 1986, the Government ended the debate over protective legislation for the time being by repealing it. The Sex Discrimination Bill received royal assent in November and took effect by stages in 1987.[100] The Sex Discrimination Act of 1986 sought primarily to make the British and EC regulations consistent (see chap. 3). The EC Commission had taken a more critical position toward protective legislation, except for provisions for childbirth and pregnancy, since 1975.[101] Since 1973, Conservative Party policy had called for the repeal of protective legislation,[102] and in line with the Government's desire to reduce regulatory burdens on industry, it repealed all the protective legislation that restricted the employment of women—repealing the ban on working at night and the special regulations on factory work.[103] The bill passed despite opposition from feminists and trade unionists. Parliament voted down an amendment proposed by the Labour Party to require employers to hold a ballot of employees before changing their terms of employment. The NCCL called the repeal of protective legislation for women "catastrophic."[104]

To summarize, the discussion of protective legislation in the nineteenth century showed that male workers and reformers supported protective legislation for a variety of reasons. In the early twentieth century, working-class

97. Jeanne Gregory, *Formal or Substantive Legality: The Future of Protective Legislation*, Middlesex Polytechnic Occasional Paper No. 3 (November 1981), 21.

98. Ibid., 22.

99. Coyle, 9.

100. Paddy Stamp, "Working Women Better Off?" *Civil Liberty* 3 (February 1987): 2.

101. Christopher Docksey, "The European Community and the Promotion of Equality," in *Women, Employment and European Equality Law*, ed. by Christopher McCrudden (London: Eclipse, 1987), 14.

102. Gregory, 24.

103. The Government also repealed legislation restricting night work for bakers.

104. Stamp, 2. See also Anna Coote, *Women Factory Workers: The Case Against Repealing the Protective Laws* (London: National Council for Civil Liberties, 1975), 2, 11.

women's resistance and feminist campaigns against the protective laws died out, and not only did the Women's Conference of the TUC support protective legislation (at least until 1986), but the main feminist campaign group on this issue, the NCCL, advocated its retention and proposed the extension of the provisions to men. After the lifting of the marriage bars, opposition to protective legislation seems to have died from both working-class women and feminist organizations, except the Equal Opportunities Commission. Even non-aligned analysts who talked about its paternalistic origins and criticized those who emphasized difference did not call for repeal. Passage of the Sex Discrimination Act of 1986 ended the fifty-year stalemate. It is unlikely that Conservatives, interested in deregulating industry, will pass restrictive laws in the future. And if Labour and the TUC are true to their commitment in leveling up rather than down, it seems unlikely that they would pass restrictions on women workers only.

The arguments about difference have shifted over the last century and a half. The TUC has rejected the relevance of the moral and political arguments about sexual differences that may have led their predecessors to call for protective legislation. For the TUC, the only difference that justified differential treatment in the 1970s and 1980s was a social one; usually, the social difference only justified the retention of the laws as a short-term strategy while the TUC sought to extend protection to men. But assertions of biological and social difference reemerge when one discusses reproductive hazards. Fear of competition, beliefs that men are more deserving of employment than women, claims about women being morally compromised in male-dominated workplaces, and worries about threats to male authority in the home, while less publicly acceptable today, lie just under the surface to reemerge in times of recession or crisis.

Protective Legislation in the United States

The history of protective legislation in Britain and the United States reveals two pronounced differences. First, in the United States, many important battles over protective legislation took place in the courts; in Britain judges played no part. Reformers in the early 1900s had to convince U.S. judges that protective legislation for women did not contradict the liberty of contract that judges had enshrined into constitutional law. To get an exception to that established legal principle, reformers had to persuade U.S. judges that the abilities and needs of men and women workers were significantly different. When Congress passed Title VII of the Civil Rights Act of 1964, feminists again turned to the courts and asked judges to declare the laws inconsistent with Title VII's prohibition against discrimination. In both eras, the U.S. courts played a decisive role in determining whether states could "protect" women in the workplace. In Britain, the TUC, Parliament, the executive branch, and even the European Community were the important decision makers.

The second difference is that during the second wave of feminism, feminist groups in the United States condemned protective legislation and called for its removal, seeking formal legal equality for women. During this time in Britain, however, feminists reaffirmed their commitment to protective legislation. Since its beginning in the mid-nineteenth century, women were always represented on both sides of the debate. But the position of groups and the broad base of support shifted. At the turn of the century in the United States, reformers such as Florence Howe had proposed and supported special protection for women, and feminists in the National Women's Party argued that protective legislation was harmful to women's interests. In the 1960s, many in the feminist movement in the United States came to believe that protective legislation restricted women's employment opportunities more than it protected them from exploitation, while many trade union women argued for its retention. Organized feminist opposition to protective legislation in Britain died out in the early twentieth century, while their counterparts in the United States won the debate. In the United States, those opposed to protective legislation saw their views become law. In Britain, the Government abolished protective legislation in 1986 over the objections of socialist feminists and trade unionists.

Making such sweeping generalizations about groups of women across time raises problems of categorization. Historians' labels for each side expose their own positions. Feminist legal scholar Barbara Babcock, for example, divided women into two groups: feminists and social reformers. Feminists opposed protective legislation, and reformers supported it. Babcock argued forcefully that reformers were most definitely not feminists.

> Female social reformers such as the leaders of the NWTUL, the NCL, and the GFWC have sometimes been viewed as an important part of the women's movement . . . and indeed, in many ways they were. They typified what a large number of women were doing in the public sphere at that time and toward the end, they became a force in the achievement of suffrage. Fundamentally, however, they were not feminists; their first and primary concern had never been an effort to change women's position in society vis à vis men, and they had joined the suffrage movement not because of the essential justice of granting women the vote, but because they believed that the women's vote would help them enact the social reforms which were their essential concern. In pursuing this latter desire, they helped change the basic strategy of the women's movement.[105]

---

105. Babcock et al., 40.

Historian William Chafe, like Babcock, divided the two opposing camps into feminists and progressive reformers.[106] William O'Neill called those who favored protective legislation social feminists.[107] Banks refers to the two sides as humanitarians and equal rights feminists; at other times she refers to both sides as simply feminists. In her study of the Women's Trade Union League of New York, however, Nancy Schrom Dye disagrees with labeling only the opponents of protective legislation feminists.

> Significantly, both league members and their opponents considered themselves feminists. In no way was the debate over protective legislation a fight between feminists and social reformers. Rather, the conflict was between two competing versions of feminism and two widely divergent ways of improving women's status in a male-dominated society.[108]

Reva Siegel agrees.

> This persistent scheme of characterization artificially divides the women's movement, ignoring the fact that those who would fight over the legislation during the 1920s together fought for suffrage in the decades prior; indeed they did so on the unquestioned premise that such legislation was a benefit the vote itself might secure.[109]

Whatever one calls them, women campaigned both for and against protective legislation throughout its history in the United States as well as in Britain.

The history of protective legislation in the United States, however, must be understood in the context of cases asserting an absolute liberty of contract, as in the landmark decision in *Muller v. Oregon*.[110] The need to work within this legal paradigm led advocates to emphasize women's differences from men—an emphasis that perpetuated a legacy of acceptance of legal classifications based on sex, most clearly seen in *Goesaert v. Cleary*.[111] The legislative history of Title VII of the Civil Rights Act of 1964, which prohibited discrimination in employment on the basis of sex, like its British counterpart, left

---

106. Chafe, 113–14.

107. See William L. O'Neill, *Everyone Was Brave: The Rise and Fall of Feminism in America* (Chicago: Quadrangle, 1969); see also Nancy F. Cott, *The Grounding of Modern Feminism* (New Haven: Yale University Press, 1987), 117–42.

108. Nancy Schrom Dye, *As Equals and as Sisters: Feminism, the Labor Movement, and the Women's Trade Union League of New York* (Columbia: University of Missouri Press, 1980), 160.

109. Reva Siegel, Review of *Origins of Protective Labor Legislation for Women, 1905–1925*, by Susan Lehrer, *Berkeley Women's Law Journal* 3 (1987–88): 180.

110. 208 U.S. 412 (1908).

111. 335 U.S. 464 (1948).

open the question of whether state protective laws for women conflicted with its provisions. The series of guidelines issued by the Equal Employment Opportunities Commission (EEOC) on protective legislation reflected legislators' ambivalence about state protective laws. In *Rosenfeld v. Southern Pacific Co.*,[112] the U.S. Court of Appeals for the Ninth Circuit ultimately declared state protective laws to be unlawful under Title VII.

Like their British counterparts, male trade unionists in the United States often saw women as dangerous competitors who could undercut their wages rather than as fellow workers to recruit into their unions. Their rhetoric also reflected their view that women belonged in the home. However, some groups of men workers, like miners, sympathized with women workers and recognized their vital contribution to family incomes.[113] Women had long debated among themselves whether they should seek state intervention or organize into unions with men. The Women's Trade Union League began by advocating organization, but its frustration with the AFL led it to favor legislation.[114] The obstacles to women's unionization were many and included the hostility and discrimination of the unions themselves. Some trade union women activists reluctantly came to support protective legislation.[115]

In response to Progressives' and trade unionists' efforts to secure state intervention to improve the wages and working conditions of workers, the Supreme Court interpreted the Constitution to confer a nearly absolute right to freedom of contract for workers and employers. *Lochner v. New York*[116] held that a New York law limiting the number of hours bakers could work each day violated liberty of contract. Yet in *Holden v. Hardy*,[117] the Court had previously decided that the Constitution permitted states to regulate employment in special circumstances, such as mining, if the work was dangerous. By 1908, nineteen states had passed protective legislation that applied only to women workers, and the decisions of state supreme courts were split over the constitutionality of such laws.[118] Several courts had struck down state regulations as violations of liberty of contract while others upheld them because women were properly placed in a separate category than men. When the Supreme Court heard a challenge to an Oregon law that limited the number of hours women could work in laundries, reformers hoped to capitalize on the

---

112. 444 F.2d 1219 (9th Cir. 1971).

113. Kessler-Harris, "Where are the Organized Women Workers?" 96–98.

114. Alice Kessler-Harris, "Protection for Women: Trade Unions and Labor Laws," in *Double Exposure: Women's Health Hazards on the Job and at Home*, ed. by Wendy Chavkin (New York: Monthly Review Press, 1984), 146. The leaders of the Women's Trade Union League shifted their focus to protective legislation when they failed to organize women (Dye, 142).

115. Kessler-Harris, "Where Are the Organized Women Workers?" 101; Dye, 140–61.

116. 198 U.S. 45 (1905).

117. 169 U.S. 366 (1898).

118. Albie Sachs and Joan Hoff Wilson, *Sexism and the Law: A Study of Male Beliefs and Judicial Bias* (Oxford: Martin Robertson, 1978), 112.

position of some judges that women belonged in a separate legal category, and thus, like miners, were an exception to the right to freely contract.[119]

The National Consumers League (NCL), an advocate of protective legislation for all workers, approached Louis Brandeis to represent it in filing an amicus curiae brief in the Oregon case.[120] Amicus briefs provide interest groups, agencies, and even members of Congress with a vehicle to lobby courts by providing legal arguments, sociological evidence, and political pressure.[121] In the end, Oregon hired Brandeis as special counsel. The NCL had a difficult task in persuading the Court to make an exception to the doctrine of liberty of contract. The brief, prepared by Josephine and Pauline Goldmark,[122] cited legal precedents only as a preliminary to providing extensive evidence about the health risks women workers faced and the physical differences between the sexes, such as the important differences between men's and women's knees.[123] To overcome the Court's disposition against state regulations that interfered with liberty of contract, the NCL emphasized that women's physical weaknesses placed them in a separate category than male workers. In addition, women's health was of public concern because of the influence of vigorous health upon the future "well-being of the race."[124]

The Court accepted the arguments of the Brandeis brief:

That woman's physical structure and the performance of maternal functions place her at a disadvantage in the struggle for subsistence is obvious. This is especially true when the burdens of motherhood are upon her. . . .

Still again, history discloses the fact that woman has always been dependent upon man. He established his control at the outset by superior physical strength, and this control in various forms, with diminishing intensity, has continued to the present. . . . It is still true that in the struggle for subsistence she is not an equal competitor with her brother. . . . Differentiated by these matters from the other sex, she is

119. See Nancy S. Erickson, "*Muller v. Oregon* Reconsidered: The Origins of a Sex-Based Doctrine of Liberty of Contract," paper presented at the annual meeting of the Association of Social and Legal Historians, Baltimore, October 22, 1983, 21.

120. Judith A. Baer, *The Chains of Protection: The Judicial Response to Women's Labor Legislation* (Westport, Conn.: Greenwood Press, 1978), 57.

121. Karen O'Connor and Lee Epstein, "Court Rules and Workload: A Case Study of Rules Governing Amicus Curiae Participation," *Justice System Journal* 8 (1983): 35–45; Ernest Angell, "The Amicus Curiae: American Development of English Institutions," *International and Comparative Law Quarterly* 16 (October 1967): 1017–44; Samuel Krislov, "The Amicus Curiae Brief: From Friendship to Advocacy," *Yale Law Journal* 72 (1963): 694–721.

122. Sachs and Wilson, 113.

123. Erickson argues that "Brandeis-type briefs" were in evidence before *Muller v. Oregon* and the so-called Brandeis brief was unique only in the amount of sociological and scientific evidence included (Erickson, 20).

124. Muller v. Oregon, 208 U.S. 412, 422 (1908).

properly placed in a class by herself, and legislation designed for her protection may be sustained, even when like legislation is not necessary for men and could not be sustained.[125]

Muller was thus part of a chain of legal precedents that found that the differences between the sexes justified legal distinctions between men and women. It differed from this tradition only in the rationale for the distinction.

Muller enshrined as constitutional doctrine three assumptions about women which recur throughout the history of special labor regulation. First, the most important distinctions between women and men are not temporary but permanent; they consist not of the social, economic, and political conditions of male supremacy but of the physical differences in strength and, especially, reproductive function. Second, women's interests are either identical with or properly subordinate to those of others, whether men, children, families, or "the race." Women are a class, but a class which is peculiarly interest-less. Third, the ability to bear children—presumably a valuable social function—does not confer privileges or benefits; instead, it diminishes the woman as citizen. Bearing children is in tension with bearing rights.[126]

Although those defending the Oregon statute sought regulation of working conditions for both men and women,[127] *Muller* had significance beyond standing as an exception to liberty of contract. Courts referred to the comments of Justice Brewer in *Muller* about the appropriateness of treating the sexes differently in law long after liberty of contract became a remnant of the past.

Once women won the vote in 1920, feminists turned their attention to an equal rights amendment to the Constitution. The differences between feminists and social reformers, no longer hidden by their common pursuit of suffrage, widened. The newly formed National Women's Party explicitly opposed laws that applied to one sex only. It responded to working women's reports that the protective laws were a convenient tool to remove them from good jobs they had filled during World War I.[128] "The first women to oppose protective labor legislation were workers in male-dominated trades—printing, polishing and grinding, coremaking, streetcar conducting—who had lost their jobs because of the so-called 'protective' laws."[129] Women printers

---

125. Ibid., 421–22.
126. Judith A. Baer, "Equality and Protection in the Twentieth Century," paper presented at the annual meeting of the Midwest Political Science Association, Chicago, April 11–14, 1984, 6.
127. Erickson, 8.
128. Chafe, 124–25.
129. Babcock et al., 249, quoting Ann Corinne Hill, "Protective Labor Legislation for Women: Its Origin and Effect" (unpublished paper, Yale Law School, 1970).

led working women in advocating equal treatment, forming the Women's League for Equal Opportunity and the Equal Rights Association. Women workers may have welcomed regulations on their working conditions, but they strenuously objected when the state then asserted the authority to restrict the kinds of work they could do.[130] The social reformer part of the suffrage movement formed the League of Women Voters and supported the retention of protective legislation.[131] The Women's Bureau in the Department of Labor, led by social reformers, issued a report in 1928 supporting single-sex laws.

The slurs, suspicions, and accusations hurled at the opposite side mirrored the debate in Britain. Reformers charged the National Women's Party with being "hysterical feminists" concerned only for the individual woman rather than working-class women as a group. Feminists saw trade union support for protective laws as a thin guise for getting rid of competition. Maximum-hours laws disproportionately reduced the employment of foreign-born women, leaving the employment of white women unaffected. Early support for maximum-hours legislation for women may have been motivated in part by hostility to immigration.[132] Feminists were convinced that protection led to discrimination and exclusion from jobs. They saw reformers as emphasizing women's differences and leaving sex roles unchallenged.

> The social reformers were committed to improving the present society, not to changing one of its fundamental divisions; for them, single-sex laws helped ease the lot of the poor woman worker by helping her get home to her children, so she could be a better mother. They did not realize that this narrow view of the woman worker's problems reinforced women's lowly position in the labor market because a society rigidly divided along sex lines demanded the same hierarchy in the labor market as in the home. In all the years of the struggle to get and keep single-sex labor laws, the reformers never confronted the essential nature of sex discrimination in the labor market—sex segregation and the undervaluation of the so-called "women's jobs." Thus the reformers actually helped preserve the status quo for the woman worker—low-paid, menial jobs with no chance for advancement out of the female labor ghetto.[133]

Yet the differences may have been overestimated.

---

130. Kessler-Harris, "Protection for Women," 145.

131. Jane De Hart Mathews, "The New Feminism and the Dynamics of Social Change," in *Women's America: Refocusing the Past*, ed. by Linda K. Kerber and Jane De Hart Mathews (New York: Oxford University Press, 1982), 399.

132. Elisabeth M. Landes, "The Effect of State Maximum-Hours Laws on the Employment of Women in 1920," *Journal of Political Economy* 88 (1980): 476–94.

133. Babcock et al., 268.

In the trade of recriminations, there were exaggerations and caricatures. The relation of sex-based legislation to the welfare of women workers was more ambiguous and complicated than either side acknowledged.[134]

The state of the economy greatly affected women's place in the labor force. During the Depression, there was hostility to women working, particularly married women, and laws banned women from many jobs. During World War II, women poured into jobs traditionally done by men. Because of the intense job segregation by sex prior to World War II, some of the restrictions may have been more protective than discriminatory. After the war, however, women were expected to vacate their new positions for the returning men. Men workers used long-standing protective laws that had been set aside during the war and passed new ones to displace women from "their" jobs.[135] Although the Supreme Court has long since stopped preventing states from regulating the employment contract, *Muller v. Oregon*, which emphasized men's and women's differences, lay waiting to be called into service.

Unions representing male bartenders sought legislation to exclude women from pouring or dispensing drinks behind bars. Michigan passed such a law, prohibiting the licensing of women bartenders except the wife and daughter of the male owner; Michigan's law did, however, allow women to serve as cocktail waitresses. Defenders of the law feigned concern for women's morals, yet the inconsistency of this arrangement was obvious to many who believed that the real purpose of the statute was to remove female bar owners from competition with men. Male bartenders openly expressed their desire to remove competition, and this motive was never denied in the ensuing litigation.

When Michigan began to enforce the law, the Goesaerts, a mother and daughter who ran a bar, and other women bar owners and barmaids filed suit. The plaintiffs claimed that enforcement of the statute would make them unable to run their businesses economically or to pursue their occupations.[136] The affidavits of women talked about how they supported invalid husbands in the next room while tending bar, or how they could not afford to hire male bartenders who were more likely to become drunk on the job. Babcock reports:

---

134. Cott, 135. For an account of differences between social feminists' vision of equality and that put forth in legal briefs, see Sybil Lipschultz, "Social Feminism and Legal Discourse, 1908–1923," in *At the Boundaries of Law: Feminism and Legal Theory*, ed. by Martha Albertson Fineman and Nancy Sweet Thomadsen (New York: Routledge, 1991), 209–26.

135. Ann Corinne Hill, "Women Workers and the Courts: A Legal Case History," *Feminist Studies* 5 (1979): 260. See also Sheila Tobias and Lisa Anderson, "What Really Happened to Rosie the Riveter? Demobilization and the Female Labor Force, 1944–47," in *Women's America: Refocusing the Past*, ed. by Linda K. Kerber and Jane De Hart Mathews (New York: Oxford University Press, 1982), 366.

136. Babcock et al., 94.

The complaint and subsequent briefs clearly reveal that this was in no sense a symbolic or educative suit, but was brought by plaintiffs desperately and immediately concerned about the impact of the statute on their ability to make a living.[137]

Goesaert v. Cleary is the clearest legacy of *Muller*. *Muller* invoked the contract clause, and *Goesaert* invoked the equal protection clause. The Supreme Court ruled in 1948 that the Michigan statute was not a violation of the equal protection clause of the Fourteenth Amendment.[138] Although the Court did not cite *Muller*, it commented:

> Michigan could, beyond question, forbid all women from working behind a bar. This is so despite the vast changes in the social and legal position of women. The fact that women may now have achieved the virtues that men have long claimed as their prerogatives and to indulge in vices that men have long practiced, does not preclude the States from drawing a sharp line between the sexes. . . . The Constitution does not require sociological insight, or shifting social standards, any more than it requires them to keep abreast of the latest scientific standards.[139]

The Court failed to address the severe economic harm to women posed by such lawful discrimination. Considering the economic consequences, one might have expected the Court to at least mention the evidence about the severe moral and social problems justifying such an exclusion. None was offered. Neither the Justices nor the legislators asked why women should be deprived of jobs rather than antisocial customers penalized.[140]

After 1937, the Court abstained from scrutinizing economic regulation except where states applied racial categories or violated fundamental rights. This abstinence may have had as much to do with the Court's attitude toward state regulation as it did its affirmation of sex differences.

> The Court indicates that it considers the issue of sex discrimination closed, but not, apparently, so much because precedents have determined that sex is always a permissible basis for classification as because the entire issue of economic regulation is closed.[141]

Whether *Muller* was significant in influencing judges or whether they were already inclined to accept differential treatment is hard to say, although

137. Ibid.

138. The Florida Supreme Court had found that a similar statute violated the equal protection clause in Brown v. Foley, 29 So. 2d 870 (1947).

139. Goesaert v. Cleary, 335 U.S. 464, 465–66 (1948).

140. Babcock et al., 96.

141. Baer, *The Chains of Protection*, 114.

they referred to the opinion as relevant, if not binding. In arguing for protective legislation for women as the way to eventually secure it for all workers, reformers lent their support to differential treatment for women, thereby reinforcing the view judges expressed in *Goesaert* and later cases. Certainly *Muller* provided a clear statement of several possible justifications for the Michigan statute. To uphold sex-based protective legislation, courts "have spun a web of myths about all women."[142] The judiciary's acceptance of sex-based categories did not change until the 1970s.

By the 1960s, restrictions still applied to women, but many benefits had been extended to men workers. Some twenty-six states prohibited women from working in mining, bartending, or other occupations.[143] When Congress passed a bill in 1964 to prohibit discrimination on the basis of sex, one would have thought that it would have given attention to protective legislation. A brief review of the history of this bill, however, reveals that not only did Congress fail to consider the significance of the bill for state protective laws, but it failed to consider the significance of its prohibiting discrimination on the basis of sex altogether.

When the U.S. House of Representatives debated a bill to forbid discrimination on the basis of race, religion, or national origin, Congressman Howard Smith from Virginia introduced an amendment on the floor of the House to add sex to the list of prohibitions.[144] His purpose was to kill the bill—to sink the bill "under gales of laughter."[145] Congressman Smith assumed that prohibiting discrimination on the basis of sex was so ridiculous that it would sabotage the prohibition of discrimination on the basis of race. The initiator of the amendment, however, misjudged the House. In fact, there was some support for prohibiting discrimination on the basis of sex, but adding sex at this late stage of the bill presented problems. Representative Edith Green of Oregon argued that neither the House Judiciary Committee nor the House Education and Labor Committee had considered adding sex to the bill, and neither had been petitioned to do so. Not only was there no testimony before the committees making up a legislative history, but there was also no discussion of sex discrimination in the committees' reports.[146]

In the brief floor debate, members argued about two points: whether the addition of sex would indeed kill the bill and what adding sex would mean for protective legislation. On this first point, Esther Peterson, Assistant Secretary of Labor in charge of the Women's Bureau, a governmental agency within the

---

142. A. Hill, 271.

143. Babcock et al., 261.

144. *Congressional Record*, 88th Cong., 2d sess., 1964, 110:2577.

145. Carolyn Bird, *Born Female: The High Cost of Keeping Women Down* (New York: David McKay, 1968), 5.

146. *Congressional Record*, 88th Cong., 2d sess., 1964, 110:2582.

Department of Labor, sent a letter that was read into the record asking that sex not be added to the bill.

> But discrimination based on sex, the Commission [on the status of Women] believes, involves problems sufficiently different from discrimination based on other factors listed to make separate treatment preferable.[147]

The American Association of University Women (AAUW) was also against adding sex to the bill.[148] Congressman Emmanuel Celler from New York opposed the amendment, suggesting that it would outlaw all state protective legislation that he saw as "favorable to women."[149] Congresswoman Martha Griffiths from Michigan argued to the contrary: "Most of the so-called protective legislation has really been to protect men's rights in better paying jobs."[150] Congresswoman Katherine St. George from New York agreed, saying protective legislation "prevents women from going into the higher salary brackets."[151] Although there was a brief discussion of the merits of protective legislation for women, it was not at all clear from the debate whether Congress intended Title VII to interfere with state laws.

The debate over Title VII revealed the divisions among women over the desirability of protective legislation as well as the intense hostility to women's equality. It was not clear how adding sex to Title VII would affect protective legislation. Although the amendment passed the House and although the Senate adopted the House version, conflicting statements about how adding sex would affect state protective laws meant that the legislative history was inconclusive about this point.

Given the ambivalence about the merits of protective legislation and the inconsistent statements in the House debates (and the absence of any discussion in the committee reports), it is not surprising that the agency created to enforce Title VII, the Equal Employment Opportunities Commission (EEOC), was hesitant to issue guidelines. Both sides immediately lobbied the EEOC for their position. Church groups and women's labor groups defended protective laws.[152] The EEOC was reluctant to infer congressional intent to override state protective laws because women's groups were divided.

The EEOC's initial guidelines reflected its position that some protective laws led to discrimination while others might prevent exploitation. Thus, the EEOC allowed employers to present evidence that state protective laws

---

147. Ibid., 2577.
148. Ibid., 2582.
149. Ibid., 2577.
150. Ibid., 2580.
151. Ibid.
152. Babcock et al., 262.

should fall under the bona fide occupational qualification exception (BFOQ) to Title VII.

> The Commission believes that some state laws and regulations with respect to the employment of women, although originally for valid protective reasons, have ceased to be relevant to our technology or to the expanding role of the woman worker in our economy. . . .
>
> The Commission does not believe that Congress intended to disturb such laws and regulations which are intended to, and have the effect of, protecting women against exploitation and hazard. Accordingly, the Commission will consider limitations or prohibitions imposed by such state laws or regulations as a basis for application of the bona fide occupational qualification exception. However, in cases where the clear effect of a law in current circumstances is not to protect women but to subject them to discrimination, the law will not be considered a justification for discrimination.[153]

The EEOC then appealed to Congress to clarify its intent[154] and to women's groups to inform the agency of their positions.[155]

By recognizing the discriminatory potential of protective legislation while refusing to prohibit it altogether, the EEOC's 1965 guidelines took the middle ground. But because the agency gave no method for determining whether state laws were protective or discriminatory, the guidelines were useless. The EEOC knew that it could not force states to amend their laws merely by declaring them inconsistent with Title VII.[156] As one commentator noted, "Perhaps in no other context has the frustration caused the Commission by its lack of enforcement powers been more apparent than in the area of state protective laws."[157]

A White House Conference on Equal Employment in 1965 had discussed the possibility that protective legislation may protect unorganized women in low-paid jobs.[158] The EEOC's reluctance to advocate getting rid of protective legislation, stemming from the absence of congressional guidance, was further reinforced by a two-day conference in 1967 that revealed strong disagreement among interest groups.[159] The National Women's Party, the International

---

153. 29 C.F.R. §1604.1 (1965), 30 *Fed. Reg.* 14927 (1965).

154. Joseph P. Kennedy, "Sex Discrimination: State Protective Laws Since Title VII," *Notre Dame Lawyer* 47 (1972): 523.

155. *Labor Relations Reporter* 65 (May 8, 1967): 20–22, quoted in James C. Oldham, "Sex Discrimination and State Protective Laws," *Denver Law Journal* 44 (1967): 351 n.35.

156. Richard K. Berg, "Title VII: A Three Years' View," *Notre Dame Lawyer* 44 (1969): 335.

157. Oldham, 348.

158. 59 L.R.R.M. 88 (1965), cited in Berg, 333 n.121.

159. Oldham, 351 n.35; citing 65 *Lab. Rel. Rep.* 20–22 (May 8, 1967).

Chemical Workers, and the National Organization for Women took a position favoring the elimination of all protective laws. The United Auto Workers declared "so-called 'protective' state laws—that is those based on stereotypes as to sex rather than true biological factors—are undesirable relics of the past."[160] Other unions and the National Consumer's League argued against repeal. The AFL-CIO opposed an equal rights amendment to the Constitution because it believed that such an amendment would eliminate protective legislation.[161] While the National Organization for Women focused on women's role as sole or cosupporters of their families' incomes, the AFL-CIO and the NCL echoed the British TUC in their concern for women's double day.

> Thus, although men workers are theoretically harmed by long hours (and must indeed take on more than their fair share since women are barred from doing so—thereby placing, incidentally, additional pressure on women to take on more than their fair share of household work), the maximum hours laws must be preserved so that women can fulfill their household duties![162]

The EEOC changed its position in 1968, declaring that it could not resolve the problems with protective legislation itself. It advised that the commission would make no findings as to reasonable cause when faced with a challenge to state protective laws, but it would advise the charging party of her rights to bring suit under Title VII, "to secure a judicial determination as to the validity of the state law or regulations."[163] Later, the EEOC decided to seek judicial interpretation and to advocate as amicus that courts declare protective legislation inconsistent with Title VII.

> Such litigation to resolve the uncertainties as to the application of Title VII seems desirable and necessary, and the Commission reserves the right to appear as amicus curiae to present its views as to the proper construction of Title VII.[164]

Meanwhile, the EEOC began to find "reasonable cause" in cases in which employed women charged loss of job opportunities because of protective laws.[165]

The EEOC soon had an opportunity in *Rosenfeld v. Southern Pacific Co.*,[166] the first case in which a federal court held a state protective law

---

160. Babcock et al., 263.
161. Kessler-Harris, "Protection for Women," 146.
162. Babcock et al., 266.
163. 13 Empl. Prac. Guide (CCH) §16.900.001 n.2 (1968), quoted in Berg, 335.
164. Ibid.
165. Babcock et al., 267.
166. 293 F. Supp. 1219 (C.D. Ca. 1968).

invalid under Title VII. Leah Rosenfeld had applied for a job as an agent-telegrapher with Southern Pacific, a job that required lifting and being on call for long hours in emergencies. Southern Pacific refused to hire her because to do so would violate California's laws that limited the number of hours women could work and how much weight they could lift. Instead, it gave the job to a male employee with less seniority. The EEOC filed an amicus brief arguing that Title VII superseded the state laws.[167] In issuing summary judgment on November 22, 1968, the U.S. District Court for the Central District of California found that Southern Pacific had not tested Rosenfeld to see if she could perform the job. It held that Rosenfeld had been discriminated against solely on the basis of sex and further concluded that the California laws did not create a bona fide occupational qualification and so violated Title VII. The court determined that, where the EEOC's guidelines conflicted with its ruling, the guidelines were void.

While Southern Pacific was appealing this decision, another case challenging state protective laws reached a federal appellate court. Lorena Weeks had challenged Georgia's weight restrictions, claiming they denied her opportunities for promotion. The District Court for the Southern District of Georgia examined the legislative history of Title VII to see if Congress intended to nullify state laws, and, following the EEOC guidelines, found that Georgia's weight restrictions created a bona fide occupational qualification (BFOQ).[168]

Weeks appealed, and the U.S. Court of Appeals for the Fifth Circuit became the first federal appellate court to invalidate a state protective law. In *Weeks v. Southern Bell Telephone and Telegraph Company*,[169] the court referred to both the EEOC's guidelines that held that state protective laws could create a bona fide occupational qualification and noted the decision of the district court in *Rosenfeld*. The court pointed out that Southern Bell had produced no evidence "that all, or substantially all, women would be unable to perform [the weight-lifting requirements]."[170] It held that the BFOQ exception should be a narrow one, referring to EEOC guidelines that prohibited employers from acting on "stereotyped characterizations of the sexes" to deny women employment opportunities.[171] The court went beyond the holding in *Rosenfeld*, stating that the employer had the burden to prove a BFOQ by showing all or nearly all women could not do the job, concluding:

> Title VII rejects just this type of romantic paternalism as unduly Victorian and instead vests individual women with the power to decide whether or not to take on unromantic tasks. Men have always had the

---

167. Babcock et al., 267.
168. Weeks v. Southern Bell Tel. & Tel. Co., 277 F. Supp. 117 (S.D. Ga. 1967).
169. 408 F.2d 228 (5th Cir. 1969).
170. Ibid., 234.
171. 29 C.F.R. §1601.1(a).

right to determine whether the incremental increase in remuneration for strenuous, dangerous, obnoxious, boring or unromantic tasks is worth the candle. The promise of Title VII is that women are now to be on equal footing. We cannot conclude that by including the bona fide occupational qualification exception Congress intended to renege on that promise.[172]

In May, 1969, a district court in Oregon invalidated that state's weight-lifting limits.[173] In July, a district court in Alabama and the Court of Appeals for the Seventh Circuit invalidated private companies' weight-lifting restrictions.[174] In response to these decisions, the EEOC promulgated new guidelines on August 19, 1969.

The Commission believes that such State laws and regulations [which prohibit or limit the employment of females], although originally promulgated for the purpose of protecting females, have ceased to be relevant to our technology or to the expanding role of the female worker in our economy. The Commission has found that such laws and regulations do not take into account the capacities, preferences, and abilities of individual females and tend to discriminate rather than protect. Accordingly, the Commission has concluded that such laws and regulations conflict with Title VII of the Civil Rights Act of 1964 and will not be considered a defense to an otherwise established unlawful employment practice or as a basis for the application of the bona fide occupational qualification exception.[175]

On appeal, the U.S. Court of Appeals for the Ninth Circuit affirmed the district court's ruling in *Rosenfeld*, saying: "the company attempts to raise a commonly accepted characterization of women as the 'weaker sex' to the level of a BFOQ."[176] The court of appeals held that the California laws "run contrary to the general objective of Title VII of the Civil Rights Act of 1964, and are therefore, by virtue of the Supremacy Clause, supplanted by Title VII."[177] The court went on to quote the new EEOC guidelines and commented, "The administrative interpretation of the Act by the enforcing agency is entitled to great deference."[178]

Congress had sent conflicting messages about the application of Title VII

---

172. 408 F.2d 228, 236 (5th Cir. 1969).

173. Richards v. Griffith Rubber Mills, 300 F. Supp. 338 (D. Ore. 1969).

174. Cheatwood v. South Central Bell Tel. & Tel. Co., 303 F. Supp. 754 (M.D. Ala. 1969); Bowe v. Colgate-Palmolive Co., 416 F.2d 711 (7th Cir. 1969).

175. 29 C.F.R. §1604.1 (b) (1970); 34 *Fed. Reg.* 13367–68 (1969).

176. 444 F.2d 1219, 1224 (9th Cir. 1971).

177. Ibid., 1225.

178. Ibid., 1226.

to state protective laws and refused to clarify its intent in response to a request by the EEOC. Therefore, it was the courts that ultimately determined that protective legislation was inconsistent with Title VII. *Weeks, Rosenfeld,* and later cases put an end to protective legislation.[179]

The second wave of feminism in the 1960s and 1970s no doubt influenced the EEOC and U.S. judges. On the whole, British feminists supported protective legislation at that time, but U.S. feminists were initially divided. The tide turned against those who favored protective legislation. Women's groups in the United States have never been totally united on protective legislation. Just as the National Woman's Party had opposed protective legislation in the 1920s, several women's groups defended it against the developing consensus in the 1960s. As the debates on Title VII and the ERA show, many women believed that protective legislation was merely a ruse to remove them from competition with men and to deny them employment opportunities. Labor historian Alice Kessler-Harris writes:

> Women fought bitterly to retain jobs from which protective legislation removed them. They understood, as did the skilled craftsmen who often supported campaigns for legislative restriction, that limiting access to jobs created a permanent disability in the labor force in that it deprived them of opportunities for advancement. Restrictive legislation therefore affirmed the job segregation of a divided labor market.[180]

The impetus in both the burgeoning feminist movement, reflected in the growing membership of NOW, and the position of the EEOC on other issues supported the view that employers should judge women according to their individual capacities rather than by applying stereotypes. That the judiciary would accept this position, however, was not a foregone conclusion. Feminists would have preferred the courts to follow the opinion of Justice Peters of the California Supreme Court in *Sail' er Inn v. Kirby,* in which six justices joined.

> Laws which disable women from full participation in the political, business and economic arenas are often characterized as "protective" and beneficial. Those same laws applied to racial or ethnic minorities would readily be recognized as invidious and impermissible. The pedestal upon which women have been placed has all too often, upon closer inspection, been revealed as a cage.[181]

The decisions in *Rosenfeld, Weeks,* and their progeny put an end, at least at that time, to the debates over protective legislation, even though the Su-

---

179. For a complete list of cases, see Babcock et al., 270–71.
180. Kessler-Harris, "Protection for Women," 147.
181. 95 Cal.Rptr. 329, 341 (1971).

preme Court never addressed the issue. The decisions of the two courts of appeals undoubtedly encouraged the EEOC to take a stronger stand against protective legislation and bolstered those feminists who opposed it. States declined to challenge the rulings and, instead, amended their statutes; the minority of feminists who favored protective legislation also acquiesced. The major barrier to support for the ERA—groups' support for protective legislation—was gone. That the decisive battles over protective legislation took place in the courts sets the United States apart from Britain, where the discussions took place in Parliament, political parties, trade unions, and governmental agencies. Judges did not decide the issue.

The dominance of the well-organized liberal feminist wing of the feminist movement, the disposition of the issue by courts rather than legislatures or executive agencies, and differences in political culture favoring formal legal equality rather than overt class politics contributed to the success of the equal treatment coalition in the United States that opposed protective legislation. The shifting attitudes toward protective legislation reflected both the rebirth of feminism and the expansion of the welfare state. While exploitation of women workers continues, concessions such as a minimum wage and overtime pay have been won for all workers.

In the United States in the nineteenth and early twentieth centuries, the debate over protective legislation represented disagreement over fundamentals: were women significantly different than men in ways relevant to their employment? Should feminists try to accept men's and women's different social roles and try to ameliorate the worst effects? Feminists also fervently disagreed about strategy. Should men and women fight together for a better workplace, banning all nonessential night work for everyone, for example, or should we differentiate between different groups of workers? Does treating women and men differently only reinforce biological and social differences, ultimately translating into total exclusion from different kinds of work? Women ardently disagreed about the effects of protective legislation; feminists saw difference as ultimately leading to disadvantage—others saw relief from exploitation.

At every turn, there was a class dimension to the debate. Middle-class feminists were accused of being insensitive to the needs of working women. Socialist feminists, the dominant group in Britain during the second wave, allied themselves with working-class women and maintained that protective legislation prevented employers from exploiting them. Liberal feminists in the United States, the dominant group, maintained that protection led to discrimination, and that working-class women were excluded from work and their wages depressed. They advocated legal equality. Working-class women found themselves on both sides of the debate. At times, they saw restrictions as beneficial. When the restrictions led to reduced job opportunities, they vigorously opposed them.

The ascendancy of liberal feminists in the United States and socialist feminists in Britain has implications for how feminists in each country respond to exclusionary policies that are a new form of protection. We can expect a stronger objection to differential treatment for men and women from U.S. feminists. We can expect working-class women excluded from jobs to fight exclusionary policies in both countries—perhaps with more support by unions and feminists in the United States. We also can expect the U.S. courts to provide an arena for resolving these disputes, but not the British courts. In the United States, the rhetoric of freedom of choice and equal employment opportunity won the day; in Britain, the Tory Government sought to end burdens on industry. Extrapolating to the case of exclusionary policies, one might predict that at least U.S. feminists might argue for women to choose, based on an informed judgment, whether or not to undergo certain kinds of work while the British Government might defer to the discretion of industry to set its own policy.

Since the debate over protective legislation began in the 1960s, the terrain has radically changed. As women's participation in paid employment and politics has become more acceptable, the focus has shifted from women to fetuses. In what has been dubbed "fetal mania" or a "fetus fetish," the state has become increasingly willing to regulate and control women's bodies, including jailing pregnant women, on behalf of "fetal rights."[182] The history of protective legislation shows how the justification for treating women differently than men in the workplace changed over time. Some argued women were inferior workers, weaker, and the mothers of the race. Later the justification was that men and women had different social roles: women's double day meant that their labor force participation must be restricted. Injecting the fetus into the argument means that women are more likely to be seen in biological terms, as vessels. Treating the matter as an issue of biological difference obscures the way that social norms about women's proper role in society determine how we interpret the "facts" of biological difference.

As middle-class feminists fought middle-class reformers, there were heavy doses of paternalism on all sides. The motives of all the players were complex and difficult to assess; groups with contradictory goals converged in support of particular pieces of legislation for different reasons. The same complex mix of motive and effect, of accusations about hidden goals, re-emerges when discussing exclusionary policies. Who should set policies for working women? Can we leave women's interests in the hands of business, ostensibly committed to formal legal equality and freedom of choice for women? In the hands of the TUC, with its checkered history of ignoring the concerns of the Women's Advisory Committee and groups of women workers? In the hands of the AFL-CIO, which supported protective legislation? In the hands of feminist interest groups? With the emergence of fetal mania we also must ask: to whom should we entrust the task of protecting fetuses?

---

182. See Gallagher; see also Katha Pollit, "'Fetal Rights': A New Assault on Feminism," *Nation* 12 (March 26, 1990): 409–18.

CHAPTER 2

Feminist Perspectives on Sex Discrimination Law

In cases on exclusionary policies, judges must decide whether asserted differences between the sexes are "real" or based on stereotypes and whether biological differences justify treating women less favorably in the workplace.[1] Differences between the way British and U.S. judges have dealt with these issues highlight important differences in the two legal and political systems. Understanding these decisions requires an understanding of the institutional structure of sex discrimination law. The different outcomes, however, mask an underlying similarity in the way judges in both countries conceptualize discrimination and apply their notions of discrimination in these cases. Thus, cases on exclusionary policies provide a unique opportunity not only for understanding how a particular institutional structure produces specific outcomes, but also for exposing and critiquing the limitations of prevailing notions of discrimination and equality.

Exclusionary policies are the new generation of protective policies, and, as such, they rest on some of the same problematic assumptions and exhibit many of the same discriminatory effects as protective legislation in the past. In the United States, courts have ruled that protective laws are inconsistent with discrimination law, apart from a qualified right to reinstatement after childbirth. In Britain, the Government employed the rhetoric of equality to justify its reduction of this "burden" on industry, leveling the protection of women down to the level of protection for male workers. Given that protective legislation is now largely discredited in the United States and that the range of permissible protection is narrowing to provisions on childbirth and maternity in Britain and the European Community, why have some judges upheld this new form of discrimination under the guise of protection while others have struck it down? The differences between men and women offered to justify exclusionary policies today differ from some of the justifications for protective legislation in the past. Employers now rely solely on claims of biological difference rather than explicit claims about social roles, economic factors, or even theological imperatives. The current perception of the fetus as

---

1. For simplicity, I use the term *judges* in this section to refer to both judges and members of industrial tribunals. In the United Kingdom, industrial tribunals have original jurisdiction over cases of employment discrimination.

separate from the mother and deserving of state protection differs from past concern for the "mothers of the race" where the health of women was intertwined with the health of their offspring. Since exclusionary policies have much in common with the discredited protective laws of the past, judicial tolerance for such policies requires an explanation.

While the final outcomes of cases on exclusionary policies in Britain and the United States differ, judges and members of industrial tribunals in both countries have adopted similar approaches to the problem. They are likely to see less favorable treatment—in some cases barring all nonsterilized, premenopausal women from many jobs altogether—as justified when they see exclusionary policies as based on real biological differences between men and women. Those who have to decide these cases, and many who comment on them, see them as hard cases—ones in which the statutes generate no obviously correct answer and that require reexamination of the purpose and meaning of the laws. Exclusionary cases are hard principally because employers are supposedly treating women differently than men because of real rather than stereotypical differences between the sexes. Furthermore, their expressed goal—protecting future generations—commands wide public support. Feminists both call into question the logic of the dichotomy between real and stereotypical differences and object to the way judges have applied it in individual cases. They claim that what judges see as real differences are the result of stereotypes.

The dominant view about the nature of sex differences within a society and how those perceptions translate into social practice varies over time and is often under challenge. In chapter 1, I discussed the history of how the views about sex differences of British and U.S. feminists, reformers, judges, and legislators conflicted and which view was dominant at different times. Some feminists argued that notions of biological differences were socially constructed—fabricated to keep women in their place. Others asserted that physical, social, moral, or even spiritual differences justified treating men and women differently in the workplace.

For feminists, exclusionary policies are examples of the same phenomenon: biological difference constructed and deployed to exclude women from lucrative jobs. Making women's procreative role appear to be dictated by biology assures the primacy of procreative roles over other roles women may choose. Cases on exclusionary policies thus provide an ideal set of cases to explore the limitations of dominant notions of what constitutes discrimination and the way those conceptions translate into legal precedent. Examining what judges write as they grapple with this issue provides insight into how they conceptualize discrimination. How does the law construct sex differences? How does a recognition of difference lead to disadvantage?

Before examining the specifics of the structural and institutional framework within which sex discrimination law operates, I first offer a theoretical approach for understanding discrimination. Feminist legal scholars, like all feminists, must decide whether to herald our differences or assert our commonality—or to reject either horn of that dilemma. Moreover, feminist legal practitioners face the fundamental questions of feminist theory in the context of how the legal system operates. Individual feminist litigators often choose their legal arguments according to what will win specific cases or what will benefit women claimants as a group in one area of law. Feminists engaged in legal reform draft their proposals according to the contingent particular facts of a city council, a state legislature, or the makeup of a congressional committee. Arguments and briefs prepared for Supreme Court cases reflect what groups believe will influence that particular court, or even a swing justice, rather than how they would frame the issue in the abstract. For most feminists interested in law, then, answers to questions of feminist theory cannot be removed from questions about current political strategy and what will succeed in the short term.[2]

One only needs to look to current debates over affirmative action (called positive action in Europe) to recognize that no consensus exists over the appropriate way to dismantle race and sex hierarchies. People disagree not only about the definition of discrimination in the abstract but also about how to interpret evidence in concrete cases. That is, they disagree about whether one may take race or sex into account to achieve a better balance in schools or workplaces, as well as whether practices on the part of employers in particular cases are discriminatory. Thus, no consensus exists about how far the government may go to end group oppression nor on the meaning of evidence of discrimination.

The concept of discrimination has changed over time. Initially, discrimination was understood to be the result of intentional acts motivated by prejudice. Employers claimed African-Americans were inferior and refused to hire them. The government claimed that married women belonged in the home and that their incomes were merely supplemental and banned them from civil service jobs. Seeing discrimination as intentional acts motivated by prejudice made sense when claims of racial and gender inferiority were unabashedly made in public and when explicit rules barred groups of people from societal privileges—when factories could post signs saying "whites only" and turn white women away as well. The remedy for prejudice was truth—more information about disadvantaged groups' abilities—coupled with gender or race blindness—disregarding the irrelevant fact about the individual and treat-

---

2. Many British feminists, however, are skeptical about "enhancing law's imperialist reach" and advocate law as a site of struggle rather than merely a tool of struggle (Carole Smart, "The Woman in Legal Discourse," Women's Studies Paper Series, University of Utrecht, May 16, 1991, 2).

ing the person as a genderless or raceless individual (i.e., a white male) rather than as a member of a disfavored group. Any person who had the qualifications of a white male, but for sex or race, merited equal employment opportunity.

As the state outlawed blatant, explicit discrimination and discourse about inferiority became less publicly acceptable, seekers of greater racial and gender equality turned their attention to structural or institutional barriers. They recognized that even if decision makers were no longer consciously acting on prejudice, certain groups were frozen in the bottom echelons of society. Where some saw only the present effects of past discrimination, others saw the continuation of subtle but effective barriers. If the course was plotted to guarantee the success of athletes with certain attributes, dismantling gender and racial hierarchies would require more basic changes than letting everyone run the race. Instead of looking at intentions or motivations, feminists and civil rights groups refocused their attention to the effects of particular practices such as height and weight requirements, veterans preferences, educational requirements, and maximum age limits. In some of these cases, evidence of intent intermingled with evidence of discriminatory effects. For example, once the U.S. Congress outlawed explicit discrimination, employers spontaneously introduced intelligence tests and literacy tests but applied them inconsistently across racial groups—clearly raising suspicions about their intent to discriminate. Intent is difficult to prove, but civil rights lawyers could prove that such tests and requirements disproportionately excluded certain racial groups and bore no relationship to job performance. Employers may have adopted other job requirements, such as height and weight minimums, unaware of their effect on women or racial groups. In either case, feminist and civil rights groups claimed that these "neutral" rules, that is, rules that do not explicitly exclude women or racial groups but that affect them disproportionately, constituted discrimination when they did not accurately predict an individual's ability to do the job.

By extending the concept of discrimination to include practices not motivated by prejudice or malice but that nevertheless put women and minority men at a disadvantage, lawmakers and judges have transformed the original concept of discrimination as arbitrariness or prejudice. Oxford legal scholar Christopher McCrudden labels this unacknowledged change in the concept a *persuasive definition*: "one which gives a new conceptual meaning to a familiar word without substantially changing its emotive meaning." By using the same word, the moral weight against discrimination as an intentional act based on malice or prejudice is at least partially carried forward to institutional discrimination.[3] Both the U.S. Supreme Court and the British Parlia-

---

3. McCrudden makes this argument with respect to racial discrimination in employment; see Christopher McCrudden, "Institutional Discrimination," *Oxford Journal of Legal Studies* 2 (1982): 345–46. He draws his definition from C. L. Stevenson, *Mind* 47 (1938): 331.

ment recognized the reality and effects of so-called institutional discrimination. Chapter 4 discusses the judicially created category of disparate impact. The British Parliament acknowledged institutional discrimination by including provisions on indirect discrimination in the Sex Discrimination Act of 1975 and the Race Relations Act of 1976.

This shift in the concept of discrimination from prejudice to structure means that employers now have both positive and negative duties—a duty not to use categories of race and sex as well as a duty to scrutinize other employment requirements and practices for potential discriminatory effects. Some judges have held employers to a high standard of justification for their employment practices. Yet evidence suggests that many judges still regard discrimination or sex stereotyping as a characteristic of bad people, a disease, rather than the result of unexamined and changeable institutional practices.[4] If judges see discrimination as prejudice, they are likely to see a finding that discrimination has occurred as stigmatizing individuals and not as calling into question certain unexamined structures.

Feminists and civil rights groups continue to seek to expand our definition of discrimination. For example, sexual harassment, a term unknown a decade ago, was considered by many to be private, harmless, or even consensual conduct that had nothing to do with women's subordination; at worst, it was the behavior of a few twisted individuals. Yet through the arguments of feminists, particularly legal scholar Catharine MacKinnon, judges in Britain and the United States came to believe that some forms of sexual harassment were unlawful sex discrimination.[5] Therefore, feminists seek to raise the consciousness of judges and legislators to produce a more expansive definition of discrimination. They seek to abolish patterns and practices that operate as barriers to women's full equality regardless of the motivation for them. Explaining how such barriers operate and why they are unfair, however, is not an easy task.

Judges' and legislators' definition of what constitutes discrimination is often narrower than that of feminist litigators and legal scholars.

The courts will often, therefore, be called upon to infer discrimination from the evidence that is available. The judge's own understanding of what amounts to discrimination is consequently of vital importance. There is evidence to show that courts do not always understand the legal

---

4. Martha Chamallas, "Listening to Dr. Fiske: The Easy Case of *Price Waterhouse v. Hopkins*," *Vermont Law Review* 15 (Summer 1990): 89–124.

5. See Catharine A. MacKinnon, *Sexual Harassment of Working Women* (New Haven: Yale University Press, 1979); Michael Rubenstein, "The Law of Sexual Harassment at Work," *Industrial Law Journal* 12 (1983): 1–16; and Michael Rubenstein, *The Dignity of Women at Work: A Report on the Problem of Sexual Harassment in the Member States of the European Communities* (Luxembourg: EC Publications, 1987).

concept of discrimination and that this lack of understanding can adversely affect the outcome of a case.[6]

Expanding the definition is a long process, and one that generates objections and backlash. Chapters 3 and 4 trace the precedents in both countries and show how the concept of discrimination evolved in the courts. In both countries, judges often see sex-based policies as unlawful and discriminatory when they rest on stereotypes or when employers treat individuals as having a group characteristic that they do not have. For example, judges have said that men who stay home to care for children after the death of a spouse should get social security benefits, that women Air Force officers should get an allowance for dependent husbands on the same terms as male officers, and that employers cannot exclude women who can lift fifty pounds (or prove they can do the job) merely because they are women. The exceptional individual who defies the gender norm deserves to be treated according to his or her situation: as full-time parent, as breadwinner, or as exceptionally strong. Sex should not be a proxy for other characteristics if the characteristics are not 100 percent sex-linked. If some women can lift fifty pounds and some men cannot, the characteristic of strength does not inhere in one sex. This conception of stereotype is easy for judges to grasp, because it denies justice to individuals because of their group status. The language of liberal individualism can be deployed to argue that everyone should be able to choose their life-style, unfettered by the inaccurate attributions of group status. Using sex as a proxy for another characteristic—breadwinner, child minder, less aggressive at selling, more likely to drive drunk, or weak—is unfair to some individual members of the group.

The term *stereotype* extends beyond the case of individuals who do not fit the gender norm; it also includes acting on the basis of untrue generalizations about a group. For example, employers may refuse to hire women because they assume women are absent more frequently than men, although they are not. The characteristic is a false generalization about the group. Judges are often able to discern the unfairness of this type of stereotyping.

The final sense of stereotyping is where employers see people as representatives of their group and judge them according to exaggerated generalizations about how that group behaves or should behave.[7] For example, men will filter their experience of the token white woman or Asian in the office through gendered and racial lenses. If a woman "acts like a man," her behavior may be

---

6. Jennifer Corcoran, "Enforcement Procedures for Individual Complaints: Equal Pay and Equal Treatment," in *Women, Equality and Europe*, ed. by Mary Buckely and Malcolm Anderson (London: Macmillan, 1988), 63–64.

7. See Rosabeth Moss Kanter, *Men and Women of the Corporation* (New York: Basic Books, 1977).

judged harshly as inappropriate or unfeminine.[8] Yet if she behaves as women are supposed to behave, she may be thought to lack the qualities necessary for success in the job. This kind of stereotyping may be the most pernicious because one cannot subtract one's gender and then judge the individual. Instead, all perceptions of the individual pass through gendered lenses. Judges cannot ask whether the employer would have treated her the same if she had all the same attributes but were a man, because the answer is that the employer would have perceived all of those attributes differently.[9]

Despite limitations in application, judges' recognition of some kinds of stereotypes has led them to find some practices unlawful. British judges and members of tribunals have been less critical of stereotypical thinking than U.S. judges.[10] British jurists are less likely to mandate individual treatment, especially if the generalizations about the group have some validity. Judges in both countries, however, have often drawn a clear distinction between stereotypes that are untrue or unfair to the individual and real differences, usually biological or physical differences. They accept a rigid distinction between sex and gender. If employers treat men and women differently because of real differences, judges behave differently than when employers act on stereotypes— only the latter is discrimination.

Feminists challenge the logic of the sex/gender dichotomy as well as the way judges categorize specific differences. Feminists emphasize that perceptions about the facts of sex differences are often shaped by social conventions. Sex differences, like gender differences, are socially constructed. There are no neutral facts or givens of biological difference. Stereotypes about men's and

---

8. See Price Waterhouse v. Hopkins, 490 U.S. 228 (1989).

9. Beautifully illustrated by Natasha Josefowitz in "Impressions from an Office," *Paths to Power: A Woman's Guide From First Job to Top Executive* (Reading, Mass.: Addison-Wesley Publishing Co., 1983), 60.

He Works	She Works
The family picture is on his desk:	**The family picture is on her desk:**
Ah, a solid responsible family man.	Umm, her family will come before her career.
He's not at his desk:	**She's not at her desk:**
He must be in a meeting.	She must be in the ladies' room.
He's having lunch with the boss:	**She's having lunch with the boss:**
He's on his way up.	They must be having an affair.

10. See Skyrail Oceanic Ltd. v. Coleman, [1981] ICR 864. Lord Justice Lawton argues, "The courts, both in the United Kingdom and in the United States, have adjudged that general assumptions, or, as they are called in the United States, 'stereotyped assumptions,' do amount to discrimination against women. That this has been accepted by the Supreme Court of the United States seems clear. . . . The authorities in this country are not so clear" (870). For more recent dicta on stereotyping see Bullock v. Alice Ottley School, [1991] IRLR 324 (EAT), Enderby v. Frenchay Health Authority, [1991] ICR 382 (EAT), and The Financial Times Ltd. v. Byrne, Case no. 701/91 (EAT) January 7, 1992.

women's appropriate gender roles often mix with our understanding of physical differences, as cases on pregnancy, statutory rape, and prison guards make clear. When employers assert that a biological difference between the sexes is the basis for differential treatment, judges may fail to recognize the socially constructed nature of sex differences. They may see physical differences rather than social differences operating.

Judges in both countries have a narrow understanding of the concept of stereotype because they presume that a clear dichotomy exists between real and stereotyped differences and tacitly accept that it is all right to treat people less favorably if they are really different. One could place judges on a continuum of whether sex differences are real, knowable, biological truths, unbiased by our values and norms or whether they are socially constructed. The cases I discuss in the next two chapters show that most judges fall closer to the biological given end of the continuum in thinking about discrimination. The extent to which judges accept this dichotomy is the first important factor in how they conceptualize discrimination.

The second continuum on which to place judges to understand how they will respond to sex discrimination complaints is how they regard the fact of sex stratification and women's subordination in our society—the meaning attached to or inferences drawn from this social fact. The antifeminist sees the division of labor by sex, for example, as inevitably stemming from biological differences between the sexes and even ordained by God. The sexes are different and unequal; equality, then, is unnatural and maybe even sinful. Feminists see gender stratification as a situation of forced inequality. MacKinnon calls this perspective the dominance approach.[11] Social differences are mapped onto biological difference; social decisions, not biological differences or even spiritual differences, relegate women to an inferior position. In between these two poles would be a position arguing that men and women are socialized to pursue different goals. Thus, for example, men and women choose certain jobs to pursue their different values about spending time with their families. Sex stratification is not the result of enforced subordination but of individual choice. Sexism inheres in the individual or in society in a diffuse way. There is, thus, a continuum about one's explanation of unequal roles and privileges in our society. Feminists see this situation and call it socially constructed, enforced subordination. Antifeminists see it as natural and God's will. A middle position might conclude that it is the result of individual choices, resulting from socialization.

---

11. See MacKinnon, "Feminism, Marxism, Method and the State: Toward Feminist Jurisprudence," *Signs* 8 (Summer 1983): 635–58, "Toward Feminist Jurisprudence: Review of *Women Who Kill*" by Ann Jones, *Stanford Law Review* 34 (February 1982): 703–37, *Feminism Unmodified: Discourses on Life and Law* (Cambridge, Mass.: Harvard University Press, 1987), and *Toward a Feminist Theory of the State* (Cambridge, Mass.: Harvard University Press, 1989).

The third continuum, or relevant factor, is one's own experience of the pervasiveness of discrimination and who its victims are. For example, many white men who hear a lot of rhetoric about affirmative action and the salaries of a few exceptional white women or minorities conclude "women and blacks have it made." Another phrase I have frequently heard is "women and blacks can write their own ticket." Yet white women and minorities look at the number of women and minority men in powerful positions, the average salaries of such groups, the statistics on advancement, and search in vain to discover these mythical people who are "writing their own tickets." People vary dramatically about whether they think groups suffer discrimination or disadvantage. Judges, too, have different views about whether discrimination is pervasive. The definition is crucial. When discrimination is seen as the result of intentional acts rather than as diffuse institutional barriers, then, if one sees no overtly prejudiced or malicious people in the workplace, it is easy to conclude that no discrimination has occurred. Others go further and conclude that since they see no discrimination in their environment, but the government or organization has demanded remedial steps to try to end discrimination, then white men are now the principal victims of discrimination.

One's view of the cause and incidence of stratification by sex— biological inevitability, free choice, or oppression—determines how one interprets the evidence in discrimination cases as well as one's view about whether the law should be an instrument for social change to end that stratification. Feminists and civil rights groups in Europe and the United States have called for reversing the burden of proof in cases of discrimination.[12] Employers fear that if the statute shifts the burden to them to prove that they have not discriminated, workers will falsely accuse them of discrimination and they will be unable to win in court. This fear will lead them to hire according to gender and racial quotas rather than to provide equal employment opportunity and to hire the best-qualified.[13] Feminists and civil rights groups, on the other hand, are likely to be suspicious when work forces are grossly disproportionate in their representation of qualified women and minority men in the labor market or applicant pool. They sense discrimination. They see this stratification as neither a biological inevitability nor the result of free choice, but the result of oppression. They want the law to remedy the problem.

If you see the division of labor by sex as the result of freely chosen acts or as stemming from social differences flowing inevitably from biological difference, you will not expect to see a proportionate representation of all groups in any given job category. You will not see sinister discrimination in a

---

12. Com. (88) 269 final. See Handels-og Kontorfunktionaerenes Forbund i Danmark v. Dansk Arbeidsgiverforening ex parte Danfoss, [1991] CMLR 8.

13. See debate over the Civil Rights Bills of 1990, and 1991, *Congressional Record*, 102d Cong., 1st sess., (1991); 137: 9505–58, 15,481–492.

workplace in which women sell the cheaper items without a commission and men sell all of the big-ticket items with a commission, earning far more on average than the women do.[14] Employers claim justice requires only equality of opportunity, not equality of results. Furthermore, if sex segregation results from individual choices, then laws forcing integration are brutally coercive. On the other hand, feminists and civil rights groups question how one can judge whether there is true equality of opportunity without looking at the "bottom line." Disagreement over how one should interpret evidence of sex segregation reflects basic disagreements about the concept of discrimination.

The core of the concept of discrimination contained in both anti-discrimination legislation and the equal protection clause of the U.S. Constitution is an Aristotelian view of equality: justice entails treating likes alike. The corollary is that if people are different, not only is it all right to treat them differently, but justice may demand it. In legal jargon, the U.S. Constitution requires the government to treat men and women the same when they are "similarly situated." Under this approach, once employers have established a relevant difference between the sexes—a real rather than stereotypical difference—treating men and women differently does not constitute discrimination. For example, only women become pregnant, making them different from men. One could argue that it would not be discriminatory to treat women differently, such as excluding them from certain medical benefits, because they are different.[15] Yet it would be discrimination if an employer paid men and women a different wage for doing the same job. In their ability to do the job, they were the same, yet the employer arbitrarily treated them differently.

MacKinnon calls this approach the difference approach; legal scholar Sylvia Law calls it the assimilationist approach;[16] legal scholar Christine Littleton calls it the symmetrical approach.[17] Feminists using this approach have tried to benefit from important precedents established in cases of race discrimination. To end race discrimination, civil rights activists sought to make race an unacceptable and irrelevant basis of classification. Skin color or ethnicity is now clearly seen as a socially constructed category used to subordinate groups of people rather than as a difference relevant to employment.

---

14. Equal Employment Opportunity Commission v. Sears, Roebuck and Co., 628 F. Supp. 1264 (N. D. Illinois, 1986).

15. This was the rationale of the Supreme Court in General Electric Co. v. Gilbert, 429 U.S. 125 (1976) and Geduldig v. Aiello, 417 U.S. 484 (1974).

16. Sylvia A. Law, "Rethinking Sex and the Constitution," *University of Pennsylvania Law Review* 132 (1984): 963.

17. Christine A. Littleton, "Reconstructing Sexual Equality," *California Law Review* 75 (1987): 1291.

No one would today suggest that slavery was instituted in order to protect Blacks because they are different than whites.[18]

> At the core of that rejection [of separate spheres] is the powerful notion that Black men are fundamentally the same as white men, and that it is irrational for such surface differences of skin color and physiognomy to carry any significant meaning, except perhaps an aesthetic one (similar to, say, eye color or foot size).
>
> The consistent message of racial equality analysis since *Brown* is that any disadvantages Black men face in participating equally with white men in this society are traceable to either irrational prejudice or socially imposed burdens growing out of previous prejudice. In other words, they face no natural handicaps and possess no natural significant differences.[19]

Drawing on this framework was useful when women could argue that they really were just like men in relevant respects. To win cases, feminists have had to draw parallels between men and women. Even if only women give birth, both parents need to bond with newborns or need time to cope with a new baby. Both can be a dependent spouse and need spousal support upon the dissolution of marriage. Both can suffer reproductive damage. Both can suffer temporary disabilities. Both should be able to resist the draft or engage in combat.

The difference approach is unsatisfactory. First, it rests on the assumption that we can separate stereotypes from true differences—it fails to recognize that sex differences are socially constructed. Once judges discover a real difference, they assume it is all right to treat men and women differently, and women's subordination continues. MacKinnon's dominance approach argues that asserted differences between the sexes are not merely silly, irrational mistakes, but that nearly all alleged differences between the sexes are socially constructed, part of a design to use minor physiological differences to justify wide differences in treatment of the sexes to oppress women. Part of what MacKinnon calls the dominance approach includes the recognition that the social meaning given to differences of gender has little or no biological foundation and focuses instead on the social construction of women's infe-

---

18. "The danger of reinforcing stereotypes may be greater in relation to sex-based classifications than in relation to race-based classifications because sex roles define appropriate ways of acting and being more comprehensively than race roles. Further sex-based classifications are especially invidious because they have often provided the protection and help of the pedestal that turns out to be a cage. No one ever defended chattel slavery as an institution adopted for the benefit of black people." Law, 1012–13 n. 215.

19. Littleton, 1289.

rior status and not on biology. Rather than seeing arbitrary irrationalities in societal arrangements, the dominance approach sees the content of sex differences as the structural and systemic subordination of women to men in all spheres.

The more damning criticism of the difference approach may be that it fails to ask, different than whom? Embedded in this approach is a male standard for what is normal. As Minow points out,

> "Difference" is only meaningful as a comparison. I am no more different from you than you are from me. A short person is different only in relation to a tall one. Legal treatment of difference tends to take for granted an assumed point of comparison: women are compared to the unstated norm of men, "minority" races to whites, handicapped persons to the able-bodied, and "minority" religions to "majorities."[20]

The difference between men and women resides in the relationship. Men and women are different than each other; but when you employ a male standard, the difference lies within the woman—something is different about her. For example, women who are, on average, shorter than men may need to lower the conveyer belt in the factory to work comfortably, or lower the podium and microphone to speak comfortably in public.[21] Under the difference approach, women gain the right to work in the factory or speak in public if they are tall or can conform to a male standard. If they need an adjustment, we focus on how they differ from the norm rather than reflect on the norm itself—set according to the size of some men and therefore not neutral. "Institutional arrangements define whose reality is to be the norm and make what is known as different seem natural."[22] Women can have the rights and privileges white males enjoy only insofar as they can show that, in all relevant respects, they are just like men. Adopting a comparative standard freezes the status quo (which employs rules that work to women's disadvantage) and assumes that the adoption of a male standard is fair and appropriate. Many people's failure to see the existence of discrimination rests on their inability to see the male norm in apparently neutral rules. For them, equal opportunity—letting women compete in a system designed to insure men's success—is enough. Feminists who challenge long-standing employment practices have farther to go to succeed than merely showing there was one bad person or prejudiced employer. Many judges require evidence of intent or malice that is difficult to show for arrangements we accept as legitimate. Minow notes, "Judges operat-

---

20. Martha Minow, "Justice Engendered," *Harvard Law Review* 101 (1987): 13.
21. These examples are drawn from Littleton.
22. Minow, 14.

ing under the assumption that the world is neutral do not find discrimination unless it is specifically proven."[23]

Finally, the difference approach cannot accommodate the reality that women and men are different in ways that *are* relevant to social arrangements. The race analogy falls short in these circumstances. Not all differences are the result of stereotypes. As Minow asks, "What, however, is equal treatment for the woman who is correctly identified within the group of pregnant persons, not simply stereotyped as such, and who is different from nonpregnant persons in ways that are relevant to the workplace?"[24] The difference approach's only solution for cases of real differences is to first seek an analogy—such as disability for pregnancy—but beyond that to allow employers to treat women differently, which usually means less favorably, thereby punishing women for biological differences. Under the difference approach, one can only be equal—claim benefits or privileges—if one is the same, or at least comparable. This is what Littleton calls the mathematical fallacy: the view that only things that are the same can ever be equal.[25]

Despite its limitations, however, the difference approach, entrenched as it is in law, has been a useful tool for women to claim rights on the same terms as men. The categories of disparate treatment in U.S. law and direct discrimination in British law have promoted greater equality. Winning equal rights and privileges for women who are similarly situated has meant that women teachers have won the right to equal pay for equal work, women students the right to admission to professional schools on equal terms, or girls the right to participate in training for the manual trades. The difference approach, however, deflects attention from the unfairness inherent in the standards themselves and cannot deal with situations in which men and women are different: cases in which women cannot or will not conform to a male standard. The difference approach does not address the question of why it is just or even permissible to disadvantage women who refuse or who are unable to conform to a male standard. Women may have won the opportunity to compete with men for high-powered jobs or train for the building trades, but granting power to the exceptional woman who does not have children does little to change the status of women who conform to a more traditional role. It does nothing to improve secretaries' pay—depressed because it is women who do this job—or to ease the economic vulnerability of women who devote their time to caring for children.

Feminist legal scholars agree on several important theoretical points. They have drawn attention to the socially constructed nature of sex differences

---

23. Ibid., 56.
24. Ibid., 40.
25. Littleton, 1282.

and have argued that many so-called real differences are the result of stereotyping. Second, feminists have drawn attention to the way that the law encapsulates and reinforces a male norm, conferring status, rights, and privileges on women only when they can conform to that norm. They have drawn attention to how institutional arrangements penalize women for being different than men. Not content with the difference approach's adoption of the language of individual rights, which sees discrimination as unfair to individuals, feminists draw on the language of group oppression. Under MacKinnon's dominance approach, discrimination consists of the systematic disadvantage of social groups. Discrimination is part of a system that defines women as inferior and penalizes them for their differences. Feminists using this approach do not seek benefits for the few individual women who do not share the group characteristics, but seek to discard the standard that penalizes women for being different than men—for example, by getting pregnant, living longer, or driving more safely.

Some judicial opinions, along with provisions for disparate impact and indirect discrimination, show traces of the dominance approach. They recognize that discrimination is institutional, that it is not an isolated, individual act based on prejudice, that groups, not just individuals, are oppressed. The cases discussed in chapters 3 and 4 show, however, how limited judges' understanding of discrimination is. While recognizing some institutional discrimination, judges still rely on the dichotomy of real versus stereotypical differences and continue to uphold a male norm.

Feminist legal scholars may agree that sex differences are socially constructed, that judges often fall prey to stereotyped thinking, that apparently neutral standards encompass a male norm that disadvantages women, and that the legal system's recognition of difference often provides the basis for less favorable treatment, but they disagree about strategies for change. Just as there were feminists on both sides of the debate on protective legislation in Britain and the United States, feminists continue to disagree about how to accommodate difference. As Littleton explains, feminists disagree about what to do about "the difference difference makes,"[26] the way that difference translates into disadvantage. Should feminists try to change the neutral rules: lower the conveyor belt or get an adjustable one; have parenting leaves for both men and women; lower exposures to hazardous substances enough to protect pregnant women and men planning to father children? Or should they seek accommodation for women: maternity leave, part-time work, and "the mommy track"?

The choice presents a serious dilemma. What Minow calls "the dilemma of difference" is that we may recreate difference either by noticing it or by ignoring it.

---

26. Littleton, 1301.

Focusing on differences poses the risk of recreating them. Especially when used by decision makers who award benefits and distribute burdens, traits of difference can carry meanings uncontrolled and unwelcomed by those to whom they are assigned. Yet denying those differences undermines the value they may have to those who cherish them as part of their own identity.[27]

Some feminists in the United States describe the debate as between those advocating special treatment versus equal treatment. Equal treatment feminists believe that if women draw attention to their differences, it will ultimately be used against them in the law. Historically, when women claimed they were different than men to gain some accommodation, that difference was ultimately used as the basis for denying them rights. If the law mandates that women get maternity leave, for example, feminists fear employers will use that as a reason not to hire women. Furthermore, if mothers stay home with newborns while fathers continue to work, this arrangement reinforces the idea that women are the primary caretakers and perpetuates unequal responsibilities for child care and housework. If women are exempt from the draft because they are more fragile or peace loving or physically weak, they will lose other important rights of citizenship for which military service has traditionally been an important prerequisite, such as holding high public office. "Feminist theorists frequently take the symmetrical approach to sexual equality, not as an ideal, but as the only way to avoid returning to separate spheres ideology."[28]

Rather than emphasizing difference, equal treatment feminists suggest that women should try to change the gender-neutral rules so they operate less to women's disadvantage. For example, both parents of newborns should enjoy parental leave; any worker with a temporarily incapacitating medical condition should win the right to job reinstatement; a spouse of either sex who performs unpaid work in the home should have that contribution recognized if the marriage dissolves; and so on.

The so-called special treatment feminists argue that, in some cases, treating women differently than men is necessary to ease women's oppression. They should have maternity leave, preferences for jobs, or whatever is necessary to secure equal status, rights, and privileges. Women should not have to assimilate to a male norm to gain equality; instead, difference should not lead to disadvantage. MacKinnon calls her approach the dominance approach, while Littleton calls her approach equality as acceptance. Rather than seeking formal equality or neutral rules, both call for an examination of the effects of practices. A difference between men and women cannot justify differential

---

27. Minow, 12.
28. Littleton, 1292.

treatment if recognizing that difference reinforces inequality. That women are different than men does not justify perpetuating women's subordination.

> The difference between human beings whether perceived or real, and whether biologically or socially based, should not be permitted to make a difference in the lived-out equality of those persons . . . . To achieve this form of sexual equality, male and female "differences" must be costless relative to each other.[29]

Other feminists, such as Law, criticize MacKinnon's approach for its complexity and are wary of her effects test.

> Professor MacKinnon's approach is ambitious, but it adds unnecessary complexity to the application of sex equality doctrine in a large number of cases. The determination of what reinforces or undermines a sex-based underclass is exceedingly difficult. Professor MacKinnon may overestimate judges' capacities to identify and avoid socially imposed constraints on equality.[30]

For example, feminists do not agree that special treatment for pregnant women promotes greater equality in the workplace or merely reinforces the belief that caring for children is women's responsibility rather than men's, the employer's, the state's, society's, or some combination. The same debate exists over affirmative action. Does it stigmatize women and preserve their token status, or does it break down barriers to equality?

If we think of the dominance approach not as an immediate guide that we can expect conservative judges to embrace readily nor as a method that all can agree how to apply, but as an important shift in thinking about discrimination, its value is clear. MacKinnon focuses our attention not on how we can pigeon-hole feminist claims into existing legal categories—all of which have considerable limitations—but on how we go about envisioning women's equality and how we avoid constraining the debate by more narrow strategic concerns. If we shift the debate about special versus equal from a debate about ideology to a debate about strategy, as Carole Smart suggests,[31] the answers lie outside the law. We then focus on the complex evidence of concrete and symbolic long- and short-term effects. The law forces the special/equal dichotomy upon us and we should resist having that structure order our thinking.

---

29. Littleton, 1284–85.

30. Law, 1005.

31. Carole Smart, *Feminism and The Power of Law* (London: Routledge, 1989); see also Nicola Lacey, "Legislation Against Sex Discrimination: Questions from a Feminist Perspective," *Journal of Law and Society* 14 (1987): 411–21.

For both institutional and ideological reasons, British and European feminists have not shown the same attachment as U.S. feminists to the equal treatment model of feminism. Nor, as a result, have they become locked into a debate between the two. Instead, they have always embraced some forms of so-called special treatment while sharing U.S. feminists' critique of stereotyped thinking, the male norm, and the way difference leads to disadvantage. European Community law contains some aspects of so-called special treatment.[32] It allows member states to treat pregnant women more favorably than other workers with disabling medical conditions, for example.

While feminists have recently been more critical of characterizing the issue as special versus equal,[33] maintaining that it is a false dichotomy, bridging the gap and drawing on both approaches may still be easier in theory than in practice. Both approaches are useful, but feminists still have strategic choices. Feminists continue to grapple with how to use legislation and litigation to promote greater equality and to eradicate women's oppression. They share many aspects of a common critique of discrimination doctrine and judges' reasoning even if they do not always agree about specific legal reforms. Feminists share a common critique if not always a common vision. Nevertheless, the differences between feminists look less significant when compared to the gulf between those engaged in feminist legal thought and criticism and the concept of discrimination applied by judges.

In Britain and the United States, the definition of discrimination is contested and evolving. In both countries the word *discrimination* can be applied to two very different scenarios: where men and women are the same in some pertinent respect but have been treated differently, or when men and women are different in some respect and women suffer a disadvantage because of this difference.

---

32. Council Directive of 9 February 1976 on the implementation of the principle of equal treatment for men and women as regards to access to employment, vocational training and promotion, and working conditions, 76/207/EEC. See article 2, secs. 2 and 3.

33. Joan W. Scott, "Deconstructing Equality-versus-Difference: Or, the Uses of Poststructuralist Theory for Feminism," *Feminist Studies* 14 (Spring 1988): 33–50.

CHAPTER 3

British Sex Discrimination Law

The history of protective legislation in both countries helps explain how each country's legal system applied its sex discrimination law to cases on exclusionary policies. It also helps us understand how feminists have reacted to exclusionary policies and why British and U.S. feminists approach the issue of protective legislation differently. British legislators considering the Sex Discrimination Act had to grapple with how the proposed legislation would affect protective laws that purportedly recognized and accommodated real differences between men and women. Legislators gave little guidance on this question, but assigned a commission the task of recommending changes to protective labor laws. Parliament left open the question of whether employers could use asserted differences between men and women as a justification for treating women differently than men beyond what protective labor laws required.

British and U.S. sex discrimination law are very similar. In fact, this chapter will show how the British Government explicitly modeled its statute on U.S. law. Yet U.S. courts have, on the whole, been more suspicious of exclusionary policies and less likely to find them compatible with sex discrimination law. What accounts for the difference?

Part of the answer lies in an institutional analysis. The differences in outcomes in the two countries can be seen as a function of differences in the two legal and political systems. This chapter describes Parliament's aims in passing the Sex Discrimination Act, the provisions of that statute, the impact of membership in the European Community, the performance of the enforcement agency, the structure of industrial tribunals, and the behavior of judges. Chapter 4 does the same for U.S. law and explicitly compares and contrasts the two. These institutional factors help explain the different outcomes in the cases that are discussed in chapters 5 and 6. In addition, comparing the opinions and holdings in Britain and the United States in cases involving discrimination brings into focus differences between the two legal systems.

Understanding the framework of sex discrimination law requires more than an understanding of the provisions of the statutes, the legislative history, and the structure of the enforcement agency. Like any body of law, one must look to see how judges have interpreted it. The discussion of cases in the next two chapters provides the necessary legal background for understanding the cases on exclusionary policies in chapters 5 and 6. They include cases where judges or members of tribunals made observations about the nature of sex differences, about the appropriate legal response, and about the nature of discrimination. For my purposes, dicta are as meaningful as the results. This section does not provide a full explication of legal doctrine nor all the rules of discrimination law. Nor is it intended to be merely a parade of horribles to string together a selection of sexist quotes that castigate individual judges for misogyny (although the evidence may warrant such a conclusion). Nor am I trying to claim that my selection is perfectly representative of current judicial thinking or, further, the judicial view over time. Instead, I have selectively gathered cases in which judges expounded on the nature of sex differences, on the definition of discrimination, and on the relationship between biological differences and discrimination law. My purpose is to cast new light on discrimination law by analyzing how some judges construct biological differences in their opinions. The next two chapters bring the theoretical questions from chapter 2 to bear on statutes and cases. Before explicitly comparing the two countries, however, I must first describe and analyze the institutional structure of sex discrimination law in Britain. The European Community is replacing British courts and tribunals and the British Parliament in defining discrimination.

The European Community and Sex Discrimination

Membership in the European Community[1] has had a profound impact on British law on sex discrimination and equal pay and contributed to passage of the Sex Discrimination Act of 1975.[2] The British Parliament has had to amend both pieces of legislation to comply with EC law. Furthermore, individual victims of discrimination have won cases in British courts by appealing to EC law when they would have failed by relying solely on the more restrictive British law. The European Court of Justice's interpretations of EC law have shaped how British courts have interpreted British law, and its activist rulings have significantly expanded the powers of the British judiciary, in effect, giving it the power of judicial review and pushing it toward more purposive interpretations. Finally, given Prime Minister Thatcher's hostility to expanded protection for workers—protection she felt posed a burden on industry—initiatives to improve discrimination law came from the EC, rather than from the British Government. In fact, Britain has sought to block such initiatives. The EC has thus eclipsed the British Parliament as the arena for innovation in this area of law.

The United Kingdom signed the Treaty of Rome and became a member

---

1. Strictly speaking there are three European Communities. The most important for my purposes is the European Economic Community created by the Treaty of Rome. The three communities are now subsumed under the name European Community (EC).

2. W. B. Creighton, *Working Women and the Law* (New York: Mansell, 1979), 145–55.

of the EC in 1973. Parliamentary recognition followed with the European Communities Act of 1973, which codified the supremacy of EC law. The EC is more than an international organization; it is a supranational organization with laws, courts, a legislature, and an executive.[3] The Council of Ministers and the European Commission share the legislative powers of the community. The Council of Ministers, made up of a representative from each member state, votes on proposals from the Commission, a body of civil servants appointed by member states but sworn to serve the interests of the community as a whole. The Commission must consult the European Parliament, but Parliament has few powers.[4] Article 177 of the Treaty of Rome gives the European Court of Justice (ECJ) the authority to hear cases national courts refer to it that raise questions of EC law. Once the ECJ rules on the points of law, national courts apply its ruling to the facts of the particular case. Article 169 of the treaty gives the ECJ the authority to hear cases referred to it by the Commission when the Commission believes that member states are violating EC law.[5] The Commission, then, has the important task of overseeing the enforcement and implementation of EC law as well as proposing legislation.

The European Court of Justice interprets several kinds of EC law. First, the Treaty of Rome lays down general rules for member states. Second, member states also must follow regulations that the Council of Ministers passes. Regulations bind member states without relying on national implementing legislation. Third, the Council also issues directives that set objectives but allow member states discretion in carrying out those objectives. The ECJ's rulings holding some directives to be "directly effective," capable of creating rights that individuals may claim against their governments and sometimes against other individuals regardless of whether a member state has fully implemented a directive through legislation, has limited the member states' discretion.[6] The Commission or Council may issue decisions, ordering someone to perform or cease some action to comply with EC law. Finally, either the Council or the Commission may issue opinions or recommendations.

---

3. See Joseph Weiler, "The Community System: The Dual Character of Supranationalism," in *The Yearbook of European Law*, ed. by F. G. Jacobs (Oxford: Clarendon Press, 1981): 267–306.

4. Although the European Parliament has primarily the power to persuade, the Single European Act gives it the power to force the Council to institute qualified majority voting rather than require unanimity on certain issues. Furthermore, the direct election of members of the European Parliament has reduced the "democracy deficit" and enhanced its credibility. See A. Campbell, "The Single European Act and the Implications," *International and Comparative Law Quarterly* 35 (October 1986): 932–39; and "Qualified Majority Vote," *Industrial Relations Legal Information Bulletin* 399 (April 19, 1990): 4.

5. See L. Neville Brown, *The Court of Justice of the European Communities*, 3d ed. (London: Sweet and Maxwell, 1989): 76–86.

6. See Pierre Pescatore, "The Doctrine of 'Direct Effect,'" *European Law Review* 2 (1983): 155–77; Anthony Arnull, "The Direct Effect of Directives: Grasping the Nettle," *International and Comparative Law Quarterly* 35 (1986): 939–46.

The ECJ has turned the Treaty of Rome into a constitution that limits what member states may do just as the U.S. Constitution constrains governmental action.[7] The Federalist Marshall Court in the early nineteenth century expanded the powers of the judiciary and the national government. Similarly, the ECJ has used its powers of interpretation to expand the powers of the EC at the expense of member states, to transfer power to domestic courts at the expense of central governments, and to promote European integration.[8] It has done this in two principal ways. First, it has upheld the supremacy of EC law.[9] In its rulings on the supremacy of EC law, the Court of Justice has made it clear that the EC is not just another international organization whose laws bind only member states who may flout or implement them as they see fit. Second, by holding that certain parts of the treaty or directives are directly effective,[10] the ECJ has tried to insure that member states cannot benefit from their own failure to implement EC law. Instead, under some circumstances, national courts must give effect to clear and unconditional parts of directives in claims of individuals against other individuals (horizontal direct effects) or in cases of citizens claiming rights against their governments (vertical direct effects), regardless of whether the government has carried out the directive or passed legislation in conflict with it.

One of the main ways the European Court has expanded EC law and sought greater integration is in its interpretations of EC law on equality between the sexes.[11] Article 119 of the treaty mandates equal pay for equal work. The Equal Pay Directive of 1975 expanded article 119 to provide for equal pay for work of equal value.[12] The Equal Treatment Directive of 1976 prohibits discrimination in promotion, training, and benefits.[13] The Council

---

7. See Brown; Vanessa Hall-Smith et al., *Women's Rights and the EEC: A Guide for Women in the UK* (London: Rights of Women Europe, 1983); Richard Townshend-Smith, "The Impact of European Law on Equal Pay for Women," in *The Effect on English Domestic Law of Membership of the European Communities and of Ratification of the European Convention on Human Rights*, ed. by M. P. Furmston, R. Kerridge, and B. E. Sufrin (London: Martinus Nijhoff, 1983), 69–107.

8. See Terrance Sandalow and Eric Stein, eds., *Courts and Free Markets: Perspectives from the United States and Europe* (Oxford: Clarendon, 1982); Bernard Rudden, *Basic Community Cases* (Oxford: Clarendon, 1987).

9. Costa v. ENEL, [1964] ECR 585; Amministrazione delle Finanzo dello Stato v. Simmenthal S.p.A., [1978] ECR 629.

10. Van Gend en Loos v. Nederlandse Administratie Belastingen, [1973] ECR 1; Defrenne v. Sabena, [1976] ECR 455.

11. See Eve C. Landau, *The Rights of Working Women in the European Community* (Luxembourg: Commission of the European Communities, 1985).

12. 75/117. Council Directive of 10 February 1975 on the approximation of the laws of the Member States relating to the application of the principle of equal pay for men and women.

13. 76/207. Council Directive of 9 February 1976 on the implementation of the principle of equal treatment for men and women as regards access to employment, vocational training and promotion and working conditions.

has also passed directives on equal treatment in social security,[14] equal treatment in occupational social security schemes,[15] and equal treatment for self-employed women (including women in agricultural work).[16] The Commission has proposed directives on reversing the burden of proof in discrimination cases,[17] extending employment rights to part-time workers,[18] and parental leave,[19] but Britain has blocked these draft directives in the Council of Ministers.[20] Thwarted in issuing a directive, the Commission has issued a recommendation on positive action.[21] Finally, it has recently proposed a draft directive on the protection of women during pregnancy.[22] The Commission has done much to promote equality for women in its recommendations of directives to the Council, in its pleadings before the ECJ in infringement proceedings, and in its interventions in individual cases.

The ECJ has interpreted the Equal Pay and Equal Treatment Directives more broadly than the British legislation they spawned. As a result, several British claimants have demanded their rights under EC law when British law alone provided them no remedy, and some have won.[23] Britain's failure to

---

14. 79/7. Council Directive of 19 December 1978 on the progressive implementation of the principle of equal treatment for men and women in matters of social security.

15. 86/378. Council Directive of 24 July 1986 on the implementation of the principle of equal treatment for men and women in occupational social security schemes.

16. 86/613. Council Directive of 11 December 1986 on the application of the principle of equal treatment between men and women engaged in an activity, including agriculture, in a self-employed capacity, and on the protection of self-employed women during pregnancy and motherhood.

17. Proposal for a Council Directive on reversing the burden of proof in the area of equal pay and equal treatment for women and men, COM (88) 269 final. See Christopher Docksey, "The European Community and the Promotion of Equality," in *Women, Employment and European Equality Law*, ed. by Christopher McCrudden (London: Eclipse, 1987): 1–22.

18. Proposal for a Council Directive supplementing the measures to encourage improvement in the safety and health of temporary workers, COM (90) 228 final, No. C 224/8 O.J.C., September 8, 1990.

19. Amended proposal for a Council Directive on parental leave and leave for family reasons, COM (84) 631 final, 316/7 O.J.C., November 27, 1984.

20. "Qualified Majority Vote," 4. Britain has consistently blocked the expansion of discrimination law and the social charter more generally.

21. Council Recommendation of 13 December 1984 on the promotion of positive action for women, 84/635/EEC, No. L 331/34 O.J.C., December 19, 1984.

22. COM (90) 406 final.

23. See especially E. Coomes (Holdings) Ltd. v. Shields, [1978] ICR 1159 (CA). The British courts have referred a number of cases to the ECJ on sex discrimination and equal pay; see Macarthys Ltd. v. Smith, [1980] ICR 672 (ECJ); Lloyds Bank Ltd. v. Worringham and Another, [1981] ICR 558 (ECJ); Jenkins v. Kingsgate (Clothing Productions) Ltd., [1981] ICR 592 (ECJ), [1981] ICR 715 (EAT); Garland v. British Rail Engineering Ltd., [1982] IRLR 111 (ECJ), [1982] IRLR 257 (HL); Burton v. British Railways Board, [1982] IRLR 116 (ECJ), [1983] ICR 544 (EAT); Marshall v. Southampton and Southwest Hampshire District Health Authority (Teaching), [1986] ICR 335 (ECJ), [1990] IRLR 481 (CA) (on appeal to the House of Lords); Roberts v. Tate and Lyle Industries Ltd., [1986] IRLR 150 (ECJ); Drake v. Chief Adjudication Officer, [1986] 3 All ER 65 (ECJ); Johnston v. The Chief Constable of the Royal Ulster Constabulary, [1987] ICR 83 (ECJ); Newstead v. Department of Transport and H.M. Treasury, [1988] ICR 332 (ECJ);

fulfill its treaty obligations has prompted the Commission to bring infringement proceedings twice,[24] and, combined with rulings in individual cases, the
ECJ's decisions have forced the British Parliament to amend the laws several
times to harmonize British law with EC law.[25] Forcing changes in British law
by individual lawsuits or action by the Commission is an expensive, slow, and
cumbersome way of producing social change; yet given the Government's
hostility to expanded protection for workers, working in the arena of the EC
has been the most effective way of altering British law in the 1980s.

More significant than the EC's pressure on Parliament to amend its
discrimination laws has been the effect of membership on British courts. Long
used to the idea of parliamentary sovereignty, lacking the power of judicial
review of legislation and a written constitution, British courts have often been
drawn to literal rather than purposive interpretations of discrimination law.
The ECJ has ruled, however, that Britain may not insulate discrimination
claims (for example against the police) from judicial review.[26] Now that the
European Court of Justice has held parts of the Equal Treatment Directive
directly effective against the state, EC law requires British courts to refuse to
give effect to aspects of domestic law that fail to implement EC requirements
fully. The ECJ has ruled that national courts must make awards that provide
victims of discrimination with an appropriate remedy and deter would-be
discriminators irrespective of what national statutes require.[27] The ECJ has
gone still further and required that judges must seek to harmonize their interpretations of domestic law with EC law.[28] "For the most part, the trend established
in 1988 towards a liberal and purposive construction of the statutes by the senior
members of the judiciary continued to be reflected in the decisions."[29]

Seeing greater equality for women as the base of its goal of social rather
than mere economic integration, the ECJ has declared such equality to be one

---

Foster v. British Gas plc, [1990] IRLR 354 (ECJ); Barber v. Guardian Royal Exchange Assurance
Group, [1990] IRLR 240 (ECJ).

24. Commission of the European Communities v. United Kingdom of Great Britain and
Northern Ireland, [1984] [1982] ICR 578 and ICR 192.

25. The Equal Pay (Amendment Regulations) 1983; see Christopher McCrudden, "Equal
Pay for Work of Equal Value: the Equal Pay (Amendment) Regulations 1983," *Industrial Law
Journal* 12 (December 1983): 197–219. Parliament amended the Equal Pay Act of 1970 to
include a right to equal pay for work of equal value—not just the same work. The Sex Discrimi-
nation Act of 1986 is discussed below. See "New Developments in the Law," chap. 2 in Equal
Opportunities Commission, *Twelfth Annual Report* (London: HMSO, 1987): 4.

26. Johnston v. RUC, [1987] ICR 83 (ECJ).

27. Marshall v. Southampton Area Health Authority, [1986] ICR 335 (ECJ).

28. Von Colson and Kamann v. Land Nordhein-Westfalen, [1984] ECR 1891. See Deirdre
Curtin, "The Province of Government: Delimiting the Direct Effect of Directives in the Common
Law Context," *European Law Review* 15 (June 1990): 220–21.

29. Michael Rubenstein, *Discrimination: A Guide to the Relevant Case Law on Race and
Sex Discrimination and Equal Pay*, 3d. ed. (London: Eclipse, 1990), 1. See Pickstone v. Freemans plc., [1988] IRLR 357 (HL).

of the foundations of EC law,[30] and on occasion it has taken a feminist line in the cases before it. Through its interpretations of EC law, the ECJ has brought into effect reforms of discrimination law that the Council could not agree on.[31] Its rulings have gone far to overcome the considerable limitations of British sex discrimination law. Despite its significant contribution to expanding equality law, the ECJ has taken an evolutionary rather than a revolutionary approach. It often leaves national courts the discretion to judge their own domestic situations. For example, in *Jenkins*, the Court ruled that paying part-time workers at a lower hourly rate might be indirectly discriminatory against women if employers could not show that a material factor other than sex justified the differential.[32] The Court left national courts to determine whether the differential was justified. In *Johnston v. RUC*, women challenged the Chief Constable of Northern Ireland's decision to fire all women officers when he decided that all officers should carry firearms.[33] The ECJ rejected the British Government's arguments that several exceptions from the Equal Treatment Directive applied in the case and insisted that Britain could not insulate the question from judicial review, but left to the Northern Ireland tribunal the question of whether the special circumstances of Northern Ireland justified refusing to arm women officers. In *von Colson*, the Court refused to rule that EC law required judges to provide the remedy of requiring employers to hire people they had discriminated against, but held that judges could go beyond domestic law to require fines or awards that would deter would-be discriminators and provide a real remedy to victims.[34] Finally, when the ECJ has expanded the protection of the law and overturned settled assumptions about what EC law requires, the Court has refused to give its ruling any retrospective effect.[35] Thus, the ECJ has often tried to find a compromise position,[36] one that allows national courts to keep a measure of discretion but continues to advance the cause of equality for women. Before discussing further the significant impact membership in the EC has had on British sex discrimination law, it is first necessary to discuss that law.

---

30. Defrenne v. Sabena, [1976] ECR 455, 472.

31. See Rinner-Kuhn v. FWW Spezial-Gebaudereinigung GmbH, [1989] IRLR 493; Handels-og Kontorfunktionaerenes Forbund I Danmark v. Dansk Arbejdsbiverforening ex parte Danfoss, [1991] CMLR 8; Dekker v. Stichting Vormingscentrum voor Jonge Volwassen (VJV-Centrum) Plus, [1991] IRLR 27. See also Josephine Shaw, "The Burden of Proof and the Legality of Supplementary Payments in Equal Pay Cases," *European Law Review* 15 (June 1990): 264.

32. Jenkins v. Kingsgate (Clothing Productions) Ltd., [1981] ICR 592 (ECJ).

33. Johnston v. RUC, [1987] ICR 83.

34. von Colson and Kamann v. Land Nordhein-Westfalen, [1984] ECR 1891.

35. Defrenne v. Sabena, [1976] ECR 455; Barber v. Guardian Royal Exchange Assurance Group, [1990] IRLR 240 (ECJ). See Deirdre Curtin, "Scalping the Community Legislator: Occupational Pensions and *Barber*," *Common Market Law Review* 27 (1990): 475–506.

36. See Dekker v. Stichting Vormingscentrum voor Jonge Volwassen (VJV-Centrum) Plus, [1991] IRLR 27; and Handels-og Kontorfunktionaerernes Forbund i Danmark (acting for Hertz) v. Dansk Arbejdsgiverforening (acting for Aldi Marked k/s), [1991] IRLR 31.

British Sex Discrimination Law[37]

Lobbying by interest groups, anticipated pressure from the European Community, and knowledge of the United States's example all contributed to the passage of the Sex Discrimination Act of 1975. The British Parliament had passed the Equal Pay Act in 1970 (which became effective in 1975), before it joined the European Community.[38] Many members of Parliament and interest groups were dissatisfied with the Equal Pay Act in 1970 and thought its provisions inadequate to combat women's inferior position in the labor market without a law forbidding discrimination on the basis of sex.[39] The Trade Union Congress, which had pushed for legislation requiring equal pay, supported the Sex Discrimination Bill. Women's groups worked together to submit evidence to the select committees as well as to lobby Parliament. Because both parties supported the bill, it did not require much support from outside groups or exceptional efforts from individual women MPs to secure passage.

An additional factor in accounting for passage of the Sex Discrimination Act of 1975 was the Labour Government's commitment to legislate on race relations and its desire to use the Sex Discrimination Act as a model. Roy Jenkins, the home secretary, had traveled to the United States to investigate its legislation, and he incorporated the lessons from the U.S. experience into the Sex Discrimination Act. In particular, he based the concept of indirect discrimination on the concept of disparate impact, enunciated in *Griggs v. Duke Power Company*,[40] and modeled the British Equal Opportunities Commission (EOC) on the U.S. Equal Employment Opportunity Commission (EEOC).

The Sex Discrimination Act prohibits discrimination in employment, housing, education, and the provision of goods and services. The first type of discrimination prohibited by the act is direct discrimination as set out in part I, section 1(1).

A person discriminates against a woman in any circumstances relevant for the purposes of any provision of this Act if (*a*) on the ground of her sex he treats her less favourably than he treats or would treat a man.

---

37. The section deals with only statutes relating to equal treatment since it is these provisions that are relevant for cases on exclusionary policies. Many of the sources in the bibliography, however, also cover the relevant statutes and cases on equal pay and social security.

38. For a full description of these events, see Elizabeth M. Meehan, *Women's Rights at Work: Campaigns and Policy in Britain and the United States* (London: Macmillan, 1985), 72–87.

39. The first Private Member's Bill was introduced by Joyce Butler in 1967 and, in the following four years, Private Member's Bills each year on the subject received increasing support. See Vicky Randall, *Women and Politics* (London: Macmillan, 1982), 183.

40. 401 U.S. 424 (1971).

The alleged victim of direct discrimination must prove three points: that an employer (or landlord or proprietor) treated her differently than he or she would treat a man; she must show that the employer treated her not just differently but less favorably from that man; and she must show that the employer treated her differently because of her sex rather than for another reason. If she proves her case, the only defense for the employer is that one of the many exceptions in the act applies, for example, that sex is a genuine occupational qualification for the job.

The prohibition against direct discrimination outlaws blatant forms of discrimination, such as prohibiting all women from certain jobs or refusing to consider applicants of one sex, but direct discrimination is difficult to prove.[41] Given time, legal advice, financial incentives, and the fear of bad publicity, most employers can enunciate some plausible, lawful reason for their practices. Whether they are successful in refuting the charges of discrimination will then depend on how carefully industrial tribunals scrutinize employers' explanations and how effectively complainants can gather and present corroborative evidence and question witnesses.

Direct discrimination has many of the pitfalls of what MacKinnon calls the difference approach and Littleton calls the assimilationist approach. As originally conceived, discrimination consisted of intentional acts of prejudice to individual men or women; the British courts have now moved several steps beyond that.[42] Thinking of discrimination this way does little to tackle the male norms for employment, but grants women the right to be judged according to male standards. If women are the same, they can demand the right to be treated as well as men. By relying on a comparative standard, the provisions on direct discrimination do not help women whose employers treat them badly because only women perform certain jobs. The decision of the House of Lords in *James v. Eastleigh Borough Council*, allowing women to compare themselves to a hypothetical man, is a welcome advancement in the law, but it still leaves a male norm entrenched.

Part I, section 1(1) of the Sex Discrimination Act prohibits indirect discrimination.

A person discriminates against a woman in any circumstances relevant for the purposes of any provision of this Act if (*b*) he applies to her a

---

41. "One point on which all were agreed was the evidential difficulty of proving a case of equal pay or sex discrimination" (Cosmo Graham and Norman Lewis, *The Role of ACAS Conciliation in Equal Pay and Sex Discrimination Cases* [Manchester: EOC, 1985], quoted in Alice Leonard, *Judging Inequality: The Effectiveness of the Industrial Tribunal System in Sex Discrimination and Equal Pay Cases* [London: Cobden, 1987], 113). See Nicola, Lacey, "Legislation Against Sex Discrimination: Questions from a Feminist Perspective," *Journal of Law and Society* 14 (1987): 412.

42. James v. Eastleigh Borough Council, [1990] IRLR 288 (HL).

requirement or condition which he applies or would apply equally to a man but—(i) which is such that the proportion of women who can comply with it is considerably smaller than the proportion of men who can comply with it, and (ii) which he cannot show to be justifiable irrespective of the sex of the person to whom it is applied, and (iii) which is to her detriment because she cannot comply with it.

Indirect discrimination has four parts: the claimant must be able to identify a specific requirement or condition; she must show that fewer women than men can comply with it; the employer must fail to justify it irrespective of sex; and the requirement must work to her detriment. The individual complainant carries the burden of identifying which requirement the employer is using and providing the statistical evidence that fewer women can comply with it. Only then does the responsibility shift to the employer to prove the requirement justifiable. The act provides no definition or criteria for industrial tribunals to apply when deciding when a rule is justifiable.

The Sex Discrimination Act's prohibition against indirect discrimination tries to combat institutional discrimination by outlawing requirements that employers may apply to both sexes, but that deny women full equal employment opportunity. The provision on indirect discrimination is also a recognition that men and women may be different, but differences should not be reasons for denying women jobs. It questions the value of the male standard and requires employers to justify its use. For example, just because women are shorter than men on average does not mean that they cannot be effective police officers. The provision on indirect discrimination embodies some of what MacKinnon calls the dominance approach or Littleton calls equality as acceptance. Discrimination disadvantages groups of people because they differ from the norm. Employers bear the burden of showing that the practice is justified.

Indirect discrimination dispenses with the need to prove a discriminatory intent; instead, it looks to effects.[43] This focus makes it difficult for employers to evade the law by setting up apparently neutral requirements (that is, requirements that employers can and do apply to both men and women) to exclude women. In some respects, indirect discrimination is easier to prove than direct discrimination if women have access to the right statistical information.[44] The employer, however, has the chance to show that its requirement is justifiable. Cases alleging indirect discrimination center on the effect of a rule on men and women, looking at groups rather than individuals. Instead of promoting an equality of opportunity that allows only exceptional women access to jobs, the provisions against indirect discrimination seek to break

---

43. Angela Byre, *Indirect Discrimination* (Manchester: Equal Opportunities Commission, 1987).

44. A big if; women have had trouble identifying the relevant pool for comparison and collecting the necessary statistical information.

down artificial barriers for all women,[45] but the provisions on indirect discrimination have not lived up to their promise. Judges and members of industrial tribunals have set a low standard of justifiability,[46] and have held complainants to a high standard of proof. In *Kidd v. DRG (UK) Ltd.*,[47] for example, an industrial tribunal refused to accept without proof that women were largely responsible for childrearing.[48] The ECJ's more recent rulings have reduced the discretion of national courts in determining whether neutral rules are justifiable.[49]

Although the provisions against direct and indirect discrimination broadly prohibit discrimination, the 1975 Sex Discrimination Act contained many exceptions before Parliament amended it to comply with rulings of the ECJ. The prohibition against discrimination did not apply when sex is a genuine occupational qualification in one of eight ways: (1) if the job required one sex because of physiology (such as a wet nurse or sperm donor) or for authenticity in dramatic performances, (2) if the job needed one sex to preserve decency or privacy, (3) if the job required an employee to live on premises not equipped for both sexes (such as on an oil rig), (4) if the nature of the work required one sex because it was a prison, hospital, or the worker would have been supervising only one sex, (5) if the holder provided personal services, (6) if laws restricted the holding of the job by a woman (protective legislation), (7) if the job was outside the United Kingdom and another country's laws or customs prevent one sex from performing the job, or (8) if the job was one of two held by a married couple.[50] The act permitted an employer to discriminate in provisions on death or retirement.

The act did not apply to single-sex schools, to private clubs that treated men and women members differently, to charities, political parties, or voluntary groups. It did not prohibit excluding women from working underground in mines or when necessary to safeguard national security. Organized religion could continue to discriminate in hiring. The act did not apply to competitive sports, insurance, or communal accommodations. These exceptions limited the act's ability to end discrimination, and the EOC called for Parliament to remove most of them.[51] I discuss how these exceptions come into play in cases on exclusionary policies in chapter 5.

---

45. See Katherine O'Donovan and Erika Szyszczak, "Indirect Discrimination—Taking a Concept to Market—I and II," *New Law Journal*, January 4, 1985, 15, and January 11, 1985, 42; Katherine O'Donovan and Erika Szyszczak, *Equality and Sex Discrimination Law* (Oxford: Blackwell, 1988), 96–120.

46. Vera Sacks, "The Equal Opportunities Commission," *Modern Law Review* 49 (1986): 575.

47. [1985] IRLR 190. The EAT refused to overturn this decision; see Sacks, 573.

48. See also Pinder v. Friends Provident, (1985) unreported; Sacks, 587.

49. Bilka-Kaufhaus GmbH v. von Hartz, [1986] 2 CMLR 701 (ECJ).

50. David Pannick, *Sex Discrimination Law* (Oxford: Clarendon, 1986), 226–71.

51. Equal Opportunities Commission, *Equal Treatment for Men and Women: Strengthening the Acts* (London: HMSO, 1988).

The European Commission brought an infringement action against the United Kingdom before the ECJ in 1982. The Court found that several of the Sex Discrimination Act's exceptions violated the Equal Treatment Directive.[52] While Parliament was considering the 1986 Sex Discrimination Bill, the ECJ handed down its ruling in *Marshall*.[53] The Court held that the Equal Treatment Directive prohibited dismissing a woman who exceeded the pensionable age (sixty for women, sixty-five for men) if the employer allowed men to continue working, and that the directive was directly effective against the state as an employer. The rulings thus called for removing certain exceptions to the Sex Discrimination Act.

The Sex Discrimination Act of 1986 removed the blanket exemption for small employers, although it retained an exemption for private households under the genuine occupational qualification.[54] It voided discriminatory provisions in collective agreements, internal rules, and rules governing professions, although it did not provide an effective mechanism for challenging them. It made dismissing women who had reached the age of sixty unfair if men could continue working until sixty-five.[55]

The Government took the opportunity provided by the 1986 bill to repeal some protective legislation for women, repealing restrictions on hours of work for women who work in factories. The act also repealed limits on the hours men could work in bakeries. In furtherance of its goal of reducing "burdens on employers" through deregulation,[56] the Government went beyond what the EOC had called for in its 1979 report. It did not protect women against employers who could now require them to work shifts or nights or lose their jobs.[57]

The British Government seized the opportunity again presented by pressure from Europe to amend the discrimination laws to deregulate rather than to seek equality.[58] The European Commission had issued a reasoned opinion

---

52. Commission of the European Communities v. United Kingdom, [1984] ICR 192.

53. Marshall v. Southampton Area Health Authority, [1986] ICR 335 (ECJ).

54. See Lyn Durward, "More Legislation, Fewer Rights—A New Sex Discrimination Bill," *Rights of Women Bulletin*, December, 1986, 20–21; Jeanne Gregory, "Sex Discrimination Bill: Update," *National Council for Civil Liberties Women's Rights Unit Newsletter* 1 (October 1986): 2.

55. It also outlawed discrimination in job offers, training, promotion, and demotion. See Hazel Carty, "The Sex Discrimination Act 1986: Equality or Employment Deregulation?" *Journal of Social Welfare Law*, 1987, 177; Barry Fitzpatrick, "The Sex Discrimination Act 1986," *Modern Law Review* 50 (1987): 939. The 1986 Act did not, however, entitle victims of discrimination to receive redundancy payments. The Employment Act of 1989 made women eligible for redundancy payments on the same terms as men after they reached the pensionable age of sixty.

56. Fitzpatrick, n.5.

57. Ibid., 949.

58. "Protective Legislation for Women in the Member States of the European Community," COM (87) 105 final.

that section 51 of the 1975 Sex Discrimination Act was inconsistent with the Equal Treatment Directive.[59] (A reasoned opinion is the step preceding infringement proceedings before the ECJ.) Section 51 exempted acts done under statutory authority from coverage under the Sex Discrimination Act. Thus, the act did not invalidate any act of Parliament passed before 1975 or a statutory instrument passed after 1975 but under the authority of a statute passed before 1975 that permitted or required discrimination. The Employment Act of 1989 amended section 51 and repealed most of the protective laws excluding or restricting women's employment (I consider the significance of the changes to section 51 in chapter 5). The broad exemption for discrimination on grounds of health and safety remain intact. Employers must link other exemptions to the protection of women to pregnancy, maternity, or "other circumstances giving rise to risks specifically affecting women."[60] The Employment Act repealed the restrictions on women working underground in mines, cleaning moving machinery, and working in the pottery industry. It retained protection for health and safety, specific restrictions for lead and ionizing radiation, and certain protection for pregnancy and childbirth. The act also provides for industrial tribunals to hold prehearing reviews and order a deposit of up to £150 if a party wants to continue to participate in the hearings.[61]

Despite the new legislation and what appears to be formal compliance, the Commission and the ECJ may conclude in the future that some of these broad exceptions in the Sex Discrimination Act conflict with the Equal Treatment Directive. Not only do the many exceptions to the Sex Discrimination Act limit its ability to eradicate discrimination, but other factors reduce its effectiveness. The requirement that claimants file within three months of the incidence of alleged discrimination provides little time for contemplation or the acquisition of legal help and advice.[62] Britain has the shortest time limit for filing of any country in the EC. Although the law gives tribunals the discretion to allow exceptions to the time limit if "in all circumstances it considers that it is just and equitable to do so," tribunals have usually declined to do so.

Although the burden of proof rests with the complainant and is supposed to be only at the level of "the balance of probabilities"[63]—the standard British judges use in civil cases—litigators and commentators report confusion over what standard judges and members of tribunals are actually applying.[64] Some

---

59. Docksey, 14.

60. Employment Act 1989, sec. 3 (3)(2)(a)(ii). See "The New Employment Bill," *Industrial Relations Legal Information Bulletin* 368 (1989): 14–15.

61. As of writing, this provision had not yet come into effect.

62. Leonard, *Judging Inequality*, 102–5.

63. The balance of probabilities means that the claim is more likely to be true than false. This is very different than "beyond a reasonable doubt," for example, the standard in criminal cases.

64. Corcoran, 63.

argue the standard is too high. "The British courts and tribunals, unlike those in the United States, have produced no theory on the evidential burden of proof in discrimination cases."[65] This failure is important because the evidence in discrimination cases is often circumstantial. Because British law allows no class action suits, women cannot benefit from the weight of evidence about an employer's practices as a whole. Instead of being able to show a pattern of discrimination, women must prove discrimination in their individual cases.[66] The Equal Opportunities Commission recently called for Parliament to shift the burden of proof so that once the applicant has proven less favorable treatment, a presumption of discrimination would arise requiring the respondent to prove such is not the case.[67] The European Commission, too, has called for reversing the burden of proof in discrimination cases.[68]

Parliament has rejected two mechanisms that U.S. advocates for civil rights see as essential to the struggle for equality: affirmative action and contract compliance. Contract compliance requires those holding governmental contracts to meet higher standards of equal employment opportunity than other employers.[69] The Sex Discrimination Act only permits affirmative action in a few situations, such as training schemes. Preferential treatment in hiring would constitute discrimination against men under the act. Parliament specifically rejected the method of using governmental contract compliance to force employers to hire and promote women,[70] and the former chairman of the EOC spoke against it in 1987.[71] The Greater London Council, before the Government abolished it, experimented with using contract compliance for London, as did several other local authorities. Under the 1988 Local Government Act, though, such requirements are illegal. As a result, the government does not require employers to keep statistics on their hiring record of women and minority men, let alone set goals and timetables for hiring, and this failure makes it more difficult to prove indirect as well as direct discrimination.

The biggest weakness of the act is the limited power industrial tribunals have to provide remedies in proven cases of discrimination. These tribunals have no power to require reinstatement, promotion, or affirmative action.

---

65. B. A. Hepple, "Judging Equal Rights," in *Current Legal Problems* 36 (London: Stevens, 1983), 80; see also Steven L. Willborn, "Theories of Employment Discrimination in the United States," *Boston College International and Comparative Law Review* 9 (1986): 243–56.

66. See David Pannick, *Sex Discrimination Law* (Oxford: Clarendon, 1986), 272–302.

67. EOC, *Equal Treatment*, 21–22. See Leonard, *Judging Inequality*, 142–45.

68. COM (88) 269 final; Corcoran, 62–63.

69. See Colin Bourn and John Whitmore, *The Law of Discrimination and Equal Pay* (London: Sweet and Maxwell, 1989): 213–21.

70. *Parliamentary Debates* (Commons), 5th ser., vol. 893 (1975), cols. 1478–82. The European Community's Council of Ministers has, however, issued a recommendation on positive action; Council Recommendation of 13 December 1984 on the promotion of positive action for women, 84/635/EEC, No. L 331/34 O.J.C., December 19, 1984.

71. "Bring Out the Stilettos," *Economist*, July 11, 1987, 59.

They may issue an order declaring the rights of the parties, may make recommendations that an employer take certain actions,[72] and may order compensation for economic loss (up to a maximum of £8,925)[73] and injury to feelings. In *Skyrail Oceanic Ltd. v. Coleman*, the Court of Appeal reduced compensation from £1,000 to £100, thereby setting a precedent for low payments for injury to feelings.[74] Before 1988, the amount of compensation that industrial tribunals ordered was small and formed no discernible pattern.[75] In 1988, however, the Court of Appeal decided two cases that reversed this pattern.[76] The court stated that awards for injuries to feelings should not be minimal and clarified when tribunals should award the maximum the statute allows. Recent evidence suggests, however, that tribunals are overcoming their reluctance to award damages, and the need to comply with the EC's Equal Treatment Directive may permit tribunals to exceed the statutory minimum for compensations.[77] A complainant may return to the tribunal to have the compensation increased if the employer does not follow the tribunal's recommendations.[78] If an employer proves that its indirectly discriminatory actions were unintentional discrimination, the tribunal can only issue a statement of rights and recommend that the employer change its practice. The act exempts an employer from paying compensation if it proves that the discrimination was unintentional. In general, tribunals avoid making recommendations that require extended supervision and intervention to insure compliance,[79] while U.S. courts may go so far as to appoint special masters, representatives of the courts who supervise day-to-day execution of the courts' order. The limited

---

72. In Prestcold Ltd. v. Irvine, [1981] ICR 777 (CA), the Court of Appeal held that an industrial tribunal could not order a company to pay increased wages to a woman until they promoted her after finding it had discriminated against her on the basis of sex. The Court of Appeal held that an industrial tribunal could order compensation but it could not make recommendations about wages (see Pannick, 88–90).

73. See "Review of 1988," *Industrial Relations Legal Information Bulletin* 371 (January 10, 1989): 15. The *Marshall* case, before the House of Lords, may alter the compensation limits; see "EEC Law Does Not Override SDA Compensation Limits," *Equal Opportunities Review Discrimination Case Law Digest* 5 (1990): 1.

74. [1981] ICR 864 (CA).

75. Leonard, *Judging Inequality*, 61; Hepple, 73.

76. Alexander v. Home Office, [1988] IRLR 190 (CA), and Noone v. North West Thames Regional Health Authority, [1988] IRLR 195 (CA), discussed in Equal Opportunities Commission, *Thirteenth Annual Report* (London: HMSO, 1988), 6. Both cases were claims of race discrimination.

77. Marshall, [1986] ICR 335 (ECJ), [1988] IRLR 325 (CA); von Colson, [1984] ECR 1891 (ECJ).

78. In Nelson and Another v. Tyne and Wear Passenger Transport Executive, [1978] ICR 1183 (EAT), the Employment Appeal Tribunal heard a claim that an employer had not complied with the recommendation of a tribunal that it give serious consideration to promoting a woman whom it had discriminated against within six months. The EAT found that discrimination could not be eradicated instantly, and the employer had justification for its delay.

79. Hepple, 85.

ability of tribunals to award compensation and their inability to order employers to act to remedy or prevent discrimination has led the Equal Opportunities Commission to call for Parliament to set a minimum figure for compensation and to give industrial tribunals the power to fine employers for each day they do not make the ordered changes.[80]

The British Equal Opportunities Commission

The 1975 Sex Discrimination Act created an enforcement body, the Equal Opportunities Commission (EOC). Although modeled on the U.S. Equal Employment Opportunity Commission (EEOC), the EOC's brief included only discrimination on the basis of sex and not race. The EOC did not have to set priorities between the two, unlike its U.S. counterpart.[81] The Sex Discrimination Act gives the EOC the responsibility to work toward the elimination of discrimination and promote equality of opportunity between men and women, to keep under review the working of the Sex Discrimination Act and the Equal Pay Act, recommending possible amendments and revisions to the acts, to review protective legislation, to conduct formal investigations and require individuals or companies to produce information, to recommend changes in practices or procedures, and to issue a report of its investigations. If, during a formal investigation, the commission is satisfied that discrimination has occurred, it can serve a nondiscrimination notice requiring the recipient to change its practices. The commission also has special powers to institute proceedings against discriminatory practices and advertisements. It may help individuals bring cases, provide information, and issue codes of practice for employers, advertisers, or providers of goods and services.

Feminists and civil rights activists have criticized the EOC for being inactive, conciliatory, and conservative.[82] The principal problem is the membership of the commission. Fourteen commissioners supervise a staff of 166.5. The EOC is a tripartite body—the Home Office appoints members from three segments: industry, trade unions, and government. By informal

---

80. EOC, *Equal Treatment*, 20–21.

81. The Commission for Racial Equality deals with claims of race discrimination. Because of the similarity between the wording and provisions of the Sex Discrimination Act and the Race Relations Act, principles established in race cases generally hold true for sex discrimination cases.

82. See Paul Byrne and Joni Lovenduski, "The Equal Opportunities Commission," *Women's Studies International Quarterly* 1 (1978): 131–47; Anna Coote and Beatrix Campbell, *Sweet Freedom: The Struggle for Women's Liberation* (London: Picador, 1982), 123–29; Francis Cairncross, "Is the EOC Worth £3 Million of Public Money?" *Guardian*, December 7, 1983; Elizabeth Meehan, "Equal Opportunity Policies: Some Implications for Women of Contrasts Between Enforcement Bodies in Britain and the U.S.A.," in *Women's Welfare, Women's Rights*, ed. by Jane Lewis (London: Croom Helm, 1983): 170–92; Vera Sacks, "Equal Opportunities Commission"; Jeanne Gregory, *Sex, Race and the Law: Legislating for Equality* (London: Sage, 1987); Evelyn Ellis, *Sex Discrimination Law* (Brookfield, Vt.: Gower, 1988): 235–79.

agreement, the Confederation of British Industry nominates three of the commissioners, as does the Trades Union Congress.[83] Some critics blame tripartism itself for leading to paralysis, but the main problem is the Home Office's determination to avoid appointing people who have shown a commitment to fighting inequality, leading Coote and Campbell to argue, "the EOC was designed to *contain* the problem of sex discrimination not to *solve* it."[84] The Home Office rejected the suggestions of women's groups who had campaigned for the legislation.[85] Furthermore, the CBI and TUC have frequently used their positions to appoint people who will uphold the status quo of current industrial relations practice rather than appoint people experienced in discrimination issues and committed to dismantling practices that lead to inequality. In fact, the opposite is the case: some commissioners have used their position to frustrate the efforts of the EOC.[86] The blandness or conservative nature of the appointments to the EOC is not unique, but is characteristic of governmental appointments to quangos (quasi-autonomous nongovernmental organizations).[87]

The blatant antifeminism on the part of some commissioners, their reported tendency to meddle in staff affairs while simultaneously failing to provide overall direction to the agency,[88] and their general lack of commitment and experience in discrimination matters has made it hard for the agency to keep committed and experienced staff. Initially, feminists applied to and served on the staff, resulting in one commissioner commenting that "there are too many people [on the staff] who are committed to the women's cause, so they can't think straight. They just go barging through."[89] The staff turnover has been extremely high (38 percent in 1978, four chief executives in the first five years), and many disgruntled feminists have left.[90] Although staff are not, strictly speaking, civil servants in that they cannot transfer to other civil service departments, the commission has expected feminists on the staff to adopt the British civil service's posture of bureaucratic neutrality and to "leave their feminist hats at home."[91] The grievances of feminist staff during the early years, leading many to quit or to file discrimination claims against the

83. Ellis, 237.

84. Coote and Campbell, 128.

85. Gregory, *Sex, Race and the Law*, 110.

86. Coote and Campbell, 127; Meehan, "Equal Opportunity Policies," 181–82; Gregory, *Sex, Race and the Law*, 137–38.

87. "The main drawback to the present system is not abuse of power or responsibility but the avoidance of risk which leads to the unimaginative and repetitive appointment of the same safe names" (Anne Davis, "Patronage and Quasi-Government: Some Proposals for Reform," in *Quangos in Britain: Government and the Networks of Public Policy-Making*, ed. by Anthony Barker [London: Macmillan, 1982]: 167–80).

88. Sacks, 562–63.

89. Coote and Campbell, 127.

90. Ibid.

91. Meehan, "Equal Opportunity Policies," 180.

agency, has contributed to the EOC's poor relations with feminist groups. Locating the headquarters in Manchester, rather than London, exacerbated the problem of finding well-qualified individuals to accept jobs both on the commission and on the staff.

From the outset, the commission took the position that it should seek to promote equality through consensus and conciliation rather than confrontation.[92] Its first annual report stated,

> the Commission has nevertheless chosen to adopt an advisory and explanatory approach, seeking from the outset as much voluntary cooperation as possible from advertisers and publishers and keeping its powers in reserve to deal if necessary with persistent or deliberate flouting of the law.[93]

Lady Howe, the first deputy chair, addressed a management conference in 1976 to reassure business interests that the EOC would not approach its task as "one-eyed egalitarians." She devoted most of her speech to explaining what the EOC would not do.

> *It is not* trying to turn men into women or vice versa. . . . *It is not* trying to rewrite the English language (hence her and Betty Lockwood's [first chairman] insistence on the term chairman) . . . . *It is not* trying to destroy the privacy of the family or the home . . . . *It is not* trying to interfere with the employer's legitimate freedom.[94]

Specifically, this approach has meant that the EOC has written to employers informing them of the law, it has produced pamphlets, and it spent £100,000 to encourage women to go into science and engineering. It prefers to warn employers who place discriminatory advertisements rather than prosecute them, though only the agency has the power to prosecute for this offense. It prefers to enter a dialogue with employers over suspicious practices rather than to start formal investigations. If it finds widespread discrimination, it prefers to allow employers to change voluntarily.[95] As Gregory notes, "The Home Office comment that the EOC has used its powers 'sensibly' and that neither Commission has 'caused too much trouble' speaks volumes."[96]

---

92. The EOC expresses and defends this position in its *Eighth Annual Report* (London: HMSO, 1983). See also *Equality Now* 3 (Summer 1984): 5.

93. Ellis, 270.

94. EOC Press Notice, February 23, 1976, quoted in Gregory, *Sex, Race and the Law*, 110; italics in the original.

95. Sacks, 580.

96. Gregory, *Sex, Race and the Law*, 142; George Appelby and Evelyn Ellis, "Formal Investigations: The Commission for Racial Equality and the Equal Opportunity Commission as Law Enforcement Agencies," *Public Law* (Summer 1984): 272.

This focus on conciliation has led to the complaint that the EOC has not used its enforcement powers to the fullest, specifically, that it has not used its authority to launch formal investigations, a potentially powerful weapon.[97] Frustrated EOC staff put pressure on the agency to undertake more formal investigations.[98] The White Paper, *Equality for Women*, which sets out the drafters' vision of the agency, saw this power as the key to its effectiveness.[99] Because British law permits no class actions, formal investigations provide the best opportunity to investigate employers who have been the target of many complaints or industries or institutions whose practices, if changed, could have a significant impact. Yet the agency "has chosen to keep its 'big guns' in reserve and to use them as little as possible."[100] Formal investigations get around the problem of having to wait for individual complaints and permit the agency to move against the big problems and seek large awards. As Sacks comments, "Since law enforcement of this kind is the sole preserve of the agency, extra resources ought to be switched to formal investigations— perhaps the £100,000 spent on W.I.S.E. [Women Into Science and Engineering] could have been spent more 'wisely.'"[101] Since Leonard found most complaints of sex discrimination were either against governmental agencies, nationalized industries, or large employers, the EOC is missing a golden opportunity to go after the large offenders.[102]

The commission, the chairman, and the courts should share the criticism for this failure. The commission's preference for dialogue and persuasion rather than legal action to force employers, companies, or educational authorities to change their behavior stands in stark contrast to the Commission for Racial Equality (CRE).[103] The EOC embarked on eleven formal investigations and issued three nondiscrimination notices; during the same period the CRE began sixty-two formal investigations and issued nineteen nondiscrimination notices.[104] Employers' challenges to the CRE's investigations provided the courts with the opportunity to obliterate the powers of formal investigation. The courts found that the agency must allow employers to make representations at every stage of the proceedings and to challenge the agency's right to continue. The subsequent delays have seriously undermined both

---

97. "The main trouble with the Equal Opportunities Commission, say its critics, is that it is simply too ladylike" ("Bring Out the Stilettos," 60).

98. Gregory, *Sex, Race and the Law*, 112.

99. "The main function of the EOC was thus envisaged as the elimination of widescale, institutionalised discrimination, aid to individuals involved in bringing their own proceedings was to be a secondary function only" (Ellis, 236).

100. Gregory, *Sex, Race and the Law*, 130.

101. Sacks, 581.

102. Leonard, *Judging Inequality*, 19.

103. In fact, the CRE has been criticized for instituting too many investigations, more than it can effectively pursue to completion.

104. Ellis, 266.

agencies' ability to conduct investigations and have eroded morale. Even if judicial rulings had not decimated the power of formal investigation in cases against the CRE,[105] the agency has not shown the will to use its statutory powers fully.[106]

Besides being hostile to the purposes the agencies are pursuing, judges are suspicious of the mixture of powers—administrative, judicial, and legislative—that the agencies have. Lord Denning characterized them as "inquisitional powers of a kind never before known to law."[107] As Evelyn Ellis notes: "The Commissions are, rightly, perceived by many members of the public as both prosecutor and judge, and this carries the inevitable taint of possible bias in the enforcement process."[108] Ian Gilmour, leading the Conservative opposition to the Sex Discrimination Bill, described the powers of the EOC as "policewoman, prosecutor, judge, jury, and even probation officer and after-care officer rolled into one."[109] The courts' hostility to entrusting all stages of the law enforcement process to one agency has led the CRE to call for an independent tribunal of fact to participate at an earlier stage.[110]

The EOC has also been slow in issuing codes of practice. Although such codes do not have the force of law, judges and members of tribunals accept them as prima facie evidence of how they should interpret the act. Only once has the EOC used this authority to define the parameters of the law, and then it diluted the one code of practice it did issue by its choice of language—by stating that a code of practice is *merely* a guideline. While the EOC scrupulously consulted and redrafted the code to accommodate various groups' comments, a CBI member on the commission bragged of the success he had had in delaying the process.[111] Ellis laments: "The Code is not (and was never expected to be) a radical restatement of the law, so that it is unfortunate that it took nearly a decade to come into effect. During this time, industrial tribunals have become accustomed to finding their own way through the sex discrimination legislation and may now be somewhat reluctant to change their ways and make full use of the Code."[112] Instead of playing down their importance and issuing few codes of practice, the EOC could try to make the act stronger by issuing codes of practice on comparable worth, insurance, sexual harassment,

---

105. See David Pannick, 272–302. See also R. v. CRE ex parte Hillingdon L.B.C., [1982] AC 779 (HL); In re Prestige Group plc, [1984] 1 WLR 335 (HL); R. v. CRE ex parte Cottrell and Rothon, [1980] 3 All ER 265 (QBD); Selvarajan v. Race Relations Board, [1976] 1 All ER 12 (CA); CRE v. Amari Plastics Ltd., [1982] ICR 304 (CA). These are cases under the Race Relations Act but they are also relevant for the Sex Discrimination Act.

106. Appelby and Ellis, 236–76; see also Byrne and Lovenduski.

107. Nasse v. Science Research Council, [1978] IRLR 352, 355 (CA).

108. Ellis, 258.

109. Gregory, *Sex, Race and the Law*, 108–9.

110. Ibid., 123.

111. Ibid., 138.

112. Ellis, 275.

and other issues, and it could also give employers specific guidance about what the law requires.

Finally, critics have accused the EOC of failing to use its authority to litigate fully and for failing to have any coherent strategy for either litigation or formal investigations.[113] The agency is now helping more complainants—but fewer than the 80 percent of complaints to the CRE that receive some form of aid.[114] Most people approaching the EOC found the quality of assistance to be high.[115] Proving discrimination has been notoriously difficult. In cases of indirect discrimination, complainants may need access to complex statistical analysis. In all cases, expert advice and representation dramatically increase the chances of success. Furthermore, only limited legal aid is available for the preparation of the case, and few private litigation groups can afford to bring cases. It is, thus, a rare victim of discrimination who can successfully pursue a case unassisted. Because the EOC has no statutory duty to inform those whose claims for help it rejects its reasons for doing so, it is not surprising that many of these unsuccessful applicants eventually withdraw their claims.[116] Intervention by the EOC is essential if the law is going to work. Furthermore, the EOC has an important role to play in seeking to shape legal precedent. Considering that participation as amicus curiae is rare in British courts, although the EOC does so occasionally,[117] the importance of defining and expanding the law through test cases and codes of practice increases.

Here again, the commission must share the blame with others, in this instance, the Home Office and the Government. Even if the EOC wanted to expand the use of litigation, it could not because the Home Office strictly limits the number of lawyers it may employ.[118] Although the EOC does merit criticism for devoting such a small part of its budget to litigation and formal investigations, the Government's failure to increase its budget ties its hands. The Commission for Racial Equality had a budget of £10.6 million in 1986 while the Equal Opportunities Commission received only £3.4 million.[119] The difference in budgets reflects the Government's view that race discrimination is a more important social problem because of its connection to civil

---

113. Sacks, 574–76.

114. Gregory, *Sex, Race and the Law*, 132.

115. Jeanne Gregory, *Trial by Ordeal: A Study of People Who Lost Equal Pay and Sex Discrimination Cases in the Industrial Tribunals During 1985 and 1986* (London: HMSO, 1989), 36.

116. Gregory, *Sex, Race and the Law*, 75.

117. The EOC has appeared as amicus curiae in E. Coomes (Holdings) Ltd. v. Shields, [1978] ICR 1159 (CA); Nasse v. Science Research Council, [1979] IRLR 465 (HL); Page v. Freight Hire (Tank Haulage) Ltd., [1981] IRLR 13 (EAT). Sacks (571) advocates wider use of this role.

118. EOC Official, interview with author, London, August 1986.

119. "Bring Out the Stilettos," 60. This budget difference reflects the salaries the CRE pays to local community relations councils.

disorder and also reflects the CRE's funding of local community relations counselors. Furthermore, the growth in the budget has not kept pace with inflation, nor risen as fast as the Government had promised.[120]

EOC Budget, 1976–86

Year	Grant (£)	Percentage Increase
1976–77	850,430	
1977–78	1,460,699	42
1978–79	1,644,650	11
1979–80	2,146,422	23
1980–81	2,520,270	15
1981–82	2,911,000	13
1982–83	3,046,000	4
1983–84	3,168,000	4
1984–85	3,387,000	6
1985–86	3,434,000	1

Since Vera Sacks's article criticizing the EOC for having no sense of direction, and since the appointment of Joanna Foster as chairman, the EOC has developed an explicit strategy for the 1990s: "From Policy to Practice: An Equal Opportunities Strategy," although its plans for implementing that strategy are less clear. It has had a well-developed legal strategy for some time.

The EOC prefers to keep its distance from feminist groups,[121] a task made easier by its location in Manchester. (Most pressure groups' headquarters are in London.) This aloofness is not surprising since the Home Office explicitly avoids drawing commissioners from the ranks of feminists and the staff reflects the commission's ambivalence about fighting for women's rights. Two chairmen of the agency have employed the same metaphor to describe their position as a "tightrope" between "the demands of the long-standing campaigners for women's equality . . . and the majority of the population who are fearful of busybodying."[122] Lady Platt dissociated herself from both groups, putting herself in the middle, between "male chauvinists" and "militant feminists."[123] Her position reflects the civil service position that a governmental agency should be neutral rather than captured, above the fray rather than an advocate. It also reflects the ambivalence or outright hostility of chairmen and commissioners to feminists and feminism.

This desire to "float above" the problems posed by inequality and desire to appear neutral reflects the greater distance between civil servants and

120. Ellis, 240.
121. Meehan, 187–88.
122. Gregory, Sex, Race and the Law, 154, quoting Betty Lockwood.
123. Ibid.

interest groups characteristic of the British civil service as a whole. A former senior staff member believes that an organized feminist group could lobby the agency and reinforce the positions taken by the few feminists within the agency. The EOC's caution in meeting feminist demands and its incremental, nonconfrontational approach stem, in part, from its vulnerability and lack of support from a Government concerned with cutting public spending, reducing burdens on industry, and lacking a commitment to fighting sex inequality.[124] Although the 1988 annual report boasts of several lunches with feminist groups, the EOC's isolation from feminist groups squanders the expertise of these organizations and leaves it without public defenders. Its distance from feminists has not led to success in getting the Government to accept its proposals, but has led to feminists publicly attacking the agency. The EOC is not accountable to any constituency outside of government. Gregory identifies this as a more general problem of quangos in Britain.

> Since 1979, the murmur of voices from the political right, demanding a drastic reduction in the numbers and powers of these administrative bodies, has become a strident, persistent chorus. The quangos have been left largely undefended from such attacks, because those political groups that favour interventionist policies have their own reservations about this particular form of implementation. The people it is established to serve frequently experience the quango as a remote and alien body which appears to make arbitrary decisions that cannot easily be challenged.[125]

If the EOC lacks friends in the feminist movement, it also has no entrenched interests in Parliament to defend it and to push it forward. In the United States, in contrast, the Democratically controlled Congress has several committee chairs who exercise their legislative and oversight functions to encourage the pursuit of equality. Congressional committees defend agencies from budget cuts, expand their budgets, scrutinize their policies and records, and oversee executive appointments to the agencies. In contrast, the British Government may easily push its program of reducing burdens on industry through Parliament.

While feminists within Britain have been highly critical of the agency, the EOC has won praise throughout the EC.[126] The EOC has successfully sponsored test cases that have advanced EC equality law and invalidated parts of the British law. The EOC's advocacy before the ECJ receives strong praise,

---

124. See *Lifting the Burden*, Cmnd. 9571 (London: HMSO, 1985).

125. Gregory, *Sex, Race and the Law*, 153.

126. Corcoran describes the EOC's ability to assist cases as "the envy of other member states" but also acknowledges how financially risky it was for the EOC to sponsor cases all the way to the European Court of Justice; see Corcoran, 62.

despite ECJ judges' critical view toward the way British judges have inter-preted British sex discrimination law. European feminists and civil rights campaigners envy the agency's ability to gather information and propose changes to the law, as well as the effectiveness with which the EOC supplies the European Commission with information.

Despite the institutional limitations posed by its existence as a quango, weak or no parliamentary committees, low budgets, and a hostile judiciary that has dismantled its powers, many of the criticisms of the agency are fair. While persuasion may have been a good strategy for the 1970s, the time for education has passed. If employers know that they can wait for the agency to put pressure on them, if they know they will get a warning long before the agency acts, and if they know the worst sanction is a slap on the wrist or one or two individual complaints, they have no incentive to act. Downplaying litigation and formal investigations sends no message to industry that it is time to obey the law. The EOC can no longer afford a "softly, softly" approach. It needs leaders well versed in sex discrimination law and policy rather than a chairman who distances herself publicly from "strident" or "militant" femi-nists. The time has come to draw on feminists for expertise, support, and ideas. Instead of sending papers to Whitehall proposing changes, the EOC needs to work with feminists and political groups to develop a strategy to see those proposals carried out.

As well as institutional constraints and internal policy choices, two other factors may help to account for the EOC's limited effectiveness. First, the public is less supportive of reducing sex inequality in Britain than in the United States, although survey researchers have not extensively studied this question.[127] In 1983, the Eurobarometer survey showed more Britons dis-agreeing with the claim: "there should be fewer differences between men's and women's roles in society" than in any other European nation surveyed.[128] Second, feminists have not only been critical of the agency for its failure to accomplish its own limited goals, but are also ambivalent about the evolution-ary liberal reform the agency seeks. British feminists, aligned with the Left more so than their U.S. counterparts, have had reservations about legislative reform, litigation as a strategy for social change, and the potential of the EC, although they are now more positive.

---

127. See Sophia Peterson, "Public Opinion and Policy Implementation: The Sex Discrimi-nation Act in Great Britain, 1976–82," paper presented at the annual meeting of the American Political Science Association, Washington, D.C., September 3–6, 1987; Pippa Norris, *Politics and Sexual Equality: The Comparative Position of Women in Western Democracies* (Boulder, Colo.: Rienner, 1987), 132–41. Norris analyzes Eurobarometer surveys as well as the those taken for the UN Decade for Women.

128. Joyce Gelb, "Feminism in Britain: Politics Without Power?" in *The New Women's Movement: Feminism and Political Power in Europe and the USA*, ed. by Drude Dahlerup (London: Sage, 1986), 104.

The British Women's Movement

In both the United States and Britain, the women's movement is a diverse coalition of groups of individuals who share only the most general aims: ending women's oppression. They share neither a common critique nor strategy for change. Thus, describing the movement as a single entity and listing its characteristics is an oversimplification: groups vary among themselves as much as they differ from country to country. [129] Despite this problem of comparison, the most striking difference between the two movements is the absence of a large, mass membership organization engaged in both protest politics and a dialogue with the state: there is no British equivalent of the National Organization for Women. British women elites are less likely than their U.S. counterparts to self-identify as feminists, and the movement misses their organizational skills, political connections, money, ability to function as articulate spokespersons, and the legitimacy they impart to the movement as a whole.

While liberal feminists are a strong presence in the feminist movement in the United States, most feminists in Britain identify themselves as radical or socialist feminists, and both groups are much more suspicious of "working within the system." Radical feminists focus on peace issues, pornography, and sexual violence and seek to set up alternative institutions rather than work within governmental agencies. Socialist feminists in Britain are engaged with the state, albeit in a more critical stance than their liberal sisters, but they lack the numbers of the U.S. organizations. Furthermore, their wider economic and social critique costs them their ability to appeal across parties and classes to form a broad coalition on a few issues. Socialist feminists work within the Labour Party, trade unions, law centers, and pressure groups such as the National Council for Civil Liberties. Both radical and socialist feminists value ideological integrity over political expediency—their more comprehensive critique of society makes them less willing to seek pragmatic compromise, particularly with a Conservative Government.

As much as ideological differences, the structure of British political institutions leads to differences in the British and U.S. feminist movements. [130] The British system discourages the formation of a mass feminist

---

129. See Joyce Gelb, "Social Movement 'Success': A Comparative Analysis of Feminism in the U.S. and U.K.," in *The Women's Movements of the United States and Western Europe: Consciousness, Political Opportunity, and Public Policy*, ed. by Mary Fainsod Katzenstein and Carol McClurg Mueller (Philadelphia: Temple University Press, 1987), 267–89; Anne Sedley, "Equal Opportunities in the U.S.A.," *Rights: The Journal of the National Council for Civil Liberties* 8 (Autumn 1984): 5; Joni Lovenduski, *Women and European Politics: Contemporary Feminism and Public Policy* (Amherst: University of Massachusetts Press, 1986); Vicky Randall, *Women and Politics: An International Perspective*, 2d ed. (Chicago: University of Chicago Press, 1987).

130. See Joyce Gelb, *Feminism and Politics: A Comparative Perspective* (Berkeley: University of California Press, 1989) for a full description of the impact of the institutional and ideological differences.

organization. Unlike the U.S. system, there are few access points for feminist lobbyists to address (such as parliamentary committees or state governments). The civil service is a career service—its members do not move in and out of business or interest groups. The bureaucracy responds to only a select few interest groups—the administration of government is more closed. Finally, the structure of Parliament, political parties with party discipline characteristic of a parliamentary system, and limited election campaigns make it difficult to form nonpartisan political groups. Socialist feminists often prefer to work within the Labour Party, trade unions, or even Labour-controlled local governments rather than campaign on a national level with women of other parties.

British feminists have not embraced litigation to promote social change to the same degree as feminists in the United States. Judges and members of industrial tribunals have neither been very sympathetic to the concerns of women plaintiffs nor seen their constitutional position as expanding equality or making public policy. Despite the limitations of the legal system, feminists in Britain have begun to organize to maximize the gains possible under the current legal structure and to campaign for legal reform. The Women's Legal Defense Fund coordinates litigation and aims to improve women's representation before industrial tribunals. The National Women's Alliance lobbies Parliament and provides a network for women's groups. The National Women's Funding Coalition seeks to raise money for feminist organizations. Finally, British feminist groups have become active in the European Network on Women to campaign for change at the EC level.[131] Such groups provide a watchdog function on governmental agencies (including the EOC), provide a channel for funneling information and criticism from the movement to government and the EC, train future feminist leaders, propose policy reforms, and help individuals with their legal problems.

Industrial Tribunals

The performance of the EOC determines, in large part, the effectiveness of the Sex Discrimination Act, as does the behavior of industrial tribunals. Industrial tribunals, not courts, have original jurisdiction over cases of equal pay or sex discrimination in employment,[132] but most of their cases are disputes over employment contracts, unfair dismissal, and redundancy. The tribunals consist of panels of three people: two lay members, one appointed in consultation

---

131. Maggie Monteith, "Women's Legal Defense Fund: A New Fund to Fight for Women's Rights," *Rights of Women Bulletin*, May 1987, 12–13; "Women's Legal Defense Fund," *Civil Liberty* 3 (April 1987): 4; Maggie Monteith, "Movement News," *Rights of Women Bulletin*, Winter 1988, 11.

132. Parliament first established industrial tribunals in 1964. See Donald B. Williams and Denis J. Walker, *Industrial Tribunals—Practice and Procedure* (London: Butterworths, 1980); John McIlroy, *Industrial Tribunals* (London: Pluto, 1983). County courts hear cases if the discrimination on the basis of sex is in the provision of goods and services.

with the Confederation of British Industry (CBI), the other in consultation with the Trades Union Congress (TUC), and a legally qualified chairman. Legally qualified includes solicitors, barristers, and those with administrative legal experience, although this experience rarely includes any knowledge of employment law or industrial relations.[133] In practice, legally qualified means old. As early as 1967, one commentator was concerned that chairmen were mostly over fifty years old, had pursued a legal rather than an industrial career, and that many were either ex-colonial or ex-county court judges.[134]

Chairmen (the statutory term) can be either part-time or full-time.[135] Industrial tribunals set out their reasons for decisions in opinions that do not have the weight of precedent, and the decisions vary in both coverage and quality. Some state the evidence available, the testimony of the witnesses, the points of law, and the reasons for the decision. Others contain little information or reasoning. Parliament also established an Employment Appeal Tribunal to hear appeals on points of law whose rulings do carry the weight of precedent. Appeals from the EAT go to the Court of Appeal and then to the House of Lords. Under article 177 of the Treaty of Rome, if cases raise a question of EC law, a domestic court (or, in this case, an industrial tribunal or Employment Appeal Tribunal) may suspend its proceedings and put the question of law to the ECJ.

Compared to courts, industrial tribunals were supposed to be a "quick, cheap, accessible, informal, and expert" way of resolving disputes.[136] Proponents of tribunals hoped to draw on the expertise of trade unionists and management in industrial relations, an area judges know little about. Trade unions and the Labour Government also feared judges' historical antipathy to unions and sought to create a legal structure at least partially separate from courts.[137] Dissatisfied with the record of the Race Relations Board and aware of the backlog of complaints at the U.S. EEOC, the drafters of the Sex Discrimination Act explicitly rejected having an agency to process claims and conciliate and, instead, permitted individuals to bring cases directly.[138] Because the aim was to avoid legal wrangling and judicial formality as well as to provide an affordable method of dispute resolution, individuals are supposed to be able to represent themselves—legal aid is not available for the hearing, although an

---

133. Justice, *Industrial Tribunals* (London: Justice, 1987): 47.

134. R. W. Rideout, "The Industrial Tribunals," *Current Legal Problems* 21 (1968): 183, 193. See also Keith Whitesides and Geoffrey Hawker, *Industrial Tribunals* (London: Sweet and Maxwell, 1975), 33.

135. Sex discrimination claims are more likely to succeed before a full-time chairman—28 percent versus 20 percent; see Leonard, *Judging Inequality*, 122.

136. Whitesides, 9, summarizing the views of the Franks Committee.

137. See J. C. McCrudden, "Discrimination Against Minority Groups in Employment: A Comparison of Legal Remedies in the U.K. and the U.S." (D.Phil. thesis, Oxford University, 1981), 41; J. A. G. Griffith, *The Politics of the Judiciary*, 3d ed. (Glasgow: Fontana, 1985).

138. Leonard, *Judging Inequality*, 2.

individual who qualifies may receive up to £50 of professional advice in preparing the case. [139] Lawmakers wanted the hearings to have the characteristics of an inquisitorial system rather than an adversarial one. [140] They placed laypersons on the panel, encouraged them to question witnesses and help them to identify the correct legal claim, declined to make legal representation available, and opted not to provide any strict rules of procedure or evidence. [141]

The industrial tribunal system has not realized its potential in sex discrimination cases. Contrary to design, employers usually have counsel to represent them. [142] Yet a study of all industrial tribunal decisions on sex discrimination and equal pay over a three-year period between 1980 and 1982 by Alice Leonard, former U.S. civil rights lawyer and current deputy legal officer for the Equal Opportunities Commission, found that nearly half of all complainants attended hearings without a representative of any sort. [143] Nearly all who have studied the system agree that cases on sex discrimination and equal pay raise sufficiently complex issues of law and fact that individuals require skilled representation to win or even to identify and articulate the right claim. [144]

Legal representation is not fungible. Our defamation law prevents me from being specific, but there can be no doubt that some key cases have been lost by complainants through the lack of competence of counsel, or more specifically for our purposes, that principles have emerged from the case that would not have been enunciated had the case been better argued. Conversely, other cases have been won through counsel's inge-

---

139. According to Justice, the Donovan Commission envisaged the availability of legal aid for complainants whose employers were represented by lawyers, but Parliament never extended legal aid to cover this situation (Justice, 14).

140. An adversarial system places judges in the role of umpire, making the parties responsible for presenting evidence and arguing their case. An inquisitorial system gives the judge the role of questioner, giving him or her responsibility for seeing that justice is done and the appropriate questions are asked. Nearly half of all EC countries have an inquisitorial system for hearing sex discrimination and equal pay cases (Leonard, *Judging Inequality*, 147).

141. Rule 8 of the Industrial Tribunals Rules of Procedure (1980) states: "The tribunal shall conduct the hearing in such a manner as it considers most suitable to the clarification of the issues before it and generally to the just handling of the proceedings; it shall so far as appears to it appropriate seek to avoid formality in its proceedings and it shall not be bound by any enactment or rule of law relating to the admissibility of evidence in proceedings before the courts of law" (Michael J. Goodman, *Industrial Tribunals Practice and Procedure*, 4th ed. [London: Sweet and Maxwell, 1987], A43).

142. Leonard, *Judging Inequality*, 24.

143. Ibid., 11, 107–8. Leonard read 298 decisions, interviewed ten tribunal chairmen, interviewed barristers, solicitors, and activists experienced in this area of law, analyzed statistics from the Department of Employment, and observed several tribunal hearings.

144. Ibid., 3. See also Justice, 36; Hazel Genn and Yvette Genn, *The Effectiveness of Representation at Tribunals: Report to the Lord Chancellor* (London: Lord Chancellor's Department, 1989).

nuity and ability; Anthony Lester's brilliant record on behalf of equal pay and sex discrimination complainants is an obvious example.[145]

This representation makes a big difference in the success rates of complainants.[146] Complainants with lawyers do better than those unrepresented; however, what is important is that the advocate is expert in discrimination claims, regardless of whether he or she is a lawyer, trade union representative, or member of the Citizen's Advice Bureau.[147] Leonard found that complainants representing themselves were often unable to identify and present the evidence that would further their case,[148] in particular, to call witnesses who would corroborate their testimony. Respondents, more likely to have legal counsel, were also more likely to produce witnesses,[149]and the success rate varied strikingly with the number of witnesses called.[150] A more recent study of several different types of tribunals, including industrial tribunals, found that representation had an independent effect on the success of the complainant and concluded that Parliament should extend legal aid rather than merely trying to make the system more inquisitorial.[151] Clearly, the hope that individuals would be able adequately to represent themselves has not been realized in cases on sex discrimination and equal pay.

Not only have individuals found the law too complex and faced well-represented respondents, but the procedure has often been formal and incomprehensible to claimants—it has also often been adversarial rather than inquisitorial, although these criticisms are less true for Scottish tribunals.[152]

---

145. Michael Rubenstein, "Beyond the Whinge," *Oxford Journal of Legal Studies* 2 (1991): 260.

146. "Several of the tribunal chairmen most experienced with sex discrimination and equal pay cases stated that knowledgeable legal representation is extremely helpful, if not necessary in such cases" (Leonard, *Judging Inequality*, 86). Complainants in sex discrimination cases who are represented by counsel were successful 39 percent of the time, while those represented by themselves were successful only 21 percent of the time between 1976 and 1983 (Leonard, *Judging Inequality*, 124).

147. "Specialization appears to be an important factor in success" (Hazel Genn, "The Myth of Informality," *Legal Action*, September 1989, 9).

148. "In fact the decisions reveal an overwhelmingly frequent failure by complainants and their representatives to identify correctly in advance the information which was necessary to support the claim, to obtain it, and to produce it in the necessary form at the tribunal hearing" (Leonard, *Judging Inequality*, 80).

149. "Clearly, respondents took witnesses to hearings much more frequently than complainants." Complainants took witnesses 27 percent of the time versus 56 percent for respondents (Leonard, *Judging Inequality*, 20).

150. In claims under the Sex Discrimination Act, when only the complainant testified, 17 percent were successful. When two witnesses testified, 78 percent of complainants won (Leonard, *Judging Inequality*, 79–80).

151. Tom Mullen, "Representation at Tribunals," *Modern Law Review* 53 (March 1990): 230–36.

152. Leonard, *Judging Inequality*, 95.

The rule of procedure informs members that it is appropriate to seek to avoid the formality in its proceedings, yet chairmen vary in the extent to which they conduct their hearings informally and actively cross-examine, elicit the necessary evidence, and help articulate the correct claim. Those who have studied industrial tribunals put forward two explanations for this variation. Chairmen and panel members may be ignorant of the provisions of the law and, thus, unable to question those before them or help articulate claims. Moreover, chairmen confessed that they feel aggressive questioning and participation compromises the appearance of fairness and objectivity. Claimants often reported that they did not experience the proceedings as informal or the panel as helpful.[153] Because of the complexity of the law and the importance of skilled representation, the Justice Committee (a nonpartisan organization of jurists) recently called for creating two tiers of industrial tribunals. Tribunals would operate in an inquisitorial way for routine cases and perform their own investigations. For most cases of discrimination, however, the parties would be represented and specially trained tribunals would hear their cases.[154]

Tribunal members have made a disturbing number of conspicuous legal errors in their reasons for decision. Leonard concluded: "Some tribunals clearly misunderstood and/or misapplied the SDA 1975 and the EQPA 1970, or were unaware of their provisions."[155] "There is overwhelming evidence from empirical research that there is a serious lack of judicial expertise in the handling of these cases, which are both complex and sensitive, and that this is one of the reasons why so many complaints fail."[156] Frequent mistakes are not surprising since cases of sex discrimination and equal pay make up only 1 percent of the workload of any industrial tribunal,[157] and two of the members are unlikely to have had any legal training. Chairmen and lay members receive little if any instruction about the law prohibiting discrimination on the basis of sex,[158] and they do not always benefit from having the issues argued before them by legal counsel. The variation of the success rate of complainants under full-time and part-time chairmen suggests that the expertise of the chairmen significantly affects the outcome of the case.[159]

The EOC recently proposed that chairmen of industrial tribunals receive

---

153. "Sex Discrimination Tribunals . . . Extracts from a Real Experience," *National Council for Civil Liberties Rights for Women Unit Newsletter*, January 1984, 4 (confirmed by Gregory in *Trial by Ordeal*).

154. Justice, 54–56. See also Linda Dickens, "Justice in the Industrial Tribunal System," *Industrial Law Journal* 17 (March 1988): 58–61.

155. Leonard, *Judging Inequality*, 29.

156. Justice, 35.

157. Leonard, *Judging Inequality*, 74.

158. Ibid., 68.

159. Ibid., 122. Twenty percent versus 28 percent. "The identity of the chair or adjudicator had a significant and independent effect on the outcome—one way or the other" ("The Myth of Informality," 9).

specialist training in sex discrimination law, and that the lay panel members should have experience before they heard cases.[160] The campaigning group Justice echoed the EOC's call for specialized training in discrimination law and for assigning cases to the most experienced members.[161] Others have called for Parliament to set up separate discrimination tribunals.[162] The assignment of discrimination cases to full-time chairmen who have expertise has varied across the presidencies of the EAT. Before 1983, this specialization resulted in a fairly clear and consistent body of interpretation, but, after 1983, assignments have been more random.[163]

Tribunals most frequently erred by using the standard of "reasonableness," the correct legal standard in unfair dismissal cases, rather than applying the Sex Discrimination Act's definition of discrimination as "less favorable treatment."[164] Parliament did not define discrimination as "less favorable treatment a tribunal finds unreasonable" but simply forbade less favorable treatment. To import the standard of reasonableness is to circumvent the purpose of the act, because, unfortunately, many practices that initially strike panel members as reasonable on closer inspection would deny women employment opportunities.

Tribunals not only import a standard of reasonableness, but they rely on their feelings about the respondents: whether they thought the employer was sincere or whether they believed he or she meant any harm, rather than whether the evidence suggested that he or she had treated a woman less favorably than a man.[165] Leonard found that tribunals were often extremely reluctant to find respondents in breach of the law, and, in fact, the success rates of the claims are low: 11 percent of all sex discrimination claims end in a finding of discrimination, 27 percent of those that proceeded to a hearing are successful.[166]

One of the more serious opinions expressed was that many lay members (possibly influenced by the previous existence of penal sanctions in race discrimination cases) attach such a stigma to a finding of discrimination, that they are extremely reluctant to find discrimination has occurred. One chairman interviewed said "effectively, they apply a standard of proof not

160. Monteith, "Tackling the Problems," 9.

161. Justice, 4.

162. Bob Hepple, "The Judicial Process in Claims for Equal Pay and Equal Treatment in the United Kingdom," in *Women, Employment and European Equality Law*, ed. by Christopher McCrudden (London: Eclipse, 1987): 157–58.

163. Justice, 52.

164. Leonard, *Judging Inequality*, 34–35.

165. Ibid., 38–39.

166. Alice Leonard, *The First Eight Years: A Profile of Applicants to the Industrial Tribunals under the Sex Discrimination Act 1975 and the Equal Pay Act 1970* (Manchester: EOC, 1986), 23.

simply of the 'balance of probabilities' but of 'not unless absolutely certain.'"[167]

Distinguishing between legal mistakes and sexism is difficult. Are panel members erroneously importing the standard of reasonableness and setting a high burden of proof because of ignorance of the law and a mistaken association with unfair dismissal cases or because they fail to appreciate the harm of discrimination? While Leonard explains the reasons panel members might make mistakes, her study also uncovered a disturbing pattern of comments revealing views counter to the purposes of the Sex Discrimination Act.

There were several tribunals which appeared to be quite unaware of the discriminatory possibilities of sex-based assumptions. In fact, there were a number of tribunals which not only accepted but expressed agreement with the generalized assumptions about women which were offered to explain an employer's actions.[168]

For example, tribunals commented that a job that required employees to go out in the evenings was "a job quite unsuitable for a woman."[169] One tribunal praised women for not asserting their legal rights: "We were impressed by the attitude of the applicant toward her job. When she left to have a baby she chose not to give the notice that would entitle her to the right to return enjoyed by pregnant employees."[170] Some members clearly preferred women who did not become angry about discrimination but who merely became upset: "It is right to say that the applicant created an extremely favorable impression upon all of us. She was in no way militant. On the contrary, she was plainly extremely emotionally upset as a result of what had occurred."[171]

Leonard found that tribunals often did not scrutinize the evidence, accepting at face value the explanations employers offered, even when there were contradictory accounts.[172]

Tribunals were found to be superficial in their analysis of the evidence, too ready to accept vague and generalised statements even where these appeared to be inconsistent with other evidence, or based on irrelevant considerations such as "benevolent" motives.[173]

---

167. Leonard, *Judging Inequality*, 72.

168. Ibid., 32–33.

169. Miss Vickers v. N. W. Electronics (Bradford) Ltd., quoted in Leonard, *Judging Inequality*, 33.

170. Mrs. Hayward v. Keg Services, Ltd., quoted in Leonard, *Judging Inequality*, 34.

171. Miss King v. Amey Roadstone Corp. Ltd., quoted in Leonard, *Judging Inequality*, 34.

172. Leonard, *Judging Inequality*, 76.

173. Bob Hepple, foreword to Leonard, *Judging Inequality*.

This failure may reflect an unwillingness on the part of tribunals to intervene in the running of businesses or simply a propensity to believe employers. Or it may reflect an inclination to disbelieve women and to doubt that discrimination occurred. Parliament could solve this problem, in part, by clarifying employment law, making its intent clear, and setting clear legal standards that nonlawyers could apply.[174]

Part of the problem may be that panel members' expertise on industrial relations does not translate into experience with discrimination or even a commitment to equality, a point made by a commentator on racial discrimination.

> Yet precisely because of their membership, use of industrial tribunals may well have been a mistake. Nothing in the background of experiences of most wingmen [lay panel members] can be expected to equip them with an understanding of discrimination or empathy with its victims. Indeed, in so far as discrimination has come about through understandings between union and management, or merely as the inadvertent result of long-standing practice, they can be expected to be instinctively unsympathetic to complainants.[175]

In its report, Justice sharply criticized the current method of selecting lay members for its failure to produce panels that are fully representative of industry or which include women and minorities. Justice lamented using a patronage system for appointment that appears unfair, undemocratic, and inaccessible. Finally, it called for an open system of appointments and for taking responsibility away from the Department of Employment.[176]

Having women chair panels, or at least having a woman on the panel, may help overcome the perception that tribunals are unsympathetic to complainants. A woman on the panel may create the appearance of justice, since a woman complaining of sex discrimination before an all-male panel may see the very situation she is contesting replicated in the panel.[177] Women chaired industrial tribunals in only 5 percent of the cases involving sex discrimination or equal pay.[178] Leonard discovered that complainants were twice as likely to

---

174. Justice, 12.

175. Laurence Lustgarten, *Legal Control of Racial Discrimination* (London: Macmillan, 1980), 195.

176. Justice, 49–50.

177. "The policy of including a woman on every panel is in accordance with the Government's 1975 White Paper on sex discrimination and is also consistent with the principle of representative membership which has long been accepted for a variety of tribunals. However, it is not being followed in England and Wales as closely as its importance should require" (Leonard, *Judging Inequality*, 69). See Justice, 3.

178. Leonard, *Judging Inequality*, 133. "Only 11 chairpersons and under 20 percent of lay members are women" (McIlroy, 7).

succeed if a woman was on the panel.[179] Most disturbing is that the number of women on industrial tribunals has not increased in the last ten years, further reinforcing Justice's conviction that the method of appointing members must change.[180]

Women not only find it difficult to win, but gain little when they do. Not only did women find the process of bringing a claim difficult, the chance of success small, and the amount of compensation minuscule,[181] but winning a case brought little tangible change in working conditions and a high chance of victimization—that is, employers punishing women for complaining.[182] A follow-up study of successful complaints concluded: "Employers rarely take a new look at equal opportunity issues and are more inclined to adopt entrenched positions."[183]

> Most [women complainants] reported at a minimum a deterioration in working relationships, mainly with management but also with fellow workers. At least ten ended up leaving their jobs as a direct result of the case; three left before the case because of the deterioration in atmosphere; three left after for similar reasons; and four believed they had been made redundant or dismissed because they had taken action. . . . Nor was there evidence of any significant benefits for other employees. . . . Most serious of all for the individual was the effect of the case on their employment opportunities outside the firm; fourteen of forty-five who had looked for a job after the case believed they had experienced difficulty in finding a new job because they were identified as troublemakers.[184]

Despite dissatisfaction with the record of industrial tribunals, it is unlikely that anyone would argue for transferring jurisdiction to the courts. In

---

179. Fourteen percent versus thirty percent (Leonard, *Judging Inequality*, 122).

180. Justice, 49.

181. Rubery reported: "The more surprising and disturbing findings of the report were the low levels of compensation, the difficulties claimants faced in actually obtaining the compensation after the ruling, the minimal influence of the cases on employers' employment practices and the damaging effects of the case on the individual's career, both at the firm where the problem had arisen, and potentially in the wider labour market" (Jill Rubery, review of *Pyrrhic Victories: Winning Sex Discrimination and Equal Pay Cases in the Industrial Tribunals, 1980–1984* by Alice Leonard, *Industrial Law Journal* 17 [March 1988]: 61).

182. "What we gained was at considerable personal cost: to our working relationships, personal life, our self-esteem, and no doubt, to our future careers within and outside the institution. We feel that any woman who undertakes such action should be in no doubt about the consequences" (Jean Woodall et al., "Don't Tell Me the Old Boys' Story," *Guardian*, September 10, 1985).

183. Gregory, *Trial by Ordeal*, 37.

184. Rubery, 61–62. Gregory's survey, reported in *Trial by Ordeal*, confirms this finding: "Of the 66 employees who left or were dismissed, only ten secured alternative work within a short time of leaving. The vast majority remained out of work for long periods and experienced considerable difficulties re-entering the job market" (37).

fact, the EOC has called for industrial tribunals to hear the cases the Sex Discrimination Act gives to county courts because the performance of the courts is even worse.[185] Women are even less well represented on the bench—reputed to be even less receptive to claims of discrimination than industrial tribunals. It is easier for feminists and those committed to ending discrimination to become lay members of industrial tribunals than to become judges. The newly formed Women's Legal Defense Fund has begun to develop a plan to propose lay members, to insure that those with knowledge and experience with discrimination are chosen, and to train and educate current members. Despite the bleak picture, the tribunal system offers several potential advantages over the U.S. system. Legal remedies may be more accessible and affordable in Britain than in the United States, as well as more quickly dispensed.

The British Judiciary

Although advocates of victims of discrimination and trade unionists prefer industrial tribunals rather than courts to decide cases of employment discrimination, the courts play an important role in shaping the contours of labor law through their appellate jurisdiction. Judges can undo what industrial tribunals do, as well as direct them on points of law. While feminists criticize both the EOC and the industrial tribunals for not being vigorous enough in their enforcement of the law and for unfavorable rulings, the criticism directed at British judges is even sharper. The British judiciary's blatant hostility to women in general and claims of sex discrimination in particular is well documented.[186] While many charge the British judiciary with being racist, classist, and sexist, there is less agreement about what causes the judiciary's poor performance in cases that matter to feminists.

In fairness to the judges, their less-than-feminist rulings in cases of

---

185. Justice, 36.

186. See Albie Sachs and Joan Hoff Wilson, *Sexism and the Law: A Study of Male Beliefs and Legal Bias in Britain and the United States* (Oxford: Martin Robertson, 1978); Polly Patullo, *Judging Women: A Study of Attitudes that Rule Our System* (London: National Council for Civil Liberties Rights for Women Unit, 1983); Melissa Benn, Anna Coote, and Tess Gill, *The Rape Controversy* (London: National Council for Civil Liberties Rights for Women Unit, 1983); Katherine O'Donovan, *Sexual Divisions in Law* (London: Weidenfeld and Nicolson, 1985); Carol Smart, *The Ties that Bind: Law, Marriage, and the Reproduction of Patriarchal Relations* (London: Routledge and Kegan Paul, 1984); Susan Edwards, *Female Sexuality and the Law: A Study of Constructs of Female Sexuality as They Inform Statute and Legal Procedure* (Oxford: Martin Robertson, 1981); Newcastle-upon-Tyne Trades Council, *Laws with Claws: Government Attacks on Women* (Newcastle-upon-Tyne, U.K., 1980); Katherine O'Donovan and Erika Szyszczak, *Equality and Sex Discrimination Law* (Oxford: Blackwell, 1988); Gregory, *Sex, Race and the Law*; Michael Zander, *A Matter of Justice: the Legal System in Ferment*, rev. ed. (Oxford: Oxford University Press, 1989); Carol Smart, *Feminism and the Power of Law*; and all issues of *The Equal Opportunities Review*. For a more optimistic account, see Rubenstein, "Beyond the Whinge."

discrimination stem partly from Parliament's failure to make its intentions clear. While the wording of the provisions of direct and indirect discrimination suggest a clear purpose—creating equality between men and women— the many exceptions Parliament included in the act suggest a much more limited commitment to social change. Parliament left the hard questions for judges to decide.[187] Does the act permit employers to recognize physical differences between the sexes? How high a standard of justification must employers offer for employment practices that have a disparate impact on women? What is the correct allocation of the burden of proof between employers and workers? In Britain, judges do not rely on the legislative record for insight into Parliament's intent. And the law, as written, reflects Parliament's ambivalence about social change and the limitations of its commitment to greater equality. In some cases, such as the Equal Pay Amendment Regulations where the need to comply with EC law forced the Government to legislate, the regulations are so vague and complex that judges are genuinely perplexed about how to proceed. Furthermore, members of Parliament—a vocal segment of British society—expressed strong views against the purposes of the act. For example, a member of the House of Lords commented: "For a man to be unemployed is a threat to his masculinity, but for a woman to be unemployed is not a threat to her femininity. It will hit her purse but not her sex life."[188]

The result of this legislative vagueness is that the personal views of the judges, their sense of what is socially acceptable, and their view of their appropriate judicial role will matter more to the outcome of the case than if the statute were clear cut. All three factors work to the disadvantage of victims of discrimination, as Jeanne Gregory notes.

> Complex legislation often results from desire on the part of the legislators to minimize the discretion of the courts and tribunals, on the argument that the more detailed the provisions, the fewer the gaps that remain for the judiciary to fill. In the case of the equality laws however, the complexity arises largely from the need to pacify those who would otherwise oppose it. The result has been to increase the discretion of the tribunal members and judges. Required by the legislators to balance conflicting considerations, their own predispositions have proved crucial in resolving those dilemmas. A careful re-drafting exercise is necessary, making it more difficult for hostile judges to frustrate the aims of the law.[189]

---

187. Simon Lee, *Judging Judges* (London: Faber, 1988), 67. Lee's point is about racial discrimination but it applies equally well to sex discrimination.

188. *Parliamentary Debates* (Lords), 5th ser., vol. 362, (1975) cols. 149–50; see discussion in O'Donovan and Szyszczak, *Equality and Sex Discrimination Law*, 33.

189. Gregory, *Sex, Race and the Law*, 104.

Not only are some parts of the law deliberately vague or confusing, but judges do not perceive a consensus to exist inside or outside of Parliament for bold new interpretations of the law. A Conservative Government commanding a large majority in Parliament wants to roll back rather than expand the burdens on employers. No mass movement feminist organization storms the courts when they issue an unfavorable ruling, nor is there widespread condemnation in the press beyond a small cadre of feminists and legal academics.[190] U.S. judges, in contrast, employ several law clerks—recent law school graduates influenced by the increase in women students and faculty in law schools—who encourage judges to issue rulings in step with current legal thinking. British judges, who have no law clerks, do not benefit from the interaction with new blood. Thus, in filling in the large gaps in the law, judges do not feel the pressure from the legislature, social movements, or public opinion to advance the law. I suspect the contrary is the case. In their Inns of Courts, dining clubs, and the legal community, the status quo, or even the past, commands more support than a radical restructuring of society.

The social and political context notwithstanding, many decisions do merit criticism on legal grounds. Leonard's finding of clear errors in law, substitution of personal views of what is reasonable rather than the law's definition of less favorable treatment, reluctance to find that respondents had discriminated, and stereotypical views about women that run counter to the purpose of the Sex Discrimination Act hold true for the British judiciary in cases of sex discrimination. Unlike members of industrial tribunals, judges cannot plead that they deal primarily with unfair dismissal cases, where the standard of reasonableness is the correct standard, or that they lack legal training, or that they do not have the benefit of having the issues presented to them by counsel. While Parliament did not clarify its intent, insofar as the demands of the Sex Discrimination Act are clear, one can reasonably expect judges to follow them rather than substitute their own preferences.

Those who criticize judges for their rulings in this area of law range broadly across legal philosophies. Pannick takes the view that judges have made mistakes, but his criticism does not extend to judges as a group or to the legal system or the statute. His tone suggests the errors are benign and can be corrected. British legal scholars O'Donovan and Szyszczak recognize that judges are wholly unsympathetic toward victims of discrimination but attribute it to their hearing one case at a time: the absence of class actions prevents judges from grasping the pattern of discrimination.[191] Sachs and Wilson maintain that male judges wrongly applied the law because of material

---

190. Michael Zander's articles in the newspapers, the Women's Legal Defense Fund Newsletter, *Between Equals*, Michael Rubenstein's articles in the *Equal Opportunities Review*, and the newsletter of the National Council for Civil Liberties are notable exceptions—strong voices raised in criticism of many judicial decisions.

191. O'Donovan and Szyszczak, *Equality and Sex Discrimination Law*, 84–86.

(economic) self-interest. Others see the behavior of judges in sex discrimination cases and labor law in general as adding to a critique of law itself, arguing that legitimation of domination is an integral part of law irrespective of the personnel of the courts. This view claims that, in some sense, the law itself is male or is only capable of incorporating a male point of view.[192] Others document the hostility and attribute it to the personal views among judges and members of industrial tribunals, recognizing a diversity of opinion despite the homogeneity of the bench.[193]

Many of the critics of judges' performance in sex discrimination cases focus on the personnel of the judiciary.[194] Anne Sedley notes: "Women lawyers argue, as NCCL [National Council for Civil Liberties] has, that it is not good enough to have laws dealing with sex discrimination if the people who administer those laws hold stereotyped views of women."[195] The claim is that judges have certain values and biases that differ from the values embodied in the statutes. "Individuals do matter. Individual judges, individual counsel, individual litigants."[196] Rubenstein comments further that "if there is recognition that the Race Relations Act, the Sex Discrimination Act and the Equal Pay Act are humanitarian laws designed to remedy the unfairness and humiliation caused by arbitrary discrimination, there is little sign of it in decisions handed down by Mr. Justice Wood in 1989."[197] Both those who see law as an instrument of domination and those who believe that judges inexplicably err in certain kinds of cases propose altering the composition of the judiciary. Such a project might be feasible in the United States;[198] in Britain, it would require a revolution. The pool from which the Lord Chancellor selects British judges is small—a select group of barristers who are Queen's Counsel, itself a small proportion of the legal profession—and provides little opportunity to broaden the personnel of the judiciary to include women and feminists.[199]

---

192. See Elizabeth Kingdom, Review of *Sexism and the Law* by Albie Sachs and Joan Hoff Wilson, in *m/f* 4 (1980): 71–88; Catharine MacKinnon, "Feminism, Marxism, Method and the State: Toward a Feminist Jurisprudence," *Signs* 8 (Summer 1983): 635–58; Robin West, "Jurisprudence and Gender," *University of Chicago Law Review* 55 (1988): 1–72.

193. Gregory, *Sex, Race and the Law*, 95–106. See Rubenstein's commentaries in the *Equal Opportunities Review*.

194. Michael Zander (103–38) describes how judges are selected and provides the breakdown by sex.

195. Sedley, 5. See also Griffith, *The Politics of the Judiciary*, and Albie Sachs, "Barristers and Gentlemen: The Roots and Structure of Sexism in the Legal Profession," Feminist Library, London, 1977, photocopy.

196. Rubenstein, "Beyond the Whinge," 260.

197. Michael Rubenstein, *Discrimination: A Guide to Relevant Case Law on Race and Sex Discrimination and Equal Pay*, 3d ed. (London: Eclipse, 1990), 1.

198. In fact, it has been the project of the Reagan administration, but in the pursuit of different goals. See Herman Schwartz, *Packing the Courts: The Conservative Campaign to Rewrite the Constitution* (New York: Scribner, 1988).

199. In 1986, 18 out of 797 Queen's Counsels were women (Zander, 114).

Those who focus on the personnel of the judiciary and industrial tribunal system further divide into two groups: those who talk about the general characteristics of the judiciary—that most judges are white, male, upper class, Conservative, from public schools—and those who are less willing to link the social characteristics of judges with a particular set of views, but instead talk about the views and ideas of individual judges and members of tribunals without lumping them together as a group. Relying on judges' sex, class, race, political background, and type of education as a predictor of how they will rule in discrimination cases fails to explain the immense variation in views among judges who share the same background.[200] In some cases, the backgrounds of the most progressive judges are indistinguishable from the most conservative. Conversely, one can find women who share the views of the most socially conservative judges. Though these characteristics are only the roughest of indicators, they do contribute to part of an explanation: Leonard, for example, found that having a woman on the panel increased the complainant's chances of winning. Class and sex alone do not determine the outcome, although they are important variables. Clearly, the specific views of the individual judge about discrimination makes an important difference to the outcome of the case, and judges do vary. Courts and tribunals change over time, as do individual judges.

There are now different judges in the Court of Appeal and House of Lords deciding the cases. The generation of judges which heard the first discrimination cases tended to regard the laws as infringements on the liberty of the subject and therefore to be interpreted restrictively. The new generation is much more prepared to accept that they are reforming statutes and therefore to be interpreted purposively. The older generation tended to view discrimination as an aberration from traditional English standards of "fair play." The new generation, if not quite prepared to accept that discrimination is "institutional," would seem to recognize that it is widespread, yet difficult to prove.[201]

The explanations for the behavior of the judiciary—the ambiguity of the statute, the limited consensus in Parliament, the absence of a strong social movement, the limited nature of public support for feminist goals, and the sex, class, and political persuasion of the individual judges—do not complete the explanation. Even if feminists managed to replace the current judiciary with those sympathetic to feminist concerns, they would not succeed in eradicating inequality. Prevailing canons of statutory interpretation in Britain favor a literal application of the law and militate against a purposive interpreta-

---

200. Lee, 67.
201. Rubenstein, "Beyond the Whinge," 257.

tion.[202] While the U.S. Supreme Court has sometimes used the purpose of the statute—ending discrimination and promoting equality—to override specific limiting provisions,[203] British judges are more likely to stick to the letter of the law.[204] "The British judiciary see their task as one of subtle linguistic analysis of the wording of statutes, and not as social engineers. This may be contrasted unfavourably with the approach of the American judiciary who treat major statutes as blueprints for social policy."[205] Membership in the EC, however, has had a significant impact on how British judges now approach sex discrimination law. They have occasionally used the mandates of EC law to adopt a more purposive interpretation of British law to harmonize British and EC law.

Part of the reason for the tendency for literalism and aversion to a purposive approach is that the United Kingdom has no written constitution or bill of rights, and, despite the constitutional effect of EC law, British judges are less likely than U.S. judges to see themselves as the defenders of fundamental rights against governmental intrusion. Instead, British judges see themselves as the defenders of the rule of law, duly carrying out the will of the

In the U.K., Parliament is supposed to be sovereign and the judges are therefore in a different relationship to the politicians. The judges are not trumping the elected representatives of the people. They are stepping into their shoes where Parliament has not provided a definitive answer to a legal problem, and they know that if Parliament does not like their solution, it can find the time to overturn the judges' answer. Hence the British judges are more like deputy legislators whereas the American judges are like super legislators.[206]

The absence of a written bill of rights or of a single written constitution combines with the absence of judicial review of legislation in Britain. Judicial review exists only for executive not legislative action,[207] although judges may

---

202. See Glanville Williams, *Learning the Law*, 11th ed. (London: Stevens and Sons, 1982).

203. The most obvious example is California Federal Savings and Loan v. Guerra, 479 U.S. 272 (1987). Although the Pregnancy Discrimination Act seemed to explicitly call for exactly the same treatment for pregnancy and disabilities, Justice Marshall's opinion for the Court held that a state law granting a limited right to reinstatement following childbirth was consistent with the purposes of Title VII, as amended.

204. This is not to suggest that interpretations based on the letter of the law or the spirit of the law are not problematic ways of describing what judges do. See Walter F. Murphy, James E. Fleming, and William F. Harris, II, *American Constitutional Interpretation* (Mineola, N.Y.: Foundation Press, 1986).

205. O'Donovan and Szyszczak, *Equality and Sex Discrimination Law*, 39. See Laurence Lustgarten, "Race Inequality and the Limits of the Law," *Modern Law Review* 49 (1986): 68–85.

206. Lee, 24.

207. See Emlyn C. S. Wade and A. W. Bradley, *Constitutional and Administrative Law*, 10th ed. (London: Longman, 1985), 57–59.

now find that British law fails to meet Britain's obligations as a member of the EC. Except for EC law, British judges cannot appeal to higher law to invalidate or fail to enforce acts of Parliament.

By U.S. standards, the British judiciary often appears excessively deferential to the government. Deference to the government of the day, commentators have noted, varies between Conservative and Labour Governments. The Labour Party has charged that the judiciary is partisan and will not fairly interpret its enactments, particularly in the area of industrial relations. It is hard to compare across systems and across time. The U.S. Supreme Court may have been more or less deferential to the president depending on the political party of the majority of judges, the number of appointments a particular president had made, and the political context. Despite wide variations in the amount of deference the Supreme Court grants the president and the government in general, at its most deferential, the U.S. judiciary is less deferential than the British. While some U.S. judges may write opinions as if they are the guardians of individual rights or the Constitution against governmental intrusion, British judges rarely, if ever, behave as a coequal branch whose purpose is to provide checks and balances.

Finally, whether it is the result of the class bias of the judiciary, the sense of the narrowness of the judicial role, judges' uncertainty about the intent of Parliament, or a personal hostility to women workers, British judges are more reluctant to interfere with businesses than their U.S. counterparts. Changes in the composition of the U.S. judiciary, in terms of class, party, and judicial philosophy, may make the two groups more similar. In any case, "the [British] judiciary seems more concerned with policing the equality laws to ensure that they do not ride rough-shod over the employers, than with policing employers to ensure that the laws are observed."[208]

This brief summary suggests that, in cases of sex discrimination, British judges will be pulled in opposite directions. Because of their backgrounds and values, they may neither be sympathetic to claimants nor suspicious of employers' policies. A preference for literal interpretation may lead them to give full force to the many exceptions written into the Sex Discrimination Act that appear to go against its purpose. Perhaps judges grasped the limited nature of Parliament's commitment? Giving full recognition to the exceptions written into the act also would put judges in accord with the present Conservative Government, which sees the law prohibiting discrimination as a burden on industry and seeks to reconcile British and EC law by making the most minimal changes necessary to prevent the Commission of the EC from instituting additional infringement actions. While pressure from the EC will pull them in one direction, moving slowly appears to have no costs. No social movement protests judicial decisions nor will Parliament overturn their rulings.

---

208. Gregory, *Sex, Race and the Law*, 101–2.

As the examples in this section will show, the strength of the judiciary's hostility to the purpose of the Sex Discrimination Act is revealed when, in interpreting the act, judges have at times abandoned a literal approach to statutory interpretation to insure that claims of sex discrimination will fail. Another example of how judges' strong political views lead them to blatantly disregard the straightforward provisions of the law is in the area of industrial relations,[209] seen most clearly during the miners' strike.[210] It may be too extreme to explain judges' behavior solely by their personal hostility to the purposes of the Sex Discrimination Act. I have suggested many other factors. Any new legislation, especially if it seeks broad social change, will begin with a "breaking-in period" in which advocates must educate the judiciary about the purpose of the legislation and how to interpret it. In response to criticism, and even amendments, judges may quickly overrule "mistaken" interpretations. Some evidence suggests that such a process took place in the United States in the late 1960s and early 1970s. Thus, we must leave open the chance that at least some of the differences between the behavior of British and U.S. judges is due to the time lag between passage of Title VII in 1964 and the Sex Discrimination Act in 1975.

Before discussing precedents that both illustrate my argument and are relevant to cases on exclusionary policies, let me offer two examples of how these competing explanations for judges' behavior apply. First, those committed to effective enforcement of discrimination law criticize the judiciary for systematically destroying the CRE's and EOC's power of formal investigations through judicial interpretation of the statute. By granting significant procedural rights to employers at every stage and holding the agency to a high standard of judicial scrutiny, the judiciary has nullified the power envisioned by the White Paper *Equality for Women* to make the EOC the strongest such body in the Western world. Critics of this line of precedent say the decisions reflect judges' personal hostility and lack of sympathy for the victims of discrimination because judges are male, upper-middle-class Conservatives. They might add that it provides another example of the judiciary overruling an act of a Labour Government. Others might suggest the possibility that judges sensed Parliament's ambivalence about greater equality and the limits of the societal consensus. If one took judges at their word, however, one would conclude that the structure that Parliament created effectively made the EOC prosecutor, judge, and jury, and that it is the consolidation of these powers in one agency rather than the content of the enforcement action that brings forth judicial wrath. Absent a sophisticated methodology for separating the effects of these three variables, no one variable alone provides an adequate explana-

---

209. See Griffith, 53–82.

210. See Frank Belloni, "Politics and the Law: Industrial Conflict in Britain," paper presented at the annual meeting of the American Political Science Association, Washington, D.C., August, 1986.

tion of judges' behavior. A more complete explanation includes all three.

Second, the judiciary has avoided defining key aspects of discrimination law; in particular, it has avoided setting up guidelines about the burden of proof. Since 1983, presidents of the Employment Appeal Tribunals have "reasserted, in the light of Court of Appeal decisions, that no guidelines are to be laid down, and that the appellate role is to be severely curtailed."[211] Critics see the Court of Appeal's rulings as an attempt to nip in the bud progressive rulings on the part of the Employment Appeal Tribunal and to permit wide inconsistency in outcomes between different industrial tribunals. The Court of Appeal's position is that the purpose of the industrial tribunals was to provide an arena for gathering facts and issuing a fair decision free from complex sets of legal rules. Thus, laying down clear rulings on these legal matters encourages more legalism and formality in industrial tribunal proceedings. In addition, the Court of Appeal is well aware that Parliament has abdicated its responsibility to direct courts on these issues, and, until the EC moves in to fill the vacuum (the Commission has proposed a directive on the burden of proof), it will refuse to enforce its own opinion on industrial tribunals. Again, the evidence offers support for all three explanations—any explanation that left out one would be incomplete.

Lacey, Rubenstein, McCrudden, O'Donovan, Patullo, Sachs and Wilson, Gregory, and Pannick have provided a more thorough critique of where judges erred in law, where dicta revealed sexism and outright misogyny, or where judges did not understand the purpose of the Sex Discrimination Act. Yet it is worth examining some examples where British judges have limited the effectiveness of the Sex Discrimination Act because, although dated and possibly unrepresentative of judges' overall performance, the precedents are relevant for cases on exclusionary policies.

Gregory's history of the early discrimination cases illustrates the variation among individual judges and members of tribunals.

When the first cases to be filed under the discrimination laws reached the hearing stage, the tribunals were frequently out of their depth and some decisions floundered badly. There can be no doubt that in the early days the EAT, under the presidency of Mr. Justice Phillips, launched a rescue operation and provided some useful guidelines for the tribunals to follow. . . . It was when the Court of Appeal began to intervene that the EAT seemed to lose its sense of purpose and direction. The Appeal Court's pronouncements on the new legislation came like a cold shower, dousing the enthusiasm of those below.[212]

---

211. *Justice,* 52.
212. Gregory, *Sex, Race and the Law,* 90–91. For commentary on the relationship between the Court of Appeal and other presidents of the Employment Appeal Tribunal, see Gregory, *Sex, Race and the Law,* 95–105.

For example, in *Automotive Products Ltd. v. Peake*,[213] an employee claimed that the company discriminated against him by letting women leave the factory five minutes earlier than men to avoid the crush as hundreds of employees left the factory. Over a year, men thus worked 2.5 days more than women. Peake claimed he had been subject to a detriment under the Sex Discrimination Act. The industrial tribunal rejected his complaint, but the Employment Appeal Tribunal upheld it on appeal. The Court of Appeal found that the practice was not discriminatory because the act permitted differential treatment based on chivalry or administrative convenience. And even if it were discriminatory, this claim was de minimis.[214]

This judgment deserves criticism on several grounds. First, the act clearly lays out many exceptions, but Parliament did not include practices based on chivalry and convenience among them. Second, using these criteria would allow the very practices and distinctions that Parliament intended to prohibit—the exception would swallow the rule. Third, the judgment is significant for what it reveals about the Court of Appeal's attitude toward the Sex Discrimination Act: that it is an unjustified interference with benign and reasonable practices. The court failed to appreciate the harm of discrimination or sensed Parliament's limited interest in changing established social and labor practices. Master of the Rolls Lord Denning's opinion makes clear that he will not interpret the act as forbidding "sensible" distinctions in treatment between the two sexes.

> Although the Act applies equally to men as to women, I must say it would be very wrong to my mind if this statute were thought to obliterate the differences between men and women or to do away with the chivalry and courtesy which we expect mankind to give womankind. The natural differences of sex must be regarded even in the interpretation of an Act of Parliament. . . . There is ample scope for the operation of the Act without trespassing on sensible administrative arrangements.[215]

The danger is that protection based on stereotypes about women as the weaker sex in need of chivalry often work to women's detriment and lead to their oppression.[216]

Lord Justice Shaw's opinion reveals his definition of discrimination to be unfavorable treatment and shows his unwillingness to see how distinctions based on chivalry could be unfavorable to either men or women.

---

213. [1977] IRLR 365.

214. The full phrase is *de minimis non curat lex* (the law does not adjudicate on trifling matters).

215. Automotive Products Ltd. v. Peake, [1977] IRLR 365, 366–67.

216. See Frances Olsen, "Statutory Rape: A Feminist Critique of Rights Analysis," *Texas Law Review* 63 (November 1984): 387–432.

The Sex Discrimination Act 1975 was not, in my judgment, designed to provide a ground for capricious and empty complaints of differentiation between the sexes. Nor was it intended to operate as a statutory abolition of every instinct of chivalry and consideration on the part of men for the opposite sex. The phrase used in all the prohibitions imposed by the Act is "discrimination against" one sex or the other. This, to my mind, involves an element of something which is inherently adverse or hostile to the interests of the persons of the sex which is said to be discriminated against. . . . In applying statutory provisions which touch human conduct and relationships in infinite ways, it is vitally important to cling to common sense.[217]

He also raised the deep-seated fear shared by opponents of the Equal Rights Amendment in the United States that ending sex discrimination will force men and women to use the same bathrooms. "Otherwise it may be argued by some troublemaker some day that the provision of separate and different arrangements for hygiene and sanitation constitutes an act of discrimination against the males or females or both."[218]

Perhaps because of widespread criticism of this decision,[219] the court recanted in *Jeremiah v. Ministry of Defence.*[220] Jeremiah, an examiner in an ordnance factory, claimed the Ministry of Defence discriminated against him by requiring all men who volunteered for overtime to work occasionally in a shell bursting shop while not requiring women to do so. The work was dirty and dusty, and workers had to wear protective clothing and shower afterward. The ministry paid the men an additional four pence per hour and paid them for forty-five minutes to shower and change. The industrial tribunal and the Employment Appeal Tribunal held that the Ministry of Defense had discriminated. Despite the extra payment, men were subject to a detriment by having to work in the shop. An employer could not buy the right to discriminate.

Lord Denning retracted his reasoning in *Peake*, saying that the only remaining grounds for the holding in *Peake* was the de minimis claim, not the reasons of chivalry or administrative convenience.[221] While *Jeremiah* removed most of the exceptions *Peake* created, judges could construe the de minimis exception widely or narrowly to prevent sex discrimination claims from succeeding depending on the judges' view that particular instances of discrimination are unimportant. For example, El Vinos Wine Bar in Fleet Street had a policy of not serving women at the bar but only if they were

---

217. Automotive Products Ltd. v. Peake, [1977] IRLR 365, 367.
218. Ibid., 367.
219. Francis Bennion, one of the drafters of the Sex Discrimination Act, complained vociferously about the ruling in a letter to the *Times*. See Gregory, *Sex, Race and the Law*, 91–92.
220. Jeremiah v. Ministry of Defence, [1979] IRLR 436.
221. Ibid., 437–38.

seated. The County Court found that a reasonable person would not object to this rule (relying on *Jeremiah v. Ministry of Defence*) and found that El Vinos had not discriminated against women.[222] This discretion may allow the judge's view that sex discrimination is harmless to diminish the effectiveness of the act. The Court of Appeal overturned the ruling saying that one should look to the words of the statute and see if women suffered a detriment. It warned that courts should not use the de minimis defense to preclude the bringing of claims of sex discrimination in the provision of goods and services, what the act prohibited. *Jeremiah* shows, however, that the Court of Appeal will interpret the act more literally and will be less willing to create exceptions than it was in *Peake*. As Lord Justice Brandon commented:

> I am not persuaded that it is right to interpret the concept of unlawful discrimination under the Act of 1975 in quite as forceful a way as he [Lord Justice Shaw in his opinion in *Peake*] did in that judgment. I think, as I indicated earlier, that the sole question to be answered in this case was whether the men examiners were put under a disadvantage by comparison with the women examiners. That was a question of fact; it was answered by the Industrial Tribunal in the affirmative; and I can see nothing wrong in law with that answer.[223]

In the United States, Canada, and Britain, men may have been more successful in vindicating their right to equal treatment than women. They have certainly brought many of the cases in Britain.[224] While feminists should applaud all efforts to break down sex-role stereotypes and barriers to equal opportunity, it would be unfortunate if judges applied the formal legal equality advocated in the statutes to conclude that discrimination was bad when it hurt men and justifiable if it hurt women.

Despite signs that the Court of Appeal is moving toward interpreting the act by determining whether there has been less favorable treatment on the grounds of sex rather than by using its own judgment about whether an employer acted reasonably, evidence still suggests that judges succumb to sex-role stereotypes. For example, Lord Denning began his opinion in *Jeremiah* by commenting:

> A woman's hair is her crowning glory, so it is said. She does not like it disturbed: especially when she has just had a "hair-do." The women at the ordnance factory in Wales are no exception. They do not want

---

222. Gill and Coote v. El Vinos Wine Bar, [1983] IRLR 206 (CA).
223. Jeremiah v. Ministry of Defence, [1979] IRLR 436, 439.
224. John Hutton, "How the SDA has Failed," *Legal Action*, 1984, 10–11.

to work in part of the factory—called a "shop"—which ruins their "hair-do."[225]

Lord Justice Brightman reinforced Lord Denning's pronouncement of sex-role stereotypes, commenting, "women . . . are more concerned with, and devote more time and attention to, their personal appearances than men."[226] He also discussed the view that differentiation does not always mean discrimination, presenting a "separate but equal" argument about ladies' carriages on trains. His comments reveal his difficulty in grasping the purposes of the legislation and his falling into the trap of sex-role stereotyping.

Lord Justice Brightman further revealed a widely shared judicial view of the Sex Discrimination Act. "The purpose of the legislation is to secure equal treatment of the sexes *so far as is appropriate.*"[227] Yet if judges are to determine what is appropriate without reflection on the specific, limited exceptions in the act, then it is likely that their prejudices, stereotypes, and notions of chivalry will limit the effectiveness of the act. Chivalry may be merely the appearance of treating women better that masks systematic inequalities.

The opinions in *Jeremiah* and *Peake* support the claim that judges' stereotypical views of women and judges' definition of discrimination limit the potential of the act. While judges may occasionally make up a new exception to the act, they have enforced existing exceptions with vigor and without any expression of sympathy to the claimant or criticism of the law that British judges occasionally express in cases on racial discrimination.[228] Happily allowing employers to discriminate if the law has created specific exceptions is consistent with preferred canons of interpretation, although it is also consistent with the low value judges place on nondiscrimination. Both factors militate against judges appealing to the general purposes of the law, or even the broader obligations of EC law, to require employers not to discriminate regardless of the statutory exceptions.

In some cases, however, women have claimed that, although their claim falls within an exception to the Sex Discrimination Act or Equal Pay Act, EC law guarantees them a remedy. In several cases, women have challenged British judges' interpretations of British and EC law before the European

---

225. Jeremiah v. Ministry of Defense, [1979] IRLR 436, 437. For a discussion of the zoological metaphors judges have used in sex discrimination cases, see Paul Robertshaw, "Semantic and Linguistic Aspects of Sex Discrimination Decisions: Dichotomised Woman," 203–27 in *Semiotics, Law and Social Science*, ed. by Domenico Carzo and Bernard S. Jackson (Liverpool: Liverpool Law Review, 1984).

226. Jeremiah v. Ministry of Defense, [1979] IRLR 436, 439.

227. Ibid., 440.

228. See Mandla v. Dowell Lee, [1983] ICR 385 (HL); Bracebridge Engineering Limited v. Darby, [1990] IRLR 3 (EAT), and discussion in Vivienne Gay, "Sex Discrimination and Sexual Harassment," *Industrial Law Journal* 19 (March 1990): 35–39.

Court of Justice and won. Not only is the sweep of the prohibition of discrimination broader in EC law (and fewer exceptions written in), but the ECJ, in contrast to British courts and tribunals, has interpreted EC law by referring to the broad purpose—the elimination of discrimination. When faced with the apparently competing demands of the two, however, British judges have been reluctant to allow the broad purposes of EC law to take precedence over the many exceptions in British law. Whether this disregard of obligations as a member of the EC represents resistance to new types of interpretation, antipathy to the supremacy of EC law, or hostility to claims of sex discrimination, the effect is the same. British women have difficulty in gaining recognition for their rights under EC law in British courts.[229]

While *Jeremiah* and *Peake* illustrate the judiciary's stereotypical views of women and its failure to appreciate the harm of sex discrimination, the cases appealed to the ECJ expose the limitations of the legislation itself as well as the British judiciary's crafted approach to interpretation. The judiciary's limited view of discrimination and insensitivity to claims of sex discrimination is further exposed if we explore cases on pregnancy. Cases about pregnancy indicate how the tribunals and courts may approach cases on reproductive hazards because both raise claims of discrimination stemming from claims about biological differences.

Pregnancy

To understand the protection the law provides to pregnant women workers, one must piece together statutes on unfair dismissal, sex discrimination, social security, and maternity benefits.[230] Employed mothers have five basic rights: the right not to be dismissed because of pregnancy, the right to time off work for antenatal care, the right to maternity leave and reinstatement after this leave, and the right to certain payments during absence from employment. The Employment Protection (Consolidation) Act of 1978 provides employed women with a limited right to reinstatement after pregnancy and childbirth (confinement). Provided they meet the conditions, women are also entitled to statutory maternity pay or maternity allowance. The law requires employers with fewer than five employees to reinstate women only if "reasonably practicable." A woman forfeits her right to return to her job under terms

---

229. This resistance, too, may reflect a sort of time lag. That is, British courts may need some time to adjust to membership in the EC and the requirements of the Equal Treatment Directive. "A conviction is growing that to avoid decisions which show a complete misunderstanding of the Directives' aims, the judges should undergo special training, and the European Commission has accepted that training of the judiciary is important" (Corcoran, 65).

230. See Jean Coussins, *Maternity Rights for Working Women*, 2d ed. (London: National Council for Civil Liberties, 1980). For an analysis of cases on maternity rights before industrial tribunals, see Johanna Fawkes, *Maternity Rights and Industrial Tribunals* (Manchester: Equal Opportunities Commission, 1983).

and conditions no less favorable by not strictly following with the requirements, such as failing to give her employer twenty-one days notice before she
plans to return, or if the employer can show that it is not reasonably practicable to reemploy her.[231] The restrictions on eligibility coupled with arduous
notification requirements mean that only 60 percent of working women are
covered,[232] and fewer than are eligible actually receive the benefits.[233] Evelyn
Ellis concludes: "[The maternity provisions] are cast in such complex and
restrictive terms as to be incapable of achieving the vital objectives which
provide their raison d'être."[234]

The Employment Protection Act of 1975 made the dismissal of an employee on the grounds of pregnancy unfair, providing she had been employed
continuously for twenty-six weeks and could do the job. Because the Employment Act came into effect on the same day as the Sex Discrimination Act, the
SDA did not stipulate that discrimination on the basis of pregnancy was sex
discrimination.[235] Subsequent legislation extended the qualifying period from
six months to two years, or five years for women who work eight to sixteen
hours per week,[236] leaving many women unprotected against dismissal on the
grounds of pregnancy. Furthermore, the Employment Act did not protect
women from discrimination because of pregnancy in hiring, promotion, or
other employment matters. Many women thus seek redress under the Sex
Discrimination Act rather than under the Employment Act (although they
cannot seek the remedy of reinstatement). Consequently, the EOC has called
for the removal of qualifying restrictions for both maternity leave and pregnancy dismissal.[237]

British industrial tribunals, like their U.S. counterparts, had trouble
thinking of discrimination against workers on the grounds of pregnancy as sex
discrimination because not all women become pregnant and no men do.
Because not all women become pregnant, early commentators characterized
the issue as "sex-plus." An employer was ostensibly not firing the woman

---

231. "Pregnancy and Maternity: 2," *Industrial Relations Legal Information Bulletin* 377
(May 23, 1989): 2.

232. "British EEO Agency Warns Employers that Discharge for Pregnancy is Illegal,"
Daily Labor Reports 175 (September 11, 1987): A–5.

233. For a study of the maternity rights provisions in practice, see W. W. Daniel, *Maternity
Rights: The Experience of Women* (London: Policy Studies Institute, 1980).

234. Evelyn Ellis, *Sex Discrimination Law* (Brookfield, Vt: Gower, 1988): 282.

235. It only refers to pregnancy in sec. 2(2), where men cannot claim discrimination
because they have not been afforded special treatment afforded to women in connection with
pregnancy and childbirth.

236. For a review of recent changes in the law, see Lyn Durward, "Changes in Maternity
Payments," *Legal Action*, April 1987, 9–11; Joanne Conaghan, "Statutory Maternity Pay Under
the Social Security Act 1986," *Industrial Law Journal* 16 (June 1987): 125–29; Lyn Durward,
"Maternity Rights in Crisis," *Rights of Women Bulletin*, December 1986, 21.

237. EOC, *Thirteenth Annual Report* (London: HMSO, 1989): 1; see also EOC, *Equal
Treatment*, 7–8.

because she was a woman, but because she was pregnant. In *Reaney v. Kanda Jean Products Ltd.*, the industrial tribunal commented: "The applicant was not dismissed on the assumed facts because she was a woman. She was on the assumed facts dismissed because she was pregnant, and it is only an accident of nature which bestows the burden and happiness of pregnancy on the female sex."[238] Other so-called sex-plus issues were when employers claimed that they refused to hire a mother of small children, not because they were women, but because they assumed them to be primary caretakers,[239] or when sexual harassers claimed they harassed only attractive women.[240] Recognizing that although not all women became pregnant, pregnancy is a sex-based characteristic precisely because no men become pregnant runs afoul of the comparative approach embedded in sex discrimination law and its implicit male norm. Discrimination can only have occurred if employers treat women less favorably than men. Because men cannot become pregnant, the early cases held that pregnant women were not the victims of sex discrimination.

The principle illustration of this reasoning is in *Turley v. Allders Department Store*.[241] Mrs. Turley had worked for Allders Department Store less than a year when she became pregnant and the store dismissed her. Because she did not meet the qualifying period for a claim of unfair dismissal under the Employment Act, she brought her claim under the Sex Discrimination Act. Before examining the merits of her case, the industrial tribunal considered the threshold legal questions of whether dismissal on the ground of pregnancy was unlawful direct sex discrimination. The tribunal concluded it was not. On appeal, the Employment Appeal Tribunal agreed. For discrimination to occur, a woman would have to receive less favorable treatment than a man; but the EAT found there was no male equivalent for pregnancy, making comparisons impossible.

> In order to see if she has been treated less favourably than a man the sense of the section is that you must compare like with like, and you cannot. *When she is pregnant a woman is no longer just a woman. She is a woman, as the Authorised Version accurately puts it, with child, and there is no masculine equivalent.*[242]

Ms. Smith, the only woman member of the panel, dissented, arguing that to give no protection to women dismissed on the grounds of pregnancy "con-

---

238. Reaney v. Kanda Jean Products Ltd., [1978] IRLR 427, 428.

239. Hurley v. Mustoe, [1981] ICR 490 (EAT); [1983] ICR 422 (EAT).

240. See Michael Rubenstein, "Law of Sexual Harassment at Work" and *The Dignity of Women at Work: A Report on the Problem of Sexual Harassment in the Member States of the European Communities* (Luxembourg: EC Publications, 1987).

241. Turley v. Allders Department Stores Ltd., [1980] IRLR 4 (EAT).

242. Ibid., 5; italics added.

tradicts both the spirit and the letter of the statutes."[243] She argued that employers should treat pregnancy as any other medical condition. The EAT should compare how an employer treats pregnant women to how an employer treats men with temporarily incapacitating medical conditions. The case would then turn on this finding of fact. Thus, the right not to be treated less favorably might be more limited than the protection under the Employment Protection Act, depending on the employer's provisions for medical conditions. The SDA would only protect women who had worked less than two years if their employers made allowances for sick men. Smith also suggested that *Turley* could have brought a claim of indirect discrimination that, like the claim of direct discrimination, would be a question of fact. She concluded that the tribunal erred in preventing any pregnant woman from pursuing a claim of discrimination.[244]

The EAT eventually accepted her argument and overruled its decision in *Turley* in *Hayes v. Malleable Working Men's Club*.[245] *Hayes* held that differential treatment on the grounds of pregnancy could be discrimination on the grounds of sex depending on how an employer treated medical conditions that incapacitated men. If an employer dismissed men for such medical conditions, then it could dismiss pregnant women. Both *Turley* and *Hayes* adopted a comparative approach, but in *Hayes* the EAT decided that pregnancy was not so unique after all. Instead, the EAT could draw an analogy between men's and women's medical conditions.

> Like Ms. Smith, we have not found any difficulty in visualizing cases— for example, that of a sick male employee and a pregnant woman employee, where the circumstances, although they could never in strictness be called the same, could nevertheless be properly regarded as lacking any material difference.[246]

Neither *Turley* nor *Hayes* acted on Smith's suggestion that the discrimination on grounds of pregnancy might be indirect discrimination. If employers demand that their employees shall not have incapacitating medical conditions or shall not be absent from work, it is easy to show that such a neutral requirement would have a disproportionate impact on women who wanted to have children. The statutory provisions on indirect discrimination would prohibit employers discriminating against women because of pregnancy unless such action was justified irrespective of sex. Employers would

---

243. Ibid., 6.
244. The effects of *Turley* were immediate. In Robinson v. Tees Components, Case no. 9/129/79 (February 1, 1980), an industrial tribunal held back its opinion that Robinson had been discriminated against because of pregnancy and issued an opinion consistent with *Turley*.
245. Hayes v. Malleable Working Men's Club and Maughan v. Northeast London Magistrates Court Committee, [1985] ICR 703 (EAT).
246. Ibid., 709.

carry the burden. A woman's claim of indirect discrimination, however, would allow the employer to argue that accommodating her pregnancy would be inconvenient, and thus it could treat her in a way that would be forbidden if the Government reduced or eliminated the qualifying period under the Employment Protection Act. If judges and members of tribunals have had trouble seeing men and women as comparable in the case of pregnancy, they have had even more trouble accepting claims of indirect discrimination. Judges would not likely conclude that a policy that allows for no medical leave would have an adverse effect on women. One commentator noted "how unsafe it is for advocates in discrimination cases to assume that they do not need to educate our judges as to the basic facts of life."[247] Feminists may thus choose to secure better maternity protection under the Employment Protection Act rather than rely on the Sex Discrimination Act.

The EOC rightly saw *Hayes* as a breakthrough, yet recognized its limitations.[248] "This decision has practical weaknesses; it affords no protection, for example, when an employer would have treated a sick man badly. It also takes no account of the very real differences between sick men and pregnant women since the latter are usually present at work, and so we believe it is rightly regarded as objectionable in principle by many women."[249] *Hayes* is an improvement upon *Turley* but it also has its limitations. Pregnancy is not an illness; it is normal, healthy, and unique to women. Oxford legal scholar Nicola Lacey observed: "This [comparison to a sick man] serves to reinforce a gravely damaging stereotyped view of women as having special weaknesses which render them comparable only with men in non-standard circumstances; the equation of pregnancy with ill health or other misfortune grossly misrepresents the nature of that condition and wilfully undervalues the importance still attached in our society to the bearing of children."[250] Furthermore, permitting employers to fire pregnant women because they also treat sick workers poorly does little to improve women's position in the workplace. Whether one adopts an equal treatment or special treatment approach to pregnancy, feminists agree

247. For the limitations of the tribunals' approach to indirect discrimination, see Michael Rubenstein, "Educating the Judges," *Equal Opportunities Review* 1 (May/June 1985): 48, where he discusses *Kidd v. DRG (U.K.) Ltd.* (EAT). In *Kidd*, the EAT considered whether a decision to select part-time workers first for redundancy (layoffs) indirectly discriminated against married women. The EAT concluded it could not assume that married women were more likely than men or single women to have child-care responsibilities that precluded full-time employment. "The real lesson of this case is not, as the EAT would have it, that it, 'Demonstrates how unsafe it is to act upon generalised assumptions about whether or not particular employment requirements or conditions are by their nature inherently discriminatory.' It is that it demonstrates how unsafe it is for advocates in discrimination cases to assume that they do not need to educate our judges as to the basic facts of life" (Rubenstein, 48).

248. "British EEO Agency Warns Employers that Discharge for Pregnancy is Illegal," 6.

249. EOC, *Equal Treatment*, 7.

250. Nicola Lacey, "Dismissal by Reason of Pregnancy," *Industrial Law Journal* 15 (1986): 43–45.

that employers ought not to be able to penalize women because they bear children, leading to cumulative disadvantages.

Despite the limitations of the comparative approach embedded in *Hayes*, several tribunals relied on its holding to find that employers who dismissed pregnant women violated the Sex Discrimination Act. After four such decisions from industrial tribunals, the EOC issued a statement in 1987 informing employers that pregnancy itself is not a valid reason for dismissal.[251] By 1988, the legal department had concluded that industrial tribunals were dealing with pregnancy discrimination sufficiently well that the EOC could concentrate its resources on other issues.[252]

A further breakthrough came in Northern Ireland when an industrial tribunal found in Donley v. Gallaher that, regardless of whether there was a male comparator and regardless of whether an employer dismissed sick employees, the Sex Discrimination Act for Northern Ireland prohibited employers from dismissing women because they were pregnant, or rather, what it called, "discrimination against motherhood."[253] The EAT referred to the EC's Equal Treatment Directive as well as statutes in effect in Northern Ireland and rejected the comparative approach of *Hayes*.[254] The Northern Ireland Equal Opportunities Commission assisted Donley, and its press release reported that

> the tribunal rejected the line of cases which allow a comparison to be made between a sick male employee and a pregnant female employee on the basis that such a comparison allows for a justification of direct discrimination which the Order does not permit. In addition it considered that comparing a pregnant woman with a sick male is invalid as pregnancy is not a sickness. It concluded that the vast majority of cases involved parental responsibilities and the correct comparison, if there is to be a comparison, is between mothers-to-be and fathers-to-be, to enable a comparison of like with like, albeit that they are different states. The Applicant was awarded the sum of £2,000 compensation.[255]

Citing Donley, a Belfast tribunal in McQuade v. Dabernig went further and concluded that discrimination against women because of pregnancy was *per se* sex discrimination.[256]

---

251. The cases, Callis-Smith v. Saunders, Cooney v. The Governors of Holly Bank School, Fyfe v. Farmer Giles Foods, and Barratt v. System 3, are discussed in EOC, *Twelfth Annual Report* (London: HMSO, 1987), 9.

252. EOC, *Thirteenth Annual Report* (London: HMSO, 1988), 20.

253. Donley v. Gallaher Limited No. 1, Case no. 66/86 (Northern Ireland), November 6, 1987.

254. The tribunal did not mention *Hayes*, nor was it bound by that decision, since Northern Ireland is covered by a separate sex discrimination law.

255. Donley v. Gallaher Limited No. 1, NI EOC Press Release, 59.

256. McQuade v. Dabernig, Case no. 427/89 (Northern Ireland), August 31, 1989.

Meanwhile, the British Employment Appeal Tribunal was reaffirming the comparative approach of *Hayes*. In *Webb v. EMO Air Cargo (U.K.) Ltd.*, an industrial tribunal found that a company did not violate the Sex Discrimination Act by dismissing a woman who became pregnant shortly after it hired her to fill in for another woman's maternity leave.[257] The tribunal concluded that if the company had hired a man as a substitute who then later needed a leave of absence, it would have dismissed him as well. Mrs. Webb's lawyer had made arguments under the provisions against direct discrimination, indirect discrimination, and under EC law.

On appeal, the only question before the EAT was whether discrimination against Mrs. Webb because of her pregnancy was direct discrimination.[258] That the company did not have a policy of dismissing pregnant employees— in fact, the company hired Webb to replace another employee on maternity leave—impressed Mr. Justice Wood, president of the EAT. The EAT considered three options: whether because men cannot become pregnant discrimination because of pregnancy is automatically *not* direct discrimination (the approach in *Turley*), whether for that same reason it *is* automatically directly discriminatory (anticipating the ECJ's position in *Dekker*),[259] or whether the SDA requires a comparison between actual or hypothetical men (the approach of *Hayes*). The EAT equated the first two options. Finding discrimination on the grounds of pregnancy to be *per se* direct discrimination would constitute positive discrimination, according to President Wood—not what the statute requires. Wood reaffirmed the comparative approach, drawing on the arguments of Pannick as amicus curiae. Wood concluded by noting that the Employment Protection Act does not confer an absolute right against dismissal on grounds of pregnancy and, therefore, neither does the Sex Discrimination Act.[260]

Not only did British tribunals continue to insist on a comparison, but unless they had contradictory evidence, they accepted the employer's statement of policy at face value. In Taylor v. Harry Yearsley Ltd.,[261] an industrial tribunal concluded that, unless a pregnant woman could present evidence to the contrary, an employer's testimony that it would fire a man who had to take a leave of absence would permit it to dismiss pregnant women without violating the Sex Discrimination Act.

Brown v. Stockton-on-Tees Borough Council gave the House of Lords the opportunity to rule on the question of the treatment of pregnant employees for

257. Webb v. EMO Air Cargo (U.K.) Ltd., [1989] IRLR 124.

258. Ibid.

259. Dekker v. VJV-Centrum, [1991] IRLR 27.

260. See "Highlights: April 1990," *Industrial Relations Law Reports* (1990): 117; "Pregnancy Dismissal Not Automatically Discriminatory," *Industrial Relations Legal Information Bulletin* 399 (April 19, 1990): 10–11.

261. Case no. 25716/88. See "Proving Pregnancy Discrimination," *Equal Opportunities Review Discrimination Case Law Digest* 1 (Autumn 1989): 2.

the first time in a 1988 case alleging unfair dismissal.[262] Mrs. Brown claimed that the Stockton-on-Tees Borough Council's Youth Training Scheme had unfairly dismissed her because she was pregnant. The Manpower Service Commission decided to cut the funding for the scheme but provided funding for a different scheme for one year. The new scheme, however, had staff positions for only three workers; one of the four on the original scheme would be redundant. Although Brown ranked third in seniority and her work was satisfactory, the scheme selected her for redundancy because she was pregnant and would require some maternity leave during the one-year contract. Side-stepping the issue of whether the scheme had discriminated against her because of sex, the industrial tribunal found that selecting Brown for redundancy because she was pregnant made her dismissal unfair.[263]

On appeal, the EAT disagreed, finding that the employer dismissed her because of redundancy, not because of pregnancy.[264] Justice Popplewell's comments are instructive. Like the tribunal opinions surveyed by Fawkes and Leonard, Popplewell considers the possibility that Brown offered or might have offered to take her maternity leave without pay, forgoing her statutory rights to keep her job.[265] He concluded, however, that even if she gave up her statutory maternity pay, and returned to work sooner than the law requires, the inconvenience and cost of finding a substitute for her made it reasonable for the scheme to pass her over for the job. Popplewell also commented that "the joys of motherhood" lead many women to decide not to return to work, implying that the scheme could not rely on Brown to return at all. Both comments reveal insensitivity and naïveté. Why should women have to give up their rights to keep their jobs? Furthermore, to suggest that it is solely the "joys of motherhood" rather than at least in part the obstacles society places in the path of working mothers that leads women to give up their jobs after having a child suggests a certain distance from the reality of working women's lives, as does the assumption that employment for women is often a choice rather than an economic necessity.[266]

The Court of Appeal affirmed the EAT's decision.[267] The House of Lords, however, found that selecting a woman for redundancy because she was pregnant violated the law. To do otherwise, Lord Griffiths wrote, would be "an abuse of language."[268] Although Griffiths begins with a literalist approach to the statute, he goes on to consider the history of its consolidation to

---

262. [1988] IRLR 263 (HL).

263. Brown v. Stockton-on-Tees Borough Council, Case no. 14414/85 (August 22, 1985).

264. Stockton-on-Tees Borough Council v. Brown, [1986] IRLR 432.

265. Ibid., 434.

266. Suzanne Bailey ("Maternity Rights," *Industrial Law Journal* 17 [September 1985]: 192) comments that Popplewell's reasoning has all the false seductiveness of Bristow's judgment in *Turley v. Allders Stores Ltd.*

267. Brown v. Stockton-on-Tees Borough Council, [1987] IRLR 230.

268. Brown v. Stockton-on-Tees Borough Council, [1988] IRLR 263, 265.

explain why Parliament did not explicitly make pregnancy a prohibited consideration in selection for redundancy. Moving on to a more purposive approach, Griffiths wrote:

> S. 34 (now S. 60) must be seen as a part of social legislation passed for the specific protection of women and to put them on an equal footing with men. I have no doubt that it is often a considerable inconvenience to an employer to have to make the necessary arrangements to keep a woman's job open for her whilst she is absent from work in order to have a baby, but this is a price that has to be paid as a part of social and legal recognition of the equal status of women in the workplace. . . . It surely cannot have been intended that an employer should be entitled to take advantage of a redundancy situation to weed out his pregnant employees.[269]

By clearly stating that pregnant women may not be singled out for redundancy, the House of Lords' decision represents a step forward in protecting pregnant workers. The emphasis in Griffiths's opinion on the inconvenience women workers cause by reproducing rather than on their contribution to society, their rights, or the double standard that permits men to be both workers and parents, shows the grudging and limited nature of the House of Lords' willingness to uphold the statute.

Employers may dismiss pregnant workers if they cannot do a large portion of their job, or if a statute prohibits them from working. For example, an employer can dismiss a shop assistant in a pharmacy whose job consists mainly of stocking shelves, involving heavy lifting, particularly if he suspects she may have a problem pregnancy.[270] If lifting is only a small portion of the job, however, an employer may not fire a pregnant woman for refusing to do it.[271] In *Grimsby Carpet Co. v. Bedford*,[272] the Employment Appeal Tribunal concluded the law permitted the dismissal of pregnant women who could not do their work, not because of the pregnancy but for reasons connected with the pregnancy. Mrs. Bedford was absent from work because of anemia, hypertension, and anxiety connected with her pregnancy.[273] In Jennings v. Burton Group plc, however, a Scottish industrial tribunal found that dismissing a pregnant worker who was absent with pregnancy-related illnesses during her probationary period violated the Sex Discrimination Act.[274]

---

269. Ibid., 265.
270. Brear v. Wright Hudson Ltd., [1977] IRLR 287.
271. Callan v. Majid, Case no. S/1829/89 (November 2, 1989).
272. [1987] ICR 975 (EAT).
273. See also Elegbede v. The Wellcome Foundation Ltd., [1977] IRLR 383.
274. Heather Williams, "Case Note: Direct Discrimination Against Pregnant Woman," *Legal Action*, January 1989, 24. See also George v. Beecham Group, [1977] IRLR 43.

In Almeida v. Cabeldu, an industrial tribunal found a sick-pay scheme that excluded "ailments peculiar to the female sex" from coverage to be discriminatory.[275] Tribunals are disposed toward requiring employers to let women use their sick pay for maternity just as they would allow men to use it for sickness. In *Coyne v. Exports Credits Guarantee Department*,[276] an industrial tribunal found that the Equal Pay Act prohibited employers from refusing to allow women to use their sick leave to extend their maternity leave when they were still physically unable to return to work. Mrs. Coyne had a baby by cesarean section and was not yet fit to return to work when her maternity leave expired. She wanted to take 2.5 weeks out of her sick pay, but the rules governing sick pay said it could not be used for complications resulting from maternity. The industrial tribunal held that the Equal Pay Act required the employer to remove the exemption.[277] However, if it appears that a woman will not be able to do the job for an indefinite period, or if she does not return to work at least for awhile at the end of her maternity leave, an employer may dismiss her.[278]

Tribunals now seem to have reached a consensus that dismissing women undergoing "normal" pregnancies violates the Sex Discrimination Act. Tribunals vary on whether they require a comparison with an actual or hypothetical male employee. The amount of damages tribunals award in these cases, however, has changed noticeably since 1986–87. In the early cases, tribunals were most likely to award small damages for injuries to feelings. Now, tribunals are more inclined to recognize the economic costs of losing one's job beyond the psychological injury of discrimination.[279] In Boyd v. Franklins Solicitors, the industrial tribunal awarded compensation of £1,550.[280] A Leeds industrial tribunal awarded compensation of £6,000, including £2,000 for injury to feelings against an employer who "callously and inconsiderately" dismissed an employee shortly before her baby was due.[281] Similarly, in Martin v. McConkey, a Belfast tribunal awarded £1,460,[282] and another woman received £4,997.89.[283]

275. Almeida v. Cabeldu, Case no. 6344/81/LS (March 16, 1982).

276. [1981] IRLR 51.

277. See also Todd v. Eastern Health and Social Services Board, Case no. 1149 (October 6, 1989) and (May 2, 1990); and discussion in *Equal Opportunities Review Discrimination Law Digest* 2 (Winter 1989): 1, and 6 (Winter 1990): 11.

278. Kelley v. Liverpool Maritime Terminals Ltd., [1988] IRLR 310 (CA).

279. Judges, too, seem to take more seriously the psychological injury of discrimination, at least of race discrimination. See Alexander v. Home Office, [1988] IRLR 190 (CA) and Noone v. Northwest Thames Regional Health Authority, [1988] IRLR 195 (CA).

280. Case no. 8909/89 (August 16, 1989).

281. Winston v. Oldham Batteries Ltd., Case no. 23237/89 (January 23, 1990). See commentary in *Equal Opportunities Review Discrimination Case Law Digest* 3 (Spring 1990): 10–11.

282. Case No. 1577/89 (March 8, 1990).

283. Todd v. Eastern Health and Social Services Board, Case no. 1149/88 (May 2, 1990).

The European Court of Justice eventually adopted the approach of the Belfast tribunal in Donley rather than the comparative approach of *Hayes*. The Equal Treatment Directive (ETD) is the EC equivalent of the Sex Discrimination Act (SDA);[284] it prohibits sex discrimination in employment. Like the SDA, the ETD contains provisions that permit member states to provide special treatment for childbirth and maternity to women only, even when they do not have similar benefits for men who are absent from work. In *Commission v. Italy*,[285] the ECJ held that the ETD did not prevent Italy from providing three months paid leave for mothers but not for fathers of adoptive children. Similarly, in *Hofmann v. Barmer Ersatzkasse*,[286] the ECJ ruled that the ETD did not prevent member states from offering a maternity leave beyond what women required to recover physically from the birth, to women only. The Court rejected the European Commission's arguments that if the leave was to provide intensive care for newborns rather than to allow for the mother to recover from the birth, the leave should be made available to either parent. The ECJ did decide, however, that the special privileges available only to mothers under French labor law (such as extra days' holiday each year for every child she bears) did violate the ETD since they were not directly related to pregnancy and childbirth.[287]

The decision of the ECJ in October, 1990, in *Dekker v. Stichting Vormingcentrum voor Jonge Volwassen (VJV-Centrum)* stated unequivocally that discrimination on the basis of pregnancy is direct discrimination on the basis of sex in violation of the ETD regardless of whether an employer disfavored men employees who were ill or required absences from work.[288] A Dutch woman applied to work for a youth center. Although the selection committee recommended hiring her, the center's board refused when they learned that she was pregnant. The center's insurer, the Risk Fund, refused to pay for her statutory maternity leave under the principle that you cannot insure a burning house—that is, Dekker's inability to work was foreseeable when the center would have hired her. The center hired another woman for the job and Dekker filed a complaint.[289]

---

284. 76/207/EEC.

285. [1984] 3 CMLR 169.

286. [1984] ECR 3047.

287. Commission v. France, [1989] 1 CMLR 408.

288. [1991] IRLR 27; see "Pregnancy Discrimination is Sex Discrimination," *Equal Opportunities Review* 35 (January/February 1991): 40–44.

289. Interestingly, a similar issue was presented to an industrial tribunal in Community Task Force v. Rimmer, [1986] IRLR 203 (EAT). If a youth training scheme had allowed Mrs. Rimmer to return to work after maternity in a suitable opening (her job was made redundant), the scheme would have lost its funding from the Manpower Services Commission. The Employment Appeal Tribunal upheld the industrial tribunal's finding that the requirement of the unfair dismissal law made offering her a suitable vacancy nondiscretionary, regardless of the funding consequences.

The Hoge Raad (Dutch Supreme Court) asked the ECJ whether refusing to hire a pregnant woman violated the ETD if the costs of hiring her, given the employer would have to replace her for part of her contract, would threaten the financial viability of the center. The Court concluded that discrimination on the basis of pregnancy was direct discrimination on the basis of sex under the Equal Treatment Directive. Furthermore, the state insurance scheme's failure to reimburse for maternity leaves did not exempt the employer from following the directive. It was up to employers to pressure the government to change the insurance scheme rather than force women such as Dekker to suffer the consequences. The decision should radically change how British tribunals apply the Sex Discrimination Act and the Employment Protection Act. British women will no longer need to wait two years or even five years to obtain protection against unfair dismissal because they are pregnant. Nor will their cases of discrimination in hiring, promotion, terms and conditions, sick leave, dismissal, or redundancy depend on how well or how badly employers do or might treat men employees. As the *Equal Opportunities Review* commented, "*Dekker* and *Hertz* are likely to mark the death-knell of the comparative approach to pregnancy discrimination requiring that like be compared with like, enunciated by the EAT in *Webb v. EMO Air Cargo (U.K.) Ltd.*"[290] Nor can the costs associated with employing pregnant women be a defense for discrimination under EC law.

With one fell swoop, through its interpretation of the Equal Treatment Directive, the ECJ has enacted important provisions of the European Commission's Draft Directive on Pregnancy.[291] Despite the Commission's effort to characterize the draft directive as a health and safety measure rather than an employment matter to invoke majority voting rather than unanimity (thereby getting around Britain's veto), the Council has not yet approved the directive. The ECJ's ruling goes a long way toward incorporating important provisions of that directive into EC law.

Dekker, however, was not a total victory for those seeking an expansion of protection for pregnant workers. In a case the European Court of Justice paired with *Dekker* and announced on the same day,[292] the ECJ considered an employer's obligations to an employee who was sick for an extended period because of complications from childbirth. Mrs. Hertz worked for Aldi Marked as a part-time cashier and was absent from work for most of her pregnancy. She returned to work after six months maternity leave and had no health problems for the next six months. During the year after that, however, she missed more than 100 days of work due to sickness caused by giving

---

290. "Pregnancy Discrimination is Sex Discrimination," 41.

291. "Implementing the Social Charter," *Industrial Relations Legal Information Bulletin* 413 (November 23, 1990): 9–11.

292. Handels-og Kontorfunktionaerernes Forbund i Danmark (acting for Hertz) v. Dansk Arbejdsgiverforening (acting for Aldi Marked k/s), [1991] IRLR 31.

birth. Aldi Marked dismissed her and she challenged the dismissal in a Danish Labor Court. The Danish court referred the case to the ECJ, asking what the Equal Treatment Directive obliged employers to do for employees incapacitated because of pregnancy and childbirth.

The ECJ held that dismissal on the basis of pregnancy or reasons connected with pregnancy (such as illness) is *per se* direct discrimination contrary to the Equal Treatment Directive. A woman dismissed because of pregnancy between the time she becomes pregnant and the conclusion of whatever statutory maternity leave the member state mandates need not compare herself to an actual or hypothetical male employee. However, once the statutory maternity leave period has expired, employers may dismiss women workers who are absent from work because of an illness associated with pregnancy or childbirth if they also would dismiss ill or incapacitated male employees. So after the statutory period has expired, if the member state's labor laws permit employers to dismiss sick employees, they may dismiss women whose absence resulted from complications from pregnancy. The result of this ruling in Britain is that women need not have worked for an employer for two years to claim that a dismissal because of an illness associated with pregnancy (while pregnant or on maternity leave) is unlawful.[293]

In the ten years between *Turley* and *Dekker*, the law on pregnancy discrimination has changed dramatically. The ECJ's interpretation of the Equal Treatment Directive requires member states to change their sex discrimination statutes so that discrimination on the basis of pregnancy is direct discrimination. The European Commission is also pushing for greater protection of the employment rights of pregnant women. The very reason British courts and industrial tribunals expanded sex discrimination law to encompass pregnancy discrimination was because the Conservative Government was restricting the rights of employed women under labor law by both increasing the qualifying period and erecting hurdles for women who wanted to exercise their statutory rights.[294] Pressure from the EC is countering the erosion of pregnant women's rights. As Britain becomes even more out of step with the maternity provisions in other EC countries, one would expect that pressure to increase. It will be interesting to watch the response of industrial tribunals and the Government to *Dekker*.

Conclusion

This chapter has provided an overview of British law prohibiting sex discrimination, set forth a framework for analyzing discrimination law, considered the

---

293. "All Pregnancy Dismissals Breach EEC Law," *Industrial Relations Legal Information Bulletin* 414 (December 7, 1990): 11–12.

294. The EOC called for a "simplification of the present excessively complicated law on maternity rights and benefits" (EOC, *Equal Treatment*, 8).

provisions of the Sex Discrimination Act, and outlined the effect of membership in the EC on British law. I have discussed how the law worked in practice by summarizing the effectiveness of the Equal Opportunities Commission, considering the record of industrial tribunals, and reviewing the behavior of judges in sex discrimination cases. Finally, I carefully analyzed one area of law: cases of discrimination because of pregnancy.

Understanding the text of the statute and how British judges and members of industrial tribunals have interpreted it enables us to predict how they will rule in cases on exclusionary policies. Knowledge of the provisions of the Sex Discrimination Act might lead us to expect that cases on exclusionary policies might fall within one of the many exceptions to the act. Even if women were successful in their claims, we would expect limited remedies and few changes in employment practices.

Knowledge of the enforcement agency, the EOC, leads us to expect that it will not be in the vanguard of demanding an end to discrimination resulting from exclusionary policies. It may be involved in litigation, but we would not expect it to have issued a code of practice or have conducted a formal investigation. Knowledge of the British feminist movement leads us to expect that it will not have interacted with the EOC on this matter. It is unlikely that a feminist pressure group will have taken up the issue although some trade unions may be active. Feminists will probably not bring test cases on this issue.

Knowledge of industrial tribunals leads us to foresee that they will make mistakes in law and be reluctant to find that discrimination has occurred, particularly if they see the employers' practices as reasonable. We can expect that employers will be better represented than women bringing claims, and there may be problems of fact development and presentation. The panel of tribunals or the courts may fail to understand the harm of discrimination or fall prey to stereotypes. They may see differential treatment as benign or even chivalrous and strictly interpret all exceptions to the act.

Finally, our knowledge of cases of discrimination because of pregnancy suggests that, when men and women are obviously biologically different, it may take a long time for courts and tribunals to find a way to compare them. For example, only in 1985 did the EAT compare pregnancy to temporarily disabling conditions. Similarly, the courts and tribunals may fail to realize that, although only women carry fetuses, both men and women can suffer reproductive injury from occupational exposure. *Turley* shows how slow tribunals have been to apply the comparative approach in a way that yields a favorable outcome for women. Even though British courts and tribunals eventually overturned *Turley*, they clung to the comparative approach in *Webb*, and only reluctantly abandoned it in unfair dismissal cases in *Brown*. Any pressure to expand the law will likely come, as for pregnancy discrimination, from the EC. It is the ECJ, not British courts and tribunals, that concluded that even if men and women are different, women should not suffer disadvantages in the workplace because of this difference.

Based on our understanding of the theory of discrimination, we might predict that judges and members of tribunals would distinguish between real and stereotypical differences between men and women. Not only are they likely to see real differences where feminists see stereotypes, but they are likely to conclude that real differences justify treating women less favorably than men, in this case denying them the opportunity to work. Because judges and members of tribunals tend to see discrimination as a characteristic of bad people rather than the result of structural arrangements, if employers appear to have good motives—protecting future fetuses—one would expect courts and industrial tribunals to conclude that no discrimination has occurred. If the employer acted reasonably, regardless of the statute, it has not discriminated. Finally, examining the theoretical literature on discrimination would lead us to expect that feminists themselves might be in some disagreement about the best way to accommodate biological differences in the workplace and have a difficult time developing a strategy that both accommodates and protects women but does not further their disadvantaged position in the workplace.

It is worth recognizing that the legal system in general, and the status of sex discrimination law in particular, is not static. I have documented some of the changes that have occurred in the approach of judges and industrial tribunals in the last fifteen years. Initially, judges and members of tribunals made what we could only call clear mistakes, setting aside the clear wording of the statute to find for the employers. In response to criticism, training, and experience, these mistakes have given way to a more favorable climate for victims of discrimination. The EOC's recommendations suggest less dissatisfaction with individuals, tribunal members and judges, and more dissatisfaction with the statutes themselves, suggesting there has been some movement and we are now approaching the limits of what can be done under the present legal arrangements. Unfortunately, it has been the EC, not the British Government, that has taken steps to improve, update, and advance the law to achieve the original goal of equal employment opportunity for men and women.

Chapter 5 takes up these predictions and discusses the British cases on exclusionary policies, but first, I must set out the U.S. law on sex discrimination.

CHAPTER 4

U.S. Sex Discrimination Law

Lawyers representing women who challenged exclusionary policies and many legal commentators have argued that such policies clearly violate the letter and the spirit of Title VII of the Civil Rights Act of 1964 as amended by the Pregnancy Discrimination Act of 1978. Their briefs and law review articles maintain that those judges who upheld exclusionary policies flouted settled Title VII precedent. To describe how and why judges sometimes bent the doctrine to find the policies lawful, I must first highlight the important parts of that doctrine. Too often, judges, commentators, policymakers, and employers concluded that because such policies struck them as reasonable, they were therefore lawful. Challengers have carried a heavy burden to persuade them that the policies were neither.

The field of discrimination law has now been well plowed, however often the landscape changes from the winds of new judicial appointments or legislative enactments. Excellent descriptions and analysis of Title VII doctrine are available in textbooks, law review articles, and theoretical texts. Here, I seek only to describe briefly those aspects of Title VII precedent that are necessary to understand cases on exclusionary policies, rather than rework that material.[1] I will also compare and contrast sex discrimination law in Britain and the United States by examining the provisions of the laws, judicial interpretations, the performance of enforcement agencies, and the role of interest groups. The exploration of the U.S. cases also continues the discussion of the theoretical issues surrounding the concept of discrimination through an analysis of specific cases.

Although the drafters of British sex discrimination law modeled the Sex Discrimination Act of 1975 on Title VII,[2] they ended up with a very different product: Title VII has fewer exceptions written into the statute or created by the judiciary; the enforcement body Title VII created, the Equal Employment

---

1. A more complete description of Title VII precedent would pay more attention to the interplay of race and sex discrimination cases. Exclusionary policies are one of the few areas of sex discrimination law where the race analogy is less relevant.

2. See Elizabeth M. Meehan, "Equal Opportunity Policies: Some Implications for Women of Contrasts between Enforcement Bodies in Britain and the USA," in *Women's Welfare, Women's Rights*, ed. by Jane Lewis (London: Croom Helm, 1983), 170–92.

Opportunity Commission (EEOC), has been more active in litigating cases and issuing guidelines than its British equivalent, although the two became more similar in the 1980s; and judges in the United States have assumed a more active role in enforcing Title VII, often expressing support for the purposes underlying the act in their opinions as well as sympathy for the victims of discrimination, and they have awarded substantial remedies. The effects of President Reagan's appointments to the federal bench on one side of the Atlantic, when combined with the liberalizing effect of membership of the European Community on the other, means that the differences between the two judiciaries are shrinking.

Feminist groups and trade unions in the United States have been more active than their British counterparts in litigating and submitting amicus briefs for a variety of institutional, legal, and political reasons. Feminists in the United States not only seek to promote women's equality through activities on the state level, but they have two additional legal avenues beyond Title VII. Since 1971, the U.S. Supreme Court has read the equal protection clause of the Fourteenth Amendment of the Constitution as prohibiting states from using some sex-based classifications. Moreover, Executive Orders 11246 and 11375 prohibit holders of contracts with the federal government from discriminating on the basis of sex. The Treaty of Rome and subsequent EC directives are the closest British workers come to having a constitutional guarantee of equal treatment. The Executive Order program has no parallel. Feminists in the United States have also clearly benefited from a powerful, organized movement to combat race discrimination—one that has skillfully used litigation and whose successes have left a well-developed law that spills over into sex discrimination doctrine.

Identifying the causes for the differences in the sex discrimination laws is more difficult than cataloging those differences. Explaining why Parliament did not pass its statute on discrimination until eleven years after Congress had acted requires an analysis of each country's civil rights movement, women's movement, legal system, political parties, legislature, and each country's political culture and social consciousness. Yet we can only learn so much about causes from effects. A review of the events leading to passage of the Sex Discrimination Act in Britain and Title VII in the United States suggests that we should be cautious about inferring either a strong legislative intent to promote equality between the sexes at that time or a broader social consensus on this issue. In Britain, pressure from the European Community and the efforts of well-placed individuals and interest groups are better explanations for the passage of the Sex Discrimination Act than a groundswell of public opinion in support of greater equality for women. One should not discern an unambiguous legislative intent or clear public mandate for equality from passage of either piece of legislation.

The comparison of the development of doctrine under each act and the performance of the enforcement agency should be tempered by a recognition of an eleven-year time difference between the passage of the two acts—perhaps we should compare the cases under Title VII in 1981 with cases under SDA in 1991. If one rereads lower courts' opinions in early Title VII cases, one finds the same sorts of comments that British commentators found so damning when British judges made them. A new law takes time to show effects and time for judges and members of industrial tribunals to adjust. Precedent evolves as higher courts deal with complex issues and opinions are subjected to public scrutiny, criticism, and legislative amendment. The time-lag hypothesis explains some of the differences between the outcomes of sex discrimination cases in Britain and the United States, but it has its limitations. The lag itself requires an explanation. Suggesting that Britain is eleven years "behind" the United States in promoting equality between the sexes obscures the fact that, in the 1980s, after one considers developments in EC law, the United States may be lagging behind Britain. The judicial appointments of the Reagan administration may shrink the gulf between the two countries still further.

Carefully connecting public opinion on sex equality to outcomes of discrimination cases would be a valuable contribution to this analysis if it could be done. What this study does is focus, instead, on the structure of the two legal and political systems and the views of judges, members of tribunals, administrators, and feminists, about the purposes of the Sex Discrimination Act, and what action is appropriate to bring about equality. The generalizations I make in this chapter about sex discrimination law in the United States help to explain the cases on exclusionary policies discussed in chapter 6.

The Legislative History of Title VII

Chapter 1 revealed how Congress passed the Civil Rights Act of 1964.[3] The Congress acted out of a concern about discrimination on the basis of race, not sex,[4] and congressional hearings reflected that concern.[5] Those who opposed civil rights legislation proposed an amendment adding a prohibition against sex discrimination to kill the bill,[6] and Congress debated that amendment only

---

3. 42 U.S.C. §2000e et seq.

4. See Robert Stevens Miller, Jr., "Sex Discrimination and Title VII of the Civil Rights Act of 1964," *Minnesota Law Review* 51 (1967): 877–97; Barbara Lindemann Schlei and Paul Grossman, *Employment Discrimination Law*, 2d ed. (Washington, D.C.: Bureau of National Affairs, 1986), vii–xiii.

5. See Francis J. Vaas, "Title VII: Legislative History," *Boston College Industrial and Commercial Law Review* 7 (1965–66): 431–58.

6. *Congressional Record*, 88th Cong., 2d sess., 1964, 110:2577–84.

briefly. The amendment was not, thus, a response to an organized feminist movement—in fact, women were divided on the issue.[7] A few well-placed women seized the opportunity presented by the enemies of civil rights to keep the amendment part of the bill and to insure acceptance by the administration.[8] Thus, the history of Title VII turns theories of legislative change upside down. An organized women's movement did not self-consciously campaign for the inclusion of sex discrimination provisions in the Civil Rights Act. Once a part of the law, however, the sex discrimination provisions of Title VII galvanized, reinforced, and strengthened the emerging organized women's movement.[9]

Two features of the amendment's history foreshadowed future problems. First, because opponents of civil rights legislation conceived the amendment rather than feminists and their supporters in Congress, no coalition was ready to oversee implementation of the provisions on sex discrimination and to insure that the Equal Employment Opportunity Commission took the provisions seriously. Second, the absence of any legislative record meant that the EEOC had little guidance beyond the wording of the statute on what ills Congress sought to remedy and how the EEOC should interpret the law.[10] Yet despite its rocky start, Title VII has been "a mighty engine that is gradually forcing the alteration of the employment practices of a nation in innumerable ways."[11]

Provisions

Title VII makes it unlawful for an employer with more than fifteen employees[12] to classify or discriminate because of sex, race, color, religion, or national origin in advertising, hiring, firing, compensating, or in setting the conditions of employment.[13] The prohibition extends to labor unions and employment agencies; it also covers apprenticeship and training schemes. The

---

7. Ibid.

8. Elizabeth Meehan, *Women's Rights at Work: Campaigns and Policy in Britain and the United States* (London: MacMillan, 1985), 62–63.

9. Paul Burstein, *Discrimination, Jobs, and Politics: The Struggle for Equal Employment Opportunity in the United States Since the New Deal* (Chicago: University of Chicago Press, 1985), 95.

10. See Richard K. Berg, "Title VII: A Three Years' View," *Notre Dame Lawyer* 44 (February 1969): 311–44.

11. Schlei and Grossman, xii.

12. Congress changed this provision in 1972 from 25 to 15 employees. To cushion the impact of the new law, Congress called for a step-by-step approach to implementation. First, employers with 100 employees were covered, then 75, then 50, then 25.

13. See Interpretative Memorandum of Title VII of H.R. 7152 Submitted Jointly by Senator Joseph S. Clark and Senator Clifford P. Case, Floor Managers, *Congressional Record*,

act also prohibits retaliation for filing a complaint. Title VII includes several exceptions. Congress, living up to its reputation as "the last plantation," exempted its own staffs.[14] Religious institutions may discriminate on the basis of religion, and private clubs are exempt. The act permits states to grant preferences to veterans, and exempts jobs for which a specific religion, sex, and national origin is a bona fide occupational qualification for the job. Congress made it clear that it was not mandating quotas and did not intend to interfere with bona fide seniority systems nor prohibit preemployment testing.

Title VII created an Equal Employment Opportunity Commission of five members, appointed by the president with the advice and consent of the Senate, to serve staggered, five-year terms. Not more than three members may be from the same political party. The President designates one commissioner as chairman and she or he administers the agency.[15]

A person complaining of unlawful discrimination files a charge with the EEOC in writing within 300 days of the incident in question.[16] The agency gives a copy of the complaint to the accused and is supposed to investigate the complaint within 60 days. After the investigation, if two or more members of the commission believe there is reasonable cause to believe that discrimination occurred, the EEOC tries to conciliate.[17] Participation in conciliation is voluntary for the parties, although the EEOC must attempt conciliation before it makes a finding of cause or files suit.[18] If conciliation fails and a majority of

---

88th Cong., 2d sess., 1964, 110:7212; Charles A. Sullivan, Michael J. Zimmer, and Richard F. Richards, *Federal Statutory Law of Employment Discrimination* (Indianapolis: Michie, 1980); Schlei and Grossman; Herma H. Kay, *Sex-based Discrimination*, 2d ed. (St. Paul: West Publishing, 1981).

14. Initially, federal and state employees were exempt from coverage of Title VII and were protected only by Executive Order. In 1972, Congress amended Title VII in order to cover federal and state employees, although political appointments are still exempt. See Paul M. Downing, *The Equal Employment Opportunity Act of 1972: Legislative History*, Congressional Research Service, July 3, 1972, 83.

15. The 1972 amendments also made the General Counsel quasi-independent and appointed by the president (Schlei and Grossman, 1146).

16. Congress extended this period from 180 days in 1972.

17. To reduce its case load, the EEOC implemented a rapid charge-processing unit in order to bring both parties together and to attempt conciliation before the complaint was investigated. In 1981, 43 percent of all complaints were settled this way. See Paul M. Downing, *Federal Protection of Equal Employment Opportunity for Racial and Ethnic Minorities and for Women in the Private Sector*, Congressional Research Service, February 17, 1983, 6.

18. "The Court views each one of the deliberate steps in the statutory scheme—charge, notice, investigation, reasonable cause, conciliation—as intended by Congress to be a condition precedent to the next succeeding step and ultimately legal action. Certainly, the EEOC does not contend that it could skip one or more of these steps at will. The language of the Act is mandatory as to each step and the Commission must complete each step before moving on to the next" (EEOC v. Container Corp. of America, 352 F. Supp. 262, 265 [M.D. Fla. 1972]).

the commission finds there is reasonable cause to believe that discrimination occurred,[19] the EEOC may then file a charge in federal court.[20] The EEOC has only 90 days after it has determined that reasonable cause exists to file a suit. One hundred and eighty days after filing, a complainant may ask for a right-to-sue notice and file suit, regardless of the status of the complaint or the findings of the EEOC. Title VII requires the agency to cooperate with those states that have fair employment laws and to determine which state laws conflict with Title VII. The EEOC also determines what type of records employers must keep, and it issues procedural regulations.

The Bona Fide Occupational Qualification (BFOQ)

Although Congress was willing to prohibit sex discrimination, it was not willing to accept that employers must open all jobs to both men and women. Instead, employers could recognize that sex differences, unlike differences of skin pigmentation, might be relevant to one's ability to perform a job and reserve some jobs for members of one sex. Section 703 of Title VII defines the bona fide occupation qualification.

> It shall not be an unlawful employment practice for an employer to hire and employ employees, . . . on the basis of . . . religion, sex, or national origin in those certain instances where religion, sex, or national origin is a bona fide occupational qualification *reasonably necessary to the normal operation of that particular business.*[21]

---

19. Congress gave little guidance on how the courts should interpret "reasonable cause." The agency recently made the standard more stringent and declared that reasonable cause means worthy of litigation. See House Committee on Education and Labor, *A Report on the Investigation of Civil Rights Enforcement by the Equal Employment Opportunity Commission*, 99th Cong., 2d sess., 1986, V–VI. "In a major change of position, on July 20, 1977, the EEOC adopted the following resolution, 'The reasonable cause decision will constitute a determination that the claim has sufficient merit to warrant litigation if the matter is not thereafter conciliated by the Commission or the changing party'" (*EEOC Compliance Manual* [Washington, D.C.: Bureau of National Affairs, May 1979] as quoted in Schlei and Grossman, 949). Former Chair Norton described the reason for this resolution: "Historically, the finding of reasonable cause meant only that there was sufficient evidence to attempt to settle the case. . . . Since this standard required less evidence than that necessary to go to litigation, few cases in which reasonable cause was found were taken to court. This means that the Commission did not secure leverage in settlement from the prospect of litigation, and that there was a double standard—one for conciliation and one for litigation" (Ibid).

20. Under the 1964 act, the EEOC had no enforcement powers, only the power to investigate and attempt conciliation. Although several bills modeled the agency after the National Labor Relations Board, giving it cease and desist powers, the EEOC did not acquire the power to bring suits in Federal District Court until passage of the 1972 amendments.

21. 42 §U.S.C. 2000e–2(e)(1); italics added.

Congress offered little guidance on how broad or narrow the exception was beyond the Senate's interpretive memorandum examples of a French chef for a French restaurant, an all-male baseball team, and a business that seeks the patronage of religious groups.[22]

The EEOC undertook the task of telling employers what the exception permitted. Stating in its interpretive guidelines that "the bona fide occupational qualification exception as to sex should be interpreted narrowly,"[23] the EEOC defined the bona fide occupational qualification exception negatively. The agency would not find the following to create a BFOQ exception: assumptions about characteristics of women in general, such as the assumption that women are absent more frequently from work than men, or stereotyped assumptions about women, such as the belief that women are more dexterous or less aggressive at selling than men. Instead, employers must treat an employee according to his or her individual attributes. The EEOC further refused to allow a BFOQ exception to cover circumstances in which customers or co-workers preferred men or women. The EEOC guidelines permit a BFOQ exception when authenticity or genuineness necessitates hiring one sex, for example actors or fashion models. The guidelines were silent on whether personal privacy might require the employment of members of one sex, a large part of the British genuine occupational qualification. Congress, unlike the British Parliament, left the task of defining the BFOQ exception to the EEOC and the courts.

Not all judges agreed with each other, nor did they all agree with the EEOC's interpretation. The first Title VII case the Supreme Court heard, *Phillips v. Martin Marietta Corp.*,[24] challenged a company's policy against hiring mothers of preschool children. The Court had to determine not only whether discrimination against mothers with preschool children was *per se* sex discrimination—that is, whether the policy discriminated on its face, but also whether, if the employer could show that mothers of preschool children were principally responsible for child care and that fact made them unreliable employees, that evidence could establish a BFOQ. The Court remanded the case, directing the lower court to hear evidence on the latter point. Rather than finding the assumption that mothers of preschool children were unreliable employees or less reliable than fathers to be the result of stereotypical thinking and forbidding employers to act on the basis of stereotyped assumptions (what the EEOC directed), the Court treated the question as one of fact. It did not hold that Title VII required employers to treat people as individuals rather than as having the characteristics of a group.

Justice Marshall dissented. He maintained that the case raised a question

---

22. *Congressional Record*, 88th Cong., 2d sess., 1964, 110:7213.
23. 29 C.F.R. §1604.2(a) (1972).
24. 400 U.S. 542 (1971).

of law, whether sex-specific rules were lawful under Title VII. He argued that Title VII mandated that employment criteria be gender neutral, claiming that Congress intended to prevent discrimination based on stereotyped assumptions about the sexes and "the exception for the bona fide occupational qualification was not intended to swallow the rule."[25] According to Marshall, the Court had improperly framed the question as whether discrimination against a subgroup of women, mothers, is sex discrimination, or whether employers may argue a BFOQ. Instead, the issue was whether employers may make one rule for mothers and another for fathers. That, he maintained, was sex discrimination. Echoing Judge John R. Brown's dissenting opinion from the court of appeals, Marshall noted that, because men could not be mothers, Martin Marietta's policy discriminated on the basis of sex. He agreed with Judge Brown that "if sex-plus stands, the Act is dead."[26]

Except for cases on exclusionary policies, the lower courts have largely followed Justice Marshall's reasoning in *Phillips* rather than the majority's. The Court's opinion left open the possibility that employers could apply sex-based categories if they were based on actual differences between men and women—such as a finding that mothers of small children had greater child-care responsibilities than fathers, on average. In *Rosenfeld v. Southern Pacific Co.*, for example, the Ninth Circuit held "sexual characteristics, rather than characteristics that might, to one degree or another, correlate with a particular sex, must be the basis for the application of the BFOQ exception."[27] Accordingly, refusing to hire women because they are not as strong as men as a group could not create a BFOQ because some women are strong enough to do the job. The *Rosenfeld* court's definition would restrict the BFOQ to such occupations as sperm donor or wet nurse, although it would permit the exception to apply when one sex was necessary for authenticity, such as actors or fashion models, or if it were not feasible to identify the exceptional individuals.

In *Weeks v. Southern Bell Telephone Co.*, the Fifth Circuit defined a BFOQ as a narrow exception.

In order to rely on the bona fide occupational qualification exception an employer has the burden of proving that he had reasonable cause to believe, that is, a factual basis for believing, *that all or substantially all*

---

25. 400 U.S. 542, 545 (1971).

26. 416 F.2d 1257, 1260 (5th Cir. 1969). Martin Marietta did not argue on remand that mothers of small children were less reliable than other workers. Instead, it settled the case and paid Ida Phillips back pay from the time she should have been hired (William Robinson, Lawyers Committee for Civil Rights Under Law, counsel for Ida Phillips, phone interview with author, July 1988).

27. 444 F.2d 1219, 1225 (9th Cir. 1971); see chap. 1.

women would be unable to perform safely and efficiently the duties of the jobs involved.[28]

The court commented in a footnote, however, that employers might be able to establish a BFOQ if they could show that it would be impossible or highly impractical to treat women individually.[29]

In a third case setting the parameters of the BFOQ, *Diaz v. Pan American Airways*,[30] Pan Am argued that only women flight attendants can handle the stresses passengers faced in coping with the special psychological environment created by flying. (Pan Am knew that its male customers preferred women flight attendants.) Presumably by fueling male passengers' sexual fantasies, women flight attendants could distract male passengers from their fear of flying. Critics of Pan Am's policy charged that Pan Am was arguing that the sexes were inherently different because the EEOC's guidelines did not permit it to put forward the real justification for its policy: customer preferences.[31] The Fifth Circuit relied on the word *necessary* in the statute and held, "discrimination based on sex is valid only when the *essence* of the business operation would be undermined by not hiring members of one sex exclusively."[32] Because the *essence* of Pan Am's business was transportation, not the enhancement of sexual fantasies, the airline must hire men as flight attendants.

The Supreme Court, however, was not as restrictive in its interpretation of a BFOQ as the courts of appeals for the Fifth and Ninth Circuits. *Dothard v. Rawlinson* showed the changes in the Supreme Court's thinking since *Phillips v. Martin Marietta*, but also revealed under what circumstances the Court believed employers could exclude women from jobs.[33] In *Dothard*, the Court held that being a man was a BFOQ for being a prison guard at one overcrowded maximum security prison. Because women might "provoke" attacks from prisoners (because of their capacity to be raped),[34] their employment in large numbers threatened the security of the prison. The Court noted that the law did not permit employers to defend a BFOQ on the basis of

---

28. 408 F.2d 228, 235 (5th Cir. 1969); italics added.

29. Ibid., n.5.

30. 311 F. Supp. 559 (S.D. Fla. 1970), 442 F.2d 385 (5th Cir.), *cert. denied* 404 U.S. 950 (1971).

31. 30 *Fed. Reg.* 14927 (December 2, 1965) §1604.1(a)(1)(iii).

32. 442 F.2d 385, 388 (5th Cir. 1971).

33. Dothard v. Rawlinson, 433 U.S. 321 (1977). For a full consideration of cases of discrimination on the basis of age that may apply to an interpretation of the BFOQ for sex discrimination, see Sullivan, Zimmer, and Richards.

34. See Catharine MacKinnon, *Feminism Unmodified* (Cambridge, Mass.: Harvard University Press, 1987), 73.

stereotyped assumptions and that Congress intended it to be a narrow exception. Although Title VII requires that employers allow women to weigh the desirability of hazardous work for themselves, in *Dothard*, not just women were at risk, but the security of the prison as a whole. Male guards were necessary for the safe and efficient operation of the business.

While the Court's rhetoric in *Dothard* defines a BFOQ as a narrow exception, the outcome suggests that the exception may be wider than lower court decisions in *Weeks* or *Diaz*. The Court limits its holding to a particular prison, but the dissenters were quick to recognize that the ruling would reverberate far beyond that context. The basis of the permissible distinction is that all men differ from all women, and the differences are "real" rather than stereotypical. The Court, however, has an instrumental role in perpetuating the naturalization of the sexual assault of women. Feminists counter that the view that men rape women because of unique anatomical differences or hormones is itself a social construction. One need not be an expert on prison life to notice that men are also at risk. Feminist critics of the decision point out that the Court failed in its project to separate the "real" sex differences from the stereotypical. *Dothard* has important implications for cases on exclusionary policies because it illustrates the Court's reluctance to require the integration of a traditionally male and dangerous workplace when employers raise the justification of biological, physical differences between the sexes— differences of sexuality and reproduction.

The Creation of Disparate Impact

From the start, the definition of discrimination in Title VII was contested terrain. In *Dothard*, the Court maintained that it was not discriminatory if employers treated men and women differently because of physical differences. Feminists challenged the way the Court constructed those "real" differences as well as pondered why these differences should lead prisons to exclude women from work rather than to punish those prisoners guilty of sexual assault. Another definitional battle was waged over the category of disparate impact. Was discrimination the result of intentional acts of prejudiced employers? Or did it include practices that were not facially discriminatory (*per se* sex discrimination) but had the effect of excluding certain groups? Early cases challenged "whites only" hiring policies and tried to dismantle explicit bars to employment. Workers, their lawyers, and civil rights activists knew that only some of the barriers to employment were of the disparate treatment variety. Title VII explicitly permitted employment tests and the use of seniority, nevertheless workers soon challenged word-of-mouth hiring, testing, and seniority systems that preserved segregated workplaces.

In 1971, the Supreme Court validated this expanded definition of discrimination and interpreted Title VII as prohibiting more than just disparate treatment. In the landmark case of *Griggs v. Duke Power Company*,[35] blacks claimed that a firm's requirement that all employees have a high school diploma closed jobs to many blacks, because they were less likely than whites to have graduated from high school. The Supreme Court overturned a lower court's finding that the practice did not discriminate.

> The objective of Congress in the enactment of Title VII is plain from the language of the statute. It was to achieve equality of employment opportunities and remove barriers that have operated in the past to favor an identifiable group of white employees over other employees. Under the Act, practices, procedures, or tests neutral on their face, and even neutral in terms of intent, cannot be maintained if they operate to "freeze" the status quo of prior discriminatory employment practices. . . . But Congress directed the thrust of the Act to the *consequences* of employment practices, not simply the motivation.[36]

The Supreme Court held that when a protected group could prove that the rule had a disparate impact on it, the burden would shift to the company to show that the rule was job-related.

> The touchstone is business necessity. If an employment practice which operates to exclude Negroes cannot be shown to be related to job performance, the practice is prohibited.[37]

Duke Power Company did not show that a high school education was necessary for many jobs or a useful predictor of employees' performance. *Griggs* created a whole new type of cases under Title VII: disparate impact.

In *Robinson v. Lorillard Corporation*,[38] the Court of Appeals for the Fourth Circuit set out the requirements for the business necessity defense for its jurisdiction, later adopted by other courts of appeals. First, the policy must be sufficiently compelling to override any discriminatory impact; second, it must effectively carry out the business purpose; and third, there must be no acceptable alternatives that would have less impact on the protected class.[39]

One of the most significant differences between disparate treatment and disparate impact was that, for the latter, a plaintiff need not prove that the employer intended to discriminate. If an employer had adopted a gender-

---

35. 401 U.S. 424 (1971).
36. Ibid., 429-30, 432
37. Ibid., 431.
38. 444 F.2d 791 (4th Cir. 1971).
39. Ibid., 798.

neutral rule with the purpose of discriminating, the rule would be a pretext for discrimination—it would be intentional discrimination on the basis of sex or race and, therefore, be disparate treatment. Once the complainant has shown the requirement has a disparate impact on a protected group, the burden shifts to the employer to show why the requirement is necessary. Yet neither in answering the charge of disparate treatment nor in defending a business necessity have the courts allowed employers to put forward any reason at all. The standard is stricter than reasonableness. The Court of Appeals for the Fourth Circuit explained that, while intent was not irrelevant to Title VII cases, merely having a reason for a given practice would not justify it if it had a discriminatory impact on a protected group.

> If a respondent's actions are otherwise determined to constitute an unlawful employment practice, the existence of a business purpose for continuing the practice will not negate its legality.[40]

The Supreme Court delivered a mortal blow to *Griggs* in *Wards Cove v. Atonio*.[41] At issue were several employment practices of an Alaskan canning factory that perpetuated a racially segregated workforce. The Court held that statistical evidence showing a racially divided workforce was insufficient to establish a prima facie case of disparate impact. Workers also must identify the specific practice that causes the imbalance and prove the link between each practice and the effect. The Court also took the opportunity to repudiate the burden-shifting element of *Griggs*. Previously, once a plaintiff proved a practice had a disparate impact the burden shifted to the company to justify the practice. Now the Court held that the burden remained with the Title VII plaintiff.

Finally, the Court lowered the standard of justification for business necessity, saying the practice need only be reasonable rather than necessary.

> Though we have phrased the query differently in different cases, it is generally well-established that at the justification stage of such a disparate impact case, the dispositive issue is whether a challenged practice serves, in a significant way, the legitimate employment goals of the employer. . . . At the same time, though, there is no requirement that the challenged practice be "essential" or "indispensable" to the employer's business for it to pass muster: this degree of scrutiny would be almost impossible for most employers to meet, and would result in a host of evils we have identified above.[42]

---

40. Ibid., 797.
41. Wards Cove Packing Company v. Atonio, 490 U.S. 642 (1989).
42. Ibid., 659.

Wards Cove made it virtually impossible to win a disparate impact case and led Congress to overturn the Court's holding with the Civil Rights Act of 1991.[43]

By 1991, employment law textbooks and judicial opinions treated the categories of disparate treatment–disparate impact as well-established doctrine with distinctive defenses (BFOQ or business necessity) and distinctive burdens of proof. The cases discussed in chapter 6 illustrate, however, that when it came to cases on exclusionary policies, judges were willing to disrupt these settled precedents and not only modify the defenses, but change how they classified policies. The Supreme Court returned to the traditional Title VII defenses (as modified by *Wards Cove*) in *UAW v. Johnson Controls*, but until 1991, courts seemed happy to ignore the cases I have discussed here.

Pregnancy

Understanding the distinction between disparate treatment and disparate impact is essential to understanding cases on pregnancy discrimination, the most important precedents for cases on exclusionary policies. Pregnancy discrimination could conceivably fall under the rubric of either disparate treatment or disparate impact, or both. Because only women get pregnant, discrimination on the basis of pregnancy is discrimination on the basis of sex (disparate treatment). Although a rule that employees who became pregnant can no longer work is not neutral because it applies only to women,[44] a policy of firing all those with temporarily incapacitating medical conditions would be neutral and would have a disparate impact on women, because they may become pregnant.

The Supreme Court addressed this question in *General Electric Co. v. Gilbert*.[45] Could an employer's policy that discriminated on the basis of a characteristic that some (but not all) women share (pregnancy) and that no men share be sex discrimination? Specifically, the Supreme Court considered whether a company's insurance scheme that covered nonoccupational illness, single-sex ailments, and elective surgery but excluded medical expenses arising from pregnancy was discrimination under Title VII.

In *Geduldig v. Aiello*,[46] the Supreme Court had considered whether a state disability scheme that covered all disabilities except pregnancy and

---

43. Pub. L. No. 102-37 (1991), 105 Stat. 1071 (1991).

44. Neutral in the sense that employers can apply them to all races or both sexes. For example, a height requirement can be applied to all races and both sexes, although groups will be able to meet the requirement in different numbers. A nonneutral rule would be one for mothers (but not fathers) of small children. It can only be applied to women.

45. 429 U.S. 125 (1976).

46. 417 U.S. 484 (1974).

childbirth and related complications violated the equal protection clause of the Fourteenth Amendment. *Geduldig* was a constitutional case, while *Gilbert* was a Title VII case. The Fourteenth Amendment does not cover private actions and Title VII, unlike the Fourteenth Amendment, explicitly prohibits sex discrimination. Yet both cases raised the question of whether discrimination against a subgroup of one sex was sex discrimination. In *Geduldig*, the Court held that,

> while it is true that only women can become pregnant it does not follow that every legislative classification concerning pregnancy is a sex-based classification. . . . The program divides potential recipients into two groups—pregnant women and nonpregnant persons. While the first group is exclusively female, the second includes members of both sexes.[47]

The Court was not obliged to apply its reasoning in *Geduldig* to *Gilbert*, although it did. *Gilbert* held that pregnancy discrimination was not sex discrimination under Title VII. Furthermore, it found that General Electric's "neutral" policy did not have an adverse impact on women employees, who, on average, received more medical benefits than male employees for their contributions.

The EEOC had issued guidelines in 1972 requiring employers to treat pregnancy the same as other temporary disabilities.[48] Previously, however, the EEOC's General Counsel had issued an opinion stating, "since maternity is a temporary disability unique to the female sex and more or less to be anticipated during the working life of most women employees," companies could exclude maternity provisions from their disability coverage.[49] *Gilbert* explicitly rejected the interpretation contained in the EEOC's guidelines. While noting, "the legislative history of Title VII's prohibition of sex discrimination is notable primarily for its brevity,"[50] the Court held that the EEOC's new guidelines did not comport with the proper interpretation of Title VII. The Court seemed concerned because the EEOC had changed its position. *Gilbert* reversed the rulings of five courts of appeals, generated a stinging dissent by Justices Brennan, Marshall, and Stevens, and provoked the criticism of many scholars as well as members of Congress.[51]

---

47. Ibid. 496–97, n.20.
48. 29 CFR §1604.10 (b)(1975).
49. 429 U.S. 125, 142 (1976).
50. Ibid., 143.
51. See Patricia Huckle, "The Womb Factor: Pregnancy Policies and Employment of Women," in *Women, Power and Policy*, ed. by Ellen Boneparth (New York: Pergamon, 1982), 144–61.

Perhaps that reaction partially explains why, in *Nashville Gas Co. v. Satty*,[52] the next case involving pregnancy, the Supreme Court moved away from *Gilbert*. Nashville Gas required its pregnant employees to take a leave of absence without sick pay. Unlike employees at General Electric, however, employees of Nashville Gas lost all accumulated seniority during their leave of absence, making it difficult, if not impossible, to bid successfully for jobs when they returned. Applying the rationale in *Gilbert*, the Court found that Nashville's policy was neutral, because discrimination on the basis of pregnancy was not discrimination under Title VII. Under the disparate impact analysis, however, the Court found that Nashville Gas, in the application of its seniority policy, imposed substantial burdens on pregnant workers that no male workers faced. Because there was no proof of any business necessity justifying the adoption of the policy, the Court found Nashville Gas in violation of Title VII.

Satty distinguished employment policies that did not provide benefits to pregnant employees from those that burdened them—a distinction Justice Rehnquist's opinion for the Court stated to be "more than one of semantics."[53] Under his analysis, the policy that denied Satty a wage during pregnancy was a refusal to provide a benefit, while the denial of seniority was the imposition of a burden.

Congress reacted quickly to *Gilbert* and *Satty*. Much had changed between 1964 and 1978. In 1964, Congress may have merely tolerated the addition of sex as a prohibited category of discrimination, yet it wholeheartedly affirmed the prohibition against sex discrimination during the debates over amendments to Title VII in 1972. In 1978, Congress not only condemned sex discrimination, but condemned pregnancy discrimination and passed the Pregnancy Discrimination Act[54] to reverse *Gilbert*.[55]

The statute defines sex discrimination under Title VII to include pregnancy, childbirth, and related medical conditions.

> The terms "because of sex" or "on the basis of sex" include, but are not limited to, because of or on the basis of pregnancy, childbirth, or related medical conditions; and women affected by pregnancy, childbirth, or

---

52. 434 U.S. 136 (1977).

53. Ibid., 142.

54. Pub. L. No. 95-555, 92 Stat. 2076 (1978).

55. For a detailed analysis of the legislative history of the Pregnancy Discrimination Act, see Hannah Arterian Furnish, "Prenatal Exposure to Fetally Toxic Work Environments: The Dilemma of the 1978 Pregnancy Amendment to Title VII of the Civil Rights Act of 1964," *Iowa Law Review* 66 (1980): 63–129. The House Education and Labor Committee criticized the reasoning underlying *Gilbert* and found *Satty* confusing (House Committee on Education and Labor, *Prohibition of Sex Discrimination Based on Pregnancy*, 95th Cong., 2d sess., 1978, H. Rep. 948, 3, quoted in Furnish, 79 n.76).

related medical conditions shall be treated the same for all employment-related purposes, including receipt of benefits under fringe benefit programs, as other persons not so affected but similar in their ability or inability to work, and nothing in section 703(h) of this title shall be interpreted to permit otherwise.[56]

The effect of the Pregnancy Discrimination Act (PDA) was to make pregnancy discrimination disparate treatment rather than a potential case of disparate impact.

The debates over the PDA focused primarily on overturning *Gilbert*, although Congress also touched on the cost of the bill and the impact it would have on abortion. Both the House and the Senate failed to consider the impact of the bill on jobs where employing a pregnant woman might damage a fetus. During the Senate hearings, a representative of the U.S. Chamber of Commerce testified that the PDA would make it illegal for an employer to discharge a pregnant worker in such a situation and leave the employer vulnerable to civil action brought for a malformed child.[57] In responding to a question by Senator Hatch, Dr. Hellegers, an expert witness, commented that working men's reproductive health was also in danger from workplace toxins.[58] The hearings touched on this issue only on these two occasions. Although Congress did not squarely address the specific issue of excluding women from toxic work environments, the general thrust of the legislative history of the PDA suggests that Congress wanted to prevent employers from denying women employment opportunities because they conceive and bear children.

One would expect that the Pregnancy Discrimination Act would make it easy for the Court to conclude that, since discrimination on the basis of pregnancy is unlawful, discrimination on the basis of the ability to become pregnant is also unlawful. Chapters 5 and 6 show how principles established in cases of pregnancy discrimination governed cases on exclusionary policies.

As well as being important for cases on exclusionary policies, *Gilbert* and the legislative history of the PDA show the extent to which Congress and the courts embrace the comparative approach, using a male standard for workers. Under the comparative approach, women must be sufficiently like men to claim employers discriminated by treating them differently. Because the Supreme Court found in *Gilbert* that pregnancy was unique (men and women were not alike), the Court allowed employers to treat pregnant women

---

56. 42 U.S.C. §2000e-(k).

57. Senate Subcommittee on Labor of the Senate Committee on Human Resources, *Discrimination on the Basis of Pregnancy: Hearings on S. 995*, 95th Cong., 1st sess., 1977, 482. See Furnish, 78 n.72.

58. Senate Subcommittee on Labor, *Discrimination on the Basis of Pregnancy*, 67.

differently than other employees. Because the law incorporates a comparative approach, feminists have argued that women are not so different from men. Instead of treating pregnancy as unique, however, as the majority of the Supreme Court did in *Gilbert* and *Geduldig*, feminists have suggested that employers should treat pregnant women the same as other employees with temporary disabilities. Setting the issue in this framework, one could argue that an employer's policy that treats a disability that only women suffer differently than disabilities from which men suffer is sex discrimination. Because the comparison is between a pregnant woman and a temporarily disabled man, it does not matter that all women do not become pregnant. Discrimination on the basis of sex has still occurred. The EEOC in issuing its second set of guidelines, Congress in passing the PDA, and feminists in amicus briefs in *Gilbert* agreed. Under the PDA, employers may treat pregnant women as well or as badly as they do men who suffer temporary disabilities. The law does not require employers to grant women special rights to reinstatement, maternity leave, or medical benefits not available to other employees.

The dominance approach or equality as acceptance would recognize that employers have long denied women employment opportunities because they bear children, and that the way employment is organized assumes a male worker who is not primarily responsible for housework, child care, and care of the elderly. Under the dominance approach, the relevant inquiry would not be whether women are different than men but what women would need to make them equal competitors in the job market. Feminists would have to weigh the possibility that employers would (unlawfully) choose not to hire women if they were to receive additional benefits against the advantages of those benefits. The comparative approach leads feminists to argue that men and women are alike in all relevant respects and should not be treated differently. The dominance approach might allow for special treatment if that special treatment would help to lessen women's oppression.

A comparative approach is embedded in the statute and in judicial opinions, although the judiciary, like the feminist movement, does not speak with one voice. Remember, in *Gilbert*, the Supreme Court reversed five courts of appeals. The Supreme Court's approach in *Gilbert* establishes the characteristics men have as the norm, measures women's deviance from this standard, and penalizes women when they fail to conform. *Gilbert* and the PDA both employ the comparative approach. Both require that women be able to compare themselves to men. *Gilbert* found pregnant women's situation unique, while the PDA requires employers to compare pregnant women to men with disabilities. Because it found there to be relevant, real physical differences between men and women, in *Gilbert*, the Supreme Court concluded that treating men and women differently could not be discriminatory. Congress overruled that decision by requiring employers to compare pregnant women to a category of male workers, but guaranteed pregnant women only the right to compare themselves with these men rather than a meaningful package of protection.

The Supreme Court considered whether a state's attempt to guarantee pregnant workers broader protection than sick employees violated the Pregnancy Discrimination Act in a case that divided feminists into so-called special versus equal treatment camps. In *California Federal Savings and Loan v. Guerra*,[59] an employer challenged a California statute that mandated that employees disabled by pregnancy have a qualified right to reinstatement following childbirth. Lillian Garland filed a complaint with the California Department of Fair Employment and Housing when the California Savings and Loan Association did not reinstate her after childbirth. Before the hearing, Cal. Fed. sought an injunction against enforcement of the statute, claiming it was preempted by Title VII. Citing the opinion in *Newport Shipping and Dry Dock Co. v. EEOC*,[60] which held that the PDA forbids employers from treating pregnancy-related disabilities less favorably than other disabilities, the Supreme Court affirmed the Ninth Circuit's finding that, in enacting the PDA, Congress intended "to construct a floor beneath which pregnancy disability benefits may not drop—not a ceiling above which they may not rise."[61]

In its amicus brief, the National Organization for Women argued the language of the PDA forbade treating pregnancy differently than other disabilities, whether more or less favorably. Petitioners contended that, given the clear language of the PDA, no reference to the legislative history was necessary. Justice Marshall, writing for the Court, insisted that it "examine the PDA's language against the background of its legislative history and historical context."[62] The legislative history did not make explicit that Congress meant to prohibit the states from enacting such laws. Marshall noted the California statute, unlike protective legislation in the past, was not based on stereotypical notions about women. Instead, it offered a limited benefit to insure that pregnant women were not at a disadvantage in the workplace. The Court voted six to three that the California statute mandating reinstatement for women after childbirth did not violate the Pregnancy Discrimination Act.

Although *Gilbert* and *Cal. Fed.* concern different problems, what a state may legislate and what Congress has commanded private employers to do, the two cases reveal the Supreme Court's ideas about discrimination and differential treatment and show the impact of changes in Title VII. The Supreme

59. 479 U.S. 272 (1987).
60. 462 U.S. 669 (1983).
61. 758 F.2d 390, 396 (1985).
62. 479 U.S. 272, 284 (1987).

Court's holdings have moved from the position that employers may provide benefits to men only to a position that, to promote equality between the sexes, states may choose to confer rights only on women. Yet the Court has divided over the form of equality the Fourteenth Amendment requires, what Title VII's provisions against discrimination rule out, and when so-called preferential treatment may be lawful.[63]

British judges and members of tribunals see no clash between the guarantees of equality and the rights of pregnant women. British and EC statutes explicitly permit employers to grant pregnant women rights not available to other workers. Neither are British feminists divided over the desirability of the right to maternity leave. Britain has had paid maternity leave and a right to reinstatement for some time, although the Conservative Government has so reduced the guarantees under employment law that more women are turning to the Sex Discrimination Act for redress. Parliament did not react to *Turley v. Allders Department Store* (the British case ruling that discrimination on the basis of pregnancy was not discrimination on the basis of sex) the same way that Congress responded to *Gilbert*. The reasoning in *Turley* mirrors that in *Gilbert*, *Hayes v. Malleable Workingman's Club* mandates a similar outcome as the PDA, and *Dekker* is similar to *Cal. Fed.* Yet the Employment Appeal Tribunal decided *Hayes* some eight years after Congress passed the PDA, supporting the theory that, besides any other differences between the two systems, a time lag exists in decisions on discrimination, or perhaps the British tribunals, and even the European Court of Justice, are influenced by events in the United States. Although courts and tribunals took the same position in each country, albeit at different times, in the United States, feminist outrage over *Gilbert* brought about legislative changes and the courts then honored those changes. Although the British Employment Appeal Tribunal reinterpreted the Sex Discrimination Act to produce the same changes in the law, neither pressure groups nor Parliament had urged them to do so. In a climate of reduced employment rights, the only pressure to expand rights of pregnant women comes from the European Community.

Airline Cases

Litigation against airlines forms an interesting subgroup of pregnancy discrimination cases. The opinions display the same confusion or blurring of Title VII categories as cases on exclusionary policies. Furthermore, these cases raise some of the same questions about who is responsible for fetal

---

63. United Steelworkers of America v. Weber, 443 U.S. 193 (1979). See also Wygant v. Jackson Board of Education, 476 U.S. 267 (1986); Johnson v. Transportation Agency, Santa Clara County, 480 U.S. 616 (1987); United States v. Paradise, 480 U.S. 149 (1987); City of Richmond v. Croson, 488 U.S. 469 (1989).

safety as cases on exclusionary policies, because airlines occasionally claimed to ground flight attendants for their own good and maintained that a concern about a small minority of pregnant women justified grounding all of them.

The airline industry has been a frequent target for complaints of sex discrimination. Before Title VII, airlines barred men from jobs as flight attendants,[64] and discharged women when they married,[65] reached a certain age, wore eyeglasses, exceeded a designated weight, or became pregnant. One by one, the courts struck down these policies as discriminatory. Although women flight attendants challenged many aspects of the airlines' maternity policies, the most relevant for cases on exclusionary policies is the challenge to the policy of grounding or putting on medical leave all pregnant flight attendants immediately upon detecting the pregnancy. Federal trial and appellate courts that heard these cases disagreed about whether the policies violated Title VII. While some held that the airline policies were justified as either a bona fide occupational qualification or a business necessity,[66] two federal district courts and the Court of Appeals for the Fourth Circuit struck down blanket flying restrictions for pregnant flight attendants.[67]

Following the approach of the Supreme Court in *Roe v. Wade*,[68] the three courts divided pregnancy into trimesters. During the first trimester, all three held that, despite testimony about morning sickness and the chance of miscarriage, because pregnant flight attendants were able to perform the duties of the job, Title VII forbade airlines from grounding them. In the second trimester, two district courts held that the airlines were to judge the flight attendants' fitness for duty individually, while the Court of Appeals for the Fourth Circuit (with four judges dissenting) upheld the airline's policy of grounding flight attendants between the thirteenth and twenty-eighth weeks of pregnancy. In the third trimester, all courts agreed that airlines could ground pregnant flight attendants.

The first problem facing the courts in these cases was to determine the

---

64. Diaz v. Pan American World Airways, 442 F.2d 385 (5th Cir. 1971), *cert. denied* 404 U.S. 950 (1971).

65. Sprogis v. United Airlines, Inc., 444 F.2d 1194 (7th Cir. 1971).

66. Harriss v. Pan American World Airways, Inc., 437 F. Supp. 413 (N.D. Cal. 1977), 649 F.2d 670 (1980); Air Line Pilots Association et al. v. Western Air Lines, Inc., 22 Empl. Prac. Dec. (CCH) ¶30,636 (N.D. Cal. 1979), 722 F.2d 744 (9th Cir. 1983), *cert. denied* 465 U.S. 1101 (1984); EEOC v. Delta Air Lines, Inc., 441 F. Supp. 626 (S.D. Tex. 1977), 619 F.2d 81 (5th Cir. 1980), *cert. denied* 465 U.S. 1101 (1984); Condit v. United Airlines, Inc., 12 Empl. Prac. Dec. (CCH) ¶11,195 (E.D. Va. 1976), 558 F.2d 1176 (4th Cir. 1977), *cert. denied* 435 U.S. 934 (1978). In *In re National Airlines*, the district court commented on the likely confusion in the airline industry generated by these conflicting opinions (434 F. Supp. 249, 253 [S.D. Fla. 1977]).

67. Burwell v. Eastern Air Lines, Inc., 458 F. Supp. 474 (E.D. Va. 1978), 633 F.2d 361 (4th Cir. 1980), *cert. denied* 450 U.S. 965 (1981); Maclennan v. American Airlines, Inc., 440 F. Supp. 466 (E.D. Va. 1977); In re National Air Lines, Inc., 434 F. Supp. 249 (S.D. Fla. 1977).

68. 410 U.S. 113 (1973).

correct framework of analysis—whether claimants had proven a prima facie case of disparate treatment or disparate impact. Because all but one of the contested policies were litigated prior to passage of the Pregnancy Discrimination Act, all but two courts, with some grumbling,[69] cited both *Gilbert* and *Satty* as controlling and treated the policies as facially neutral, as disparate impact rather than disparate treatment. The courts relied on the benefits and burdens distinction as outlined in *Satty*, and, bolstered by the constitutional case of *LaFleur*,[70] concluded that the policies had a disparate impact because the effect of the policies was to deprive pregnant women of employment opportunities and, in some instances, medical benefits and seniority. *Gilbert* and *Satty* notwithstanding, two courts applied the rubric of disparate treatment.[71] They then looked to see if the airlines had proven BFOQ, the defense for disparate treatment, rather than business necessity, the defense for disparate impact.

Passage of the Pregnancy Discrimination Act did not end the confusion and conflict over the right way to apply Title VII to the airlines' policies. The district court in *Harriss v. Pan Am* held that, before the PDA, the correct analysis was disparate impact–business necessity, but after, only the defense of a BFOQ would apply.

The three courts that struck down part of the blanket restriction on pregnant women flying made different decisions on whether the airline had to prove BFOQ or business necessity, but that choice did not control the outcome. *Maclennan* held that the airline met neither the requirements of BFOQ nor the more lenient standard of business necessity for grounding pregnant flight attendants in the second trimester; *Burwell* held that such a policy was a business necessity. *In re National Airlines* held that during the second trimester, airlines must evaluate pregnant women's fitness individually, but grounding them at twenty weeks satisfied the requirements of a BFOQ. The courts

69. In *In re National Airlines*, the district court took issue with the Supreme Court's opinion in *Gilbert*, both in its finding that pregnancy discrimination was not sex discrimination and in its disregard for the EEOC's guidelines, which called for pregnancy to be treated like all other disabilities. Implying that it would have decided *Gilbert* differently, the district court argued EEOC's guidelines were due great deference because they were promulgated shortly after the passage of the 1972 amendments to Title VII (434 F. Supp. 249, 256–57 [1977]).

70. In Cleveland Board of Education v. LaFleur, 414 U.S. 632 (1974), the Supreme Court held that requiring a woman to begin maternity leave at a predetermined point in her pregnancy, without regard to her individual ability to work, constituted a violation of the due process clause of the Fourteenth Amendment.

71. Although the district court reluctantly accepted that *Gilbert* was controlling, because pregnancy is sex linked, because National's policy deprived females of their means of support during pregnancy, and because its policy impinged on all women's decisions as to when to become pregnant, the court flouted *Gilbert* and treated the case as a prima facie case of disparate treatment rather than disparate impact (434 F. Supp. 249, 258 [1977]). See also Maclennan v. American Airlines, Inc., 440 F. Supp. 466 (E.D. Va. 1977).

did not even agree that the choice of rubric made a significant difference. In *Burwell*, for example, the Court of Appeals for the Fourth Circuit suggested that the two defenses were roughly the same.

> It would seem, in such cases, that the judicial flexibility which has evolved in Title VII cases should permit the application of either theory and, except in race cases, either defense. . . .The potential for violations is so variable that the Supreme Court has simply devised new judicial tools for [the] analyzing of Title VII cases. It is significant that although the Court throughout Title VII opinions speaks in terms of disparate treatment, disparate impact, BFOQ, business necessity, etc., that it cites the same general principles of Title VII law in all types of cases.[72]

Although the courts disagreed about the significance of the difference between the two defenses, they all agreed that the central issue was whether there was evidence that pregnancy interfered with the woman's ability to perform her job and thus threatened the safety of the passengers. The U.S. District Court for the Eastern District of Virginia and the Court of Appeals for the Fourth Circuit dismissed the argument that the airlines' concern for fetal health might create a business necessity defense, the latter stating: "in the area of civil rights, *personal risk decisions not affecting business operations are best left to individuals who are the targets of discrimination*."[73] The U.S. District Court for the Southern District of Florida noted that no fetal anomalies had occurred as a result of Northwest Airlines' policy of allowing pregnant flight attendants to fly. (At that time, all trunk airlines except Northwest grounded pregnant flight attendants.)[74]

> The question of harm to the fetus is basically a decision to be made not by this court, but *by the mother of the fetus.* . . . The key question posed by the issue of cabin altitude is whether it adversely affects the work performance of flight attendants so that her capability to discharge her safety responsibilities is impaired.[75]

One can only speculate why the courts found the employers' concern for fetal health unpersuasive, particularly since other courts found the opposite in exclusionary cases (see chap. 6).[76] Clearly, the thrust of the two defenses was

---

72. 633 F.2d 361, 370 n.16 (1980).

73. Ibid., 371; italics added.

74. 434 F. Supp. 249, 252 (1977).

75. Ibid., 261; italics added.

76. The companies may not have pushed this point because to do so would be to discourage pregnant women from flying.

that the issue is the individual's ability to perform the job—as established in *Weeks* and reiterated in the EEOC's guidelines. Perhaps the courts were impressed by Northwest Airlines' experience flying with pregnant flight attendants or found the medical evidence unconvincing. Plaintiffs had countered in one case that a concern for fetal safety and the safety of passengers was a thin cover for a concern about customer preference.[77] Pregnant flight attendants do not exude the "Fly Me" image of glamour and sexual availability deemed so essential to selling tickets. On the other hand, while one may not readily take to the image of extremely pregnant women circling on luggage carousals, the job is female dominated. There is nothing shocking or anomalous about women holding those jobs; women do not look out of place, even if pregnant women might. Another possibility is that counsel gave little emphasis to the arguments concerning fetal health. Because the airline tried to justify its policy through a concern for passenger safety and not fetal health, the court may have responded accordingly.

Whatever standard the courts ultimately adopted, and despite their disagreement over the facts, they did give the policies careful scrutiny. The U.S. District Court for the Eastern District of Virginia commented:

> the incantation of a safety rationale is not an abracadabra to which this Court must defer judgment. The defendant must prove that the policy is reasonably necessary, not merely that it is "reasonable," as the defendant apparently contends.[78]

The Ninth Circuit agreed that it must go beyond finding the policy reasonable, finding it reasonably necessary and faulted the lower court for failing to apply this high standard.[79]

Challenges to the airlines' policies on pregnancy forced courts to consider the legality of excluding pregnant women from certain jobs. The conflict and confusion over which Title VII framework to apply as well as the disagreement over the significance of the difference between the defenses of BFOQ and business necessity reappear in cases on exclusionary policies. Only two courts directly addressed the question of whether employers can justify excluding women out of concern for fetal health, concluding that they may not. Judges recognized the importance of passenger safety, yet carefully scrutinized the medical evidence. Some concluded that, in the second trimester, employers must treat pregnant women as individuals. Judges' careful scrutiny of scientific evidence shows a commitment to enforcing the goals of

---

77. See Levin v. Delta Airlines, 730 F.2d 994 (5th Cir. 1984), as discussed in J. Ralph Lindgren and Nadine Taub, *The Law of Sex Discrimination* (St. Paul: West, 1988), 140–42.

78. Maclennan v. American Airlines, Inc., 440 F. Supp. 466, 472 (E.D. Va. 1977).

79. Harriss v. Pan Am, 649 F.2d 670, 677 (9th Cir. 1980).

Title VII that contrasts with the behavior of British judges and members of tribunals in the cases considered in chapter 5.

Manhart

Pregnant flight attendants are different than their nonpregnant co-workers, male and female, and airlines may ground them at certain stages of pregnancy. The cases turned on at what stage in pregnancy pregnant flight attendants are no longer comparable to their nonpregnant co-workers in their ability to perform their jobs safely. In *Dothard*, because women were different than men, allegedly more likely to provoke attacks, employers could lawfully bar them from jobs. In passing the PDA, Congress amended Title VII to require that employers treat pregnant women like others with temporary disabilities, adopting a comparative approach. In *Cal. Fed.*, however, the Court upheld a state law that said under some circumstances employers must treat pregnant women better than disabled employees. In these cases, the "fact" that men and women were different was not disputed, although the significance attached to the differences, and whether they justified less favorable treatment, were.

City of Los Angeles Department of Water and Power v. Manhart[80] raised the question of whether employers could treat individual men and women employees differently on the basis of true differences between the two groups. Women employees at the Los Angeles Department of Water and Power contended that the department's policy of requiring women employees to make greater contributions to the pension fund than men violated Title VII. The department tried to justify its policy by pointing out that women, as a class, live longer than men, as a class, and claimed that the policy discriminated on the basis of longevity, not sex, just as the policy at issue in *Gilbert* discriminated on the basis of pregnancy, not sex. Because women live longer on average than men, they receive more pension benefits, therefore, the department argued, the policy did not disadvantage them.

Although the basis of the differential treatment, differences in longevity, was a "true" one, that is, the employer was acting on the basis of "real" rather than stereotypical differences, the Court held that the department discriminated against women on the basis of sex. In this case, however, the "real" rather than stereotypical difference was true for the group. The Court interpreted Title VII as requiring fairness to *individuals* and prohibiting the treatment of all women as if they share the characteristics of the class.

The statute's focus on the individual is unambiguous. It precludes treatment of individuals as simply components of a racial, religious, sexual,

---

80. 435 U.S. 702 (1977).

or national class. . . . Even a true generalization about the class is an insufficient reason for disqualifying an individual to whom the generalization does not apply. . . .Practices that classify employees in terms of religion, race, or sex tend to preserve traditional assumptions about groups rather than thoughtful scrutiny of individuals.[81]

In *Manhart*, unlike *Gilbert*, the Court agreed with the EEOC's guidelines. The justices distinguished *Manhart* from *Gilbert* by saying that the basis of the classification in *Gilbert* was pregnancy, not sex. Under the department's policy, however, all women had to pay more than all men, therefore the policy was discriminatory. Despite protestations to the contrary, the Court in *Manhart* moved away from its reasoning in *Gilbert*.[82]

The justices disagreed about how to determine congressional intent in interpreting Title VII. The majority held that unless Congress explicitly exempted sex-based actuarial tables, the plain words of the statute prohibited such a policy.

We conclude that Senator Humphrey's isolated comment on the Senate floor [that sex-based actuarial tables would not be prohibited] cannot change the effect of the plain language of the statute itself.[83]

The minority would have read the general language of the statute as not overturning this established practice; instead, they would have found the use of sex-based actuarial tables legal unless the statute explicitly prohibited them.

The justices also differed in their recognition of the harm of sex discrimination. Some were suspicious of sex-based categories while others were inclined to see them as reasonable. Some maintained there has been a long history of oppression against women equal in severity to discrimination against racial minorities. These views influence how they interpret Title VII and the Fourteenth Amendment. In *Manhart*, the dissenters appeared to call for a "reasonable" test for when sex discrimination should be prohibited. In this case, because the practice had been longstanding, because the difference between men and women was a true one, and because of a perceived lack of harm to women who may receive more benefits than men, the minority saw the policy as reasonable. They refused to recognize the distinction as discrimi-

---

81. 435 U.S. 702, 708–9 (1977).

82. "I therefore must conclude that today's decision cuts back on *General Electric*, and inferentially on *Geduldig*, the reasoning of which was adopted there, and, indeed, makes the recognition of those cases as continuing precedent somewhat questionable" (Opinion of Chief Justice Burger, 435 U.S. 702, 725 [1977]).

83. 435 U.S. 702, 714 (1977).

nation, that is, according to the minority's definition, unjustified or unreasonable differentiation.

Manhart is now most cited for the proposition that cost concerns do not answer proven cases of disparate treatment (although the justices argue about whether this is a correct interpretation in *UAW v. Johnson Controls*). Los Angeles was using a facially discriminatory classification: every woman employee paid more than every man. The only defense for disparate treatment is BFOQ. The danger of the holding, rightly regarded as a major feminist victory, is that, in focusing on an individual's right to nondiscrimination, the underlying assumptions go unchallenged. Individuals who can meet the male standard and who are not "really different" than men win the same rights and privileges as men. The rest do not. The same implied male standard, comparative approach, and acceptance of difference as a justification for disadvantage appear in constitutional cases.

Constitutional Cases

The preceding sections make clear that not all judges in the United States share a common conception of discrimination. Differences over the definition of discrimination and the role of the judiciary in prohibiting it are also evident in cases alleging violations of the Fourteenth Amendment's guarantee of equal protection of the laws. Judges disagree more about how to apply the equal protection clause to sex discrimination than they do about how to interpret Title VII. Judges' views about the nature and extent of sex discrimination, their more general views on the Constitution's protection of individual rights, and their position on whether the Constitution changes over time all play a part in their decisions.

Drafters of the Thirteenth, Fourteenth, and Fifteenth Amendments were especially concerned about discrimination on the basis of race. Although nothing in the wording of the Fourteenth Amendment's guarantee of equal protection of the laws suggests that it disfavors only racial classifications, the Supreme Court did not hold that the equal protection clause prohibited states from drawing some distinctions based on sex until 1971. What had changed between passage of the Fourteenth Amendment and 1971 was society's awareness of the extent and harm of women's oppression and growing pressure to end it.

The guiding principle for interpreting the equal protection clause in 1971 was that the Court would defer to legislative distinctions among citizens as long as those distinctions were rationally related to a legitimate governmental purpose, the so-called rational basis test. When states violated fundamental rights or used suspect classifications, however, the Court applied strict scrutiny, requiring states to prove a necessary relationship to a compelling state interest. The only suspect categories that activated this higher level of scrutiny were race and national origin. Susan Deller Ross and Ann Barcher describe this distinction in operation.

> In the past, the Supreme Court's decision about which test to apply has almost invariably determined the outcome of the case. If it used the "reasonableness" test [rational basis], the state law was valid. If it used the "strict scrutiny" test, the law was invalid.[84]

Before 1971, whenever the Supreme Court applied the rational basis test to classifications based on sex, it always found them to be constitutional. In *Reed v. Reed*,[85] however, the Supreme Court held that an Idaho statute that favored males over females as estate administrators violated the equal protection clause because it provided dissimilar treatment for men and women who were similarly situated.

In *Sail'er Inn, Inc. v. Kirby*,[86] the California Supreme Court also held that a sex-based classification, a prohibition on women tending bar, violated the Fourteenth Amendment. The California Supreme Court went further than the U.S. Supreme Court and declared that because sex, like race, was an immutable trait that frequently bore no relation to an individual's ability to contribute to society, and because classifications on the basis of sex relegate a whole class of persons to an inferior status, sex, like race, should be a suspect category subject to strict scrutiny.

Reed signaled that the Court would no longer automatically find sex-based classifications constitutional; however, a majority of the Court was unwilling to imitate the California Supreme Court and declare sex a suspect classification, the position a plurality of four pressed for in *Frontiero v. Richardson*.[87] Between those justices who favored making sex a suspect classification and those who believed that many sex-based classifications passed the rational basis test stood Justices Powell, Blackmun, and Burger. Justice Powell wrote that, because the country was considering ratification of the Equal Rights Amendment to prohibit sex-based classifications, the Court should not preempt the democratic process by declaring sex to be a suspect category. The three justices did, however, agree that allotting military benefits differently for men and women, the issue in *Frontiero*, was unconstitutional; but they preferred to hold merely, as the Court had in *Reed*, that the classification did not pass the rational basis test.

---

84. Susan Deller Ross and Ann Barcher, *The Rights of Women* (New York: Bantam, 1983), 8.

85. 404 U.S. 71 (1971).

86. 95 Cal.Rptr. 329 (1971).

87. 411 U.S. 677 (1973).

At the same time the Court was reconsidering its jurisprudence on equal protection and sex-based classifications, it greatly expanded the constitutional right to privacy established in *Griswold v. Connecticut*.[88] In its landmark decision, *Roe v. Wade*, the Supreme Court held that the constitutional right to privacy left the choice of whether to have an abortion between a woman and her physician in the first trimester of pregnancy. During the second trimester, states could regulate abortions to protect the health of the mother, and in the third trimester, states could regulate abortions in order to protect potential life. The Court's decision rendered unconstitutional the abortion restrictions of many states that banned or severely restricted abortion. Although feminists considered *Roe* a major victory for women's rights, the Court's decision to locate the woman's right to an abortion in the constitutional right to privacy, rather than equality, reflected not only the limited nature of women's constitutional right to equal protection at that time but also, more importantly, how the Court conceptualized women's constitutional rights.[89]

It was not until 1976, in *Craig v. Boren*,[90] that the Court explicitly abandoned the rational basis test for sex-based classifications. In *Craig*, however, the Court did not make sex a suspect category but, instead, created an intermediate tier of scrutiny. For a sex-based classification to survive this heightened scrutiny it would have to meet two requirements: the governmental objective would have to be an important one, and the classification would have to be substantially related to the achievement of that objective. A minority of the Court, led by Justice Rehnquist, objected to the creation of this third tier.

> The Court's conclusion that a law which treats males less favorably than females "must serve important governmental objectives and must be substantially related to achievement of those objectives" apparently comes out of thin air. The Equal Protection Clause contains no such language, and none of our previous cases adopt that standard. . . . Both of the phrases used are so diaphanous and elastic as to invite subjective judicial preferences or prejudices relating to particular types of legislation, masquerading as judgments whether such legislation is directed at "important" objectives or, whether the relationship to those objectives is "substantial" enough.[91]

---

88. 381 U.S. 479 (1965).

89. See Sylvia A. Law, "Rethinking Sex and the Constitution," *University of Pennsylvania Law Review* 132 (1984): 955–1040.

90. 429 U.S. 190 (1976).

91. Ibid., 220–21.

Although the Fourteenth Amendment sweeps beyond the employment arena, its prohibition encompasses only state and not private action. What the Supreme Court determined the equal protection clause to prohibit and what it has interpreted Title VII to prohibit differ significantly. For example, the Court did not find that the Fourteenth Amendment prohibited states from passing neutral laws that had a disproportionate impact on a protected group, unless plaintiffs could prove a discriminatory intent. In *Washington v. Davis*,[92] the Court declared:

> even if a neutral law has disproportionately adverse effect upon a racial minority, it is unconstitutional under the Equal Protection Clause only if that impact can be traced to a discriminatory purpose.[93]

Griggs, however, held that Title VII prohibited private employers from using such rules unless they were justified by a business necessity. The Court found that Title VII provides more explicit prohibitions against discrimination and reaches further than the Fourteenth Amendment.

In *Personnel Administrator of Massachusetts v. Feeney*, the Court applied *Washington v. Davis* to a case in which a state law giving preferences in hiring to veterans had a disparate impact on women. The justices refused to strike down the statute because it was not motivated by a discriminatory purpose, though the preference significantly reduced women's employment opportunities. The Court commented, "the Fourteenth Amendment guarantees equal laws, not equal results."[94] *Feeney* not only held that the preference was not motivated by a desire to discriminate, but also found that the preference was not a sex-based classification because both men and women were veterans and nonveterans.

Cases that directly challenge the most fundamental societal views about sex differences—differences in sexuality, reproduction, and participation in combat—reveal the limitations on the Constitution's guarantee of equality, as interpreted by the Supreme Court.

> This model [the intermediate tier] has one main exception. It does not apply where the Court perceives what it believes to be "real differences" between the sexes. In those situations, the deferential, rational relations standard is applied.[95]

---

92. 426 U.S. 229 (1976).

93. As discussed in Personnel Administrator of Mass. v. Feeney, 442 U.S. 256, 272 (1979).

94. Ibid., 273.

95. Lindgren and Taub, 74.

Michael M. v. Superior Court upheld California's law on statutory rape,[96] which made it unlawful for a man to have sex with a woman under eighteen who was not his wife. Justice Rehnquist's plurality opinion held that the state, in pursuing the laudable goal of reducing the incidence of teenage pregnancy, could punish men to deter them from sexual intercourse with minors.[97] Because the risk of pregnancy was enough to deter women, the state could choose not to punish them as well. Justice Rehnquist, who opposed the creation of the intermediate tier in *Craig*, did not explicitly address the degree of scrutiny for sex-based classifications, noting only that the rational basis test takes on a "sharper focus" when the Court applies it to gender-based classifications.

Justice Brennan, in a dissenting opinion Justices Marshall and White joined, maintained that California must do more than merely point to physical differences between the sexes to justify a sex-based classification. The state must show that a sex-neutral law (which it had for other sexual offenses) would be difficult to enforce and would not be a greater deterrent. Justice Brennan noted that the California legislature initially wrote and recently defended its law on statutory rape with the premise that only young men, and not young women, can consent to sexual intercourse. The law, he said, furthered "outmoded sexual stereotypes." Legal scholars suggested that the difference between men and women that was the basis for the statute was cultural, not physical: men initiate sexual contact and are held responsible for the consequences of extramarital sexual intercourse.[98]

In *Rostker v. Goldberg*, the Court refused to declare unconstitutional a male-only registration for the draft. The justices gave great deference to the decision of Congress not to include women (Congress had explicitly addressed the question) because it was a military matter. Justice Rehnquist, writing for the majority, held that, because Congress had excluded women from holding combat positions, it could require only men to register for the draft once it had determined that any draft would be characterized by a need for combat troops. Justice Marshall, dissenting, argued that the Court had not applied sufficiently exacting scrutiny and that, by excluding women from a basic civil obligation, the Court placed its "imprimatur on one of the most potent remaining public expressions of 'ancient canards about the proper role of women.'"[99]

Dothard showed when the Court believed sex differences might justify excluding women from work under Title VII. Similarly, *Rostker* and *Michael*

---

96. Michael M. v. Superior Court of Sonoma County, 450 U.S. 464 (1981).

97. Justice Rehnquist was joined by Chief Justice Burger and Justices Stewart and Powell; Justice Blackmun concurred in the judgment.

98. Lindgren and Taub, 78.

99. 453 U.S. 57, 86 (1981).

M. show the limits the Court will interpret the Constitution as placing on formal legal equality for men and women. The opinions also reveal how justices think about sex differences and discrimination, and what they believe to be the judiciary's role in dismantling oppressive practices.

> The Court is willing to permit laws that treat men and women differently if they are based on any difference between the sexes, provided that those differences appear valid to a majority of the justices. . . . First, is there an objective and logically consistent basis for distinguishing between those differences between the sexes that are "real" and those that are not, or does that distinction depend solely upon the "life experiences" of those individuals that become justices? Second, if there is such a basis, is that basis itself rooted in outmoded cultural stereotypes?[100]

Although the Court has struck down some sex-based categories, it is only willing (and able) to go so far in challenging widely held views on sex equality and sexual difference. The limitations of the Court's interpretations notwithstanding, the Fourteenth Amendment has been a fruitful avenue for women to use to begin to break down some legal distinctions between the sexes, particularly in the 1970s.[101] As such, it has no real British counterpart, apart from article 119 of the Treaty of Rome, which covers employment only.

The Equal Employment Opportunity Commission

No account of sex discrimination law in the United States is complete without an analysis of how the enforcement agency Title VII created, the Equal Employment Opportunity Commission, has defined the law, helped to implement it, and shaped doctrine. Nor is any comparison of British and U.S. sex discrimination law complete without comparing the two enforcement agencies. As discussions in chapters 5 and 6 show, both enforcement agencies played a part not only in litigation on exclusionary policies but also in shaping policy on that issue.

Considering the source of the amendment adding discrimination on the basis of sex to the civil rights bill and the absence of legislative history, it is not surprising that the first chairman of the EEOC did not see sex discrimination as part of the agency's brief and allotted it a low priority.[102] At first, only 25 percent of the complaints received by the agency were about sex discrimi-

---

100. Lindgren and Taub, 80.
101. See Jane J. Mansbridge, *Why We Lost the ERA* (Chicago: University of Chicago Press, 1986), 45–59.
102. Meehan, *Women's Rights at Work*, 99.

nation.[103] Following the settlement of claims of sex discrimination for large sums against AT&T ($38 million) and General Electric, the EEOC, urged by feminist groups, joined a growing section of the population in its belief that sex discrimination was a serious problem.[104] Feminist pressure groups and the EEOC made Title VII into a "magna carta for female workers."[105]

The British EOC never faced this problem of competing protected groups (nor accrued the benefits of cooperation) because a separate agency, the Commission for Racial Equality, handles race discrimination. Neither does the EOC have to evaluate the fair employment practice laws of states or work with state agencies. Because the United Kingdom is not a federal system, the national government does not share power. While coordination may be a problem, the EEOC does benefit from sharing the workload with state agencies and could benefit even more from a division of labor.[106] In practice, however, because the EEOC pays state agencies according to the number of cases they complete, the current arrangement may provide a financial incentive for state agencies to find that no discrimination has occurred and to close case prematurely, without a full investigation.[107] Furthermore, the EEOC's ability to monitor the quality of state agencies' reviews has diminished because the unit that performed this task has been abolished, and, in 1987, the job was being done by one person.[108]

The criticisms of the EEOC's oversight of and incentives for state agencies illustrate an important point about the EEOC's implementation of Title VII. The agency, like all governmental agencies in the United States, is profoundly affected by who the president appoints as chairman and commissioners as well as the overall philosophy of the administration on civil rights. A president such as Carter, who was committed to equal employment opportunity, can bring in someone to activate the agency. The laws are not self-enforcing, nor is the agency immune to steering from the top. While the EOC crawls along making slow but steady progress, the EEOC may gallop ahead or

103. Vicky Randall, *Women and Politics* (London: Macmillan, 1982), 189; see Jo Freeman, *The Politics of Women's Liberation: A Case Study of an Emerging Social Movement and its Relation to the Policy Process* (New York: MacKay, 1975).

104. Meehan, *Women's Rights at Work*, 100.

105. Donald Allen Robinson, "Two Movements in Pursuit of Equal Employment Opportunity," *Signs* 4 (Spring 1979): 427.

106. Title VII mandates that the EEOC give some deference to State Fair Employment Practice laws, as long as they are not in conflict with Title VII, and the EEOC works out a work-sharing arrangement with state offices. Section 706 requires that before a charge may be filed with the EEOC, it must first be filed for sixty days with the state or local fair employment practices agency.

107. Herbert Hill, "The Equal Employment Opportunities Commission: Twenty Years Later," *Journal of Intergroup Relations* 11 (Winter 1983): 55.

108. Terri Schroeder, Legislative Assistant for the House Education and Labor Committee, interview with author, Washington, D.C., July 23, 1987.

stop dead in its tracks, depending on the political appointments to the agency. One commentator reflected on the effect of the Reagan administration on the agency.

> Its boldness has been curtailed as much of the substance given to the law has been whittled, and sometimes stripped, away as a result of the permeation into all corners of the right wing coalition that put President Reagan into office.[109]

While we can make overall observations about the EEOC's twenty-eight-year record, it is important to keep in mind which administration was in power during successive developments.

Some members of Congress initially proposed making the EEOC a strong enforcement body, similar to the National Labor Relations Board, by giving it the power to issue cease and desist orders. Congress chose, instead, to make the agency's primary focus conciliation, vesting the attorney general with the power to bring "pattern and practice" cases. Partly because of civil rights groups' dissatisfaction with the Justice Department's enforcement record,[110] in 1972, Congress transferred enforcement powers to the EEOC, expanding the powers of the general counsel to supervise a staff of lawyers, bring cases, and submit amicus briefs.

This action reflects the tendency in the United States to resolve disputes through the courts. Yet giving the agency the power to initiate legal action, when combined with the then sympathetic response of some courts, has made the EEOC more effective than its British equivalent in securing compliance and obtaining relief. Ironically, although Roy Jenkins (Labour Home Secretary) thought he was setting up a more vigorous enforcement agency with strong powers to issue codes of practice and nondiscrimination notices, in practice the EEOC has often been the more aggressive enforcement agency while the EOC has been more conciliatory.

Both agencies, however, draw criticism for their conciliatory approach. The legislative creation and funding of a legal branch of the EEOC in 1972 stands in sharp contrast to the British Home Office's cap on the number of lawyers the EOC may hire, clearly showing the different emphases the two political systems place on government-sponsored litigation. While the EEOC has been a more active litigator than the EOC, it has not dominated the legal scene, bringing only 7 percent of all Title VII cases.[111] The British EOC has been very successful with litigation before the European Court of Justice.

---

109. Meehan, *Women's Rights at Work*, 101.
110. Ibid., 127.
111. Hill, 52.

Critics, moreover, argue that the EEOC needs to become a stronger enforcement agency rather than a bureau to process complaints.[112]

Congress did not give the EEOC the power to issue substantive regulations carrying the weight of law, but Parliament delegated to the EOC the power to issue codes of practice that do have the force of law. Yet again, in practice, the EEOC has outshone the EOC in issuing guidelines that, on the whole, the courts have favorably received.[113] Not only has the EEOC produced more guidelines than the EOC, but on the subjects of protective legislation, discrimination because of pregnancy, insurance premiums, sexual harassment, affirmative action, and, after much controversy and delay, exclusionary policies, the EEOC has advanced the feminist agenda and Congress and the courts have eventually adopted its positions. It is fair to say that, while many criticize its implementation of Title VII, the EEOC has developed policies favored by the civil rights community.[114]

In addition to bringing suits and issuing guidelines, the EEOC has intervened in important discrimination cases as amicus,[115] trying to shape the development of precedent.[116] In contrast, participation as amicus curiae is so rare in Britain that when the EEOC's equivalent, the EOC, intervened in one case,[117] the British Employment Appeal Tribunal felt obliged to justify why it had allowed the agency to participate. Unlike the EEOC, which has clearly advocated for its own interpretation of the law, the EOC adopted a posture of distance from the case, aiming at "objectivity" rather than advocacy.

In addition to bringing individual cases, issuing guidelines and intervening in cases as amicus, the EEOC can bring class action suits, something that has no counterpart in British law. In fact, the EEOC does not even have to fulfill the requirements of a class action to bring a systemic action of discrimination.[118] It has a special unit to monitor and develop systemic actions. Under the Reagan administration, filings of such systemic cases declined.[119] In fact,

---

112. Ibid., 48.

113. U.S. Commission on Civil Rights, *Federal Enforcement of Equal Employment Requirements: The Equal Employment Opportunities Commission* (Washington, D.C.: U.S. Government Printing Office, 1987), 15–16.

114. But see Commission on Civil Rights, 33, on the EEOC's policy on comparable worth.

115. Commission on Civil Rights, 94. The number of amicus briefs, however, dropped from 89 in 1980 and 61 in 1981, to 16 in 1985 and 26 in 1986.

116. See Karen O'Connor, *Women's Organizations' Use of the Courts* (Lexington, Mass.: Lexington Books, 1980); Jane Beard and Marcia D. Greenberger, "Women and the Law," in *Women in Washington: Advocates for Public Policy*, ed. by Irene Tinker (Beverly Hills: Sage, 1983), 165–76; Margaret A. Berger, *Litigation on Behalf of Women: A Review for the Ford Foundation* (New York: Ford Foundation, 1980).

117. Page v. Freight Hire (Tank Haulage) Co. Ltd., [1981] IRLR 13 (EAT).

118. Schlei and Grossman, 1149; see also General Telephone Co. of the Northwest, Inc. v. EEOC, 446 U.S. 318 (1980).

119. B. Dan Wood, "Does Politics Make a Difference at the EEOC?" *American Journal of Political Science* 34 (May 1990): 525 n.22.

the Reagan administration and Chairman Clarence Thomas believed that only identifiable victims of discrimination should win relief. It saw the EEOC's function as one of processing individual claims rather than attacking institutional discrimination and pursuing the large offenders.

Although on the whole it compares favorably to the EOC,[120] the EEOC has had, and continues to have, serious difficulties, and "disappointment with its performance has been widespread."[121] Managerial problems have plagued the agency. Title VII granted the agency a year to prepare for complaints before the law took effect, but because the president did not make timely appointments, the agency was not prepared to deal with cases when Title VII became effective.[122] Since then, a turnover of staff and of directors has hurt the agency, leading one commentator to refer to the "revolving door nature of the Director's position."[123]

Yet the biggest problem has been the backlog of cases. Director Eleanor Holmes Norton reorganized the EEOC and established a rapid charge-processing unit to reduce that backlog, emphasizing a quick settlement before an investigation.[124] The EEOC abandoned its past practice of seeking to broaden most charges.[125] In addition, the Commission delegated to district directors authority to issue letters of determination when a precedent (called "Commission decision precedent" or CDP) exists. Cases that are "non-CDP" are subject to even longer delays than other cases.[126]

Rapid processing was a mixed blessing. While complainants benefited from the EEOC's investigating their cases quickly, the desire to reduce the enormous backlog put pressure on all staff to conciliate, close cases without a full investigation, and not to look for patterns of discrimination. Although the EEOC did reduce the backlog, the many new cases means that equal opportunity specialists are under pressure to "get the numbers up" and to close cases administratively or find "no cause" on the basis of a perfunctory investiga-

---

120. "Implementation, in the sense of actions taken to apply the legislation, has been more vigorous [in the United States] although it is difficult to estimate the ultimate effects on women's lives" (Randall, 187).

121. Meehan, *Women's Rights at Work*, 99.

122. Schlei and Grossman, 933.

123. Hill, 50. "Only one of the five EEOC Commissioners first appointed was a woman, a black who resigned after a year because of the Commission's lack of interest in helping women" (Randall, 189).

124. Peggy Lamson, "Eleanor Holmes Norton Reforms the Equal Employment Opportunities Commission," in *Women Leaders in American Politics*, ed. by James David Barber and Barbara Kellerman (Englewood Cliffs, N.J.: Prentice-Hall, 1986), 340–44. Rapid charge-processing is no longer used.

125. That is, to see if the complainant has been discriminated against in other ways beyond what is complained about or if other employees in the same company have suffered discrimination.

126. Section 1601.21(d); see Schlei and Grossman, 964.

tion.[127] While the British EOC may avoid formal investigations and avoid litigating cases because of a conscious philosophy favoring conciliation over confrontation, the EEOC's preference for settling cases rather than litigating is a pragmatic response to the number of complaints and limited resources. Settling may not always be in the best interests of complainants. Because of pressure from the civil rights community, in September, 1984, the EEOC claimed that it would put increasing emphasis on litigation.[128]

Critics in Congress and the civil rights community focused both on the policies of the Reagan administration on equal employment opportunity in general and the management and performance of the EEOC in particular. While the Department of Justice was trying to dismantle affirmative action and rescind Executive Order 11246, EEOC Chairman Clarence Thomas was similarly questioning some important policies.[129] The General Counsel ordered EEOC attorneys not to use goals and timetables in consent decrees and restricted class actions to cases with "identified victims." The agency adopted a higher standard of proof for what constituted reasonable cause, downgraded many equal opportunity specialists, and instructed staff to close out cases without investigation to get the numbers of completed reviews up and the backlog down. Training at the agency came to a standstill and morale plummeted.[130]

Differences between the two legal and political systems account for some of the differences in the performance of the EEOC and the EOC. The EEOC, until late in the 1980s, faced a more supportive judiciary. The agency benefited from the convention of permitting amicus participation and the ability to file class actions. The different styles and strategies of the agencies also reflect differences between the civil services. The U.S. civil service is more politicized, both in the sense of being more partisan as well as seeing itself as an advocate of interests, rather than being above the fray. British civil servants

---

127. See U.S. General Accounting Office, *Equal Employment Opportunity: EEOC Birmingham Office Closed Discrimination Charges Without Full Investigation*, Report to Congressional Requesters, June 1987.

128. Commission on Civil Rights, 41.

129. Ibid., 35.

130. For a thorough and damaging investigative report on the EEOC, see House Committee on Education and Labor, *Civil Rights Enforcement by the EEOC*, Staff Rep. See House Subcommittee on Employment Opportunities of the Committee on Education and Labor, *Oversight Hearings on the Federal Enforcement of Equal Employment Opportunity Laws*, 98th Cong., 1st sess., 1983; House Subcommittee on Employment Opportunities of the Committee on Education and Labor, *Oversight Hearing on EEOC's Proposed Modification of Enforcement Regulations, Including Uniform Guidelines on Employee Selection Procedures*, 99th Cong., 1st sess., 1985; House Subcommittee on Employment Opportunities of the Committee on Education and Labor, *Hearings on Equal Employment Opportunity Commission Policies Regarding Goals and Timetables in Litigation Remedies*, 99th Cong., 2d sess., 1986.

are not drawn from interest groups, do not move in and out of government, and are not specialists in the area they are currently working. Because strong and committed people such as Eleanor Holmes Norton have occasionally headed the EEOC, it has greater potential to promote change, although that potential is not always realized. It is difficult to tell whether changes in the party in power would lead to changes in the EOC in Britain, because the Conservatives have been in office except the first four years of the agency's existence, and both Labour and the Trades Union Congress record of appointments to the agency is mixed. Two additional factors that affect the EOC and the EEOC deserve closer analysis: the role of legislative oversight and interaction with pressure groups.

Congress, the Civil Rights Commission, and outside groups monitor the EEOC, while only the Home Office seems to monitor the EOC. Congressional interest in the agency is contingent upon the views of individual members in important oversight and budget positions. As Chairman of the House Subcommittee on Employment Opportunities and then as Chairman of the House Education and Labor Committee, Augustus F. Hawkins took an active interest in equal employment opportunity and held many oversight hearings and issued committee reports on the performance of both the EEOC and the Office of Federal Contracts Compliance Programs. Despite dramatic changes in the philosophy of the Civil Rights Commission in 1981, in 1986 it began the task its predecessors performed of monitoring the enforcement of civil rights by the federal government.

Several pressure groups monitor the EEOC, propose appointments, and lobby for changes. The degree of interaction between the EEOC and interest groups is very different from that which occurs in Britain,[131] and it is consistent with the general differences between the two countries' bureaucracies. While civil rights groups have complained that the EEOC is merely a bureau to process complaints, companies have protested that the EEOC is too much of an advocate for plaintiffs. The courts have upheld the EEOC's role as advocate.[132] Courts have also commented that the EEOC brings suit in the public interest and not merely to vindicate private rights.[133] In addition, the Supreme Court has upheld the EEOC's authority to show its investigative file to the charging party, even over objections from the employer.[134] Thus, the courts have upheld the role for the EEOC that civil rights groups want—the

---

131. See Schlei and Grossman, 947, 967.

132. In an early case against Sears, company attorneys alleged that the EEOC was too closely involved with NOW (Meehan, 126). See also *Wright v. Olin* in chap. 6.

133. EEOC v. Associated Dry Goods Corp., 449 U.S. 590 (1981).

134. "When the EEOC acts, albeit at the behest of and for the benefit of specific individuals, it acts also to vindicate the public interest in preventing employment discrimination" (General Telephone Co. of the Northwest, Inc. v. EEOC, 446 U.S. 318, 326 [1980]).

EEOC as an active force to fight discrimination rather than a neutral and detached arbiter of disputes.

In the late 1960s, shortly after Congress created the EEOC, staff encouraged the formation and efforts of feminist groups, which then lobbied the agency. Staff who saw the EEOC giving nearly all its attention to racial discrimination actively encouraged women to file claims of sex discrimination. In fact, it was the lack of importance the agency initially attached to sex discrimination that precipitated the formation of the National Organization for Women.[135] This interaction between pressure groups and enforcement agencies has been absent in Britain.

> Britain has failed to evolve the kind of policy network between feminists inside government and women's organisations outside that has become so conspicuous in the United States since the mid-1960s. This is partly because of the different administrative styles of the implementing agencies. But it is also due to the absence of a substantial contingent of reformist feminists in the British women's movement.[136]

Even something as simple as the availability of information separates the two agencies, although it is consistent with the politics of secrecy surrounding the British state. The British equivalent of *Ms.*, *Spare Rib*, rarely includes any information on the EOC, although there was more coverage in the 1970s. Not all industrial tribunal decisions are reported. Since Parliament does not confirm the appointment of commissioners or chairmen, there is no public opportunity to debate the performance or mission of the agency. Although there is no British equivalent of the *Daily Labor Reports*, *The Equal Opportunities Review* and *Women's Legal Defense Fund Bulletin* have emerged to try to bridge the information gap. The absence of information about the British EOC impedes effective interaction with the public and interest groups, although it may well be the objective of the agency to keep a low profile.

Contract Compliance and Affirmative Action

An important difference between Britain and the United States is that Parliament outlawed contract compliance, while it is still required in the United States. Several British advocates for equality have studied the program with

---

135. "NOW was created when the Citizen's Advisory Council on the Status of Women failed to shake the first chairperson of the EEOC out of his reluctance to do more for women than insist on a narrow interpretation of the bona fide occupational qualification clause of the Civil Rights Act" (Meehan, 125).

136. Randall, 198.

great enthusiasm and sought to borrow it, although the program has been ineffective as administered in the 1980s.

The Executive Order prohibiting discrimination by those who hold contracts with the government began as an attempt to more effectively use labor in the defense industry in World War II.[137] This has since evolved into a moral imperative: those companies doing business with the government should meet more demanding standards to insure equal employment opportunity than those standards applied to companies that do not do business with the government.[138] Executive Order 11246,[139] issued in 1965, not only required holders of contracts with the government to abstain from discriminating against their employees and insert a clause into all contracts clearly stating nondiscrimination as the company's policy, but also that contractors take affirmative action to promote employment of protected groups. Executive Order 11375,[140] issued in 1967, extended this protection to women. Enforcement of the Executive Order is now the responsibility of the Office of Federal Contract Compliance Programs (OFCCP), housed in the Department of Labor.[141] Because contractors employ more than 30 million workers and they hold contracts worth more than $167 billion,[142] these orders have enormous potential to bring about equality in employment for women, minority groups, persons with disabilities, and victims of age discrimination.

The Executive Orders surpass Title VII in their potential for combating systemic discrimination. The OFCCP receives individual complaints as well as compiles employment statistics to target large employers, the most fre-

---

137. Executive Order 8802, 6 *Fed. Reg.* 3109, 3 C.F.R. 1938–43 Comp. 957 (June 25, 1941).

138. For a history of the executive order program, see House Subcommittee on Employment Opportunities of the House Committee on Education and Labor, *A Report by the Majority Staff on the Investigation of the Civil Rights Enforcement Activities of the Office of Federal Contract Compliance Programs*, 100th Cong., 1st sess., 1987, 31–40; House Subcommittee on Employment Opportunities of the Committee on Education and Labor, *Oversight Review of the Department of Labor's Office of Federal Contract Compliance Programs and Affirmative Action Programs*, 99th Cong., 1st sess., 1985, "Statement of Richard T. Seymour, Lawyers Committee for Civil Rights Under Law," 169–204; House Subcommittee on Employment Opportunities of the Committee on Education and Labor, *Oversight Hearings on the OFCCP's Proposed Affirmative Action Regulations*, 98th Cong., 1st sess., 1983, "Testimony of Barry Goldstein, Assistant Counsel, NAACP Legal Defense and Education Fund," 453–505; Schlei and Grossman, 871–929; Senate Committee on Labor and Human Resources, *Committee Analysis of Executive Order 11246*, Staff Report, 97th Cong., 2d sess., 1982.

139. 30 *Fed. Reg.* 12319 (1965); 3 C.F.R. 169, 42 U.S.C. §2000e.

140. 32 *Fed. Reg.* 14303 (1967).

141. Executive Order 12086, 43 *Fed. Reg.* 49240 (1978).

142. House Subcommittee on Employment Opportunities, *A Report on the OFCCP*, 1987, 2.

quently complained against, and those industries with the most serious under-utilization of women and minorities. By focusing on sectors with the worst records, such as the construction industry, the OFCCP has the potential to remedy discrimination against classes of workers and to win real changes in employment practices. The OFCCP requires contractors to keep detailed records, and when contractors discover underutilization among the workforce, to develop goals and timetables.[143] Whatever the enforcement record of the OFCCP, at a minimum contractors must monitor their workforces and keep records. Although the OFCCP almost never bars a contractor, the risk of losing lucrative contracts is a stronger incentive for employers to promote equal opportunity than is the fear of losing a suit under Title VII and having to pay backpay.

The Executive Orders, however, did not live up to their potential. The OFCCP has declined to use its hard-won enforcement powers to the fullest, has been plagued by managerial problems, and has always been the target of those who oppose affirmative action.[144] Before Reagan, every president since Franklin Roosevelt had supported and strengthened the Executive Orders. The Reagan administration's deep hostility to affirmative action, however, resulted in an unsuccessful effort by the Justice Department to rescind Executive Order 11246 in 1981. After losing that battle, the administration let the OFCCP atrophy. The agency took few enforcement actions and employers perceived that the OFCCP lacked the will and ability to enforce the law.

Some local authorities in Britain instituted contract compliance on a trial basis until the Thatcher Government banned its use through legislation. The previous chairman of the EOC, Baroness Platt, did not support it.[145] Although the OFCCP has consistently failed to use most of its sanctions, and must fight efforts to dismantle the agency, it has been successful in negotiating back pay for victims of discrimination, requiring employers to monitor their workforces, and producing some changes in employment practices. Contract compliance is a tool for fighting discrimination that is simply not available in Britain.

An important part of the Executive Order's requirements for contractors is that they carry out affirmative action. Specifically, they must set goals and timetables and aggressively seek to hire and train women and minorities. The

---

143. 41 C.F.R. sec. 60-2.11(b) (1986). Section 60-2.11 discusses affirmative action programs and defines underutilization as, "having fewer minorities or women in a particular job group than would reasonably be expected by their availability." The section then sets out, in detail, how the employer should determine underutilization.

144. U.S. Department of Labor, Office of Inspector General, *OFCCP Can Do More Enforcement and Have Greater Impact Using Fewer Dollars*, September 30, 1985; U.S. Commission on Civil Rights, *The Federal Civil Rights Enforcement Effort: The Office of Federal Contract Compliance Programs*, Summer 1987.

145. "Bring Out the Stilettos," *Economist*, July 11, 1987, 59.

courts' interpretation of Title VII and the Fourteenth Amendment to permit race- and sex-conscious hiring under some circumstances has been a powerful tool for groups seeking to break down structural inequality. While affirmative action is by no means noncontroversial in the United States, the tolerance and even support of some judges and the public, as shown by acts of Congress, stands in sharp contrast to the situation in Britain, where it is prohibited. While affirmative action bears little direct relation to cases on exclusionary policies, it does show the extent to which judges and legislators support vigorous efforts to promote equality.

The U.S. Judiciary and Sex Discrimination

One of the biggest differences between the laws prohibiting sex discrimination in Britain and the United States is the response of the two judiciaries. For a period, U.S. courts were expansive and faithful to the goal of fighting discrimination in their interpretations of Title VII compared to British courts and tribunals' interpretations of the Sex Discrimination Act. First, judges in the United States awarded more money to successful complainants than did British courts, as Title VII permitted. Judges in the United States seemed committed to the principle of "make-whole relief,"[146] provided relief for a broad class rather than merely identified victims, and took seriously the use of damages to encourage compliance and deter discrimination.[147] This support for plaintiffs has declined as Reagan's appointments made up more than half of the federal judiciary. Second, the opinions reveal sympathy for the victims of discrimination and a recognition of the country's long history of sex discrimination. Certainly, exceptions to this generalization exist at all levels of the judiciary, but the number of judges who share these sympathies creates a different climate than the one found in British courts and tribunals. Judges continue to express sympathy for individual victims of intentional discrimination while they are also making it more difficult to challenge institutional discrimination.

The outcomes of cases are in part a reflection of the different values of the two judiciaries. Noting that judges in the United States tend to be more sympathetic than British judges is not to suggest that U.S. judges' dedication to sex equality is unlimited. Cases such as *Rostker* and *Michael M.* show the limited nature of the U.S. Supreme Court's conception of discrimination and make it clear that the differences between the two judiciaries are ones of degree.

---

146. Title VII permits claims for back pay from two years prior to filing a claim of discrimination.

147. See Albermarle Paper Co. v. Moody, 422 U.S. 405 (1975); but see also City of Los Angeles, Water and Power v. Manhart, 435 U.S. 702 (1978). See Schlei and Grossman, 1418–30.

Finally, the two judiciaries vary in their construction of the concept of discrimination. U.S. courts are more suspicious of sex-based categories, scrutinize employers' behavior more searchingly, more carefully dissect employers' justifications for practices, and hold employers to the narrower exceptions to the law. British judges are likely to find that employers have not discriminated as long as their actions strike judges as reasonable, regardless of the wording of the statute.

There are at least three explanations for the differences between the two judiciaries. First, the bench is more male-dominated in Britain than the United States.[148] More important, however, judges in Britain are chosen from a much smaller pool than in the United States,[149] and the bench is composed of white, upper-middle-class males from Oxford and Cambridge. Of course, federal judges in the United States are also mainly white, upper-middle-class men from select schools, but because the president can make appointments to the bench from a wide pool, he can select women, such as Ruth Bader Ginsburg, or African-Americans, such as Thurgood Marshall, to inject a more progressive perspective. In addition, in the United States, the president nominates judges after a careful scrutiny of the candidate's views on important issues as well as his or her views about the role of the judiciary in the political system and modes and methods of constitutional interpretation. In Britain, because Queen's Counsel represent a very narrow range of political views, because the party that controls the executive also controls the legislature and no legislative confirmation of judicial appointments takes place, and because judges have a less important role in the political system, judicial appointments are not subject to partisan debate.[150]

Second, the British judiciary is not a constitutionally created third and coequal branch of government with the power to review legislation for its constitutionality. Instead, Parliament is supreme and the judiciary's role is one of applying the law. While judges in the United States may conceive their role

---

148. See Sachs and Wilson, *Sexism and the Law*, 170–97; Equal Opportunities Commission, *Women in the Legal Services: Evidence Submitted by the EOC to the Royal Commission on Legal Services*, March 1978; Hattie-Jo P. Mullins, "Women and the Law: Will Real Life Catch Up to TV?" *Ms.*, June 1987, 64–66.

149. J. A. G. Griffith, *The Politics of the Judiciary*, 2d ed. (Glasgow: Fontana, 1981), 19. In 1976, there were 31,250 solicitors in Britain and 4,076 barristers (R. S. Sim and D. M. M. Scott, *A-Level English Law*, 5th ed. [London: Butterworths, 1978], 105–9).

150. "While there may be the same kind of back-room jockeying for judgeships as there often is for university professorships and other posts in the hands of the government, partisan political considerations have played little part in the appointment of judges during this century" (Martin Shapiro, *Courts: A Comparative and Political Analysis* [Chicago: University of Chicago Press, 1981], 111). This is not to suggest that the Lord Chancellor does not consider the political views and attitudes of potential judges at all in making the decision, but, because the range of candidates is already very narrow, such political considerations play a vastly reduced role in judicial selection.

as protecting the constitutional rights of individuals from governmental intrusion, pitting themselves against states or the federal government, British judges see their role as upholding the rule of law and carrying out what Parliament commands. British judges are less likely to create bold new legal rights, such as the right to an abortion, and do not declare acts of Parliament unconstitutional. Although some evidence suggests that courts are increasingly striking down administrative acts, and that now that Britain has joined the European Community, the Treaty of Rome may have a "constitutional" effect, the differences in the role of the two judiciaries in the two political systems and their perceptions of their roles accounts for some of the differences in cases on discrimination.

Third, British courts are not engaged in a dialogue with pressure groups. British judges do not come from the ranks of interest-group litigators. Judges have chosen not to encourage the use of the amicus brief. Because interest groups do not see the courts as a vehicle for social change, focusing instead on Parliament or political parties, they bring far fewer test cases and file few amicus briefs. British courts fail to get the perspective and the analysis of pressure groups; often they will have only counsel's arguments to inform their opinion. Nor do British judges have the benefit of law clerks, interjecting the latest trends in legal scholarship into their opinions. U.S. courts, on the other hand, are often influenced by amici's arguments, which furnish valuable scientific and sociological evidence. While feminists in Britain are organizing to use litigation to further their aims as far as it is possible, they rightly recognize that, for a variety of reasons, courts are an arena where they can have only limited success. Litigators, too, in the United States are turning to other avenues for their policy objectives as the judiciary grows less sympathetic to the civil rights agenda.

Feminist Groups

While judges shape and define the law and determine whether it is fruitful or pointless to litigate, feminists, too, have an important role to play in defining, enforcing, and changing sex discrimination law. Feminists help define issues and place them on the public agenda, publicize judicial rulings by heralding victories or criticizing failures, draw attention to the need for changes in the law, bring test cases, lobby the enforcement agency, and engage in protest politics. These groups may advise women on their rights and encourage them to litigate by providing free counsel. Neither in the United States nor in Britain is there a single feminist position or ideology. Instead, feminist groups offer a wide variety of strategies and visions of change.

Feminists in the United States have been more sharply divided over the so-called special versus equal treatment debate, particularly over the question of pregnancy and maternity policies. While some early feminists celebrated women's differences from men and sought equal rights of citizenship to "feminize" politics, other feminists demanded an end to special treatment for women. Although feminists were divided over the issue of protective legislation in the early 1900s, the new wave of feminism in the 1960s usually saw this special treatment as discrimination. In the 1970s, feminists pushed for formal legal equality and brought test cases using existing law to expand women's rights. These feminists seized the opportunity provided by the law's incorporation of the comparative approach and the judiciary's greater willingness to hear claims of sex discrimination.[151] They argued before the courts that women and men were more alike than different and that all should be treated as individuals. To have the possibility of winning cases, feminist litigators adopted the liberal rhetoric of equality, focusing on the rights of individuals.

The legal strategy feminists employed in the 1970s was motivated by both a genuine belief that successful results in these cases would produce the desired legal doctrine on sex equality as well as a strategic concern that progress in the legal arena, while not ideal, was the best way to safeguard women given current legal and political constraints. As well as seeing men and women as more alike than different, some feminists also believed that men were injured by sex-based discrimination and that what was necessary was merely to treat everyone as an individual and give them equal opportunity. The concern was that any legal recognition of difference would ultimately be used against women. If women are given pregnancy leave that men with disabilities did not have, for example, then employers might use that extra benefit as a reason not to hire women. If the law recognized differences, the result might benefit women in one instance, but the courts might later exploit the same reasoning to draw a distinction that disadvantaged women.[152] Feminists may have doubted that the law could be used to draw distinctions between men and women that would help to ease the oppression of women. Recognizing that the law prohibiting discrimination incorporates a comparative approach and recognizing the male-dominated nature of the judiciary, they tried for only limited victories. Feminists, then, may have adopted the assimilationist model in arguing cases either because of their vision of the good society or as a pragmatic strategy.

The view that the terms of law should be sex-neutral and that sex dis-

---

151. See Herma Hill Kay, *Sex-Based Discrimination*, 2d ed. (St. Paul: West, 1981), 138, citing R. Wasserstrom, "Racism and Sexism," *Philosophy and Social Issues* 11 (1980): 24; Alison Jaggar, "On Sexual Equality," *Ethics* 84 (1974): 276.

152. See Joan E. Bertin, Review of *Double Exposure: Women's Health Hazards on the Job and at Home*, ed. by Wendy Chavkin, *Women's Rights Law Reporter* 9 (Winter 1986): 89–93; see also response of Wendy Chavkin in *Women's Rights Law Reporter* 9 (Spring 1986): 179–80.

crimination is harmful to both men and women was clearly dominant in the 1970s, defended by the ACLU Women's Rights Project and the NOW Legal Defense and Education Fund. As a result of feminist pressure for formal legal equality, many states rewrote their criminal statutes changing rape to sexual assault, passed sex-neutral divorce laws and criteria for custody, and abolished sex-based credit requirements. Yet a different view of sexual difference, which has always been present in the women's movement, has become more pronounced in the last ten years. Feminists began to discover that, while many men were benefiting from sex-neutral standards in benefits and criteria for custody, women could be disadvantaged by sex-neutral standards that favored attributes that men had.[153] It appeared that the very victories feminists had won were now perverted and applied to women's detriment. In addition, other feminists were extolling women's difference from men.[154] Some feminists rejected a liberal approach and maintained that equal rights under the law would not end women's oppression. Although the issue of protective legislation may have been put to rest, the equal versus special or even preferential treatment debate became more heated. Examples included the evidence in *EEOC v. Sears*,[155] debates over *Cal. Fed.*, and proposals for federal legislation requiring parental leave.

Feminists in the United States differ from their British sisters in seeking so-called equal treatment and rejecting special treatment. They also differ in their willingness to seek change through mainstream political institutions and the energy and resources they bring to bear. The differences between the British and U.S. feminist movements result from ideological and philosophical differences between the two movements as well as differences in the two countries' political institutions and class structures. U.S. political institutions, courts, legislatures (state and federal), and executive agencies are more open to pressure group activity, while the British courts, civil service, and Parliament seek less contact and interact less frequently with pressure groups. While certain pressure groups such as unions and industry may have a favored status in tripartite institutions such as the EOC and Health and Safety Executive, feminist groups find it hard to participate in these organizations or to win representation in their own right. Because there are more battlegrounds in the United States, power is dispersed. Feminists in the United States can win some skirmishes and, as a result, extol the virtues of mainstream politics and

153. Lenore J. Weitzman, *The Divorce Revolution: The Unexpected Social and Economic Consequences for Women and Children in America* (New York: Free Press, 1986), 338.

154. Carol Gilligan, *In a Different Voice: Psychological Theory and Women's Development* (Cambridge, Mass.: Harvard University Press, 1982).

155. Equal Employment Opportunity Commission v. Sears, Roebuck and Co., 628 F.Supp 1264 (N.D. Ill. 1986), *affd.*, 839 F.2d 302 (7th Cir. 1988). See Sandi E. Cooper, "Introduction to the Documents," *Signs* 4 (Summer 1986): 753–79.

seek to raise money to support their activities. British feminists, seeing less opportunity for success within a closed, centralized system, are more likely to adopt the politics of protest.

Nowhere is this distinction clearer than in feminist groups' use of the courts. Feminist groups have mushroomed in the United States to finance the bringing of test cases to expand the parameters of the Fourteenth Amendment and Title VII. The only British equivalent was the Women's Rights Project of the National Council for Civil Liberties until 1988, when feminists formed the Women's Legal Defense Fund. The difference in the expenditure of energy and money on legal projects is stark. The differences in the legal system make litigation a less fruitful line of attack in Britain, and, partly as a consequence, feminist groups often eschew such a reformist approach to political change. In fact, British feminists may well argue that U.S. feminists have devoted far too many resources to legal change through litigation and amending the Constitution. Certainly, litigation will be a less important feature of feminist activity in the 1990s, or it will be employed defensively rather than with the hope of producing social change. The eleven-year difference in passage of the Sex Discrimination Act and Title VII, however, may have also contributed to the variation in the resources feminists in Britain and the United States bring to bear to promote legal changes.

Comparing and contrasting the two feminist movements, and understanding their different strategies as a function of both ideological and institutional differences, is essential for understanding both countries' sex discrimination law. This chapter has offered a survey of discrimination law in the United States as a necessary background to understanding the cases discussed in chapter 6.

CHAPTER 5

British Cases On Reproductive Hazards

Few women have brought their challenges to exclusionary policies before the courts in the United States, and still fewer have done so in Britain. While it is impossible to draw firm conclusions on the basis of one principal case, *Page v. Freight Hire* provides an example of an industrial tribunal's willingness to find that sex discrimination has not occurred if the tribunal believes the employer acted reasonably. [1] What falls within the realm of reasonableness is influenced by individual tribunal members' gender stereotypes. *Page* also shows how exceptions written into the 1975 Sex Discrimination Act and the absence of an explicit statutory prohibition against pregnancy discrimination limit its effectiveness. The lack of participation of feminist groups and trade unions in the case is also consistent with the findings discussed in chapter 3.

Page illustrates the comparative approach in practice and shows the problems with so-called protective policies. A close inspection of Freight Hire's policy reveals that it is based on unexamined assumptions about physical differences between the sexes and may be based on judgments about the appropriate role for women in society. A careful look at the policy in operation reveals many similarities between exclusionary policies and protective legislation. In chapter 1, I argued that supporters of protective legislation often justified it on the grounds of physical differences, when closer inspection revealed that supporters' conceptions of men's and women's different social roles were the actual driving force. Their understanding of physical differences was colored by their values about appropriate gender roles. Thus, analyzing this one case not only links past protective policies with exclusionary policies, but provides an opportunity to examine one particular exclusionary policy more carefully.

Page v. Freight Hire

In Britain, employers' actions removing women from the workplace to protect a potential fetus have been the subject of litigation in only one case, *Page v.*

---

1. Page v. Freight Hire (Tank Haulage) Ltd., Case no. 1381/80, March 26, 1980; [1981] IRLR 13 (EAT).

Freight Hire. A haulage company allegedly dismissed a woman truck driver from her job hauling dimethylformamide (DMF) on the basis of the client chemical company's instruction that women should not haul DMF because it may be embryotoxic. Despite the complexity of the facts of the case and the tentative nature of the industrial tribunal's opinion, those who reported and commented on the case presented it as a clear precedent that reasonable actions to protect the health and safety of the potential offspring of the worker take priority over any statutory duty not to discriminate on the basis of sex.[2] That conclusion was an overstatement; yet the reports make this area of law appear settled, making another test case unlikely.[3] The British media's treatment of women is a subject for a thesis in and of itself. The *Northern Echo* began its article on *Page* with: "*Attractive* Jackie Page always wanted to be a lorry driver."[4] The *Daily Star* headline read, "I Got the Sack for Being a Girl—Jackie." Its opening sentence read: "*Pretty* divorcee Jackie Page had one love in life—driving heavy lorries."[5]

Jacqueline Page had always wanted to be a truck driver, an unusual occupation for a woman in Britain, particularly in the North of England where attitudes about women's role in society are very traditional and male unemployment is high.[6] Her uncle and father, both truck drivers, encouraged her. After completing a training course and obtaining her license in June, 1979, she began to work full time for Freight Hire Company in July, 1979.[7] In September, 1979, Freight Hire laid her off. Page continued to work on a casual basis: the company would occasionally phone her during the evening to see if she could work the next day. In October, 1979, the managing director asked her if she would work more jobs, because another driver had broken his

---

2. See Alan J. P. Dalton, *Health and Safety at Work* (London: Cassell, 1982); "Ban On Woman Transporting DMF Not Unlawful Discrimination," *Health and Safety Information Bulletin* 62 (February 1981): 18–19; Norman Selwyn, *Law of Health and Safety at Work* (London: Butterworths, 1982), 205; "No Discrimination Against Woman Lorry Driver," *Times*, November 5, 1980; "Chemical Ban on Woman Driver Upheld," *Evening Gazette*, May 28, 1980; Charles D. Drake and Frank B. Wright, *Law of Health and Safety at Work: The New Approach* (London: Sweet and Maxwell, 1983), 77.

3. Much of the commentary criticized the decision. See Katherine O'Donovan, *Sexual Divisions in Law* (London: Weidenfeld and Nicolson, 1985), 168–69; Tess Gill and Larry Whitty, *Women's Rights in the Workplace* (Harmondsworth, England: Penguin, 1983), 267–68; *Health and Safety Information Bulletin* 62 (February 1981): 18–19.

4. March 27, 1980; italics added. She actually spells her name Jacky.

5. March 27, 1980; italics added.

6. This information is based on an interview with Jacqueline Page, April 15, 1985. I also interviewed Mr. and Mrs. Lewis (from Freight Hire) and their son, who helps manage the company.

7. Unlike the cases discussed in chap. 6, Freight Hire did not begin to hire women due to pressure from a governmental agency such as the Equal Employment Opportunity Commission or from trade unions.

leg. When she accepted, Page said she believed that Freight Hire was re-employing her full time.

On her runs, she carried a variety of hazardous substances including dimethylformamide,[8] a product manufactured by Imperial Chemical Industries (ICI). On Wednesday, October 17, a senior manager from the petrochemicals division saw Page hauling a load of DMF into ICI. He phoned the freight company and informed it that, because of the danger to women of childbearing age, it should not assign Page to haul the product again. When the manager informed Page that she could no longer haul DMF because of this danger, she offered to sign an indemnity form that would clear the company of any responsibility if she should miscarry or bear a deformed child. At the time, she was twenty-three years old and divorced. Freight Hire refused her offer.

Although an industrial tribunal later claimed that Page did not pursue a grievance with her union, the Transport and General Workers Union, Page maintains that when Freight Hire prohibited her from hauling DMF she did seek her union's support and her father encouraged her to pursue a legal claim. According to Page, her union refused to help, claiming that her case would not benefit most members, who were men. Furthermore, she reported that union members suggested that she was taking the case merely for money and not for the sake of improving working conditions—an interesting claim, given the meager amounts of money that industrial tribunals award in such cases.

Page claimed that Freight Hire Company had directly discriminated against her on the basis of sex contrary to the Sex Discrimination Act of 1975. The first issue before the industrial tribunal was whether Freight Hire had dismissed Page—she claimed that the company had dismissed her when the manager decided that she could no longer haul DMF. Freight Hire claimed that it had only conveyed there would be a reduction in work. The manager assumed that she had resigned one week later when she turned in her log

---

8. The hazards of DMF have been the subject of review in at least two authoritative sources; see S. M. Barlow and F. M. Sullivan, *Reproductive Hazards of Industrial Chemicals* (London: Academic Press, 1982), 355–58. Barlow and Sullivan write:

> The lack of teratogenicity of DMF is at first sight surprising since it is metabolized to the highly teratogenic MMF. . . .It is interesting also to note that testicular lesions have been found in rats and mice after F or MMF administration, but not after DMF. Thus it is these two compounds in the formamide series which may pose a reproductive hazard. . . . Formamide and more clearly, MMF have been shown to be both embryolethal and highly teratogenic in rodents and to a limited extent, embryolethal in rabbits. DMF is much less active in this regard in animals and the majority of studies suggest that it is not teratogenic, but may be embryolethal in high doses.

See also A. C. Fletcher, *Reproductive Hazards of Work* (Manchester: Equal Opportunities Commission, 1985), 57.

book. The tribunal found that Freight Hire had not dismissed her, but, rather, that she had resigned when she learned that she could no longer haul DMF.

After the industrial tribunal decided that Page had resigned and there was no case of unfair dismissal, it considered whether refusing to allow her to haul DMF constituted discrimination. The tribunal held that it did, using the criterion that discrimination on the basis of sex is "less favourable treatment than a man."

> By withdrawing from the applicant the opportunity of carrying the DMF traffic the respondent company were discriminating against her on the ground of her sex and that a male employee would have been allowed to carry the DMF traffic.[9]

Finding that Freight Hire had treated her less favorably than a man, however, did not end the matter. Counsel for Freight Hire had argued that *Peake v. Automotive Products Ltd.* applied, and the industrial tribunal agreed.[10] In *Peake*, the Court of Appeal had held that arrangements made in the interests of safety or administrative convenience were not infringements of the law even though they may be more favorable to one sex. The industrial tribunal decision quoted the statement of Lord Justice Shaw.

> It may be argued by some trouble makers some day that the provision of separate and different arrangements for hygiene and sanitation constitutes an act of discrimination against the males or females or both. . . . Some acts of differentiation or discrimination are not adverse to either sex and are not designed so to be. Nor without surrendering to absurdity can they be so regarded.[11]

Despite recognizing that the Court of Appeal had later rejected the reasoning in *Peake* when it decided *Jeremiah v. Ministry of Defense*,[12] the industrial tribunal nevertheless decided that it was "bound by the decision of *Peake*."[13] Because refusing to allow Page to haul DMF was in the interests of safety, the action was not unlawful. By relying on *Peake*, the tribunal was free to disregard whether the employer's differential treatment of men and women was necessary or whether the employer could insure safety and sound admin-

---

9. *Page*, 1381/80, 3.

10. The industrial tribunal has incorrectly referred to the case as *Peake v. Automotive Products Ltd*; when the case reached the Court of Appeal, however, it was Automotive Products Ltd. v. Peake, [1977] IRLR 365 (CA).

11. *Page*, 1381/80, 3–4.

12. [1979] IRLR 436 (CA).

13. *Page*, 1381/80, 4.

istration in a less discriminatory way. The tribunal accepted Freight Hire's assertion that excluding women was reasonable at face value.[14] The industrial tribunal, in relying on *Peake*, adopted a comparative approach. Treating women less favorably than men is not discriminatory if the treatment stems from a "real" difference. Once the difference is established, it is permissible to disadvantage women workers. The tribunal wasted little time probing the accuracy or relevance of the asserted difference, that women are more vulnerable than men to the reproductive hazards of DMF.

The industrial tribunal next considered whether DMF was a reproductive hazard, and, if so, whether it was hazardous to women only. British law requires employers to inform workers about the hazards of the job.[15] In practice, the information available to workers is minimal and rarely includes any information about reproductive hazards. ICI issued a "trem card" (transport emergency) stating, in very general terms, the hazards of the substances truck drivers are carrying and what action a driver should take in an emergency such as an accident or spillage. The trem card for DMF states that it is a skin irritant and advises what to do if there is skin contact or inhalation. It says nothing about the reproductive hazards of DMF.

At the time of the hearing, litigants, members of the tribunal, and reporters were confused about the exact hazards of DMF. The only evidence specifically about the reproductive hazards of DMF before the tribunal was an *Industrial Hazards Bulletin* that ICI published in January, 1976.

Recent publications have suggested that there may be an embryotoxic effect *at levels of exposure greater than the T.L.V.* [The threshold limit value is the maximum recommended exposure as set by the Health and Safety Executive.] Precautionary measures must therefore be rigorously applied when women of childbearing age are likely to be exposed to the material. Regular monitoring of the atmosphere is essential.[16]

Page believed that DMF might cause sterility in women or induce a miscarriage. Another employee of Freight Hire testified that he believed DMF could make men sterile.[17] The bulletin suggests only that DMF *might* be embryotoxic, that is, hazardous to a developing fetus, but not that it would

---

14. See the discussion of *Peake* in chap. 3.

15. The Health and Safety at Work Act, 1974, Section 2(2)(c); see Drake and Wright, 78.

16. *Page*, 1381/80, 2; italics added.

17. The industrial tribunal did not refer to the testimony of Wilkinson, a former employee of Freight Hire, but the Employment Appeal Tribunal mentioned it. "Evidence was given by a Mr. Wilkinson as to what he understood the position to be. He had been a driver but was employed as a fitter. He said that he knew that if the vapour of this chemical was absorbed it could make one sterile. He thought that it affected men and women; that both were at risk of sterility" ([1981] IRLR 13, 14).

cause sterility in women—yet the industrial tribunal concluded: "the material was particularly hazardous to women."[18] Strictly speaking, the evidence suggested that DMF would be hazardous only to a fetus and not to women.

This confusion was also evident in the newspaper accounts of the hazard.[19] The *Northern Echo* reported that Page lost her job because DMF could make women sterile, later adding that it might cause pregnant women to abort. Both the *Evening Gazette* and the *Daily Star* reported the hazard as sterility. The industrial tribunal was content that Page knew what the hazards were, even though it had little evidence about the hazards of DMF before it and Page's stated beliefs conflicted with that evidence.

> Although in the warning card issued by the manufacturer attention was drawn to the fact that the DMF was a hazardous liquid the precise nature of the hazards were not fully explained on the card although the tribunal are satisfied that the applicant had become aware of the dangers at some time prior to mid-October 1979.[20]

Page's barrister did not present evidence as to whether DMF was embryotoxic, whether it made women sterile or caused them to miscarry, or whether it affected men's reproductive capacity. Other than the conflicting beliefs of the various witnesses, the tribunal had virtually no scientific evidence before it. Page's barrister contended that ICI had the burden of proving that DMF was hazardous and that the hazards were specific to women.

> ICI were not, as far as I know, invited to testify for the respondents. I argued that they should have been called to give evidence, but it was not in the interests of the applicant to lead evidence concerning DMF unless we had specific evidence which could show that the fluid was not embryotoxic. I simply had no idea whether this was the case or not. I cannot remember whether I advised the Union or Ms. Page to carry out research in this area. In our system, this kind of work is left very much to the solicitors.[21]

Freight Hire did not call ICI to present evidence to justify its directive. The managers for Freight Hire feared that dragging ICI into the proceedings, even if doing so would have enhanced their case, would have damaged their

---

18. *Page*, 1381/80, 2.

19. "Lorry Driver Jackie Loses Out," *Northern Echo*, March 27, 1980; "I Got the Sack for Being a Girl—Jackie," *Daily Star*, March 27, 1980; "Chemical Ban on Woman Driver Upheld," *Evening Gazette*, March 28, 1980.

20. *Page*, 1381/80, 2.

21. Page's barrister, letter to the author, February 18, 1986.

good working relationship with ICI, and the company could have easily switched its business to another hauling firm. It was Page's view that ICI had left Freight Hire "out in the cold" to face the tribunal alone. Yet even without ICI's testimony, the industrial tribunal gave great weight to its directive.

> I think the Industrial Tribunal (rather than the EAT) were particularly influenced by the fact that the warning as to the hazards of DMF came from ICI who are probably the largest industrial concern on Teesside and whose business would be vital to the respondent employers. I rather feel that the Industrial Tribunal sympathised with a view expressed for the employers that they simply had to go along with every safety directive (if that is the right word) from ICI so as to secure their transport business.[22]

In fact, in a letter to the *Health and Safety Information Bulletin*, ICI later denied any involvement in the case and denied that they had evidence suggesting that DMF was embryotoxic.

> *HSIB* has been in correspondence with ICI over this point and we have received a letter from the company which points out that ICI was not involved in the case and confirms that "we do not know of any information available which creates uncertainty about the safety of fertile women when exposed to *any* concentration of DMF. We believe that the TLV of 10 ppm is a reasonably safe standard."[23]

The industrial tribunal rejected the arguments of Page's barrister and held that Freight Hire did not have the burden of proving that DMF was a reproductive hazard affecting women but not men. With minimal scrutiny, the industrial tribunal accepted Freight Hire's evidence as a legitimate basis for its exclusionary policy.

Even if DMF were embryotoxic at levels *above* the threshold limit value, one would assume that Freight Hire would have to show that the level of exposure on the job placed Page at risk. And even if it did, surely it is the employer's duty to at least first try not to exceed the limit recommended by the Health and Safety Executive. The industrial tribunal did not consider the levels of exposure or the employer's responsibility for meeting a certain level. No party presented evidence on the effects on men. Freight Hire never established that, by hauling the material, Page was likely to be exposed (she left the area while the substance was loaded and unloaded, having merely driven the truck). Even if she was exposed, there was no evidence of exposure above

---

22. Ibid.
23. "In Brief," *Health and Safety Information Bulletin* 62 (March 1981): 2.

the threshold limit value. The freight company had never determined the level of exposure.

Encouraged by her barrister, who thought she could win, Page appealed her case to the Employment Appeal Tribunal (EAT) and sought the support of the Equal Opportunities Commission. Both Page's barrister and the EOC as amicus curiae argued there was not enough evidence to justify barring her from driving—that Freight Hire had not met its burden of proof. Page's barrister wrote:

> Very sparse evidence concerning DMF was presented to the tribunal. That was the main plank of my appeal. The information in the ICI warning leaflet was very tentative, saying in effect that recent research had suggested that DMF may be embryotoxic. Frankly, I argued that it was up to the employers to produce more cogent evidence to justify their discrimination.[24]

The EAT did not accept the argument that the industrial tribunal should have required additional evidence. It found, although the evidence presented in the *Industrial Hazards Bulletin* alone was not enough to prove that women should not haul DMF, that ICI had instructed Freight Hire to remove Page from hauling DMF was sufficient to meet the employer's burden of proof, although ICI had not testified or presented evidence to justify its directive and later denied that such evidence existed. The EAT noted, however,

> if there had been material which suggested that this was an act of excessive caution on the part of the employers, that it was being used as a device to prevent Mrs. Page from being employed, then the situation would be very different.[25]

Page therefore had the burden of proving either that DMF was not harmful to women's reproductive capacity or that it was harmful to men's reproductive capacity as well.

Page's barrister and the EOC had argued that the tribunal should have demanded that Freight Hire present this sort of evidence, but the EAT disagreed.

> It does not seem to us that, once discrimination is established, it really is for the Tribunal itself (as has been suggested here) to ensure that all the scientific information which might be relevant is brought before the

---

24. Page's barrister, letter to the author, February 18, 1986.
25. [1981] IRLR 13, 16 (EAT).

Tribunal. The Tribunal was to decide the matter on the evidence which is there.[26]

The EAT next addressed the industrial tribunal's reliance on *Peake*. Because the Court of Appeal had recanted its position in *Peake* in *Jeremiah*, the EAT ruled that the industrial tribunal had erroneously applied the law. Instead of concluding that employers were no longer free to disregard the command of the Sex Discrimination Act if they asserted that to do so was in the interests of safety or good administration, the EAT arrived at the same result as if it had relied on *Peake*. The EAT referred to section 51 of the Sex Discrimination Act.

> Nothing in Parts II to IV shall render unlawful any act done by a person if it was necessary for him to do it in order to comply with a requirement . . . (a) of an Act passed before this Act.[27]

Parliament had passed the Health and Safety at Work Act in 1974, creating a general duty on the part of employers to provide a safe and healthy workplace. The EAT interpreted section 51 of the Sex Discrimination Act as a blanket exemption that allowed employers to meet their obligation to provide a safe workplace in a discriminatory way. Furthermore, the EAT accepted Freight Hire's assertion that excluding women was *necessary* at face value, and chose not to remand the case to an industrial tribunal to gather additional evidence.[28]

The EAT warned, however, against reading its findings too broadly:

> It is important to bear in mind that we are here dealing with a case where the only evidence upon which reliance can be placed was that there was a danger of embryotoxic effects at certain levels of exposure. This is not a case (despite the evidence given by Mr. Wilkinson)[29] where the Tribunal had to decide what would happen if both men and women were subjected to the same kind of risk and the employers had decided that it was more desirable to protect the woman than to protect the man: wholly different

---

26. Ibid., 16.

27. Ibid., 15. See Hugh-Jones v. St. John's College, Cambridge, [1979] ICR 848 (EAT) and Greater London Council v. Farrar, [1980] ICR 266 (EAT).

28. "Accordingly, in all the circumstances, it seems to us that this is not a case which we need to remit to an Industrial Tribunal. The evidence was such that this Tribunal would have come to the same conclusion, for the reasons the Tribunal gave, but on the basis of S. 51 of the Act of 1975 rather than of what was said in *Peake*" (Ibid., 16). For a comparison with section 41 of the Race Relations Act, see Colin Bourn, "The Defense of Justifiability," *Industrial Law Journal* 18 (1989): 170–73.

29. Wilkinson, an employee of Freight Hire, testified that he believed that DMF made men sterile ([1981] IRLR 13, 14 [EAT]).

considerations would arise in that kind of case. Here we are not concerned with a situation where a man's ability to procreate is involved; and it does not seem to us to be material in any way that both men and women were liable to be affected by this chemical in other ways, i.e., in relation to their digestive organs, their liver and so on.[30]

This caveat in the EAT's opinion about the limitations of the decision's value as a precedent, however, did not appear in press reports of the case.

The EOC had argued that Freight Hire should have to prove that the *only* way of complying with the Health and Safety at Work Act was by excluding women. Although the EAT decided that the employer should have to offer some justification for the policy, it rejected the EOC's argument that the employer must show that exclusion was the only alternative. If doubt existed about various courses, the employer may choose the course it decides is best.

Moreover, the EAT stated that, in deciding what course an employer must pursue, all circumstances must be taken into account, including the wishes of the person not to have children, but concluded—with virtually no comment or analysis—that these wishes "cannot be a conclusive factor."[31] Freight Hire never claimed that DMF exposure harmed Page, only that it could possibly affect a fetus she might carry. According to Page, she has never wanted children, so it was not an agonizing decision to offer to sign the indemnity form. Twelve years later, Page had not changed her mind, had no desire to have children, and her partner had been sterilized. She did not consider sterilization as an option because she believed it to be difficult to have done through the National Health Service and too expensive to get privately. Neither the EAT nor the employer, however, considered Page's wishes. She believes that her desire not to have children made her monstrous in the eyes of the tribunal and prejudiced them against her case.[32] The press quoted the solicitor for Freight Hire as saying, "She formed the view, as women's libbers and pro-abortionists do, that she had the right to decide the future of her own body and her own unborn."[33] He had argued before the

---

30. Ibid., 16.

31. "We accept that the individual's wishes may be a factor to be looked at—although, in our judgment, where the risk is to the woman, of sterility, or to the foetus, whether actually in existence or likely to come into existence in the future, these wishes cannot be a conclusive factor" ([1981] IRLR 13, 15).

32. Her barrister's opinion, on the other hand, is that what was decisive was the directive from ICI. As a large employer in the area and one on which the freight company was dependent for business, what ICI said went, regardless of what Freight Hire would have liked to do. The EAT recognized the importance the industrial tribunal placed on the ICI directive: "But it would appear here that, on the material, this Tribunal was very concerned with the question of safety; its members attached great importance to what they described as 'the arrangements dictated by ICI' " ([1981] IRLR 13, 16).

33. *Northern Echo*, March 27, 1980.

tribunal that the decision to have children was not a decision for Page to make, but a decision for her future husband.

Page illustrates many of the findings about the 1975 Sex Discrimination Act discussed in chapter 3. First, it illustrates confusion over who has the burden of proof and what that burden is.[34] The industrial tribunal admitted that Page had shown that she had been treated less favorably on the grounds of sex. Freight Hire then argued it did so because of a concern for Page's future offspring's health. Which party then has the burden? It appears that Freight Hire had merely to assert a reason for its action.

Second, Leonard's study found that tribunals were reluctant to find that discrimination occurred, a reluctance the industrial tribunal showed in *Page*. This reluctance may be the result of tribunals erroneously importing a "reasonableness" standard from the other employment cases that they hear, and the policy in this case struck members as reasonable. Or it may arise because tribunals fail to scrutinize employers' reasons because of an aversion to meddling in employment policies and limiting managerial discretion. Or tribunal members may believe a finding of discrimination carries such a stigma that they are reluctant to make such a finding. In any case, the result is clear. *Page* is a further example of the findings chapter 3 reports: tribunals are often reluctant to scrutinize employers' explanations for differential treatment.

Third, the industrial tribunal in *Page* was not inquisitorial, nor did the EAT admonish it for being passive or demand that the industrial tribunal ask for new evidence on remand. While Leonard found that some tribunals, particularly those in Scotland, asked questions and required parties to present relevant evidence, most tribunal panels were passive, deciding cases on the basis of what the parties chose to present. The EAT's decision not to require additional evidence contrasts sharply with that of the EAT in *Hayes v. Malleable Working Men's Club and Institute*,[35] discussed in chapter 3. In *Hayes*, once the EAT determined that the industrial tribunal needed to consider a different range of facts, specifically, the employer's treatment of men with incapacitating medical conditions and the specific concerns of the employer about the individual pregnancy, it required the industrial tribunal to start afresh. In *Page*, the EAT could have directed an industrial tribunal to hear evidence on the effects of DMF on men's reproductive capacity, the actual level of exposure, and the possibility of alternatives to excluding women.

Fourth, Leonard found that industrial tribunals made frequent errors of law, and *Page* illustrates that point. The industrial tribunal relied on *Peake* although the Court of Appeal had changed its position in *Jeremiah*. This reliance on *Peake* was not the result of poor training, inexperience, or ignorance; the tribunal knew about *Jeremiah* but chose to disregard it. Disturbing,

---

34. See Leonard, *Judging Inequality*, 142–45.
35. [1985] ICR 703 (EAT).

too, is the EAT's decision to interpret section 51 of the 1975 Sex Discrimination Act to exempt not only administrative rules under the 1974 Health and Safety at Work Act that may set different health and safety standards for men and women, but *any* employment practice that treats men and women differently for the alleged purpose of promoting safety and health. Under this interpretation, section 51 swallows the Sex Discrimination Act. Such an interpretation reflects undue deference to employers and lack of sympathy for victims of discrimination. Not requiring employers to consider alternatives to exclusion that might advance health and safety equally well is an example of the finding that members of tribunals give little weight to the harm of discrimination. The principle of proportionality established under EC law in such cases as *Johnston v. RUC* would require tribunals to balance the necessity for excluding women against the discriminatory effect of such exclusion. The decision in *Page* is striking for the absence of any recognition of the consequences of Jacky Page losing her job. She received hate mail as a consequence of the case and, although well qualified, found it impossible to get a job driving in the area for two years. In 1986, she had a job delivering auto parts on a part-time basis. Ironically, her job now requires her to provide information on health and safety.

Finally, *Page* confirms Leonard's conclusion that specialized representation is necessary but not sufficient to successfully pursue a claim of sex discrimination, a requirement that is contrary to the design of the tribunal system. Page was lucky not only because a barrister represented her, but also because the EOC intervened on appeal. She was thus better represented than the average claimant. Yet, as Leonard forcefully argues, representation is not enough: it must be *skilled* representation by advocates with knowledge of sex discrimination precedent as well as knowledge about the behavior of tribunals in sex discrimination cases. The function of the barrister in the English system is to be a specialist in oral advocacy. Although some do specialize by subject, in 1980, only a handful of solicitors and barristers could claim specialist expertise in discrimination law. Page's barrister admitted that he collected no scientific evidence on DMF,[36] believing that Freight Hire had the burden of proof. He did not specialize in discrimination law.

> Jackie Page's case was a very interesting one and one which I am still convinced was wrongly decided. However, you must not make the mistake of thinking that I am a specialist in sex discrimination cases. This case was perhaps the only substantial sex discrimination case I have ever had.[37]

---

36. As he again pointed out, this is not the function of a barrister in the English system.
37. Page's barrister, letter to the author, February 18, 1986.

Although the EOC intervened, it was stuck with the industrial tribunal's findings of fact. The EOC had to be satisfied with making a legal argument in the hopes that the EAT would request that the case be reheard. The EOC became involved with the case at the last minute and without making full use of its resources. The EOC's barrister reported getting the materials for the case and preparing on the train on the way to the hearing, having argued a case before the European Court of Justice the day before. Late receipt of the papers prevented him from advising Page's barrister to further investigate the hazards of DMF for men, the level of exposure, and the alternatives to exclusion. Furthermore, the EOC and Page's barrister did not coordinate their arguments.

I knew nothing about the Equal Opportunities Commission becoming involved until the day of the hearing, I think, when [the barrister] presented himself at the tribunal. I did not know this at the time, but there was a practice whereby the EOC was granted leave by the EAT to appear to argue cases which took their fancy. He was involved as amicus curiae because he was not instructed by Ms. Page.[38]

The last minute appearance of the EOC's barrister increased Page's sense of alienation from the process because she did not believe that he was familiar with the details of her case.[39]

Page not only illustrates many of the points made in chapter 3 about the 1975 Sex Discrimination Act; it is also consistent with the comparisons of British and U.S. laws prohibiting sex discrimination and comparisons of the two countries' feminist groups. The EEOC and EOC intervene in the legal process in very different ways. The EOC made it very clear that, in its participation as amicus, it was as a neutral party and not an advocate for Page. Richard Collins, health and safety expert for the EOC, and the barrister representing the EOC as amicus curiae, commented that the EOC was not representing Page, but was amicus curiae and therefore had to be impartial. This neutrality contrasts sharply with the EEOC's approach in *Wright v. Olin*, to be discussed in chapter 6. In *Olin*, the EEOC was an active participant from the start and intervened on the side of Theresa Wright.

Page was not a beneficiary of a sex discrimination law specialist's advice until a very late stage in her appeal. The record shows that her case also could have benefited from the presentation of scientific evidence that, in U.S. cases, has been supplied by feminist litigators, as counsel and amicus, and by trade union. *Page* thus illustrates further the findings discussed in chapters 3 and

---

38. Ibid.

39. This is not to suggest that he is not an extremely able barrister or that he departed from standard practice in Britain. Barristers often argue cases after having a cursory briefing by solicitors who are familiar with the facts of a particular case.

4. While the ACLU and others brought test cases on exclusionary policies and submitted amicus briefs in the United States, no feminist groups helped Page. Feminists in Britain, in part responding to Leonard's study, are only just beginning to organize a legal defense fund to share expertise in discrimination law and to bring test cases.

Leonard also documented how trade unions may not have the necessary expertise in discrimination law and, in some cases, the interests of the union conflict with the interests of women bringing claims because the union is colluding with the employer to perpetuate the discriminatory practice.[40] Page's union, the Transport and General Workers, has not made health and safety a high priority in general, nor has it been actively concerned with reproductive hazards in the workplace.[41] While several unions in the United States have been the instigators and supporters of test cases on this issue, in Britain, the largest union in the country declined to support one of its members' challenge to an exclusionary policy.

The third point of comparison borne out by *Page* is the difference between the tone of the opinions in cases in the United States and Britain. The British tribunals expressed no sympathy for Page as a victim of discrimination, nor were they skeptical about an employment policy treating men and women differently. Neither the industrial tribunal nor the Employment Appeal Tribunal appeared particularly sympathetic to Page's loss of employment or suspicious of the employer's justification for the policy. Some judges in the United States—the district judge in *Olin*, the lower court judges in *UAW v. Johnson Controls*—also failed to acknowledge the effects of exclusionary policies on individual women. Other judges in the United States have recognized the harm of discrimination and expressed sympathy for the plaintiffs. *Page* confirms the finding that most British judges and members of tribunals are less concerned about the harm of discrimination than U.S. judges have been in the past.

Fourth, comparing *Page* to cases in the United States shows the harm of the statutory exceptions to equal treatment written into the Sex Discrimination Act. While some U.S. judges invented exceptions to Title VII, section 51 gave British tribunals grounds to permit employers to refuse to hire women. (Of course, the industrial tribunal needed no such license—only the EAT referred to section 51 in *Page*.) After the EC Commission concluded that such a sweeping exception violated the Equal Treatment Directive, Parliament ostensibly narrowed the exception in the 1989 Employment Act. Acts done under statutory authority which call for treating men and women differently are now only permissible on the part of employers or those engaged in vocational training if their purpose is to protect women as regards pregnancy,

---

40. Leonard, *Judging Inequality*, 110–13.

41. As of 1986, for example, the Transport and General Workers Union was the only large union not to have a health and safety officer. See "TGWU Action," *Hazards* 11 (1986): 10.

maternity, or other circumstances giving rise to risks specifically affecting women. The Employment Act gives the secretary of state for employment (in consultation with the EOC) broad powers to determine whether treating men and women differently is protective or discriminatory. The act specifically permits different standards of exposure to lead and radiation for men and women, and allows employers to discriminate in pursuit of their general duty to provide a safe workplace. While creating the appearance of conformity with the principle of equal treatment, the 1989 Employment Act's modification of section 51 would most probably not have insured that Page would have won her case. On the contrary, the balancing of the employer's need to discriminate against the harm to workers is still left to industrial tribunals, with some oversight by the secretary of state. In cases of exclusionary policies, we may expect the same result as in *Page*.[42]

Page also exposes several important characteristics of exclusionary policies. They arise in traditionally male-dominated industries where women are only beginning to hold jobs. The manager of Freight Hire commented that he actually preferred women drivers because they were tidier, but, after the case, he would no longer hire them because they were too much trouble. Because these women are "out of place," employers may be more likely to concentrate on the differences between men and women workers. Although he was not there and this is not an account of what happened, a former medical officer of ICI comically described his imagined scenario.[43] He pictured a woman driving into the plant. The medical officer looks out the window and exclaims: "There's a woman driving that lorry! Women don't drive lorries. It's unsafe for a woman to drive a lorry."

While this account is by no means an accurate report of what happened, it does illustrate how a former ICI employee perceived the company officers: as men who see women as "out of place." According to Page, she was one of only two women drivers who ever hauled chemicals into ICI. The other woman was older (in her fifties) and drove for her husband's small freight operation. The result may be that employers focus only on reproductive hazards that affect women. One type of reproductive hazard becomes sui generis, and employers emphasize it not only over other reproductive hazards, but also over other health hazards. DMF is a dangerous substance and exposure to it leads to serious health risks. Assuming there were an exposure to

42. See Richard Townshend-Smith, *Sex Discrimination in Employment: Law, Practice and Policy* (London: Sweet and Maxwell, 1989), 130–33; Simon Deakin, "Equality Under a Market Order: The Employment Act of 1989," *International Law Journal* 19 (1980): 7–11; "The Employment Act of 1989," *Industrial Relations Legal Information Bulletin* 391 (December 19, 1989): 2–3; "The New Employment Bill," *Industrial Relations Legal Information Bulletin* 368 (1989): 14–15.

43. Interview with author, October 10, 1985.

DMF through an accident or spillage, the potential reproductive hazards would pale in significance when compared to other health hazards. It is discriminatory to raise some health risks over others in importance. An employer cannot lawfully elevate the importance of certain health risks over others when doing so leads to the exclusion of women workers. The law should not permit employers to assume one level of risk for cancer, liver damage, or male sterility and another for fetal damage.

It is precisely when women take up these traditionally male jobs that the pressure to emphasize their role as childbearers becomes strongest. Exclusionary policies treat all women as if they are continuously pregnant, despite their personal choices about life-style and parenthood, and ignore men's contribution to reproduction. Not only do employers who institute exclusionary policies usually not examine the levels of exposure, but they also usually fail to consider engineering controls, product substitution, or temporary transfers as alternatives to banning women from the workplace.

This setting apart of one kind of reproductive hazard from all other hazards has significance for how judges apply legal categories to the policies. As explained in chapter 3, the way courts and tribunals have interpreted the 1975 Sex Discrimination Act is as follows: if men and women are the same in some relevant respect, but one sex is treated less favorably (assuming no exceptions apply), discrimination has occurred. Under this analysis, only substances that affect women and fetuses, but not men, could justify the exclusion of fertile or pregnant women from the workplace. Banning women from the workplace because a substance caused sterility would be discrimination if the substance caused sterility in men as well. Therefore, the confusion on the part of counsel, the members of the tribunal, and the parties to the case over what sort of hazard DMF is and, particularly, the ignorance of its effects on men is significant. Because most members of tribunals and judges embrace a comparative approach, the only way for women to succeed in combating exclusionary policies is to persuade the judges that men and women are more alike than different: they are both vulnerable to reproductive hazards despite the different form the damage may take—damage to eggs versus damage to sperm.

One can make a persuasive argument using the comparative approach that exclusionary policies are discriminatory—if women are really more like men than we think, because men are at risk too, then it is no longer permissible to exclude women from jobs. If, however, employers, members of tribunals, and judges believe that women's proper place is in the home, that their proper role is as childbearer, and their participation in the paid labor force is secondary, it may be even harder to get them to rethink their assumptions about reproduction, even when faced with scientific evidence. When judges and tribunal members talk about exclusionary policies and justify them by appealing to physical differences between the sexes, what may really be operating is a willingness to justify the perpetuation of social differences—a contemporary example of the way social inequality is naturalized. To submit this possibility is not to suggest that these individuals are lying about their reasoning, but, rather, that it may be possible that their well-established ideas about men's and women's social roles and their assumptions about physical differences between the sexes may color their interpretation of the arguments and evidence before them.

Unless they weigh both feminist arguments about the requirements of the law and the importance of women's jobs with evidence that men, too, are at risk for sterility, and that men's exposure can lead to malformations through chromosomal mutations, and that men's exposure may lead to a higher mis-carriage rate for their partners, judges and employers will accept exclusionary policies as reasonable, and, under British law, reasonable comes to mean lawful. Because the burden of forcefully making the legal argument to show how differential treatment is discriminatory, of combating judges' assumptions about what is reasonable, and of educating them about the facts of reproduction and the effects of exposure to reproductive hazards falls on the claimant, specialist counsel and amicus curiae are crucial.

The dominance approach would require more than that judges and members of tribunals accept that, by law, women have a right to a job and that men and women are sufficiently similar biologically in their vulnerability to reproductive damage. It also would require them to acknowledge that, even if men and women are different biologically and only women can carry fetuses into workplaces, employers must accommodate this difference and insure that it does not lead women to suffer disadvantages in employment. The dominance approach might demand that if men and women are different in some relevant respect, then employers must allow women to transfer to another job during pregnancy or lower exposure levels or use less-hazardous products. The dominance approach would critique the characterization of women as always pregnant as oppressive and point out that not all women want children nor are all women equally likely to be pregnant. It would question the equation of woman with pregnant woman as well as the notion that women's primary role is childbearer, not breadwinner. Furthermore, the dominance approach might conclude that women are best suited to judge the risks for themselves and their offspring and to behave responsibly when given enough information. Legal strategists, however, must recognize that most British judges and members of tribunals adopt the comparative approach and not the dominance approach.[44]

---

44. This question of litigative strategy is addressed in Sally J. Kenney, "Reproductive Hazards in the Workplace: The Law and Sexual Difference," *International Journal of the Sociology of Law* 14 (1986): 393–414.

Johnston v. Highland Regional Council

While *Page* is the only reported case in Britain about the exclusion of fertile, as opposed to pregnant, women, a second case did address an employer's duty to protect workers from reproductive hazards.[45] Unlike *Page*, the complainant in Johnston v. Highland Regional Council[46] was a clerical worker working in a female-dominated occupation. In male-dominated occupations where women are "out of place," employers and members of tribunals characterize men and women as differently situated and allow employers to exclude women. In female-dominated workplaces, however, they are more likely to accommodate women workers' needs. In both cases, however, the tribunals acted to do what they thought would protect a potential or actual fetus.

Hazel Johnston worked in an Inverness library as one of twelve library assistants. The library acquired four visual display units,[47] and each librarian worked on one for about four hours per day. When Johnston discovered that she was pregnant, she asked the senior library assistant who assigned duties to excuse her from the shifts on the VDUs. She said that she did not mind working on them occasionally. Several of the other library assistants offered to fill in her time. Her supervisor contacted the acting regional librarian and explained that Johnston was worried about the effects of the VDU on her pregnancy. The officials consulted the medical director who stated that, to the best of his knowledge, radiation from the VDU did not affect pregnant women. He referred to the Health and Safety Executive's document, *Visual Display Units*,[48] that reported that conclusion.[49] The supervisor informed

---

45. The EOC received at least one additional request for assistance in a similar case, but the case did not go to an industrial tribunal and the EOC is not able to release the information. In Deignan v. Lambeth, Southwark and Lewisham Area Health Authority, a pregnant woman claimed a hospital discriminated against her when it required her to have a chest X ray as a condition for employment. She refused, out of concern for the fetus. The industrial tribunal commented that "she was an unsatisfactory witness" and found the hospital's requirement reasonable and not discriminatory (Case no. 22152/79/D [December 21, 1979]).

46. Johnston v. Highland Regional Council, Case no. S/1480/84 (July 31, 1984).

47. In Britain, the term is *visual display units* (VDUs); in the United States, it is video display terminals (VDTs).

48. Health and Safety Executive, *Visual Display Units* (London: HMSO, 1983).

49. The Health and Safety Executive's publication and position has been widely criticized by the Hazards movement. "Despite continuing reports of clusters of abnormal pregnancies, the Health and Safety Executive have not agreed to carry out the sort of large-scale investigation that is needed to determine whether VDUs pose a hazard to pregnant users or not. At present the Health and Safety Executive consider that 'on balance,' there is no risk to pregnant women. It is difficult to see what they base this view on as all the studies conducted to date have been inconclusive" (Women's Health Information Centre, Broadsheet no. 11, *VDUs and Pregnant Women* [London: WHIC, 1985]).

Johnston that she could not be excused from working on VDUs, and Johnston said that she would rather quit than work on them. While these discussions were taking place, Johnston had early contractions and bleeding, threatening a miscarriage, and left on sick leave.

When she returned, the supervisor warned Johnston again that he could not exempt her from working on VDUs because it would set a bad precedent. The industrial tribunal wrote:

> In their various departments the respondents had 110 VDUs and 90 percent of the operators were female. The transfer of the applicant to other duties might have led to applications from dozens of operators for transfers. There were however at least two pregnant operators who had no objection to working on VDUs. If the respondent had granted the applicant's request, they would have been admitting that there was a danger.[50]

Johnston did not return to work and, after exhausting the library's appeal procedures, brought a claim of unfair dismissal.

The industrial tribunal found that the library had not properly followed its own disciplinary procedure and was critical of the way the library responded to Johnston's concerns, saying, "the respondents gave no more than perfunctory consideration to the matter."[51] The tribunal considered evidence presented on the effects of VDUs and noted that other unions, both in the United Kingdom and Canada, allowed pregnant women to decline work on VDUs and to move to other positions. Yet the tribunal did not decide the merits of the scientific issue, stating, "it is not our task to decide or to offer any opinion on this controversial matter. It is sufficient that we were satisfied that the applicant's apprehension was by no means ill-founded."[52]

Furthermore, the tribunal carefully scrutinized the employer's claim that exempting Johnston from working on VDUs was not practical, finding "there was no evidence that if the applicant's wish had been met, there would have been a flood of similar requests."[53]

> We decided unanimously and without difficulty that in all the circumstances the respondents did not act reasonably. Accordingly the applicant's dismissal was unfair. She did not contribute to her dismissal.[54]

---

50. Johnston, S/1480/80, 4.
51. Ibid., 6.
52. Ibid.
53. Ibid.
54. Ibid., 7.

Johnston's baby died three days after birth. She stated:

I wish very much this issue had been sorted out before I became pregnant. The arguments I had with my employer and then being sacked was
very traumatic, and I now find myself wondering if stress could have had
an effect on my pregnancy as well. It's something I'll never know, but I
hope other women don't find themselves in the same predicament.[55]

Johnston is very different than *Page*. First, the industrial tribunal had
more evidence to consider on the hazards of VDUs. The evidentiary burden
was different. Johnston had only to prove that a scientific debate existed, but
Page had to either disprove the evidence presented on women or present
evidence on the effects on men. Thus, Johnston's case was easier to make.
Nevertheless, the industrial tribunal that heard Johnston's case did consider
the scientific evidence about the hazard in greater depth, no doubt because
counsel presented more evidence to it.

Second, the tribunal in Johnston was much more concerned about alternatives short of discharging Hazel Johnston. It carefully scrutinized the employer's claim that exempting her from working on a VDU was impractical.
Page left the employer free to chose among alternatives, and the tribunal did
not probe further.

Third, the disposition of the employer to risk was startlingly different.
Any evidence that the fetus, or rather a potential fetus, was at risk led the
employer to err on the side of caution in *Page*; in Johnston, the employer
stubbornly asserted there was no risk, despite some evidence to the contrary.
Perhaps the significant difference is that women were dispensable in the
freight business while nearly all VDU operators were women. The caution of
Freight Hire is seen as even more pronounced when we consider that Page was
not (and did not intend to become) pregnant, while Johnston was. Fourth,
Freight Hire was adopting a mandatory exclusion policy while Johnston was
only requesting a voluntary and temporary transfer.

Perhaps the differences between the two cases can be explained by the
fact that Johnston was a case of unfair dismissal while *Page* was a case of
discrimination. Thus, in Johnston, the industrial tribunal correctly invoked the
"reasonableness" test, carefully considering disciplinary procedures to see if
the employer acted reasonably. It may be that members of tribunals are disposed to exercise extreme caution when faced with hazards to reproduction
that result from women's exposure. The comparison reveals the difference
between treatment of hazards to reproduction resulting from women's ex-

55. Women's Health and Information Centre, *VDUs and Pregnant Women*, 2. See also
"Sacked Mum in Screen Victory," *Daily Record*, September 20, 1984.

posure in male-dominated versus female-dominated workplaces and shows how tribunals' approach to cases varies. The care, however, that the industrial tribunal took in evaluating the evidence, in scrutinizing the employer's behavior, and in considering possible alternatives in Johnston notwithstanding, *Page* carries greater weight as a precedent because it was eventually decided by the Employment Appeal Tribunal.

CHAPTER 6

U.S. Cases on Reproductive Hazards

This chapter explores the cases filed in the United States and compares them to those in Britain. In the United States, the Supreme Court has declared that exclusionary policies violate Title VII, while the British Employment Appeal Tribunal has interpreted the Sex Discrimination Act as allowing them. Most striking about the comparison, beyond the different outcomes, is the number of cases and complaints. More than forty women have filed complaints on exclusionary policies with the EEOC in contrast to the two cases brought to industrial tribunals and the handful of inquiries made to the British EOC.[1] The level of court or tribunal that decided the case also differs. In Britain, the Employment Appeal Tribunal decided the principal case, *Page v. Freight Hire*, while the highest federal court, the U.S. Supreme Court, recently decided *UAW v. Johnson Controls*.[2] Consistent with their perceptions of their judicial role as well as with their attitudes toward sex discrimination, U.S. courts assumed a central role in evaluating the merits and legality of such policies; the British tribunal deferred to employers.

Comparing the cases reveals the importance of the clear language of the Pregnancy Discrimination Act in the United States and the effect of the absence of such a legislative mandate in Britain. Some lower courts were willing to ignore the statutory language, but the Supreme Court demanded it be applied in *UAW v. Johnson Controls*. The comparison also shows that U.S. judges have been more willing to delve into scientific and policy issues and that litigants presented them with more scientific evidence than have their British counterparts. In contrast to British tribunals, the opinions of U.S. judges are more likely to include a careful consideration of the scientific justification for exclusionary policies. Judges in the United States are also more comfortable dictating employment practices, for example, requiring employers to consider less drastic alternatives to excluding women from the workplace such as introducing protective clothing, substituting another product, or temporarily transferring the worker.

---

1. House Education and Labor Committee, *A Report by the Majority Staff on the EEOC, Title VII and Workplace Fetal Protection Policies in the 1980s*, 101st Cong., 2d sess., April 1990: 16.

2. 111 S.Ct. 1196 (1991).

Although the record is mixed, judges in the United States have been more committed to formal legal equality between the sexes and more suspicious of justifications for differential treatment than their British counterparts. Judges in the United States carefully scrutinized employers' rationales for treating men and women employees differently, although they occasionally uphold such policies. U.S. courts required employers to justify treating men and women differently; British industrial tribunals assumed differential treatment to be justified if it struck them as reasonable. This difference reflects U.S. judges' lower tolerance for discrimination, their greater willingness to scrutinize employment policies, different cultural approaches to equality, and differences between feminist movements. It also may reflect the importance of the statutory mandate of the Pregnancy Discrimination Act.

These differences are differences of degree and may be shrinking in importance as President Reagan's appointments to the federal bench make their presence felt. In some of the cases, judges in the United States have deferred to employers, while British tribunals intervened. In Johnston v. Highland Regional Council,[3] for example, the British industrial tribunal found that the employer should have considered less discriminatory alternatives; in Wright v. Olin,[4] on remand, a federal district judge refused to scrutinize the facts or comply with guidelines set down by the Court of Appeals for the Fourth Circuit. (The Court of Appeals subsequently vacated this opinion and deprived it of any legal significance.) Despite these exceptions, the differences between the cases vividly illustrate differences between the U.S. and British legal and political systems, judges and members of tribunals, sex discrimination statutes, enforcement agencies, and feminist movements.

An important difference between the two systems that helps explain the different results in cases on exclusionary policies is the role of interest groups, both in sponsoring litigation and putting their views before courts and tribunals as amicus curiae. U.S. judges have the benefit of experienced counsels' oral arguments and amicus briefs that carefully argue a feminist perspective. The virtual absence of evidence before the British industrial tribunal in Page v. Freight Hire[5] and the impact of the absence of counsel in the remanded case of Wright v. Olin show how important it is to have scientific evidence and feminist perspectives before judges and members of tribunals in both countries.[6] To persuade judges and members of tribunals that exclusion-

---

3. Johnston v. Highland Regional Council, Case no. S/1480/84, July 31, 1984; see chap. 5.

4. 24 Fair Empl. Prac. Cas. (BNA) 1646 (W.D. N.C. 1980); 697 F.2d 1172 (4th Cir. 1982); on remand 585 F. Supp. 1447 (W.D. N.C. 1984), vacated without opinion, 767 F.2d 915 (4th Cir. 1984).

5. Page v. Freight Hire (Tank Haulage) Ltd., Case no. 1381/80, March 26, 1980; [1981] IRLR 13 (EAT).

6. Lord Denning, for example, blames an erroneous ruling that was subsequently overturned on the fact that no counsel had pointed out the relevant statutory provision for him.

ary policies are discriminatory, litigants in both countries must counter perceptions about women's proper place in society as well as stereotyped assumptions about the reproductive process. While traditional or even oppressive views about the role of women may be more frequently, strongly, and unashamedly stated by British judges and members of tribunals, stereotyped views appear all too often in legal opinions in the United States as well. Since, for many judges and members of tribunals, stereotyped views are their starting point, counsels' and amici's only chances of overcoming these predispositions are through rigorous arguments. When courts and tribunals only hear the employer's side of the argument, the exclusionary policies seem justifiable—even progressive.

Counsel for women plaintiffs seek to persuade judges or members of industrial tribunals to apply the categories of discrimination consistently in cases on exclusionary policies, however apparently reasonable the policy. They must engage in a complex scientific debate to educate judges about the magnitude of risk to a developing fetus, including the risks from men's exposure. Counsel are also asking judges to rethink their preconceptions about the nature of biological differences as well as their views about how strong employers' justifications must be to continue employment practices that disadvantage women. Because judges and members of tribunals are grappling with several questions at once and on many different levels, in analyzing their written opinions the similarities in the reasoning may be more interesting than the contrasts in the outcomes.

As in chapter 5, I will analyze cases on exclusionary policies and explore the theoretical issues presented in chapter 2. I will also explore judges' and industrial tribunal members' thinking about stereotypes, views about the sex/gender dichotomy, and views about how to apply the comparative approach in cases on exclusionary policies. The cases in both countries show that judges and members of tribunals have been willing to abandon, ignore, or blur previous interpretations of sex discrimination law to permit employers to justify exclusionary policies under a lower standard of justification. The Supreme Court denounced this move in *UAW v. Johnson Controls*. Under both countries' laws, one could argue persuasively (by referring to the stated purpose of legislation, judicial precedents, and scientific evidence) that exclusionary policies violate both statutes prohibiting discrimination on the basis of sex and regulations promoting health and safety in the workplace. Yet courts and tribunals have not universally found exclusionary policies inconsistent with sex discrimination law. This chapter argues that judges' and tribunal members' views of what is reasonable, their opinions on the proper place of women in society, and their understanding of the significance of biological

---

Jeremiah v. Ministry of Defense, [1979] IRLR 436, 437 (CA). See Jerome Gregory, *Sex, Race and the Law: Legislating for Equality* (London: Sage, 1987), 101.

differences between men and women lead them to uphold some of the policies and to refuse to categorically rule out such policies altogether. Judges' and tribunal members' widespread acceptance of the reasonableness of excluding women from hazardous jobs in both countries cause them to depart from established legal doctrine. When judges and members of tribunals see a legitimate motive for excluding women from exposure to reproductive hazards rather than an intention to discriminate against women, they conclude, perhaps erroneously, that exclusionary policies do not violate sex discrimination statutes. Although British and U.S. laws differ, as does the behavior of each country's judges and members of tribunals, both British and U.S. judges and members of tribunals share this tendency.

Given this tendency to consider the employer's motives rather than to apply the statute, why then did the Supreme Court, composed of a majority of conservative members, choose to issue such a strong condemnation of exclusionary policies in *UAW v. Johnson Controls*? Why did conservative members of the court of appeals vote against upholding the company's policy? Although *UAW v. Johnson Controls* is a victory for the men and women litigants and a resounding victory in the area of sex discrimination law, one can criticize the reasoning on several grounds. This chapter tries to explain the outcome as well as examine the opinions.

Before proceeding to the cases, it is worth making clear how few there are. Analyzing them allows me to explore a complex public policy question of importance to women, explore the concept of discrimination, apply feminist theory to a particular legal question, and illustrate differences between the British and U.S. legal systems. The findings of my study are, nevertheless, limited by the small number of cases. Furthermore, in common-law systems, legal development is likely to be contingent on the particular facts of individual cases, especially the characteristics of the people challenging the policies and the sympathies their individual stories evoke. Women who have brought cases in the United States wanted jobs. In chapter 7, I show how difficult it was for women workers (and the same is true for men) to vindicate their right to a safe workplace. Furthermore, antidiscrimination law, unlike the guarantee of a safe workplace in the Occupational Safety and Health Act, is within the control of individual workers. The development of the law on exclusionary policies, then, reflects the fact that workers find it easier to challenge a health and safety policy as discriminatory than as not protective of their health and safety. It is easier for women to demand access to hazardous work than to demand that employers *not* require them to perform tasks that exposed them to hazardous substances.

In *Fancher v. Nimmo*,[7] the District Court for the Eastern District of

---

7. 549 F. Supp. 1324 (E.D. Ark. 1982).

Arkansas concluded that a hospital discriminated against a pregnant woman by refusing to allow her to continue light duty in the nuclear medical services department, which exposed her to less radiation than her regular job, and by forcing her to transfer permanently to another department outside her area of expertise. The court objected to the hospital's failure to administer its own sound personnel policies properly. In Johnston v. Highland Regional Council, the British industrial tribunal had to decide whether a failure to offer alternative work to a pregnant woman was unlawful. In another case in Britain that did not reach a tribunal, women were exposed to the sheep dip oxfendozle, a potential reproductive hazard. Rather than complaining that the employer shut them out of jobs, women complained bitterly about being exposed to the hazardous drug. But in Britain, as in the United States, their claim to a safe workplace was a complaint made through their union; a discrimination complaint, however, could have been made to an industrial tribunal.[8] This contingency of law, making it easier to complain of discriminatory access to hazardous work than to protest the hazardous work itself, is what creates the false impression that, in bringing cases on exclusionary policies, women seek the right to poison themselves and their children. Instead, getting rid of exclusionary policies removes an obfuscation of the issue: employers cannot create the appearance of a safe workplace by banning women and pretending men are immune to toxic substances. Only then can the issue of men's and women's shared vulnerability to toxic substances be properly addressed.

The same legal contingency, which causes plaintiffs to protest the discriminatory access to unhealthy work rather than providing the opportunity to protest the nature of the work, may well have influenced the development of sex discrimination law on protective legislation. As I explained in chapter 1, although women disagreed about the desirability of protective legislation, women who wanted access to jobs and to end protective legislation were the ones who litigated. If women had, instead, demanded the enforcement of protective legislation, the courts might have interpreted the law differently. The development of the law on both protective legislation and exclusionary policies is contingent upon the kind of cases before the courts and the particular claims women made.

Feminist theory reminds us to consider differences among women rather than trying to develop the one "women's position" on exclusionary policies. Feminist litigators would be among the first to point out the costs and risks of putting women workers' fates in the hands of the courts and having to manipulate women's concerns into legal claims judges will accept. But if the methodology of feminist theory is listening to women's experience, we must be very careful to ask what women workers want. When analyzing what we

---

8. Bill Robb, ASTMS Safety Representative, interview with author, January, 1986.

think to be the limitations of the victory women have won in the courts, we must keep in mind why women workers felt strongly enough about the issue to see their cases through. Those women want good jobs and a safe workplace. Exclusionary policies offer them neither. Outlawing exclusionary policies gives them a chance at the first, and takes the first step toward the second.

The cases analyzed in this chapter follow the pattern of development of sex discrimination and pregnancy discrimination law laid out in chapter 4. Before passage of the Pregnancy Discrimination Act, the outcome hinged on whether employers had considered alternatives short of firing women exposed to hazardous substances. The first case after passage of the Pregnancy Discrimination Act turned on a matter of procedure. Three cases in the Fourth, Eleventh, and Sixth Circuits addressed the appropriate framework for deciding such cases under Title VII. In its ruling, the Court of Appeals for the Fourth Circuit established guidelines for evaluating particular exclusionary policies—guidelines the Eleventh Circuit grudgingly followed and the Sixth rejected. A case in arbitration about an exclusionary policy also raised interesting points about the scientific evidence underlying exclusionary policies and competing theories of discrimination. Finally, the Supreme Court's opinion in *UAW v. Johnson Controls* departed dramatically from the legal analysis employed by lower courts and the EEOC. Although some of the British and U.S. cases are very similar, contrasting *UAW v. Johnson Controls* with *Page v. Freight Hire* shows significant differences.

The first cases discussed in this chapter are about the exclusion of pregnant, rather than fertile, women and are similar to the airline cases discussed in chapter 4. In those cases, the employer claimed pregnant women could not perform the job. In the cases considered here, however, the employers claimed that women's exposure put potential fetuses at risk, although the women could perform the job. I am using whether employers explicitly justified their policies by reference to an existing or potential fetus as the defining feature of an exclusionary policy, although the airline cases and the early cases on exclusionary policies are both about discriminating against pregnant women rather than women whose infertility is not medically documented.

Equal Employment Opportunity Commission Decision 75-055

The commission decided two complaints about removing pregnant women from hazardous work before Congress passed the Pregnancy Discrimination Act in 1978.[9] Both cases turned on whether hospitals that fired pregnant technicians who worked with radiation had considered less drastic alterna-

---

9. The Equal Employment Opportunity Commission refers both to the entire enforcement agency as well as a body of commissioners who actually decide the outcome of cases. I shall use commission to refer to the adjudicative body and EEOC to refer to the enforcement agency.

tives. A technician who had worked for three years in a hospital's thyroid laboratory informed her employer she was pregnant. The hospital gave her the alternative of taking a leave of absence without pay or resigning. Afraid of losing both her pay and unemployment benefits, she resigned and filed a complaint with the EEOC.[10] The commission found that the employer should have considered laying her off, which would have preserved her unemployment benefits as well as her seniority, or it should have considered transferring her to another position in or outside the laboratory. The hospital had not only failed to offer her a transfer but frustrated her attempts to obtain one on her own initiative. The commission found she could have moved to one of some thirty-two open positions. The hospital's unwillingness to accommodate her contrasted sharply with its treatment of a man who had contracted hepatitis. The hospital transferred him to another job when he could no longer perform his laboratory job and permitted him to keep the higher rate of pay.

Although its opinion referred to the permissible level of exposure set by the National Council on Radiation Protection and Measurements, the charging party did not question whether removing her from exposure was reasonable, nor did the commission. It only questioned the decision to fire her rather than consider alternatives. The commission had no hesitation in treating the policy as disparate impact. Before passage of the Pregnancy Discrimination Act, discrimination on the basis of pregnancy fell under the rubric of disparate impact, and thus the employer had to prove that the policy was a business necessity. The commission dispensed with consideration of whether the justification for the policy was sufficiently compelling to override its impact on women and whether the challenged policy effectively carried out the business purpose in seeking to protect the fetus, assuming both to be the case. Instead, it jumped directly to the question of whether the hospital could have pursued less discriminatory alternatives. On this point, the hospital did not satisfy its burden, and thus the commission concluded reasonable cause existed that the employer violated Title VII.

Zuniga v. Kleberg County Hospital

The second case on exclusionary policies the commission decided also turned on whether the employer had considered less discriminatory alternatives.[11] Kleberg County Hospital hired Rita Zuniga as an X-ray technician in 1971— the first woman to hold that position. Two years later she asked about the hospital's policy for pregnancy leave. The administrator made it clear that, despite the hospital's discretionary policy of granting time off without pay for medical or family reasons, if she became pregnant, the hospital would fire her

10. 78 E.E.O.C. Dec. (CCH) 4182 ¶6,443 (October 29, 1974).
11. C.A. No. 77-C-62 (S.D. Texas, January 23, 1981), 692 F.2d 986 (5th Cir. 1982).

because of potential hazards to the fetus. She would not be allowed to take a leave of absence, and her job would not necessarily be available should she return to work. Nor would the hospital permit her to use sick leave or avail herself of maternity benefits that were available to women outside the X-ray department. The administrator had never before denied an employee medical leave.

Zuniga filed a charge with the EEOC, claiming that the hospital's policy constituted unlawful sex discrimination. Three months later, she discovered she was pregnant. The administrator told her to resign or he would fire her. She resigned, losing her job and her medical insurance. The commission found that, because the hospital did not consider alternatives to firing her, reasonable cause existed that the employer had discriminated. It noted that neither party actually presented evidence about what dosage of radiation Zuniga would actually receive, although it acknowledged the controversy over the safe level for a fetus and disagreement about whether a lead shield would effectively lower her dosage. The commission did not find persuasive the hospital's claim that it could neither move her to another post or hire a temporary replacement, since the hospital had not tried to do so and was located near a school that trains X-ray technicians. The commission argued that the hospital had an obligation to produce the least discriminatory impact possible, and thus, at a minimum, the hospital should have let her use her sick leave or maternity leave.

After receiving a right-to-sue notice from the EEOC,[12] Zuniga brought suit in federal district court, claiming that Kleberg County Hospital's unwritten policy violated Title VII of the Civil Rights Act of 1964 as well as the Fourteenth Amendment. Her case was the first time a federal court considered the legality of an exclusionary policy under Title VII. The U.S. District Court for the Southern District of Texas found that the hospital had not discriminated against Zuniga. District Judge Owen D. Cox, a Republican appointed by Richard Nixon, found the administrator's "termination of the Plaintiff as an X-ray technician was based on its fear that exposure of the Plaintiff to X-rays would possibly harm Plaintiff's unborn child and in addition, that such harm might ultimately result in a lawsuit against the hospital."[13] Unlike the EEOC, Judge Cox noted that the hospital had offered her a lower-paying job as a nurse's aid.[14] He also pointed out that the hospital offered to reemploy her after the birth of her child. He accepted the hospital's claim that it could

---

12. It seems apparent from the details of the case that EEOC Commission decision 75-072 was Zuniga's EEOC complaint. 78 E.E.O.C. Dec. (CCH) 4180 ¶6,642 (November 14, 1974).

13. Zuniga v. Kleberg County Hospital, C.A. No. 77-C-62 (S.D. Texas, January 23, 1981), 2.

14. The court of appeals subsequently noted that the proffered job would not become available until more than a month after Zuniga was fired (692 F.2d 986, 988 [1982]).

neither transfer her nor afford to hold her job open. Citing expert testimony, Judge Cox concluded that a one-time exposure to radiation could damage a fetus and that no preventive measures could guarantee its safety. Judge Cox never mentioned the risk to the fetus without reiterating the risk to the hospital of lawsuits.

Although the findings of fact are straightforward, if contested, the judge's legal reasoning is less clear. He merely asserted that the hospital's policy did not discriminate against Zuniga because of sex or deny her employment opportunities, without any reference to precedent or the categories of disparate treatment or disparate impact. He concluded that the hospital's decision was "based upon a legitimate, non-discriminatory business reason or purpose and was not a pretext for discrimination."[15] Citing several precedents suggesting the hospital would be liable for prenatal injuries, Judge Cox concluded: "the hospital's objective to avoid damage and litigation was neither arbitrary nor discriminatory."[16] One might infer that Judge Cox considered Zuniga to have failed to prove disparate treatment, her claim refuted by the existence of a valid business purpose. Yet his opinion also contains traces of a disparate impact analysis in his conclusion that the hospital's policy was the most efficient, indeed the only way, of pursuing its legitimate aims of preventing injury and tort actions.

The American Civil Liberties Union's Women's Rights Project filed an amicus curiae brief when Zuniga appealed her case to the Court of Appeals for the Fifth Circuit.[17] The ACLU's participation in cases on exclusionary policies has been both constant and effective, starting with its representation of the Cyanamid women in the 1970s (see chap. 7). The ACLU was concerned that exclusionary policies fail to protect men and worried about the ramifications of such policies for women's employment opportunities. It challenged the stereotyped assumption that "women are the only appropriate objects of policies designed to protect the health of future generations."[18]

The ACLU's brief contested the hospital's and district judge's conclusions about the risks of exposure to radiation as well as the hospital administrator's ability to make such a scientific assessment.[19] Submitting evidence that the low level of exposure an X-ray technician received posed no danger to a developing fetus, the ACLU criticized the hospital for not more carefully

---

15. C.A. No. 77-C-62, 5.

16. Ibid., 5.

17. Both feminist groups and unions signed onto the ACLU's brief, including AFSCME, two chemical workers unions, ICWU and OCAW, NOW, and the Women's Legal Defense Fund.

18. ACLU brief, ii.

19. The administrator, Wayne Aycock, was a high school graduate who sold hospital supplies and equipment before becoming the hospital's administrator. He disclaimed any expertise on assessing the hazards of exposure to radiation (ibid., 6–7).

matching the medical evidence about levels of exposure to the amount of radiation Zuniga received. The ACLU also presented evidence that future offspring were at risk from a father's exposure to radiation because evidence showed that radiation caused mutations in men's chromosomes that can be transmitted through sperm to the fetus. Protective devices would have lessened Zuniga's exposure; in fact, the ACLU pointed out that the hospital subsequently used these devices for a pregnant employee it later permitted to continue working as an X-ray technician. Because the hospital could accurately monitor Zuniga's exposure level with a radiation badge, it could frequently check to insure that her exposure remained below acceptable limits.

The brief exposed the inconsistency of the hospital's posture toward acceptable health risks for its employees. Men could assume some risk to their reproductive health, women none. The ACLU maintained that this inconsistency was discrimination—the hospital treated men and women differently. If the hospital were genuinely motivated to protect employees' future offspring and not to purge pregnant women from its workforce, it should have guarded against all reproductive hazards affecting men and women, and not just those affecting the fetus through pregnant women's exposure.

The ACLU countered the hospital's claim about the likelihood of expensive lawsuits for malformed children, injured as a result of the mothers' exposure, which Judge Cox found so persuasive despite the paucity of evidence. The administrator had made his assessment that the hospital would be vulnerable to expensive lawsuits that it would lose without consulting a lawyer or the hospital's board of directors. The ACLU argued that the medical evidence showed no cause for concern about the level of exposure Zuniga received. Furthermore, the hospital had improperly ignored the risk from men's exposure, both from damage and from litigation. Not only was men's exposure likely to lead to malformed offspring, men were more likely to sue.[20] The hospital's policy of firing pregnant women while ignoring risks to offspring posed by men's exposure was discriminatory because the hospital tried to insulate itself from lawsuits from women but not lawsuits from men. In any case, the ACLU argued, the hospital's fear of future liability was hypothetical and unsupported.[21]

---

20. "Lawsuits brought by male veterans who served in Vietnam and were exposed to the herbicide agent orange exemplify this point. Some actions allege birth defects in subsequently born children, miscarriages, and 'serious maladies in servicemen.' . . . Male workers at a plant in Renssalaer, N.Y. also allege that their exposure to the herbicide oryzalin has resulted in birth defects in their children. They have filed complaints with OSHA and the Environmental Protection Agency" (ibid., 32 n.50). The ACLU argued that the hospital had liability insurance and also that cost considerations do not provide a defense to a prima facie case of discrimination (ibid., 12, 14).

21. Ibid., 14.

The ACLU also challenged the district judge's findings of law. The hospital had never argued or shown that Zuniga could not do her job—required by the business necessity defense—only that it believed the fetus was at risk (and the hospital at risk from litigation). The ACLU contested whether concern about tort liability could be included in the business necessity defense. The hospital had not shown excluding Zuniga to be necessary, a further requirement of business necessity. The ACLU revealed the recklessness with which the administrator had refused to consider such alternatives as protecting Zuniga on the job or finding a short-term replacement.

The Court of Appeals for the Fifth Circuit first addressed Zuniga's legal claims. Placing the issue squarely within the category of disparate impact, Judge Homer Thornberry, a Democrat appointed by Lyndon Johnson,[22] noted that the district judge had not stated whether he thought Zuniga had made out a prima facie case of sex discrimination before he concluded that the hospital acted on a valid business purpose.[23] When the hospital fired Zuniga, Congress had not yet passed the Pregnancy Discrimination Act (PDA) that made discrimination on the basis of pregnancy disparate treatment.[24] As described in chapter 4, before the PDA, courts considered discrimination on the basis of pregnancy to be disparate impact. Zuniga, therefore, had to claim that the hospital's "neutral" policy had a disparate impact on women and that the hospital had not established a business necessity defense. The court of appeals recognized that, after *General Electric Company v. Gilbert*,[25] pregnancy discrimination was not disparate treatment, but drew instead on *Satty*,[26] which held that Title VII forbade employers from imposing burdens on pregnant employees, such as stripping them of seniority for taking maternity leave. Applying *Satty*, Zuniga had established a prima facie case of discrimination because the hospital's policy of requiring pregnant employees to resign deprived them of employment opportunities.[27]

Briefly mentioning (without reference to the brief) the ACLU's concern that the business necessity defense requires employers to show that the individual cannot perform the job, Judge Thornberry skipped the question of whether concern about harm to the fetus or fear of lawsuits would make the exclusion of pregnant women "necessary to the safe and efficient operation of the business." Only in a footnote did the court address the ACLU's concern about whether the

---

22. The two other judges were Judge Thomas Gibbs Gee, a Republican, Richard Nixon appointee, and Judge Will Garwood, appointed by Ronald Reagan.

23. 692 F.2d. 986, 989 n.3 (1982).

24. The act was passed on October 31, 1978.

25. 429 U.S. 125 (1976); see chap. 3.

26. 434 U.S. 136 (1977).

27. 692 F.2d 986, 991 (1982).

hospital's fear of tort liability could constitute business necessity. On the one hand, it held that these decisions were normally left to the mother. On the other hand, the court noted such litigation could be financially devastating, precisely what the ACLU had argued the hospital's administrator had concluded without any reference to legal reality. Yet Judge Thornberry did not rule on the factual or legal issues raised by the employer's fear of tort liability. Like the Equal Employment Opportunity Commission before it, the court of appeals focused on whether the hospital had pursued less discriminatory alternatives. Because it had not, Judge Thornberry found the hospital's business necessity defense to be a mere pretext for discrimination. The hospital's high turnover rate for X-ray technicians, its policy of finding temporary replacements for other employees on medical leave, and its location forty-five miles from an X-ray technician school led the court to conclude that the hospital could have found a replacement for a short period. Even if doing so were inconvenient, the law required employers to consider alternatives with the least discriminatory impact. At a minimum, the hospital should have permitted Zuniga to take medical leave, something it permitted other employees to do.

Because *Zuniga* was decided before passage of the Pregnancy Discrimination Act, it has little value as a precedent for the other cases in this chapter. The hospital's policy, however, is typical of exclusionary policies. Employers usually adopt exclusionary policies in traditionally male workplaces.[28] We may now think of X-ray technicians as a position held by women, but Zuniga was the first woman to do the job at Kleberg County Hospital. Also typical is the flimsy scientific basis for the policy. Aycock, the hospital administrator, was a high school graduate with no medical training, and he had no idea what the medical evidence said about the risk of low levels of radiation to the fetus. He had no idea how much radiation an X-ray technician received or how to reduce exposure. In developing this policy, he was ignorant of the possible risk to men's reproductive capacity. He made a stereotyped assumption about the medical evidence—that only women could damage their offspring.

Also typical is the harshness of the policy. The unwillingness of the hospital to accommodate Zuniga in any way convinced the court of appeals that the hospital's real goal was to discriminate. Because the EEOC and court of appeals decided the case on the question of alternatives, the opinions are notable for the absence of any discussion of the scientific disputes over whether women were actually at risk or of the relative risks of women's and men's exposure. The court of appeals avoided having to decide whether the

---

28. See sample policies in U.S. Congress, Office of Technology Assessment, *Reproductive Health Hazards in the Workplace* (Washington, D.C.: Government Printing Office, 1985). See also Maureen Paul, Cynthia Daniels, and Robert Rosofsky, "Corporate Response to Reproductive Hazards in the Workplace: Results of the Family, Work, and Health Survey," *American Journal of Industrial Medicine* 16 (1986): 267–80.

hospital's desire to protect the fetus or its desire to absolve itself from tort liability created a legitimate defense to discriminatory practices. The district judge wasted little time pondering how to classify the hospital's policy under Title VII—the court of appeals skipped immediately to the question of alternatives. This legal muddle may be typical of early Title VII cases on sex discrimination.[29] Judges' failure to distinguish clearly between the categories of disparate treatment and disparate impact is typical of cases on exclusionary policies. *Zuniga*, however, is atypical of exclusionary policies because the hospital's policy sought to protect existing, rather than potential, fetuses. It restricted only pregnant women rather than women whose physical inability to bear a child was not medically documented.

Doerr v. B. F. Goodrich Co.

Doerr v. B. F. Goodrich Co.[30] was the first reported case challenging an exclusionary policy after Congress passed the Pregnancy Discrimination Act. The District Court for the Northern District of Ohio in *Doerr*, like the courts deciding *Zuniga*, did not directly address either the legal or the scientific questions raised by exclusionary policies. Instead, the case turned on the question of the procedural requirements for obtaining injunctive relief under Title VII.

Goodrich hired Carole Doerr in 1973 as a bagger. In 1976, the company promoted her to a position where she was regularly exposed to vinyl chloride. Less than a week later, however, Goodrich returned Doerr to her previous position, following its new policy of forbidding women of childbearing age from working in areas where they would be exposed to vinyl chloride. Goodrich's medical personnel had determined that vinyl chloride posed a significant health risk to the "unborn children of female employees."[31] Doerr was then thirty years old. She would have retained the higher rate of pay and benefits for one year.

Doerr filed a complaint with the Equal Employment Opportunity Commission and requested a right-to-sue notice, a prerequisite for bringing a case under Title VII. To recap the procedure described in chapter 4, after receiving a complaint, the EEOC is supposed to investigate the claim, determine whether there is reasonable cause to believe discrimination has occurred, and attempt conciliation—all within six months. If conciliation fails, the EEOC may file suit for the charging party or issue a right-to-sue letter. If the EEOC

29. See Richard K. Berg, "Title VII: A Three-Years' View," *Notre Dame Lawyer* 44 (1969): 311–44.

30. Doerr v. B. F. Goodrich Co., 22 Fair Empl. Prac. Cas. (BNA) 345 (N.D. Ohio, 1979).

31. Ibid., 346.

has not completed this process within six months, or if it has found "no cause," the charging party may request a right-to-sue letter and proceed to federal court on her own. Doerr did not wait for the EEOC to act. She filed for injunctive relief the day after filing her complaint with the EEOC, claiming that the loss of job experience would irreparably injure her career opportunities if the policy remained in force pending the EEOC's investigation.

Because Doerr did not follow the procedure Title VII prescribed, the central issue before the district court was whether the statute permitted courts to create exceptions to the mandatory procedures Title VII established and, if so, what did plaintiffs have to show to obtain preliminary injunctive relief?[32] After citing conflicting precedent, Judge Krupansky momentarily set aside the question of whether plaintiffs could bypass the EEOC altogether and considered what Doerr would have to show if she were to do so.[33] To override Congress's intent to have a mandated conciliation and cooling-off period, Doerr would have to show both irreparable injury and a likelihood of success on the merits. Judge Krupansky not only concluded that Goodrich's exclusionary policy had not irreparably damaged Doerr, but he was also not sure she was really injured at all, calling the damage to her career opportunities "remote" and "speculative."[34] Nevertheless, he noted that Title VII gave the courts wide powers to issue relief. Should Doerr convince the EEOC and a court that the policy harmed her, the court could fashion a remedy that would make her whole.

The most interesting part of the opinion, however, is not the procedural discussion but Judge Krupansky's view about the likelihood of Doerr succeeding on the merits. He found nothing in the record to refute Goodrich's contention that requiring the company to reinstate Doerr would damage the company. In footnotes near the end of his opinion, he considers whether exclusionary policies are justifiable. Although Doerr was contemplating sterilization, Judge Krupansky thought the chance that she, or a damaged child she might bear and whose rights she could not waive, would sue put the company at a high risk of liability.[35]

Judge Krupansky commented on Doerr's claim that Goodrich was inconsistent in its policy because it excluded only women despite evidence that vinyl chloride harmed men's reproductive capacity. He stated that a decision on the legality of the policy would no doubt turn on the medical and scientific evidence. Yet he gave his opinion on the likely result.

---

32. The Court of Appeals for the First Circuit addressed this issue in Bailey v. Delta Airlines, 722 F.2d 942 (1983). See also Wagner v. Taylor, 836 F.2d 566 (D.C. Cir. 1987).

33. Richard Nixon appointed Robert B. Krupansky, a Republican, to the district court in 1970, and Reagan elevated him to the Sixth Circuit in 1982.

34. 22 Fair Empl. Prac. Cas. (BNA) 344, 348 (1979).

35. Ibid., 350 n.3.

The comparative risks of transplacental carcinogenesis on the one hand and male mutagenesis on the other resulting from exposure to vinyl chloride at the current permissible levels are not well established as the medical evidence to date appears largely inconclusive. To the extent *it can be subsequently demonstrated* that the risk of fetal damage associated with transplacental carcinogenesis is substantially greater than that associated with male mutagenesis, it might appear that defendant's policy is grounded upon a legitimate, nondiscriminatory factor.[36]

Judge Krupanksy's way of describing what the medical evidence would have to show for the employer's policy to be lawful suggests that he assumes the evidence will show that men and women are not similarly vulnerable to the reproductive hazards of vinyl chloride. The court did not consider whether the focus in the scientific community on hazards from women's exposure might itself be the result of gender bias—researchers neglecting to investigate the effects of men's exposure. Neither did it consider the question of whether Goodrich assumed a different posture toward risk for hazards to a potential fetus caused by men's exposure to hazardous substances than for hazards to a potential fetus caused by women's exposure, allowing men to assume some risk while allowing women to assume none. Goodrich, of course, also assumed a different posture toward the legal risks: it sought to protect itself against lawsuits from women employees and their offspring but not from men employees and theirs.

What should employers' policies be, given the uncertainty of the scientific evidence? Does Title VII permit them to assume risks from women's exposure and assume no risk from men's if there is little evidence? Given the impact of this policy on working women, should the would-be discriminator not also have to prove that men are *not* affected by exposure? Should the employer treat a thirty-year-old woman who is contemplating sterilization as if she were always pregnant? What amount of exposure to vinyl chloride do workers receive? Can Goodrich control, monitor, and reduce the exposure to safe levels? The district court answers none of these questions in *Doerr* because the threshold issue is whether she followed the procedures Title VII mandates. Because she did not, and because she could not show irreparable injury, Doerr lost her case. The Court of Appeals for the Fourth Circuit addressed many of these questions and established a framework for deciding cases on exclusionary policies in *Wright v. Olin*.[37] That precedent stood until the Supreme Court decided *UAW v. Johnson Controls*.

---

36. Ibid., n.4; italics added.
37. 24 Fair Empl. Prac. Cas. (BNA) 1646 (W.D. N.C. 1980), 697 F.2d 1172 (4th Cir. 1982), *on remand*, 585 F. Supp. 1447 (W.D. N.C. 1984), *vacated without opinion*, 767 F.2d 915 (4th Cir. 1984).

Wright v. Olin

The Court of Appeals for the Fourth Circuit was the first court to fully explicate the legal issues exclusionary policies raised after Congress passed the Pregnancy Discrimination Act. The court established a framework for analyzing exclusionary policies and remanded the case. The legal analysis in *Olin* not only differs from *Zuniga* and *Doerr*, but so do the hazards the policy seeks to control. Olin's policy protected women whose infertility was not medically documented from the hazards of lead and benzene rather than radiation. Radiation is unusual in that scientists have studied it extensively for reproductive effects, and employers can easily and accurately monitor exposure. Most reproductive hazards have not been the subject of extensive study nor are they easy to monitor. Moreover, like Goodrich, Olin sought to exclude all women who could not medically prove they were physically incapable of bearing a child, not just pregnant women. Its policy is thus more representative of exclusionary policies.[38]

The EEOC-assisted challenge to Olin's "fetal vulnerability policy" was just one piece of a broad challenge to the company's employment practices. Having received more than fifty charges against the company, the Equal Employment Opportunity Commission filed suit against Olin in September, 1978, alleging many instances of race and sex discrimination in violation of Title VII.[39] Five months later, the EEOC filed a much broader amended charge for Theresa Wright. After receiving a right-to-sue notice, Wright and Howell (the representative of the class of Black employees) filed separate class actions. Consolidating the cases, District Judge Jones found that Olin had not discriminated.[40] In the four paragraphs of the opinion devoted to Olin's policy on "fetal vulnerability," Judge Jones described the policy and concluded that Olin could not sufficiently lower exposures.

The Court finds that the policy was instituted for sound medical and humane reasons and is based upon sound medical knowledge and research and years of monitoring of levels of chemical exposure at Olin's plant. The Court further finds that it was not instituted or maintained with the intent or purpose to discriminate against females because of their sex. The evidence shows that the purpose of the policy is to protect the unborn fetus at a time when it is most vulnerable to exposure to harmful chemicals. The policy has been conducted in a reasonable manner, and

---

38. Office of Technology Assessment, *Reproductive Hazards in the Workplace*, Appendix 8A: Reproductive Health Protection Policies.

39. 24 Fair Empl. Prac. Cas. (BNA) 1646, 1650 (W.D. N.C. 1980).

40. Ibid., 1658–59. Lyndon Johnson appointed Judge Woodrow Wilson Jones, a former Congressman and Democratic Executive Committee member, in 1967.

the Company has counselled with females who have indicated their desire to enter restricted or controlled areas. The record shows that very few female employees have indicated a desire to work in the "restricted" areas. No female employee has filed a charge of discrimination with the commission alleging that this policy discriminates against females because of sex.[41]

On appeal, the court of appeals found that the EEOC could not legally pursue charges for which it had not made a reasonable cause determination. On the charges properly before the court, the court of appeals upheld the district court's judgment for Olin in all respects except its holding on the "fetal vulnerability policy." Had either court ruled differently on the other claims of discrimination, Wright might have more easily proven that Olin's exclusionary policy was a mere pretext for sex discrimination—part of a pattern of practices that produced a workplace segregated by race and sex.

Olin had instituted its exclusionary policy in 1978, after four years of planning. The company's Department of Hygiene and Toxicology had determined that Olin should restrict women's exposure to several hazards, principally lead, to protect potential fetuses. The program created three job classifications: restricted jobs exposed workers to known teratogens and abortifacients, and Olin excluded from these jobs all women who did not have medical proof that they were physically incapable of bearing a child; controlled jobs involved some risk, and pregnant women could only work them after consideration on a case-by-case basis (nonpregnant women could work after signing a form stating that they recognized the job posed some risk); and unrestricted jobs posed no hazard to a fetus. Olin's policy effectively barred nonsterilized women from access to many unrestricted jobs, since restricted and controlled jobs were often stepping stones to unrestricted jobs. Olin warned men orally about the reproductive hazards posed by lead, but did not restrict the jobs they could hold.

Since the agency had such a large stake in the broad range of charges against Olin, only one of which remained, it is not surprising that the EEOC actively helped Wright in the preparation of her case. Olin objected, but the court of appeals ruled that the intervention was lawful. The EEOC's brief discussed all the charges it appealed and thus devoted only a few pages to Olin's "fetal vulnerability policy."[42] Although the arguments were not enough

---

41. 24 Fair Empl. Prac. Cas. (BNA) 1646, 1659 (W.D. N.C. 1980). In a 1979 arbitration case against Olin, however, the arbitrator upheld Olin's policy of excluding women aged eighteen to fifty who did not have medical proof of infertility from jobs that exposed them to lead. One woman had herself sterilized to keep her job. In re Olin Corporation and International Association of Machinists and Aerospace Workers, 72 Lab. Arb. 291 (August 7, 1979).

42. EEOC brief, 13–17, 46–50.

to convince either court that the company had discriminated, the EEOC's brief did show that Olin's workforce was segregated by race and sex.

The EEOC's brief questioned the credibility of the two witnesses who developed the policy and testified, neither of whom were experts. Neither could identify any of the medical or scientific literature supporting the policy, a point emphasized in the court of appeals's opinion. One expert testified that women have been known to bear children from age five to sixty-three. The agency pointed out that Olin had conducted no studies of its own or entertained alternatives to excluding women, although no woman who had held a controlled job had ever become pregnant.

The brief devoted one paragraph to legal analysis and equivocated about how to classify the policies under discrimination doctrine. While the paragraph began with a declaration that Olin's policy was facial discrimination (that is, explicit discrimination—the policy, on its face, discriminates) in violation of the Pregnancy Discrimination Act (therefore disparate treatment), the footnote mentioned both the BFOQ and business necessity defenses and the citations referred to disparate impact cases. The EEOC moved on quickly to the claim that Olin's policy was not necessary to carry out its legitimate business purpose. The agency Congress created to enforce and define the law, the agency the courts turn to for guidance as the experts in discrimination law, invited the court to misapply Title VII precedent and blur the line between defenses. The EEOC seemed content merely to argue that, although protection of the unborn is a legitimate employer interest, Olin's policy was not necessary to carry out that purpose and the company should have explored alternatives.

The brief contrasted Olin's policy of merely counselling men about the reproductive hazards posed by lead while removing all women: "At trial, Olin failed either to explain why women should not be considered equally responsible or to justify the different treatment of similarly situated male and female employees."[43] The EEOC referred to Congress's intent to end discrimination based on stereotypes and pointed out that good intentions do not redeem discriminatory practices. The thrust of the EEOC's very brief argument was that, although such policies are facially discriminatory, this policy cannot be justified as a business necessity. The EEOC clearly hoped to gain by placing the policy in the context of widespread employment practices that discriminated on the basis of sex and race.

The legal issues were thrashed out in the briefs of the ACLU and the Equal Employment Advisory Council, rather than in the briefs of the parties or the EEOC. By rejecting the legal analysis advocated by Wright and the ACLU, the *Olin* court diverged from previous interpretations of Title VII that

---

43. Ibid., 49.

set out the two categories of disparate treatment and disparate impact. Exclusionary policies are clearly disparate treatment because they are *per se* discriminatory. The only defense for proven disparate treatment is that sex is a BFOQ. The EEOC defines the BFOQ as a narrow exception, and courts have applied the test set out in *Weeks*: whether all or substantially all women are incapable of performing the job. By noting the broad purposes of Title VII and pointing to precedent such as *Weeks*, one could argue that exclusionary policies are not lawful because being potentially pregnant does not make one incapable of performing a job.

Judges have also construed the business necessity defense to be a narrow one because many acceptable business practices may have an adverse impact on a protected group. On the other hand, because the neutral requirements that have a disparate impact are not intentional discrimination (otherwise they would be disparate treatment), the business necessity defense is broader than the BFOQ defense. The test for business necessity is whether the practice in question is necessary for the safe and efficient operation of the business, not that it serves some other beneficial private or societal purpose. *Olin* was decided before the Supreme Court lowered the standard of proof for business necessity. Yet in *Olin*, the court of appeals gave employers wider scope to treat women differently than the business necessity defense had allowed.

The court claimed that it could not apply traditional Title VII analysis and that it was trying to determine what Congress intended. Congress had only briefly addressed the question of exclusionary policies in its hearings. The hearings on the Pregnancy Discrimination Act (PDA) were a prompt and pointed effort to overturn the Supreme Court's decision in *Gilbert*. Although the main purpose was to overrule *Gilbert*, the plain language of the PDA admits no exceptions. Furthermore, the main theme of those hearings was that women should not suffer a reduction in employment opportunities because they bear children.[44] The plain language of the PDA does not say that Congress intended to create an exception to allow employers to exclude women ostensibly to protect fetal health. Nor had there been prior rulings allowing defenses other than the BFOQ for cases of disparate treatment. Without evidence that the wording of the statute was ambiguous or that Congress intended such an exception, the court could have concluded that employers would have to seek legislative change if they wanted to treat women differently than men.

The evidence on the reproductive hazards of lead, while limited, is more extensive than on any other hazard except, perhaps, radiation. The evidence that men's reproductive capacity is at risk from lead exposure was sufficiently

---

44. For a detailed discussion of the hearings, see Hannah Arterian Furnish, "Prenatal Exposure to Fetally Toxic Work Environments: The Dilemma of the 1978 Pregnancy Amendments to Title VII of the Civil Rights Act of 1964," *Iowa Law Review* 66 (1980): 63–129.

convincing to lead OSHA to set a single standard of exposure for men and women.[45] The Court of Appeals for the District of Columbia Circuit upheld the single standard and expounded at length on reproductive hazards to men posed by lead exposure.[46]

Because the legal question before the court of appeals—do exclusionary policies constitute disparate treatment or disparate impact—was "an open one," Judge Phillips sought "to put the rulings in the proper conceptual framework for analysis,"[47] recognizing "the parties are in hopeless conflict on this fundamental point."[48] Olin relied on *McDonnell Douglas v. Green* and *Texas Department of Community Affairs v. Burdine*,[49] which held that, after an employee had proved a prima facie case of sex discrimination, an employer could offer a defense by claiming a legitimate, nondiscriminatory reason explained its action. Olin argued that its legitimate concern for fetal health answered the charge of discrimination. Wright countered that *McDonnell Douglas* and *Burdine* were both cases of covert discrimination, while Olin's written policy overtly discriminated on the basis of sex.[50] Thus, *Burdine* and *McDonnell Douglas* were cases in which the courts permitted an employer to argue that discrimination did not occur because it had a more convincing explanation. Yet Olin's policy explicitly treated women differently than men, and the employer was trying to justify the differential treatment rather than deny it existed. The policy was facial or *per se* discrimination.

The court agreed with Wright that *McDonnell Douglas* was not controlling, finding it "wholly inappropriate" for deciding cases involving exclusionary policies.[51] The court distinguished *Olin* from cases where courts had to infer an intent to discriminate and further recognized rulings that held that good intentions are not enough to justify discrimination.[52] Once the court concluded that Olin's policy was facially discriminatory, it then had to decide what burden Olin must meet to defend its policy: BFOQ or business necessity. Wright argued that the only defense for facial discrimination, disparate treatment, was the BFOQ defense.

---

45. 29 CFR §1910.1025.

46. United Steelworkers of America v. Marshall, 647 F.2d 1189, 1256–58 (1980), *cert. denied*, Lead Industries Association v. Donovan, 453 U.S. 913 (1981). See chap. 7.

47. Jimmy Carter appointed J. Dickson Phillips, a Democrat, in 1978. The other two judges were Francis D. Murnaghan, Jr., and James M. Sprouse, both Democrats appointed by Carter.

48. 697 F.2d 1172, 1183 (1982).

49. McDonnell Douglas v. Green, 411 U.S. 792 (1973); Texas Department of Community Affairs v. Burdine, 450 U.S. 248 (1981).

50. I will adopt the court of appeals's approach of discussing arguments presented by amici curiae in favor of Wright's case as arguments presented by Wright (697 F.2d 1172, 1183 n.16 [4th Cir. 1982]).

51. Ibid., 1185.

52. Ibid., n. 20.

The court decided, however, that the facts did not "fit with absolute precision into any of the developed theories."[53] The court found: "it is often appropriate to assess particular Title VII claims and defenses alternatively under different theories," concluding

> these theories [disparate treatment/BFOQ, disparate impact/business necessity] were not expected nor intended to operate with rigid precision with respect to the infinite variety of factual patterns that would emerge in Title VII litigation.[54]

Judge Phillips suggested that the courts could freely choose which category to apply, constrained only by the general principles underlying Title VII and the need to make the doctrine as stable and predictable as possible.[55]

He found the BFOQ defense too narrow because it did not provide Olin the opportunity to justify its policy. He called the logical dispute over whether the policy can be considered under disparate impact theory because it is not neutral, that is, it explicitly applies only to women, "mere semantic quibbling." The most appropriate analogy, he thought, was *Satty*. In that case, the Supreme Court held that although the practice of stripping the seniority of women who left work to have a child was "neutral," it had an overwhelmingly disparate impact on women and was not justified by business necessity. Judge Phillips's choice to analyze Olin's policy under the disparate impact framework led him to deduce backwards that Olin's policy, like the one at issue in *Satty*, was facially neutral. The continued use of the word *neutral* for either policy is a most astounding misuse of language, despite the correctness of its logic under Title VII doctrine in *Satty*. Phillips's use of *Satty*, however, is particularly interesting because the Pregnancy Discrimination Act legislatively overturned the reasoning of *Satty* and placed pregnancy discrimination squarely in the category of disparate treatment. Phillips wrongly returned to pre–PDA principles to decide the case. Although Olin's policy was not neutral (therefore not disparate impact), Judge Phillips concluded that Olin should still have the opportunity to justify its policy by relying on the business necessity defense. His previous statement that good intentions do not redeem discriminatory policies notwithstanding, Judge Phillips employed the framework of disparate impact because he believed Olin's concern for its women employees' offspring had some validity, despite its clear impact. The unstated conclusion, of course, is that regardless of logic and Title VII doctrine, the discriminatory impact of Olin's policy was an unintended consequence of

---

53. Ibid., 1184.
54. Ibid.
55. "While the loose equation—overt discrimination/only BFOQ defense—is therefore properly descriptive of a paradigmatic litigation pattern, it is not an accurate statement of any inherent constraints in Title VII doctrine" (ibid., 1186 n.21).

Olin's good intentions rather than a deliberate act of discrimination by bad people acting on prejudice and stereotyped assumptions.

After deciding that Olin should have a chance to offer a business necessity defense, the court of appeals considered whether protection of fetal health could be contained within the scope of that defense. In previous cases involving hazardous work, the courts let women decide for themselves whether they wanted to assume the risk on the same basis as men. The court ruled, however, that the health of a future fetus could not properly be left to the decision of the mother. Instead, employers were entitled to treat yet-to-be-conceived fetuses as "legitimate business visitors" or "personal service customers."[56] Other courts had recognized that employers' legitimate concern for the safety of passengers, clients, or customers could establish the business necessity defense.[57] Judge Phillips's opinion glides over the question of why fetuses who are not yet conceived as well as actual fetuses should both be considered analogous to an invited guest.

After establishing that the appropriate framework was disparate impact and that the yet-to-be-conceived fetus could be likened to a "business visitor," the court set out guidelines for determining when the risk to potential fetuses would constitute a business necessity justifying the exclusion of all nonsterilized women. First, the employer had the burden of proving that women's occupational exposure posed a significant risk to the fetus. An employer's mere belief that this was the case was not enough—it would have to prove the risk by independent, objective evidence. Although reputable scientific evidence must underlie the policy, consensus need not exist. Second, the employer must show that the risk exists only through exposure of the mother and not the father. Otherwise, the policy is underinclusive as well as unlawful under Title VII. Third, the employer must show there are no less discriminatory alternatives to exclusion.[58] If there were obvious alternatives, claimants might be able to prove that the concern about fetal health was just a pretext for discriminating against women.

Although the court of appeals only ruled on the question of law, remanding the case for the district court to apply its legal ruling to the facts of the case, it did note that the evidence Olin presented would not have been enough to prove business necessity. The three Olin employees who testified did not have the necessary scientific expertise to develop such a policy, and none of the three could cite any of the medical literature undergirding the policy. The court did not, however, comment on Olin's failure to consider alternatives or

---

56. 697 F.2d 1172, 1189 n.25 (4th Cir. 1982).

57. Burwell v. Eastern Air Lines, Inc., 633 F.2d 361 (4th Cir. 1980), *cert. denied*, 450 U.S. 965 (1981); New York City Transit Authority v. Beazer, 440 U.S. 568 (1979).

58. In a footnote, the court recognized that the burden of demonstrating acceptable alternatives fell on the claimant (697 F.2d 1172, 1191 n.29 [1982]).

the inconsistency of its policy toward reproductive hazards to women and men exposed to lead. It acknowledged the medical and scientific evidence amici curiae presented, but left it to the district court to sort through on remand.

The EEOC was out of the case because it had not made a reasonable cause determination about Olin's exclusionary policy, and Wright was no longer able to represent the class. Legally and jurisdictionally barred because she was no longer a "woman of childbearing age," Wright asked to be excused as a representative of the class. Lawyers for amici curiae were concerned that important evidence had not been collected in discovery and felt it was unlikely Judge Jones would allow them to reopen the record.[59] They thought there was no reasonable likelihood of further favorable development of the law.

Although Wright was excused and no other class member came forward, Judge Jones heard evidence from Olin in defense of its policies and wrote an opinion as if Wright were present, had called witnesses to testify on her behalf, and as if her lawyers had submitted briefs and cross-examined witnesses. Although the law requires a judge to dismiss the case if no other class member comes forward, Judge Jones went ahead with the case without a class representative, without counsel on one side, and without anyone to cross-examine witnesses.

The court of appeals's skepticism about the need for a policy restricting only women, its statements about the high burden of justification employers must meet to have a sex-specific policy, and its criticisms of the paucity of evidence supporting the policy did not change Judge Jones's mind. He found that the company had tried to reduce exposure as much as possible. Altering his approach to consider the case under the disparate impact rubric and noting the court of appeals's guidelines, he went first to the third guideline, concluding that Olin had considered several less-discriminatory alternatives, none of which were satisfactory.

The court of appeals's comments, however, were not wasted on Olin. It presented several outside medical experts who had analyzed the scientific basis for its fetal protection policy. They testified that the fetus was most at risk in the first weeks of pregnancy, before a woman may know she is pregnant. They also testified that the risks posed by maternal exposure existed at lower levels than for paternal exposure, and that the hazards posed by paternal exposure were less well documented. (Of course, alternative evidence was never presented, nor were the experts cross-examined.) Judge Jones concluded that a substantial risk existed for a fetus and that the risk was confined to women, and he admonished women to be grateful for Olin's policy.

---

59. Joan Bertin, ACLU Women's Rights Project, telephone interview with author, November 1, 1988.

An employer such as Olin can justifiably choose a policy of fetal protection as a moral obligation to protect the next generation from injury, and it is a social good that should be encouraged and not penalized. Women in general should applaud the effort and there is every indication that most of the women employees at the Olin plant appreciate and support the policy.[60]

Notably absent from both of Judge Jones's opinions, as well as Judge Phillips's, is any discussion of the risk of tort liability as a justification for the policy.

The court of appeals later vacated the district court's decision on the grounds of due process, depriving the district court's opinion of any legal significance.[61] Olin remained bound by the Fourth Circuit's ruling but lacked an explicit determination that its policy could be justified under the Fourth Circuit's guidelines.[62]

Two features of *Wright v. Olin* invite comparison with the British case of *Page v. Freight Hire*. Judge Jones's original opinion and his opinion on remand reached the same result as the Employment Appeal Tribunal in *Page*. The U.S. district court, the British industrial tribunal, and the British EAT all assumed the policies to be justified rather than holding employers to a high burden of proof. The British tribunals were reluctant to examine employers' policies or interfere with the conduct of their businesses. Despite the Fourth Circuit's determination that Title VII required courts to scrutinize exclusionary policies carefully, Judge Jones mimicked the British courts and tribunals.

As pertinently observed in *Furnco Const. Corp. v. Waters*, "courts are generally less competent than employers to restructure business practices, and unless mandated to do so by Congress, they should not attempt it."[63]

The district court and British tribunals were similarly disposed to favor exclusionary policies, expressed little recognition of the impact on women's employment opportunities, and offered little scrutiny of the employer's justifications. While the court of appeals was both more suspicious of the policy and

---

60. 585 F. Supp. 1447, 1453 (W.D. N.C. 1984).

61. 767 F.2d 915 (4th Cir. 1984). Judge Murnaghan wrote, "Given the circumstances, it was hardly a surprise that Olin's unilateral showing of business necessity remained unrebutted, resulting in the judgment of dismissal with prejudice."

62. Judge Jones dismissed the complaint on August 12, 1985, when no other class member came forward.

63. 585 F. Supp. 1447, 1452 (1985), *vacated without opinion*, 767 F.2d 915 (4th Cir. 1984).

more concerned about its impact, the court's opinion is similar to the EAT's in one key respect: both bodies were prepared to stray from previous legal analysis on discrimination in evaluating exclusionary policies. And both created new exceptions that were, arguably, inconsistent with the broad purposes of the statutes. Even though Olin's policy explicitly treated men and women employees differently, the court of appeals deviated from the conventional analysis under Title VII and analyzed the exclusionary policy under the rubric of disparate impact rather than disparate treatment. One commentator characterized this maneuver as "analytical gymnastics to attempt to fit the claim into disparate impact theory."[64]

Presumably because the court of appeals perceived the motivation for Olin's policy as laudable, the judges not only allowed the company a business necessity defense but also expanded that defense to incorporate a general societal goal of protecting fetal health. Before, that defense covered only the pursuit of business goals.[65] The court of appeals in *Olin* was surprisingly like British courts and industrial tribunals who found employment practices to be lawful when they seemed reasonable, regardless of whether they treated women or men less favorably because of their sex. In the courts and tribunals that heard cases on exclusionary policies in both countries, judges and members of tribunals not only looked upon them favorably but also changed legal doctrine to find them lawful.

The court of appeals, however, was more ready to scrutinize the scientific justification for the policy, or at least to order the district court to do so, than was the British EAT. Although the court in *Olin* modified traditional Title VII categories to allow employers to defend an exclusionary policy, in practice, the court established a gantlet for any particular policy to run. The small sample makes it hard to explain differences, either between the British and U.S. courts and tribunals or between the district court and court of appeals. Unlike the British tribunals, the court of appeals had the benefit of amici's legal and scientific analysis. However, District Judge Jones also had the benefit of at least some of this information, so why was his approach so different than the court of appeals? The differences between the district court and the court of appeals in *Olin* are intriguing; and they reveal the limitations of using broad systemic explanations for outcomes in individual cases.

The court of appeals's decision in *Olin* was not a clear victory for either party. Wright and the ACLU would have liked the court to declare exclusionary policies discriminatory as a matter of law. Olin would have liked the court to have set a low evidentiary standard for such policies to be lawful. By opting

---

64. Diane Sanders Peake, "Employment Discrimination *Wright v. Olin Corp.*: Title VII and the Exclusion of Women from the Fetally Toxic Workplace," *North Carolina Law Review* 62 (June 1984): 1083.

65. This precedent was watered down in Wards Cove v. Atonio, 490 U.S. 642 (1989).

for a decision between those two positions and by resting the lawfulness of the policy on the nature of the scientific evidence, the court of appeals made it likely that parties would again bring exclusionary policies before the courts. It did, however, create a narrow exception and place the burden of justification squarely on the employer. In contrast, the opinion of the EAT in *Page* insured that aggrieved British women would be unlikely to see legal action as an effective way to fight exclusionary policies. Although the EAT played an important role in setting public policy by interpreting the Sex Discrimination Act as permitting exclusionary policies, the decision discouraged future litigation on this issue. By ruling that some exclusionary policies might be lawful under Title VII, courts in *Olin* and *Hayes* insured an important position for themselves as the arbitrators of future disputes. The Fourth Circuit's legal framework was the starting point for opinions in other circuits and was the legal standard for nine years, until the Supreme Court decided *UAW v. Johnson Controls*.

Hayes v. Shelby Memorial Hospital

The Court of Appeals for the Fourth Circuit had not yet handed down its decision in *Olin* when the District Court for the Northern District of Alabama heard *Hayes v. Shelby Memorial Hospital*.[66] On appeal, however, the Court of Appeals for the Eleventh Circuit referred to the Fourth Circuit's opinion. The facts of *Hayes* are the same as *Zuniga*, but Hayes, unlike Zuniga, was fired after Congress passed the Pregnancy Discrimination Act. *Hayes* is significant for three reasons. First, the district court and court of appeals clearly applied post–Pregnancy Discrimination Act doctrine to the case. Second, the firing of pregnant X-ray technicians is a recurring problem. Third, the *Hayes* court was much more critical of the *Olin* court's approach and more suspicious of the value of exclusionary policies in general. The Court of Appeals for the Eleventh Circuit in *Hayes* both fully analyzed the legal issues exclusionary policies raise and determined whether Shelby Memorial Hospital's policy violated Title VII.

The Court of Appeals for the Eleventh Circuit distinguished its ruling from the Fourth Circuit's in *Olin* and came closer than any court to the position advocated by feminist commentators and amici supporting Hayes. Yet its criticism of *Olin* obfuscates the fact that the Eleventh Circuit adopted the same legal framework, making its own analysis seem confusing and contradictory. Although Hayes won her case, and the court declared that Shelby Memorial Hospital's policy violated Title VII, the court did not insist

---

66. 546 F. Supp. 259 (N.D. Ala. 1982), 726 F.2d 1543 (11th Cir. 1984), *rehearing denied*, 732 F.2d 944 (11th Cir. 1984).

on analyzing exclusionary policies under the rubric of disparate treatment. It did not fulfill the expectations that its bold rhetoric and critique of *Olin* created.

Shelby Memorial Hospital's radiology department hired Sylvia Hayes as a staff technician on August 11, 1980. She worked taking X rays on the 3:00 to 11:00 P.M. shift because she was attending nursing school in the mornings.[67] In October, 1980, her doctor confirmed that she was two months pregnant. After discussing her occupational duties with her, he determined that it would be safe for her to work until about April 24, 1981, if she followed safety precautions. When Hayes told the hospital radiology department's medical director (who had held that position for only two days)[68] that she was pregnant, the hospital fired her the same day. Testimony at the trial revealed that the hospital was satisfied with her job performance and the only reason it dismissed her was because of a fear that her exposure to radiation would damage the fetus and the hospital might be subject to a lawsuit. The hospital had no written or formal policy requiring it to exclude pregnant women from allegedly hazardous work,[69] nor had anyone ever told Hayes that she would lose her job if she became pregnant.[70] Hayes was the sole support of her family, her husband had been laid off, and she had two children.[71]

The United States District Court for the Northern District of Alabama heard Hayes's complaint that she was the victim of sex discrimination. The morning of the trial, Judge Guin revealed his predisposition,[72] stating "the grandfather in me feels that what the hospital did is right."[73] By the end of the trial, after considering the medical and scientific evidence, and learning about how Shelby Memorial made its decision, he concluded that its action was "paternalistic and extreme."[74] He found that distinctions among employees based on pregnancy were *per se* violations of Title VII, as amended by the Pregnancy Discrimination Act, and ruled that Hayes had established a prima facie case against the hospital. After reaching the conclusion that the hospital's policy was facial discrimination, he turned to *Texas Department of Community Affairs v. Burdine* to determine the employer's burden of proof. But as Theresa Wright's lawyers had pointed out in *Olin*,[75] in *Burdine*, the company denied that sex was the basis of the differential treatment. Under the *Burdine*

---

67. Hayes reported that, despite being enrolled in classes, she would have accepted a transfer to the day shift if that was the only way she could keep her job (EEOC brief, 6).

68. Ibid., 4.

69. ACLU brief, 1.

70. Appellee brief, 7.

71. EEOC brief, 5–6.

72. J. Foy Guin, Jr., a Republican, was appointed by Richard Nixon.

73. Appellee brief, 47.

74. Ibid.

75. The EEOC's and ACLU's briefs both mentioned this point.

framework, employers can provide evidence of a lawful, nondiscriminatory reason for their actions. In this case, as in *Olin*, the hospital did not deny that its policy discriminated, but claimed that differential treatment was justified and therefore lawful. The hospital defended its policy by arguing both the business necessity defense as well as the BFOQ defense. Judge Guin ruled that, because the case involved deliberate discrimination rather than a neutral employment practice, traditional interpretations of Title VII prevented the hospital from arguing a business necessity defense. Nevertheless, the court considered both defenses.

Relying on *Dothard v. Rawlinson*,[76] the court held that to prove a business necessity defense the hospital must show that the employment practice was necessary to safe and efficient job performance. Judge Guin found that Hayes's pregnancy in no way undermined her ability to take X rays. He refused to extend the business necessity defense to include an employer's desire to avoid tort liability, saying, "such an unwarranted extension would shift the focus of the business necessity defense from a focus of concern for the safety of hospital patients to a focus of concern for hospital finances."[77] The court found that even if such an extension were made, the hospital's claim would fail because it had refused to investigate such alternatives to firing Hayes as moving her to other duties or moving her to the day shift. He attached much significance to the hospital's decision to allow two other pregnant radiology technicians to continue working. Those two technicians were white and Hayes was black.[78]

Judge Guin also rejected the hospital's BFOQ defense, saying "potential for fetal harm, unless it adversely affects a mother's job performance, is irrelevant to the BFOQ issue."[79] The hospital had argued that, even if it met the standards of neither defense, the court should recognize a valid desire on the part of the hospital to avoid litigation.

The defendant's suggestion that it be allowed to terminate at will any pregnant employee merely because there is a possibility that the employee's child might later sue the hospital is untenable. The Constitution

---

76. 433 U.S. 321 (1977).

77. 546 F. Supp. 259, 264 (1982).

78. "Evidence adduced at trial revealed that prior to the termination of the plaintiff's employment, two white radiology technicians at Shelby Memorial had become pregnant but were not fired; instead, one technician simply took greater precautions, and the other was allowed to read X-ray films during the course of her pregnancy" (ibid., 264). Appellant's brief objected to Hayes's attorney's continual reference in the brief to the race of Hayes, the other technicians, and the medical director, given that the trial judge made no findings about the allegation of racial discrimination (Brief, 3).

79. 546 F. Supp. 259, 264 (1982).

and the laws of the United States recognize higher values than mere avoidance of speculative liability.[80]

The district court held that firing Hayes was an unnecessarily extreme measure and that the hospital had not considered possible alternatives, saying "its paternalistic and extreme treatment of the plaintiff was unwarranted."[81] The court awarded damages of $7,361.76,[82] and the hospital appealed.

The beginning of Judge Tuttle's opinion for the Court of Appeals for the Eleventh Circuit instantly reveals how he approached exclusionary policies.[83]

Historically, an effective means for employers, legislatures, and courts to limit the equal employment opportunities of women was to restrict their employment out of a professed concern for the health of women and their offspring. See *Muller v. Oregon.*[84]

Not only did Judge Tuttle explicitly draw the analogy between exclusionary policies and the paternalism of *Muller* (quoting the same passage of *Muller* presented in the ACLU's brief),[85] but he repeatedly quoted an article by feminist legal scholar Wendy Williams, "Firing the Woman to Protect the Fetus."[86] Williams analyzed exclusionary policies under traditional Title VII doctrine but, as her title suggests, sought to reconcile the competing policy goals of fetal protection and equal employment opportunity. Since the policies discriminate on their face, the employer should have to prove BFOQ, something it cannot do because being potentially pregnant does not interfere with job performance. Williams suggested, however, that if an employer could prove that the hazard posed a risk to future generations only through maternal but not paternal exposure, it could justify such a policy if the company could also show that it could not accomplish its goal through less discriminatory

---

80. Ibid., 265.

81. Ibid., 266.

82. The district court denied her claim to backpay under Title VII because she had not looked for a job after the hospital fired her. It did, however, award her damages under section 1983 of the Civil Rights Act of 1871 as well as the difference between her pay after returning to work and what she would have earned if the hospital had taken her back.

83. Elbert P. Tuttle (a liberal, described as one of the four who helped the South accept desegregation) was appointed by Dwight Eisenhower. The other two judges were Frank M. Johnson and R. Lanier Anderson, III, both appointed by Jimmy Carter.

84. 726 F.2d 1543, 1545 (1984).

85. ACLU brief, 17.

86. Wendy Williams, "Firing the Woman to Protect the Fetus: The Reconciliation of Fetal Protection with Employment Opportunity Goals Under Title VII," *Georgetown Law Journal* 69 (1981): 641–704. The Fourth Circuit's opinion also cites Williams and Finneran, but only in a footnote.

alternatives. For both questions, the burden of proof would remain with the employer. Williams argued, however, that the scientific evidence would make it very unlikely that an employer could meet its burden of proving that a hazardous substance had teratogenic but not mutagenic effects and exposed the view that only women can damage their offspring as a stereotype. She also discussed the harm caused by forcing women to choose between having children, being sterilized, and having a good job. Consistent with her commitment to gender-neutral rules, Williams concluded that a gender-neutral policy that sought to protect the reproductive health of both men and women would better serve the dual goals of health and safety and equal employment opportunity.

Judge Tuttle had to first decide what rubric he would apply to the case. He referred to *Zuniga* and *Olin* in a footnote, complaining

> *Olin* did not make clear . . . whether it was applying pre– or post–Pregnancy Discrimination Act principles. Although we believe *Olin* reaches a correct result, we have endeavored to present a clearer picture of the overall framework under which such a case should be analyzed.[87]

Judge Tuttle rejected the hospital's claim that its concern for the health and safety of Hayes's fetus was a legitimate, nondiscriminatory reason answering the charge of discrimination under *Burdine*. Shelby Hospital had cited several pre–Pregnancy Discrimination Act cases.[88] Since Congress passed the Pregnancy Discrimination Act, however, treating employees differently because of pregnancy is facial discrimination. Classifications based on pregnancy are no longer neutral, which the plaintiff must then show to be a pretext for discrimination. *Burdine* is irrelevant, and concern for the fetus does not rebut the charge that the policy discriminates on the basis of sex on its face.

Despite the Eleventh Circuit's rejection of the relevance of *Burdine* and its clear determination that the hospital's policy was facially discriminatory, "to ensure complete fairness to the Hospital,"[89] it, like the *Olin* court, permitted the hospital to defend its policy as a business necessity, as if the policy were gender neutral. Agreeing with the district court that the hospital's policy was *per se* discrimination (disparate treatment), Judge Tuttle analyzed the hospital's policy under the guidelines set out in *Olin*. Yet, in a footnote, he rejected the Fourth Circuit's decision to consider the case under the rubric of disparate impact that allowed Olin to offer a business necessity defense.

87. 726 F.2d 1543, 1546 n.2 (1984).
88. Appellant's brief, 28–29.
89. 726 F.2d 1543, 1548 (1982).

We borrow these requirements from the showing of "business necessity" required in *Wright v. Olin*. Because we approach this case differently than did the *Olin* court, we do not label these requirements as "business necessity." Nevertheless, our approach and that of *Olin* require an identical showing by an employer for the employer to prevail.[90]

Judge Tuttle was only willing to entertain arguments about the business necessity defense after an employer proved that maternal exposure posed a significant risk to the fetus, and that only maternal exposure posed a hazard. Relying on the *Olin* guidelines, he recognized that an employer could argue that it sought to protect the offspring of all its employees, but an exclusionary policy was the most effective means for achieving this because offspring were only affected through women's exposure and women's exposure represented a significant risk. Judge Tuttle did not believe the policy is gender neutral, however, if the employer satisfies the burden of proving both these points, yet he is willing to conceptualize the policy as gender neutral and permit the employer to try to justify it as a business necessity.

We begin by establishing a *presumption* that if the employer's policy by its terms applies only to women or pregnant women, then the policy is facially discriminatory. That presumption may be rebutted, however, if the employer can show that although its policy applies only to women, the policy is neutral in the sense that it effectively and equally protects the offspring of all employees.[91]

Should the employer fail to show a substantial risk confined to women, the only defense for a facially discriminatory policy would be BFOQ. Because an employer would not be able to show being pregnant or potentially pregnant interferes with one's ability to perform the job, it could never succeed in establishing this defense. Judge Tuttle reiterated how narrow the BFOQ exception was and agreed with Williams and amici curiae that the court should not expand it further. He agreed with Williams that denying the employer the opportunity to present a BFOQ defense would work to the advantage of both men and women workers. If unable to exclude women, Williams argued, employers would develop gender-neutral policies that protected all workers' reproductive health.[92]

After discussing Shelby Memorial Hospital's policy and the scientific

90. Ibid., n.8.
91. Ibid., 1548.
92. Ibid., 1549.

justification for the policy, Judge Tuttle returned to the legal issue of the scope of the business necessity defense. He adopted the arguments of feminist commentators and amici and expounded on the narrowness of the defense, finding that the hospital had not established such a defense because it could not prove the essential element: that Hayes's pregnancy interfered with her job performance.[93] He found unsatisfactory the *Olin* court's analogy between the fetus and a business invitee or licensee but arrived at the same conclusion: "we simply recognize fetal protection as a legitimate area of employer concern to which the business necessity defense extends."[94]

Judge Tuttle was prepared to extend the business necessity defense beyond the strict criterion of job performance to encompass a genuine concern for protecting fetal health. He was not prepared to extend the defense, however, to allow employers to exclude pregnant women to avoid a risk of tort liability. He agreed with the district court that the hospital appeared to be motivated by a concern to avoid litigation rather than with protecting fetal health. After noting that the hospital was free to avoid liability by purchasing insurance and taking the necessary degree of care, he commented that a genuine desire to protect the fetus—presumably supported by hard scientific evidence and reflected in a carefully drafted written policy[95]—could trigger the business necessity defense.

To summarize the legal significance of *Hayes*, the court of appeals rejected the relevance of *Burdine*, agreed that the exclusionary policies were facially discriminatory, acknowledged that the employer could not substantiate a claim to a BFOQ, denied that fetuses were analogous to customers, and expressed its dissatisfaction with the *Olin* court's treatment of the issue under the rubric of disparate impact. Nevertheless, the court held that a legitimate concern for fetal health, as opposed to mere concern for tort liability, could create a business necessity defense. Blurring the line between disparate treatment and disparate impact and expanding the business necessity defense were precisely the outcomes the ACLU wanted to foreclose. Instead, the Court of Appeals for the Eleventh Circuit, while uncomfortable with the reasoning in *Olin*, abandoned the traditional analysis of Title VII—where the only defense for disparate treatment was a BFOQ—and allowed Shelby Memorial Hospital to try to justify the policy under an expanded definition of business necessity.

The Equal Employment Opportunity Commission's amicus brief may well have influenced Judge Tuttle. The EEOC criticized the district court's reliance on *Burdine* along the same lines as the court of appeals ultimately

---

93. In a footnote, it considered the framework established in *Olin* for treating the fetus as a business invitee or licensee that might create a business necessity defense (ibid., 1552 n.14).

94. Ibid.

95. The hospital had no policy for dealing with pregnant X-ray technicians and treated each case on an ad hoc basis (ibid., 1549 n.10).

did. The EEOC had also taken the position that "safeguarding the health of male and female workers' reproductive systems, and the health of their unborn children, is a legitimate concern of employers."[96] On the crucial issue of how to categorize and analyze exclusionary policies, the EEOC did not care.

Whether such proof is deemed to go towards establishing a "BFOQ" defense or a "business necessity" defense is, the Commission believes, a relatively inconsequential question. In our view, the formulation of each of the defenses has been essentially the same. Inasmuch as this case involves overt discrimination, the conceptually appropriate defense is BFOQ rather than the judicially developed business necessity defense to facially neutral employment policies having a significant disparate impact on women.[97]

The EEOC's main concern was that regardless of whether the hospital had to show BFOQ or business necessity, it would not succeed because its policy was unreasonable. The EEOC devoted most of its brief to explaining why the policy was not justified scientifically—calling the assessment of the doctor who testified for the hospital "utterly subjective and idiosyncratic."[98] Like the court of appeals, the EEOC had argued that mere economic considerations, such as fear of tort liability, would not alone justify the policy.

Contrary to the view of the EEOC, the legal distinctions were extremely important, as the ACLU consistently argued throughout these cases. The EEOC too quickly abandoned an opportunity to clarify the law and stress the importance of the distinctions between the defenses. At the time the court of appeals decided *Hayes*, however, the EEOC was correct in that the defenses were not as far apart as they are now. Courts had held employers to a high standard to prove job relatedness for the business necessity defense, as well as holding that the burden of proof shifted to the employer once a complainant had shown disparate impact. In the 1980s, however, as the influence of Reagan's appointments to the bench became felt, courts eroded the employer's burden for proving business necessity until the Supreme Court decimated it in *Wards Cove*. The importance of classifying exclusionary policies as facial discrimination (disparate treatment) rather than a neutral classification (disparate impact) grew as employers more easily met the lowered standards for proving business necessity.

The outcome in *Hayes* turned not on these legal issues, but on the scientific evidence about the effects of radiation on the fetus. Both the EEOC and the ACLU devoted considerable space to presenting and analyzing scien-

---

96. EEOC brief, 21.
97. Ibid., 21–22.
98. Ibid., 26.

tific evidence in their briefs. As cases testing the legality of exclusionary policies, *Hayes* and *Zuniga* were excellent choices for litigators seeking to prove that exclusionary policies were unlawful because the scientific evidence strongly supported the case of women who wanted to work. First, the harmful effects of radiation on men's reproductive capacity is documented in the medical literature and the evidence on the harmful effects on the fetus at low levels of exposure is sketchy and speculative. Because radiation is mutagenic it would be nearly impossible to establish that the hazard to a potential fetus existed only from women's exposure. Second, employers can easily and accurately measure the level of exposure to radiation on the job by having employees wear film badges. Third, an established scientific standard exists for what is an acceptable exposure level for the fetus, and both Hayes and Zuniga were beneath that threshold. Fourth, safety practices can effectively reduce exposure, thereby making exclusion less justifiable.

The court of appeals applied the first requirement of the *Olin* guidelines: the employer must show a significant risk to the fetus posed by the woman's exposure. The court rejected letting a hypothetical and speculative risk justify excluding women. The hospital's doctor had stated in his deposition that even sunbathing in a bikini posed an unacceptable risk to the fetus—that *any* risk was unacceptable. Like *Olin*, if one reads the testimony in *Hayes* and listens to the reasoning of the policymakers and their explanations of how their policies—often unwritten and inconsistently applied—are developed, their actions seem less justified than if one analyzes the policies in the abstract. If the hospital's sole motive was to protect offspring, its policy of allowing men to assume some risk to their reproductive capacities did not make sense. When this inconsistency was combined with the hospital's refusal to even consider such alternatives as changing the shift Hayes worked (which would lower her exposure), providing protective clothing, moving her to another job, or even laying her off with pay for the few months of pregnancy, the hospital's policy looks more like a pretext for firing pregnant women or an irrational fear of pregnant women's vulnerability, rather than a genuine desire to protect employees' offspring. The extreme position of allowing women to assume no risk, which is out of step with scientific opinion, probably swayed the court of appeals against the hospital.

The court of appeals concluded that Hayes's fetus was not exposed to an "unreasonable risk of harm."[99] Testimony about the standards set by the National Council on Radiation Protection and Measurements (NCRP) for exposure to the fetus probably persuaded the court that the risk was low. Moreover, the NCRP did not support the hospital's zero-risk approach and explicitly rejected the policy option of excluding all women or all pregnant

---

99. 726 F.2d 1543, 1550 (1984).

women from low-exposure jobs. Judge Tuttle cited Williams in support of the position that the scientific evidence itself was subject to "a certain amount of subtle bias" because scientists were likely to look only for female hazards.[100] Judge Tuttle is the first and only judge to question the "facts" of sex differences that may themselves be the result of a gendered production of knowledge. The court stated that it need not consider whether there was evidence of a female-only hazard, the second test in *Olin*, because the hospital had not met the first requirement. Judge Tuttle did, however, suggest that if the hospital had been able to prove that offspring were at risk only from one sex's exposure, its policy would not have been discriminatory.

Not only had the hospital failed to prove that Hayes's actual exposure was excessive, but it had failed, in the court of appeals's opinion, to investigate alternatives to firing her, *Olin*'s third requirement. Shelby Memorial had argued that to allow her to transfer or modify her job would have been giving her "preferential treatment" that would erode employee morale.[101] Although the EEOC's brief was devoted almost entirely to arguing that Hayes's fetus was not exposed to a significant risk, the EEOC did briefly question whether the hospital adequately considered alternatives, arguing that "there were feasible alternatives,"[102] and the ACLU agreed. While *Zuniga* turned only on the question of failure to consider alternatives, the Eleventh Circuit, in *Hayes*, did not get to that question. The hospital's failure to prove that Hayes's exposure posed an unreasonable risk to her fetus and the court's doubts about the hospital's sincerity in pursuing its legitimate goal ended the case.

To conclude, although at first glance the Eleventh Circuit appeared to have adopted the feminist rhetoric of Williams and amici and to have taken issue with the Court of Appeals for the Fourth Circuit's decision in *Olin*, it adopted a similar legal framework for evaluating exclusionary policies. It cited *Muller*, quoted Professor Williams, commented on the gender bias evident in the focus of scientific research on reproductive hazards, and agreed that employers should have to protect both male and female workers. Yet, like the Court of Appeals for the Fourth Circuit, the Eleventh Circuit rejected the counsel of Williams and the ACLU and followed the Fourth Circuit in interpreting Title VII in a new way, permitting Shelby Memorial Hospital to defend its policy under the business necessity defense while concluding that it had not met the requirements for that defense. Judge Tuttle adopted the rhetoric of the ACLU but the content of *Olin*, and, more significantly, agreed with the EEOC that distinguishing the categories was not important. An employer's concern for fetal health was now a legitimate business concern that could be encompassed by business necessity.

---

100. Ibid., 1548–49.
101. Appellant brief, 41.
102. EEOC brief, 27.

Like *Page v. Freight Hire*, *Hayes* accepted the goal of protecting fetal health as laudable, however insincere or inconsistent the employer's policy. Unlike the EAT in *Page*, however, the Eleventh Circuit carefully scrutinized the scientific evidence before it on the risks to the fetus, the level of exposure Hayes received, the effects of radiation on men, and the possibility of using protective equipment.

> To avoid Title VII liability for a fetal protection policy, an employer must adopt the most effective policy available, with the least discriminatory impact possible. To require any less would be to return to the days of *Muller v. Oregon*.[103]

Although British and U.S. courts and tribunals coincide in their willingness to expand the sex discrimination law to encompass an employer's legitimate concern for the health of employees' offspring, the two U.S. courts appear more willing to insure that the employers' policies are more narrowly tailored and justified by scientific evidence. An important difference between *Hayes* and *Page* is the evidence before the courts and tribunals. While both the ACLU and the EEOC presented weighty evidence on the effects of exposure to radiation, the British Equal Opportunities Commission and Page's attorney claimed the employer had the burden of proof and presented no contradictory scientific evidence.

Grant v. General Motors Corp.

Grant v. General Motors Corp.[104] and *UAW v. Johnson Controls*, like *Olin* and *Hayes*, worked their way through the system simultaneously. The Sixth Circuit's opinion in *Grant* referred to dissenting opinions of the Seventh Circuit in *UAW v. Johnson Controls*. Pat Grant began work at the General Motors Foundry in Defiance, Ohio, in 1976. She had worked as an iron pourer for two to three years, including once until she was four months pregnant. In December, 1981, General Motors revised its "fetal protection policy," first instituted in 1952. The company then transferred Grant to a lower-paying job that exposed her to less lead. The new policy excluded all women who did not have proof of infertility from jobs where lead-in-air levels exceeded thirty micrograms of lead per cubic meter of air (30 $\mu g/m^3$). The company would permanently transfer women whose blood levels of lead exceeded twenty micrograms per deciliter (20 $\mu g/100$ dl) over several tests to

---

103. 726 F.2d 1543, 1553 (1984).
104. Grant v. General Motors Corp., 743 F. Supp. 1260 (N.D. Ohio 1989), *vacated* and *remanded*, 908 F.2d 1303 (6th Cir. 1990).

nonlead–exposure jobs, and it would warn women of the possible dangers (and transfer pregnant women) in areas where the amount of lead in the air exceeded ten micrograms. None of these standards applied to men working at the foundry.

Grant filed a complaint with the EEOC in 1984, alleging that General Motors discriminated against her by removing her from her job as an iron pourer and by refusing to license her as a hot metal crane operator. She also filed an equal pay claim, alleging that her transfer cost her $7,683 in lost wages and overtime work, and the denial of the opportunity to pursue the other job cost her $33,320. She later filed a complaint with the EEOC claiming the company retaliated against her for filing the initial claim. The EEOC did not issue her a right-to-sue letter until May, 1988.

District Judge Richard B. McQuade for the district court of the Northern District of Ohio granted General Motors's motion for summary judgment on April 28, 1989.[105] He placed great weight on the opinion of General Motors's consultant, Dr. Lerner, who took the position that the fetus was at risk from air-lead levels exceeding 10 micrograms, and that no evidence existed that men's reproductive capacities were damaged at blood lead levels lower than 50 $\mu g/100$ g. He relied on *Wright v. Olin* in concluding that the disparate impact analysis was correct. In his view, the company's expert provided enough evidence that only the offspring of women employees were at significant risk at levels from 10–30 $\mu g/100$ dl. Because Judge McQuade concluded that neither Grant nor her attorney were experts, he did not consider the sources she cited in her affidavit refuting Dr. Lerner's testimony. Grant had therefore not shown that "there is a genuine issue of material fact regarding the scientific and medical data which forms the basis of General Motors's fetal protection policy."[106]

Grant appealed, and by the time the Sixth Circuit Court of Appeals heard the case, the Seventh Circuit had issued its *en banc* ruling in *UAW v. Johnson Controls* (to be discussed subsequently). Judge Guy's opinion began with the legal issue of whether the court should analyze General Motors's policy as disparate treatment or disparate impact.[107] Explaining away the Fourth Circuit's position in *Olin* by its occurrence before the Supreme Court decided *Newport News*,[108] Judge Guy restated Judge Easterbrook's assessments of the

---

105. McQuade is a Republican appointed by Ronald Reagan.

106. 743 F. Supp. 1260, 1262 (N.D. Ohio 1989).

107. Ronald Reagan appointed Ralph B. Guy, Jr., a Republican, in 1985. The *Almanac of the Federal Judiciary* lists *Grant v. General Motors Corp.* as one of Judge Guy's noteworthy rulings. The other two judges were Judge Danny J. Boggs, a Republican appointed by Reagan in 1986, and Judge Thomas L. Gadola, a district judge sitting by designation, appointed by Governor William Milliken to the Genesee County Probate Court (Michigan) in 1977.

108. Newport News Shipbuilding and Dry Dock Co. v. EEOC, 462 U.S. 669 (1983).

Olin and *Hayes* courts' position as: "this must be a disparate impact case because an employer couldn't win it as a disparate treatment case,"[109] and cited Judge Cudahy's comment that *Wright* was "result-oriented gimmickry"[110] (see my subsequent discussion of *UAW v. Johnson Controls*).

After stating clearly that policies such as General Motors's could only be analyzed as facial discrimination, Judge Guy concluded that the company could not satisfy its burden of proof, since being fertile does not interfere with one's ability to do the job. If sound public policy dictated allowing employers to exclude women who did not have proof of infertility, Congress, not the courts, should act. "To hold otherwise would be to usurp congressional power to regulate pregnancy discrimination on the basis of public policy."[111]

The court of appeals agreed with the district court that the equal pay claim standing alone failed, since Grant was getting paid the same as the men who did the job she was transferred to. The court remanded the case to the district court to hold a trial on the factual matters and to apply the legal framework of disparate treatment/BFOQ. Judge Guy did not address the medical evidence or mention whether Grant had adequately put the medical and scientific evidence before the court, merely stating that the district court had accepted General Motors's evidence and dismissed the evidence Grant cited. The ACLU's brief, however, devoted two-thirds of its space to discussing the scientific issues in dispute. It argued that even if the court of appeals accepted the district court's dismissal of the evidence Grant had merely cited rather than presented to the court, evidence in the *Federal Register* from the Occupational Health and Safety Administration as well as the Environmental Protection Agency was properly before the court. Both agencies had explicitly rejected exclusionary policies because the evidence on lead suggested that the offspring of both men and women, as well as adults, were at risk from low levels of exposure to lead. Although the ACLU's brief remained in the case file, the court of appeals had refused it permission to participate in the case as amicus curiae, the first time that organization had been excluded from participating in a case on exclusionary policies.

After the Supreme Court issued its ruling in *UAW v. Johnson Controls* the parties filed a proposed settlement with the court for back pay, attorneys' fees, and costs totaling $50,000. Attorneys expected the court to approve the settlement.[112]

---

109. 908 F.2d 1303, 1308 (6th Cir. 1990), citing 886 F.2d 871, 910 (7th Cir. 1989) (Easterbrook, J., dissenting).

110. Ibid., 1310 n.16 (Cudahy, J., dissenting).

111. 908 F.2d 1303, 1310 (6th Cir. 1990).

112. "Fetal Protection Issues Remain After Ruling in *Johnson Controls*," 17 *Daily Labor Reports* (January 27, 1992): A-1.

Arbitration: UAW v. General Motors Corp.

Grant was not the only challenger of General Motors's exclusionary policy. The United Autoworkers, the same union litigating *UAW v. Johnson Controls*, also fought General Motors's policy, but through arbitration. Looking at the arguments in the arbitration case allows us to trace the development of the UAW's position and analyze the umpire's opinion, one that deals more thoroughly with the complex legal and scientific matters than some judges' opinions.[113] This opinion is interesting because the umpire, Arthur Stark, spelled out his conception of discrimination and applied it to exclusionary policies. Because bringing a grievance is less expensive and less time consuming than litigation under Title VII, arbitration may be a more important arena for challenging exclusionary policies. Since arbitration cases may evolve into challenges under Title VII, like EEOC complaints, they may offer a glimpse of the future. General Motors Assembly Division-Norwood was such a case; the UAW moved on to challenge Johnson Controls's exclusionary policy, drawing on and extending the scientific and legal arguments it used against General Motors.[114]

Grievances that go to arbitration differ from suits filed under Title VII, and the umpire is not bound by the concept of discrimination embodied in that statute. Instead of proving that the policies violated a statute, the employee must show that the action, in these cases the decision to remove women who could not prove infertility, was arbitrary and capricious and violated the nondiscrimination clause of their negotiated employment contract. Employers can more easily meet the burden of justification under the employment contract than under Title VII: the employer has only to prove that the policy is reasonable—that it is based on scientific evidence. *Olin*'s guidelines, on the other hand, require that an exclusionary policy be necessary, not just reasonable, to survive scrutiny under Title VII. Employers must provide objective evidence that the hazard poses a significant risk to the fetus, that the hazard does not affect men, and that the employer must first consider less discriminatory alternatives.

The UAW, a leader among trade unions in challenging exclusionary policies, brought an arbitration case against the General Motors Assembly Division Plant in Norwood, Ohio (GMAD-Norwood) in 1976. The UAW

---

113. An umpire is the person who decides arbitration cases in which General Motors is involved. Arthur Stark was then the umpire for General Motors Corporation and the UAW, as well as coumpire for General Motors and the IUE.

114. United Automobile, Aerospace and Agricultural Implement Workers of America Local 674 and General Motors Corporation, General Motors Assembly Division (GMAD)-Norwood, Umpire Decision Q-6, Appeal Case Q-160, Grievance nos. 843841 and 993833, filed June 11, 1976, and September 9, 1976.

objected to the exclusion of women from jobs exposing them to lead, a known reproductive hazard for both men and women. After General Motors removed two women from jobs where they might be exposed to lead, the women filed grievances. General Motors had always excluded women from battery plants where exposure to lead is highest.[115] As more women were hired in manufacturing and assembly plants in the mid-1960s, General Motors reevaluated its policy and extended the exclusion to other areas where workers might be exposed. The company maintained that its policy was not sex-based because it would continue to employ postmenopausal women or women incapable of conceiving.[116] (General Motors instituted its policy before passage of the Pregnancy Discrimination Act.) The company argued that the policy was justified on moral grounds, because "to knowingly allow the potential infliction of such an injury of a fetus is morally irresponsible."[117] The company further argued that "rather than discriminatory, the policy should be viewed as protective; protective of the well-being of the fetus."[118]

General Motors also divulged that women had filed similar complaints with the EEOC challenging the exclusion of women from the Anaheim Battery Plant and the Muncie Battery Plant. The company argued that the EEOC's decision not to pursue the charges vindicated its policy as non-discriminatory.[119] The umpire noted, "Certainly, a ruling on the Corporation's female exclusion policy by the agency which oversees federal sex and race discrimination laws would be helpful in deciding the instant controversy. But the record is short on facts and citations."[120] The union contended that in one of the cases, the EEOC found cause, and the woman received a monetary payment in federal district court.

The umpire had to determine whether General Motors's exclusion of women was arbitrary, capricious, and violated the terms of the employment contract prohibiting discrimination. The parties agreed that the jobs in question did involve the exposure to lead; the union argued, however, that many of the jobs did not involve high exposure, and that General Motors could institute engineering controls to reduce exposure. Despite the union's argument that General Motors should take into account the amount of exposure when

---

115. Employer's statement, 1.

116. Ibid., 16.

117. Ibid., 14.

118. Ibid., 16.

119. Ibid., 17.

120. Umpire's opinion, 19. Nor did I find these complaints, or any record of their resolution, when I did the research for the House Education and Labor Committee Report on Fetal Protection Policies. The complaints may have been too old, resolved by the regional office rather than headquarters, not tagged as discrimination resulting from exposure to hazardous substances, or nonexistent. In any case, given the EEOC's abysmal record of handling this issue, its failure to act is hardly a stamp of approval of the policy.

deciding whether or not to remove a worker, the umpire did not discuss the disputed level of exposure of the jobs in question. Nor did he comment on neither side providing evidence on the actual level of exposure. The umpire ruled that one could safely assume that women working in these areas would have a higher amount of lead in their blood than the general population.[121]

The union argued that General Motors had selectively and inconsistently applied the scientific evidence. Specifically, the company had ignored strong evidence that men's reproductive capacity is at risk from exposure to lead. While only women can carry a fetus, the union tried to show that men and women are not different enough to warrant excluding women. The umpire disagreed. He distinguished between the hazards posed to a developing fetus caused by the mother's exposure and the hazards to men's reproductive capacity posed by exposure to lead. "It is apparent that the focus of the disputed policy is on the fetus. Therefore, much of the evidence concerning the deleterious effects of lead absorption on adult males and females is not directly in point."[122]

Even if the fetus were at risk from paternal as well as maternal exposure to lead, the umpire believed that the evidence suggested that the damage occurred at different levels of exposure. After considering each of the studies cited by the union and the corporation, the umpire ruled there was strong evidence that the fetus was in danger even at low levels of lead in the mother's blood. While there was some evidence that lead causes lowered sperm counts, there was little evidence that male exposure leads to malformations or that hazards to men occurred at low levels of exposure. The umpire did not voice the same concern as Judge Tuttle (in *Hayes*) that the different level of scientific evidence on male and female effects was itself the result of gender bias in scientific studies. Nor did the umpire find that the company bore the burden of proving that fetuses were *not* at risk from paternal exposure before it instituted its policy. Instead, without evidence to the contrary, the umpire allowed General Motors to presume there to be no risk to a potential fetus from men's exposure. Although he criticized the company for not referring to the evidence on male effects, the umpire ruled that, until there was more evidence, the policy was not arbitrary or capricious.

The umpire expressed his frustration at the lack of guidance from courts or governmental agencies. Relying on *General Electric v. Gilbert*'s holding that differential treatment on the basis of pregnancy was not sex discrimination,[123] the umpire commented that

---

121. Prior to 1978, OSHA regulations set a maximum exposure level as that resulting in 80 $\mu g/g$ of lead in the blood. General Motors removed workers who registered 69 $\mu g/g$.

122. Umpire's opinion, 11.

123. 429 U.S. 1251 (1976); The Pregnancy Discrimination Act of 1978 legislatively overturned the Court's reasoning in *Gilbert* (see chap. 4).

neither the parties, the Umpire, nor any court of law or legislative forum can alter the fact that a fetus grows only within its mother's body. . . . If scientific evidence showed that a fertile male exposed to lead could cause injury to a fetus, conceived by him, in a manner and degree similar to that of a lead-exposed mother, then a policy which distinguishes between fertile males and females would be invalid.[124]

In his view, it was not enough to show that men and women were similarly vulnerable to damage to their reproductive capacities resulting from exposure to lead. Instead, to prove men and women were sufficiently alike such that treating them differently was discriminatory, one would have to show that men and women were equally capable of injuring a potential or actual fetus as a result of exposure to lead.

The umpire considered cases under Title VII, such as *Harriss v. Pan American World Airways, Inc.*,[125] which held that prohibiting pregnant women from working as flight attendants was not defensible as a business necessity because no correlation between pregnancy and incapacity existed. The umpire rejected claims from the union that concern for the health of a fetus could not create a business necessity, but he also rejected the company's analogy between a pregnant woman and a worker who is incapable of doing his job because of a back injury, holding,

the analogy is not directly in point; the policy here is specifically designed to cover non-pregnant women. It is indeed difficult to find a relevant analogy in industrial life because the circumstances are unique.[126]

The umpire briefly considered whether the policy was overinclusive by excluding all fertile, rather than all pregnant, women and therefore was unfair to women who did not want children. He dismissed this concern by noting that women might change their minds. In addition, because it takes time for the body to excrete lead, removing only pregnant women would not adequately protect potential fetuses. Women planning to conceive would have to avoid lead exposure for some time to reduce their blood levels of lead to a level safe for the fetus. The umpire echoed the EAT in *Page*, commenting, "it would appear to be unrealistic to deal with women on an individual basis with respect to their childbearing intentions."[127] He did not discuss the apparent inconsistency in allowing men to weigh the risk for themselves and act re-

---

124. Umpire's opinion, 22.
125. 437 F. Supp. 413 (N.D. Cal. 1977).
126. Umpire's opinion, 21.
127. Ibid., 24.

sponsibly, given their preferences about parenting, while the company acted paternalistically to "protect" women regardless of their choices about parenting. Although the umpire dealt with the issue in a cursory fashion, unlike the EAT in *Page* or the court of appeals in *Olin*, he at least addressed the question of whether employers could treat all fertile women as if they were pregnant.

Compared to *Hayes* and *Olin*, the umpire conducted an impressively thorough analysis of the scientific issues presented, moving directly to the heart of the issue of whether mutagenic and other male reproductive hazards (such as lowered sperm counts) were comparable to teratogenic effects caused by women's exposure to hazards. Moreover, by declaring the facts before him unique, the umpire distinguished GMAD-Norwood from other cases of discrimination. He ignored *Weeks*'s holding that employers must treat women as individuals, not as a class, and *Burwell*'s and *Harriss*'s holdings that a concern for fetal health was not a legitimate business concern establishing a business necessity defense. The umpire's comments reveal that he shared the same conception of discrimination as some British tribunals and courts: that differential treatment, if based on real differences between men and women and if motivated by a legitimate concern, is not discrimination. His ruling is a perfect example of what MacKinnon would call the difference approach: women can only claim the right to hazardous work as long as they are only as vulnerable as men to the dangers of reproductive hazards. They can only gain employment opportunity insofar as they are exactly like men. The umpire's refusal to draw an analogy between men's and women's vulnerability to reproductive hazards was critical for his decision, as was his failure to examine whether the employer had been inconsistent in ranking some risks above others in its policy.

Because GMAD-Norwood was an arbitration case rather than a claim brought under Title VII, the case did not turn on the employer's obligation to consider less discriminatory alternatives. Instead, the employer needed only to show that the policy was reasonable. Despite the umpire's limited scope of inquiry, namely the reasonableness of the policy, he was thorough. The twenty-five-page opinion sharply contrasts with the four-page opinion of *Page v. Freight Hire*. While both bodies were considering whether the policy was reasonable rather than whether it was less favorable treatment on the basis of sex, the umpire devoted far more attention to the scientific issues involved than did the British EAT. The umpire's careful consideration of what discrimination is is surprising because the case was brought in 1976. He gave more attention to the question of discrimination than did the District Court for the Southern District of Texas in *Zuniga*, concerned mainly with whether the hospital had considered alternatives, and the District Court for the Western District of North Carolina in *Olin*, which cursorily reviewed the policy before declaring it lawful. When the UAW took its challenge of exclusionary policies to the courts, they were initially no more successful than they had been in arbitration.

UAW v. Johnson Controls

In 1984, the UAW filed a class action suit in the U.S. District Court for the Eastern District of Wisconsin alleging that Johnson Controls's adoption of an exclusionary policy at its fourteen plants that manufacture batteries violated Title VII.[128] Before 1964, Johnson Controls (then Globe Union) employed no women in its battery manufacturing process.[129] In 1977, the company began to hire women for jobs that exposed them to lead, advising against employment for women who planned to conceive and requiring women to sign a waiver stating the company had informed them of the risks. Although the company stated that it was better not to take the chance of exposing one's fetus to lead, it stated that the risks were less well documented than the relationship between cigarette smoking and cancer, perhaps inadvertently linking a risk women might not be willing to take with a risk that many people accept every day.

> Protection of the health of the unborn child is the immediate and direct responsibility of the prospective parents. While the medical profession and the company can support them in the exercise of this responsibility, it cannot assume it for them without simultaneously infringing their rights as persons. . . . Since not all women who can become mothers wish to become mothers (or will become mothers), it would appear to be illegal discrimination to treat all who are capable of pregnancy as though they will become pregnant.[130]

Between 1979 and 1982, eight employees whose blood lead levels exceeded 30 μg/dl became pregnant.[131] In 1982, Johnson Controls began to exclude all women who did not have proof of infertility from jobs in which

---

128. International Union, United Automobile, Aerospace and Agricultural Implement Workers of America, UAW v. Johnson Controls, Inc., 680 F. Supp. 309 (E.D. Wisc. 1988).

129. Johnson Controls purchased Globe Union, Inc., in 1978 and created its battery division, consolidating two battery companies.

130. 111 S.Ct. 1196, 1199 (1991).

131. Judge Coffey's opinion specifies the number as six, Judge Posner and Judge Easterbrook both put the number at eight. Justice Blackmun puts the number at eight. The number of children allegedly injured is also disputed. Judge Coffey reported that one child was born with an elevated blood lead level and was hyperactive. Justice Blackmun merely notes that one child had an elevated blood lead level at birth.

any employee had recorded blood lead levels in excess of 30 µg/dl,[132] or where air samples exceeded 30 µg/m³, as well as jobs that fed into high–lead exposure jobs. Women holding such jobs were allowed to continue as long as they maintained blood lead levels below 30 µg/dl. The company's policy discouraged women from having themselves sterilized to keep their jobs.

One of the plaintiffs, Mary Craig, had herself sterilized to keep her job. Another, fifty-year-old Ginny Green, worked at the Bennington, Vermont, plant at a job that included lifting twenty-five-pound stacks of batteries. The $9-per-hour job included many opportunities for overtime at time-and-a-half, which allowed her to provide for her nine-year-old daughter. She was divorced. When the company transferred her to a job as a respirator sanitizer (glorified laundress) she became the butt of "fertility jokes from all the Archie Bunkers."[133]

Not all of the plaintiffs were women.

> Among the men on the battery assembly line, lead divides the generations. Those who have worked for years at Johnson Controls don't talk much about the dangers, because safety still carries a sissy taint, but the younger workers think differently. There are recruits who sit through the mandatory safety lecture, then turn down the job.[134]

Donald Penney and his wife, Anna May Penney, used to work at the Middletown, Delaware, plant. Anna had a low-lead job, while Donald worked on the assembly line. In March, 1984, he asked for a three-month leave of absence to lower his blood lead so he could father a healthy child. Johnson Controls refused, and, according to his complaint, the personnel director told him, "If you feel this way, quit."[135]

The company argued that the district court should grant it summary judgment because *Hayes* and *Olin* were controlling and the facts were clear.[136] The UAW argued that summary judgment was inappropriate because the parties disagreed about whether the levels of exposure women received

---

132. The Supreme Court used the measure of deciliter rather than 100 g, as in the OSHA Lead Standard.

133. David L. Kirp, "Toxic Choices," University of California, Berkeley, Working Paper no. 172 (January 1990): 1.

134. Ibid., 7.

135. Ibid.

136. "Rule of Civil Procedure 56 permits any party to a civil action to move for a summary judgment on a claim, counterclaim, or cross-claim when he believes that there is no genuine issue of material fact and that he is entitled to prevail as a matter of law. The motion may be directed toward all or part of a claim or defense and it may be made on the basis of the pleadings or other portions of the record in the case or it may be supported by affidavits and a variety of outside material" (*Black's Law Dictionary*, 5th ed. [St. Paul: West, 1983], 748).

would harm a fetus and whether men were at risk from low levels of exposure. The UAW submitted three affidavits of experts in lead toxicology who challenged the scientific basis of Johnson Controls's policy.

The UAW further contended that significant legal as well as factual differences separated the parties. The union argued that the courts in *Hayes* and *Olin* had mistakenly interpreted Title VII. Drawing on the arguments of the ACLU in prior cases, as well as law review articles critical of *Olin*, the UAW argued that the appropriate rubric for exclusionary policies was disparate treatment. Once Congress passed the Pregnancy Discrimination Act, a classification based on childbearing capacity could never be neutral. Johnson Controls's policy was facially discriminatory. The UAW cited *Rosenfeld* and other cases to point out "even a benevolent intent cannot transform overtly discriminatory policies into neutral ones."[137] The company could not prove a BFOQ, the only defense available to it, because having the capacity to give birth does not affect job performance. The union further argued that the district court should deny the motion because the company had not argued either that sex was a BFOQ for the job or that no less discriminatory alternatives were available.

Although disparate treatment was the correct classification, the UAW maintained that Johnson Controls had also not met the requirements for business necessity. Neither a concern for fetal safety nor fear of tort liability could establish such a defense. Drawing on Emily Buss's article in the *Yale Law Journal*,[138] the UAW maintained that the *Olin* court erred in saying that Congress had not legislated to deal with the problem of reproductive hazards. The Toxic Substance Control Act (TSCA) covered precisely this problem.[139] Noting that "the TSCA mandates the elimination of an unreasonable risk of injury to health caused by chemical substances or mixtures, including those used in the workplace,"[140] the UAW maintained that it was the responsibility of the Environmental Protection Agency, which administers TSCA, and not employers to fulfill the general societal goal of protecting fetal health. The combination of TSCA and Title VII requires employers to make the workplace equally safe for men, women, and their offspring. The UAW acknowledged that both *Olin* and *Hayes* had been correct in recognizing a societal interest in fetal health, but had erred in stretching Title VII to permit employers to advance this goal on their own through exclusionary policies. The

---

137. Brief for Plaintiffs, UAW et al., in opposition to Johnson Controls's Motion for Summary Judgment, 9–10.

138. Emily Buss, "Getting Beyond Discrimination: A Regulatory Solution to the Problem of Fetal Hazards in the Workplace," *Yale Law Journal* 95 (1986): 577–98.

139. 15 U.S.C. §2601–29 (1981).

140. Brief of the Plaintiffs, UAW et al., in opposition to Johnson Controls's Motion for Summary Judgment, 4.

UAW maintained that courts were not qualified to judge whether the hazards posed to a potential fetus by either maternal or paternal exposure were real or pretextual; instead, Congress had delegated this authority to the EPA. In the UAW's opinion, courts should further refrain from "countenancing employers' ad hoc response to the problem of fetal hazards."[141]

The UAW then tried to prove that Johnson Controls's alleged concern for fetuses was a mere pretext for discriminating against women. The company had not removed women who held jobs that exposed them to lead when it instituted its policy; instead, it allowed them to remain in the job as long as their blood levels of lead were below a certain level. Second, the policy was inconsistent because it did not afford protection to men exposed to lead who were planning to become parents. The three experts expressed their views that lead-exposed males could damage their offspring. Third, the policy was overkill. Mocking the company's decision to exclude even postmenopausal women by calling it the "fertile octogenarian approach," the union commented that "the current policy completely disregards the current reality— that pregnancy and child-bearing are largely the result of discretionary acts."[142]

The union offered further evidence of pretext by pointing out that no mothers of deformed children had filed lawsuits;[143] in fact, Johnson Controls spent more in workers compensation claims as a result of men's exposure to lead than of women's. The union further attempted to discredit the company's concern for fetal health on the basis that it had not reported its concerns to the EPA, pursuant to its statutory duty under the TSCA. Finally, the union observed that Johnson Controls, by removing women not only from all lead-exposure jobs but all jobs that feed into lead-exposure jobs, revealed that its true goal was to discriminate against women. The UAW posed several alternatives to exclusion and requested that the district court grant it summary judgment.

Johnson Controls responded by pointing out that *Hayes* and *Olin* allowed an employer to justify an exclusionary policy under the rubric of disparate impact. The UAW's proposed analysis would have made all exclusionary policies unlawful, however carefully drafted—a position that was "wrong morally as well as legally."[144] Johnson Controls cited scientific studies that

---

141. Ibid., 16, quoting Buss at 591.

142. UAW brief, 23.

143. When the UAW wrote this brief, no mothers had filed suit in the United States claiming damages for a malformed child as the result of an occupational exposure. See Jarvis v. Providence Hospital, 444 N.W.2d 236 (Mich. Ct. App. 1989); Security National Bank v. Chloride, 602 F. Supp. 294 (D. Kansas 1985); and Dillon v. S.S. Kresge Co., 192 N.W.2d 661 (Mich. Ct. App. 1972). For additional cases, see "Fetal Protection Issues Remain After Ruling in *Johnson Controls*," 17 *Daily Labor Reports* (January 27, 1992): A-1.

144. Reply Brief of Defendant Johnson Controls, in Support of its Motion for Summary Judgment, 4.

suggested that the level of exposure that damaged the fetus was much lower than the level of exposure that damaged adult workers. Furthermore, citing *Dothard v. Rawlinson*, the company argued that "traditional Title VII analysis has *always* recognized that where there is an *objective, factual* basis to distinguish men and women in the workplace, an employer may treat the sexes differently."[145] At stake in this case was not merely women's employment choices, but the health of unborn children. Johnson Controls cited *Olin* to further its position that Title VII defenses were not meant to operate with rigid precision. Rejecting the UAW's claim that the TSCA precluded judicial involvement, Johnson Controls noted that, even under TSCA, courts would be deciding cases brought by the Environmental Protection Agency. Furthermore, it referred to *OCAW v. American Cyanamid* (see chap. 7) that held that an exclusionary policy was not a violation of the Occupational Safety and Health Act.

On January 21, 1988 (amended on February 24), district judge Robert W. Warren granted Johnson Controls's motion for summary judgment.[146] His opinion summarized the medical evidence and agreed with the company's experts that the fetus was at risk from low levels of maternal exposure, even lower levels than would injure a child. Although he recognized that the parties had presented conflicting studies on the risk of exposure to men, this dispute was not "outcome determinative." He held that *Olin* only required that there be a considerable body of scientific opinion, not consensus. In his view, the body of evidence showed that the fetus was at significant risk at low levels, concluding that "the Court simply cannot overlook this possibility of severe harm only to the fetus. As a concern for society and future generations this Court must uphold the fetal protection policy."[147] He took no position on whether men's exposure could damage their offspring and acknowledged that this evidence was in dispute. Noting that many pregnancies were unplanned and that lead stays in the body for some time after removal from the workplace, he ruled that Johnson Controls could exclude fertile as well as pregnant women. According to Judge Warren, blood lead levels of 10 μg/dl could cause stillbirth, even if the woman removed herself from the lead exposure immediately upon learning she was pregnant.

Once Johnson Controls satisfied Judge Warren that the fetus was at risk, and the risk was confined to women's exposure, under *Olin* and *Hayes*, its policy was no longer facially discriminatory, but neutral. "Because of the fetuses possibility of unknown existence to the mother and the severe risk of harm that may occur if exposed to lead, the fetal protection policy is not

---

145. Ibid., italics added.
146. Judge Warren was appointed by Gerald Ford in 1974.
147. 680 F. Supp. 309, 316 (E.D. Wis. 1988).

facially discriminatory."[148] Judge Warren's logic suggests that, since women are different than men, a policy that treats them differently is not discriminatory. He did not argue that the explicit discrimination was justified, but that the policy did not constitute discrimination at all. Because the policy was now deemed neutral, he did not consider whether the company had satisfied the requirements for a BFOQ defense, but considered whether the company had proven business necessity.

Despite showing no relationship between being potentially pregnant and job performance, Johnson Controls persuaded Judge Warren that its policy was necessary because the company would not have exposed customers to lead (drawing on the *Olin* analogy) and the company was legitimately concerned about tort liability. Further, the EPA would probably never get around to protecting fetuses from exposure to lead, thus the company could not wait for TSCA to take its course. Nor would engineering controls enable the company to lower exposure. Finally, Judge Warren concluded that the UAW had not shown that acceptable alternatives existed—the burden rested upon the union.

The UAW appealed and William Bradford Reynolds, Assistant Attorney General for Civil Rights, urged Solicitor General Charles Fried to file an amicus brief for the government supporting Johnson Controls.[149] Reynolds argued that

> society has a compelling interest in protecting unborn children. . . . As this case illustrates, there seems at present to be no feasible way to avoid the effects on unborn children of exposure to high levels of lead in the workplace other than to keep fetuses out of such an environment; and there also seems to be no way to exclude fetuses other than to bar presumptively fertile women from jobs involving exposure to such dangerous lead levels.[150]

Reynolds argued that the policy did not discriminate on the basis of sex. Johnson Controls's policy treated people differently because of a sex-linked characteristic: the risk of injury to a fetus being carried by an employee. A "classification on the basis of a condition causally related to sex is not in itself classification 'because of' sex."[151] Conceding that Congress had legislatively overturned the interpretation offered by the Supreme Court in *Gilbert* by

---

148. Ibid., 316.
149. Memorandum for the Solicitor General re Amicus Participation in *International Union, United Automobile, Aerospace and Agricultural Implement Workers, UAW, et al. v. Johnson Controls, Inc.*, April 28, 1988.
150. Ibid., 5.
151. Ibid., 7.

passing the Pregnancy Discrimination Act, Reynolds concluded, nevertheless, that fertility was not a medical condition related to pregnancy. He distinguished the capacity to become pregnant from the condition of being pregnant.

> Congress was plainly concerned with the "medical condition" of *women*, not with that of *fetuses*, and the unlawfulness of discrimination against a woman because of *her* "medical condition" should not be transformed into a ban on measures designed to protect the health and safety of *another* individual.[152]

Addressing the contrary ruling in *Newport News*, Reynolds argued that Johnson Controls's policy was not discriminatory because the policy's focus was children, not women.[153] He went on to say why he believed the company had satisfied the requirements of both the BFOQ and business necessity defenses.

Reynolds's views in support of Johnson Controls were not put before the Court of Appeals because of counterarguments made by the EEOC's General Counsel, Charles Shanor. Shanor argued that the facial discrimination analytical framework enunciated in *Hayes* "offers the best available judicial articulation of a methodology for handling the issue."[154] The company would not be able to meet the demands of the customary facial disparate treatment defense of BFOQ, and the EEOC argued strongly against recommending that courts expand that defense to accommodate employers' concerns. The agency would, however, support a reformulation of the business necessity defense. Shanor argued that the district court's decision to grant summary judgment was inappropriate and that it may have "improperly resolved a key factual issue against the non-movant i.e. whether the offspring of male employees were similarly affected by lead exposure."[155] Shanor's position rather than Reynolds's prevailed, and the Solicitor General did not file a brief.[156]

The American Civil Liberties Union, the American Public Health Association, Queen Elizabeth Foster (who challenged Johnson Controls's policy under California law) and the Employment Law Center did file amicus briefs.[157] The ACLU made many of the same arguments it had made in previous cases, attacking the unfounded stereotype that "all women inevitably bear children" and challenging the assumption that the fetus is more vulner-

152. Ibid., 9.
153. Ibid., n.10.
154. Letter from Charles Shanor, General Counsel, EEOC, to Charles Fried, Solicitor General, May 24, 1988, 1.
155. Ibid., 3.
156. See Memorandum to the Solicitor General from Glen D. Nager, May 26, 1988.
157. Both the ACLU and the APHA were joined by a variety of other groups.

able to toxins than adult workers. It criticized the policy's creation of an "irrebuttable presumption of permanent pregnancy" that forced women to choose between unwanted sterilization and their livelihood. The ACLU argued for consideration of the case under the disparate treatment/BFOQ rubric, and emphasized OSHA's and the EPA's findings about the risks posed by low levels of lead to men's health and reproductive capacities.

The American Public Health Association, representing groups and individuals who had scientific expertise about the adverse health effects of lead exposure, argued that the scientific evidence did not support Johnson Controls's policy.

> Amici do not believe that the scientific literature on the toxic effects of lead, taken as a whole, supports the conclusion that the most significant risk from lead exposure is experienced by the fetus, or that such a risk occurs at significantly lower exposure levels than other risks.[158]

The APHA called for a balancing of all of the health data, questioned the inferences the district court made about the absence of evidence on men, and called for protection of all segments of the population without assuming that one person or group was more worthy of protection than another. The EPA's evidence suggested that cardiovascular risks to men were significant at very low blood levels—below that which may harm a developing fetus. Were yet-to-be conceived fetuses more worthy of protection than adult men? Furthermore, the APHA was critical of how Johnson Controls had used certain scientific studies out of context to support conclusions explicitly rejected by the authors of those studies. In any case, the APHA argued that the significant disputes over the scientific evidence made summary judgment inappropriate.

Not only did Johnson Controls's policy conflict with the conclusions of federal regulatory agencies, but the APHA maintained that its assumption about pregnancy among working women was insupportable. The district court had relied on three stereotypes: (1) that only women's exposures can affect pregnancy outcome; (2) that women and their families derive no health-related benefits from their employment; and (3) that all women of childbearing capacity will become pregnant. In fact, the birth rate is near zero for women older than forty, and 83.2 percent of all sexually active women between fifteen and forty-four years of age who are not intentionally seeking pregnancy use contraceptives.[159]

On appeal, a panel of the Court of Appeals for the Seventh Circuit

---

158. APHA brief, 2.

159. "There is a 0.39 percent probability that a woman between the ages of 40 and 44 will give birth, and a 0.02 percent probability that a woman age 45 to 49 will give birth in a given year" (ibid., 18).

conducted oral argument and circulated its opinion. Before publication of the opinion, a majority of the court voted to hear the case *en banc*.[160] At the opening of the oral argument, Judge John L. Coffey[161] leaned over the bench and remarked: "This is the case about the women who want to hurt their fetuses."[162] Judge Coffey wrote the opinion for a seven to four majority affirming the district court's decision to grant summary judgment to Johnson Controls.[163]

Judge Coffey began his opinion by stating that the parties agreed that fetuses were at substantial risk from exposure to lead. Citing experts, he noted that the fetus was at least as susceptible as children were, and noted that the Centers for Disease Control had lowered its blood lead standard for children from 30 to 25 μg/dl. Because it takes a long time to excrete lead from the body, and because women may not know they are pregnant, a policy that removed women from exposure once they became pregnant would not protect fetuses.

Having concluded that Johnson Controls satisfied the first plank of the *Olin* guidelines, that the evidence demonstrate a substantial risk to the fetus, Judge Coffey turned to the legal issues. He began by citing cases in which the Supreme Court rejected the rigid application of judicially devised proof patterns—in other words, he called for flexibility in applying Title VII doctrine to the case of exclusionary policies because of "the reality that only the female of the human species is capable of childbearing."[164] Because a moral concern for the protection of future life (as well as legitimate concerns about tort liability) led the company to adopt the policy, Judge Coffey agreed with the *Olin* and *Hayes* courts that disparate impact was the proper category. Because the employer sought to protect fetuses rather than discriminate against women, the court should not find the policy to be facially discriminatory but think of it as neutral. Judge Coffey quoted the EEOC's 1988 Policy Statement acceding to the opinions in *Hayes* and *Olin* in support of his decision to analyze the case under the rubric of disparate impact.

Convinced that the requirements of the business necessity defense "balance the interest of the employer, the employee and the unborn child in a manner consistent with Title VII,"[165] Judge Coffey addressed the lowered

---

160. The rules dictate that if a panel of the court adopts a position which would overrule a prior decision of the court or create a conflict between the circuits it must first be circulated to the full court. Only if a majority do not vote to rehear the issue *en banc* may it be published.

161. John L. Coffey was appointed by Ronald Reagan in 1982.

162. David L. Kirp, "The Pitfalls of 'Fetal Protection,'" *Society* 28 (March/April 1991): 70.

163. Joining Judge Coffey's opinion were Chief Judge Bauer, Judges Cummings, Wood, Jr., Ripple, Manion, and Kanne.

164. 886 F.2d 871, 883 (1989).

165. Ibid., 886.

standard of business necessity established by *Wards Cove*. Under this decision, the Title VII plaintiff maintains the burden of proof, the burden does not
shift to the employer once the plaintiff shows disparate impact, and the Court
lowered the level of justification from necessary or essential to reasonable.
The burden of proof in *UAW v. Johnson Controls*, then, always rested with the
UAW and the employees. They agreed that a fetus would be at risk, but
disagreed that the risk to offspring comes only from maternal exposures.
Judge Coffey dismissed the evidence on the effects of exposure to men as
"speculative and unconvincing," principally because the evidence came from
animal studies. To have persuaded him, the UAW would have had to show
that men's exposure posed the same danger to an unborn child as women's.[166]
Johnson Controls had met the second *Olin* guideline, showing that the risk
was confined to women.

By applying *Wards Cove* to the framework of *Olin* and *Hayes*, Coffey
reversed the burden of proof *Olin* had placed on the employer. Under *Wards
Cove*, the employer's burden is to produce evidence of a legitimate business
reason for the policy. Plaintiffs must then prove that less discriminatory alternatives exist. Judge Coffey did not believe that the UAW had presented
convincing alternatives to Johnson Controls's fetal protection policy. On the
contrary, Johnson Controls had tried another policy and it had not worked.
The union had not met its burden of proof. Citing *Furnco* repeatedly throughout his decision, Judge Coffey concluded that "courts are generally less competent than employers to restructure business practices."[167]

Johnson Controls had not only met its burden under the business necessity defense, but it had met the more rigorous requirements of BFOQ. While
giving lip service to dicta on the narrowness of the BFOQ, Judge Coffey
argued against the assertion that the company would never be able to prove
job relatedness. Instead, the BFOQ defense should be expanded to give
"meaningful and thoughtful consideration to the *interests of all those affected
by a company's policy, in this case the employer, the employee and the unborn
child.*"[168] Judge Coffey believed Johnson Controls's policy to be a narrow one
because it only applied to the high–lead exposure areas of the battery division.

Judge Coffey argued that Title VII permits distinctions between men and
women if they are based on "real" differences. Fictitious or stereotypical
differences, on the other hand, would not justify treating men and women
differently. He cited constitutional cases in support of this proposition: "the
Supreme Court has never hesitated to recognize sex-based differences, partic-

---

166. Ibid., 889.
167. Ibid., 893, citing Furnco Construction Corp. v. Waters, 438 U.S. 567, 578 (1978).
168. 886 F.2d 871, 893 (1989).

ularly in cases involving physiology, marriage, childbirth, or sexuality."[169] He warned against "either using traditional stereotypes or falling into the equally unsatisfactory alternative of ignoring the real differences between men and women."[170] Just as the Pregnancy Discrimination Act does not preclude states from mandating a qualified right to reinstatement after childbirth (*Cal. Fed.*) or outlaw separate men's and women's teams for contact sports, the act does not prohibit Johnson Controls from recognizing "innate physical differences between men and women."[171]

Dothard showed that some physical differences between men and women might justify excluding women from certain occupations, despite the narrowness of the BFOQ defense. Because more was at stake than just women's health and safety in both *Dothard* and *UAW v. Johnson Controls*, women could not choose to assume the risks for themselves. Judge Coffey believed that women worked to "better their family's station in life,"[172] and they might discount the risk to their offspring because they needed the money. Finally, Judge Coffey drew an analogy between women undertaking hazardous jobs and couples refusing blood transfusions for their children because of religious concerns. Both cases require intervention to protect fetuses or children.

OSHA's standard for exposure to lead, which rejected setting a differential standard for men and women or excluding women altogether, recognized that men's reproductive capacities were at risk from low levels of exposure to lead. Yet Judge Coffey found OSHA's findings superseded by more recent evidence suggesting that even very low blood levels of lead injured children. Johnson Controls had done all it could to clean up the workplace and had no alternative to excluding all women who could not prove infertility.

The four dissenting justices on the court of appeals included Reagan-appointed conservatives of the law and economics school. They argued that summary judgment was inappropriate—important matters of fact and law were in dispute. They also did not accept that Johnson Controls's policy was neutral and should be analyzed under the rubric of disparate impact. Judge Cudahy referred to this as "result-oriented gimmickry." He thought the correct defense was BFOQ, and the company might be able to justify its policy under this defense, but only after a full trial. The most interesting part of his opinion is his reflection on the composition of the judiciary.

It is a matter of some interest that, of the twelve federal judges to have considered this case to date, none has been female. This may be quite

---

169. Ibid., 890.
170. Ibid., 894.
171. Ibid., 895.
172. Ibid., 897.

significant because this case, like other controversies of great potential consequence, demands, in addition to command of the disembodied rules, some insight into social reality. What is the situation of the pregnant woman, unemployed or working for the minimum wage and unprotected by health insurance, in relation to her pregnant sister, exposed to an indeterminate lead risk but well-fed, housed and doctored? Whose fetus is at greater risk? Whose decision is this to make? We, who are unfortunately all male, must address these and other equally complex questions through the clumsy vehicle of litigation. At least let it be complete litigation focusing on the right standard.[173]

Judge Posner, writing a separate dissenting opinion, also lamented that this important issue was decided on summary judgment, given the scientific complexity of the case. He criticized the majority and other courts for "stitching a new defense," that is, allowing employers to defend their policies as a business necessity. This "legerdemain" was wrong, because the policies are clearly facially discriminatory, and also unnecessary because employers might be able to defend their policies as a BFOQ. The Pregnancy Discrimination Act makes such policies facially discriminatory and the only defense is BFOQ. Furthermore, cost considerations cannot be an answer to proven disparate treatment. But employers' ethical concerns about their operations' effect on third parties, when combined with fears of tort liability, might make exclusionary policies reasonably necessary to the normal operation of a business.

Judge Posner talked about the length of time it takes to excrete lead and about the high number of "careless pregnancies." He warned about being "deceived by superficial historical analogies or facile invocations of 'paternalistic.'"[174] A paternalistic measure "protects a person against himself [*sic*]." Johnson Controls, however, sought to protect fetuses. Yet he had many questions about the company's policy. What proportion of women employed by the company became pregnant? What if Johnson Controls made its warning grim rather than merely comparing the risks to smoking and cancer? How do other companies deal with this problem? He wanted more information on the evidence on men as well as the profitability of manufacturing batteries under current conditions.

On the evidence before him, Judge Posner determined Johnson Controls's policy to be excessively cautious by presuming any woman under seventy to be fertile and by excluding women from jobs that fed into high–lead exposure jobs but were not themselves exposing workers to lead. He concluded with a call for a cautious and moderate approach after a full hearing of the evidence.

173. Ibid., 902.
174. Ibid., 906.

The issue of the legality of fetal protection is as novel and difficult as it is contentious and the most sensible way to approach it at this early stage is on a case-by-case basis, involving careful examination of the facts as developed by the full adversary process of a trial. The record in this case is too sparse. The district judge jumped the gun. By affirming on this scanty basis we may be encouraging incautious employers to adopt fetal protection policies that could endanger the jobs of millions of women for minor gains in fetal safety and health.[175]

The concurring justices on the Supreme Court echoed Judge Posner, but it was Judge Easterbrook's position that Justice Blackmun drew upon in his majority opinion. Judge Easterbrook no doubt grabbed the attention of the Court initially by writing: "this is the most important sex-discrimination case this circuit has ever decided. It is likely the most important sex-discrimination case in any court since 1964 when Congress enacted Title VII. If the majority is right, then by one estimate 20 million industrial jobs could be closed to women."[176]

Judge Easterbrook, joined by Judge Flaum, called for interpreting the statute rather than for the court to offer its own solution to a public policy problem. He strongly rejected treating Johnson Controls's policy as neutral— it was facially discriminatory. The *Olin* court wrongly concluded that because the policy was good, it had not used sex as a ground of decision: "A court's belief that a good end is in view does not justify departure from the statutory framework."[177] Judge Easterbrook summarized *Olin* as saying, "In other words, this *must* be a disparate impact case because an employer couldn't win it as a disparate treatment case."[178] He suggested that "if the rigors of the BFOQ suggest the need for a fresh approach, that is a job for another branch."[179]

Judge Easterbrook drew on *Manhart* for support in rejecting the company's arguments. *Manhart* established that employers must treat people as individuals rather than as members of a group: although some women live longer than some men, individual women cannot be charged more for their pensions than men. Similarly, although some women who are capable of bearing children do so, employers may not treat all women as pregnant. In addition, *Manhart* supports his argument that cost concerns cannot justify explicit sex discrimination. Even if it costs more to employ women, Title VII does not permit cost as a defense to intentional discrimination.

---

175. Ibid., 908.
176. Ibid., 920.
177. Ibid., 909.
178. Ibid., 910.
179. Ibid.

Judge Easterbrook dismissed the calls for flexibility in the district court's and majority's opinions. The cases they cited referred to the order of proof and methods of inference. Yet the discriminatory nature of Johnson Controls's policy did not need to be inferred or proven through a complex process: the policy explicitly treated women differently than men. He also rejected the majority's claim that the EEOC had sanctioned the court's analysis of exclusionary policies under disparate impact as the correct interpretation of Title VII, commenting that the agency was merely advising its employees about the practice of circuit courts rather than defining what Title VII, in its view, required. "If the EEOC's statement is designed as an interpretive rule, it is neither reasoned nor consistent with Title VII."[180]

Judge Easterbrook pointed out that the *Olin* court had concluded that an exclusionary policy could not be justified as a BFOQ, and, for that reason, it had turned to the business necessity defense. He compared Johnson Controls's defense of its policy with the stereotypical thinking revealed in *Muller v. Oregon*.

No legal or ethical principle compels or allows Johnson to assume that women are less able than men to make intelligent decisions about the welfare of the next generation, that the interests of the next generation always trump the interests of living woman [*sic*], and that the only acceptable level of risk is zero.[181]

Judge Easterbrook argued that most women in the industrial labor force do not become pregnant, particularly those over thirty, and, one would expect, few who had been fully informed about the risks. Furthermore, although some employees in a given area might have blood lead levels above 30 $\mu g/dl$, not all would. Those who practiced good industrial hygiene might keep their blood lead levels much lower. He thought the company's risk of tort liability had been inflated, but, in any case, it might only mean that the cost of employing women would be higher than for men—not a defense to proven disparate treatment.

Like Judge Posner, Judge Easterbrook wanted more information to decide the scientific disputes. What levels of exposure harm fetuses and at what stage of pregnancy? Some say the fetus is most at risk during the early weeks of pregnancy, others claim lead does not cross the placenta until the late stages. Furthermore, how did the slight risk compare with such other risks as smoking, using artificial sweetners, driving a car, or driving a taxi? He rejected the "zero-risk" strategy of the company when it came to fetal hazards.

---

180. Ibid., 912.
181. Ibid., 913.

Who could say whether women were safer working at some risk or unemployed with no health insurance? The net risk to the fetus might increase as a result of Johnson Controls's policy, but the company would not be legally responsible. Judge Easterbrook asked, "Surely Title VII does not allow an employer to adopt a policy that simultaneously makes both women and their children worse off."[182]

Judge Easterbrook argued that litigation was not the best way of quantifying risks and determining acceptable levels of risk. The district court and the majority were wrong to do just that and, in so doing, reject the findings of OSHA and the EPA without even having a trial. He was also startled at the quickness with which they rejected animal studies—studies that determine the risks posed by most foods and drugs. In any case, the evidence did not justify excluding women from jobs that exposed them to no lead, but fed into high–lead exposure jobs. Although "the presence of thoughtful persons on the other side suggests caution,"[183] he concluded that

> risk to the next generation is incident to all activity, starting with getting out of bed. (Staying in bed all day has its own hazards.) To insist on *zero* risk, which the court says Johnson may do, is to exclude women from the industrial jobs that have been a male preserve. By all means let society bend its energies to improving the prospects of those who come after us. Demanding zero risk produces not progress but paralysis. Defining tolerable risk, and seeking to reduce that limit, is more useful—but it is a job for Congress or OSHA in conjunction with medical and other sciences. Laudable though its objective be, Johnson may not reach its goal at the expense of women.[184]

Johnson Controls v. Foster

While the appeal of *UAW v. Johnson Controls* was pending before the Supreme Court, the Court of Appeals of California was considering whether California's discrimination law outlawed Johnson Controls's exclusionary policy. Globe Battery, a division of Johnson Controls, had refused to hire Queen Elizabeth Foster for a lead battery production job at its Fullerton plant in 1983. At the time Foster applied for the job, she was neither pregnant nor planning to become pregnant. The twenty-eight-year-old woman was enticed by the opportunity to earn twice what she had earned working at a bank.[185] Unlike the other plants, Fullerton never adopted the guidelines issued in 1977,

---

182. Ibid., 918.
183. Ibid., 920.
184. Ibid., 920–21.
185. Kirp, "Toxic Choices," 1.

informing women of the risks, recommending that they not take high–lead exposure jobs if they were planning to conceive, and making them sign a waiver noting they had been informed of the risks. Dr. Benjamin Culver, the medical consultant, declined to carry out the policy and thus, from 1972 onward, he refused to hire women who could not medically document infertility.[186]

The California Fair Employment and Housing Commission found Johnson Controls's policy to be facially discriminatory under the California Fair Employment and Housing Act. The commission noted that California law also expressly prohibited employers from requiring that employees be sterilized as a condition of employment, but since Foster had not been sterilized, the provision was not found to be applicable to the case. The BFOQ defense in California was similar to the defense under Title VII; it is a narrow defense, all or substantially all women must be shown to be unable to perform the job and the essence of the business operation must be undermined for employers to condition the holding of a job on one sex. Since there was no question whether fertile women were capable of performing the job, the commission concluded that Johnson Controls had not met its burden. Citing *Burwell v. Eastern Airlines*, the commission concluded that "the clear import of the Act, therefore, is that consideration of risks to fetuses is to be left to the sound discretion of these workers themselves."[187]

The commission doubted the company could have proven a BFOQ in any case, because of the evidence suggesting men's reproductive capacities were also at risk from exposure to lead, and because fear of tort liability would not have been enough to undermine the essence of the business. The commission rejected the possibility that the company could offer a business necessity defense, commenting that *Hayes* and *Olin* "distort the concepts of 'facially neutral practice' and 'business necessity' out of any recognizable shape in order to reach their results."[188] In any case, the federal courts' rulings were not binding on California courts interpreting California statutes.

The commission ordered Johnson Controls to hire Queen Elizabeth Foster, pay her $16,600 back pay plus interest for lost wages, and post a notice that its fetal protection policy was discriminatory and the commission had held it to be in violation of the law. The Superior Court of Orange County overturned the commission's decision.[189] Judge McDonald held that the proper framework was disparate impact, relying on *Hayes*, and found that Johnson Controls had shown a substantial risk to fetuses from women's but

---

186. Department of Fair Employment and Housing v. Globe Battery, FEP 83-84 K1-0262s L-33297 87-19 (September 1, 1987), 6.

187. Ibid., 10.

188. Ibid., 12.

189. Case no. 545241, William F. McDonald, Judge.

not men's exposure. He remanded the case to the commission to consider the business necessity defense and, in particular, whether there were acceptable alternatives to excluding women.[190] Foster appealed this decision.

The California Court of Appeals for the Fourth Appellate District reversed, finding Johnson Controls's policy to be unlawful sex discrimination under California law.[191] Judge Staniforth recognized that the court must balance the public policy goals of protecting the fetus with securing equal employment opportunities for women. Judge Staniforth noted first that the courts should defer to the commission's findings of facts as long as they are supported by strong evidence on the record considered as a whole. He then turned to the legal matter of whether the exclusionary policy was facially discriminatory.

> The evidence here is uncontradicted: Before a woman could obtain work under the Fetal Protection Program, she must demonstrate, in effect, there is medical certainty that she is sterile. The code sections and regulations adopted and legal precedents are clear, plain and unambiguous. Gender based discrimination—a refusal to hire based upon sex—violates the letter and spirit of the law and all modern precedent. The Commission determined that a *"possibility of pregnancy"* as basis for refusal to hire should not be treated differently than a "gender based discrimination." We agree.[192]

Judge Staniforth argued that although pregnancy was a condition unique to women, it was not descriptive of all women. He had no doubt that the policy was blatantly and overtly discriminatory.

He gave great weight to OSHA's rejection of the proposition that lead posed greater dangers to women's reproduction than men's, and cited the medical evidence on men. Mentioning the Seventh Circuit's opinion in *UAW v. Johnson Controls*, he noted that it "simply ignored the evidence relied upon by OSHA."[193] Like the dissenters on the Seventh Circuit, Judge Staniforth was dissatisfied with the company's medical director's ability to quantify the risk, finding his review of the evidence "speculation."

Although neither the court nor the commission was bound by federal precedent because this was a case under state discrimination law, Judge Staniforth went on to criticize the federal courts' rulings on exclusionary policies, saying "each . . . took different approaches in analyzing the issue.

---

190. 267 Cal.Rptr. 158, 163 (Cal.App. 4 Dist. 1990).

191. Ibid., *cert. denied*, Supreme Court of California, 1990 Cal. LEXIS 2107 (May 17, 1990).

192. 267 Cal.Rptr. 158, 165–66 (Cal.App. 4 Dist. 1990).

193. Ibid., 168 n.3.

Each case manifested great legal skill in refusing to enforce the plain language of Title VII,"[194] and he labeled the construction of the policy as neutral as "pure sophistry."[195] Johnson Controls had not met the requirements of the BFOQ, the only defense available to it because being fertile does not affect one's ability to do the job. Even if some women's exposure might put a fetus at risk, that does not mean all or substantially all women's does, and it is not clear that by putting some fetuses at risk the essence of the business is undermined.

Not wanting to adopt a cavalier attitude toward the "potential" youth of the nation, Judge Staniforth commented,

> We simply decline to engage in judicial engineering in an area clearly within the province of the Legislature. . . . It is not for this court in a surge of unjustified judicial activism to create statutory exceptions where the Legislature has not, for whatever reason, done so itself.[196]

He rejected Johnson Controls's argument that the BFOQ analysis was a recognition of real differences between men and women that would justify differential treatment, calling it a "largely male-created rationale [that] has grown ever less fashionable and acceptable in the latter half of the twentieth century."[197] He concluded that "the Company's FPP does not discriminate on the basis of 'objective differences' between men and women; it discriminates on the basis of unfounded scientific stereotypes."[198]

Finally, Judge Staniforth noted that the EEOC had revised its guidance following the Seventh Circuit's decision in *UAW v. Johnson Controls* and agreed with the EEOC's criticism of the ruling. In concluding his opinion, Judge Staniforth condemned the rationale for the company's exclusionary policy in language stronger than any other judge had used. He attacked the assumption that, because women can become pregnant, the only safe way to treat them is as if they are pregnant. "We are in an era of *choice*. A woman is not required to be a Victorian brood mare. She may, with constitutional basis, prefer not to have children."[199] He rejected the view that "society's interest in fetal safety is best served, not by fully informing women of the risks involved and allowing them to make informed choices, not by fixing the workplace, but rather by removing from women the opportunity to make any choices that matter at all."[200] Judge Staniforth's forceful arguments, combined with Judge

194. Ibid., 170 n.7.
195. Ibid., 171 n.8.
196. Ibid., 171 n.10, 173.
197. Ibid., 174 n.13.
198. Ibid., 177.
199. Ibid., 177 n.16.
200. Ibid., 178.

Easterbrook's and Judge Posner's, provided an interesting backdrop to the decision before the Supreme Court.

The Supreme Court's Ruling in *UAW v. Johnson Controls*

Justice Blackmun defined the question as: "May an employer exclude a fertile female employee from certain jobs because of its concern for the health of the fetus the woman might conceive?"[201] Justice Blackmun suggested that the Supreme Court had granted *certiorari* because the Seventh Circuit's holding in *UAW v. Johnson Controls* that an employer could justify an exclusionary policy as a BFOQ put it in conflict with the Fourth and Eleventh Circuits.[202] That Justice Blackmun, a liberal justice by 1992 standards and the author of *Roe v. Wade*, should have written the majority opinion indicated that the employees had been victorious. His opening left no doubt. "The bias in Johnson Controls's policy is obvious."[203] Justice Blackmun forcefully stated that the policy explicitly discriminated against women on the basis of their sex and created a facial classification based on gender. Likening Johnson Controls's policy to Martin Marietta's decision to refuse to hire mothers of pre–school age children, Justice Blackmun declared there could be no doubt that the policy constituted disparate treatment. The *Olin* and *Hayes* courts erroneously classified the policy as neutral, and the absence of a malevolent motive was not enough to convert a facially discriminatory policy into a neutral one. All nine justices agreed that Johnson Controls's exclusionary policy was facially discriminatory and the lower courts erred in granting the company summary judgment.

Justice Blackmun cited the EEOC's revised policy guidance in support of his position that the only defense available to the company was BFOQ. He was equally strong in his conclusion that the company could not meet the rigorous requirements of the BFOQ defense because being potentially pregnant did not interfere with one's ability to manufacture batteries efficiently. Johnson Controls could not force women, but not their male counterparts, to choose between a job and sterilization. He rejected the analogy between unconceived fetuses and customers and third parties.

The unconceived fetuses of Johnson Controls' female employees, however, are neither customers nor third parties whose safety is essential to the business of battery manufacturing. No one can disregard the possibility of injury to future children; the BFOQ, however, is not so broad that

---

201. 111 S.Ct. 1196, 1199 (1991).
202. Ibid., 1202.
203. Ibid.

it transforms this deep social concern into an essential aspect of battery making.[204]

Justice Blackmun argued that expanding the BFOQ defense would run counter to both the clear wording of the statute and the congressional intent that women not be excluded from their jobs because of their capacity to bear children. The plain wording of the statute precluded employers from banning pregnant women, as well as women whose infertility was not medically documented, even if the evidence showed that the offspring of female employees were at greater risk from lower exposure levels than male employees.

Justice Blackmun drew upon the opinions of courts deciding cases about whether airlines could ground pregnant flight attendants as well as the legislative history of the Pregnancy Discrimination Act to support his view that it was up to the parents, not the employers, to decide to conceive or whether to work while pregnant. Perhaps the most quoted part of his opinion (because of its significance for the abortion debate) is the following passage.

> Decisions about the welfare of future children must be left to the parents who conceive, bear, support, and raise them rather than to the employers who hire those parents. . . . Title VII and the PDA simply do not allow a woman's dismissal because of her failure to submit to sterilization.[205]

Justice Blackmun argued further that Johnson Controls could not meet its burdens under the BFOQ defense because it could not show that "all or substantially all" women would be unable to perform the duties of the job safely, even if one assumed that protecting unconceived fetuses was part of the essence of the business of manufacturing batteries. Although eight employees did become pregnant at Johnson Controls, the company never revealed what percentage of workers that was, nor did it show any of the children to have been harmed by the exposure. Since only 9 percent of women workers nationally become pregnant each year, and only 2 percent of blue collar workers over thirty become pregnant, the company's policy was excessively overbroad in treating all women as if they were pregnant.[206]

Finally, Justice Blackmun considered whether an employer's fear of tort liability could justify its exclusionary policy. In 1978, when the Occupational Safety and Health Administration set standards of occupational exposure to lead, OSHA explicitly rejected excluding women or setting different standards for men and women. Instead, OSHA concluded that the evidence warranted

---

204. Ibid., 1206.
205. Ibid., 1207.
206. Ibid., 1208 citing Mary E. Becker, "From *Muller v. Oregon* to Fetal Vulnerability Policies," *University of Chicago Law Review* 53 (1986): 1233.

setting a single standard for men and women and allowing workers of either sex the right to transfer to another job if they were planning to start families. Justice Blackmun maintained that employers who met OSHA's standards and informed workers of the risks would not be considered negligent. The question of whether the requirements of Title VII would preempt state tort law need not be answered because Johnson Controls had presented no factual evidence about the likelihood and costs of such actions, let alone proven that they would cripple the firm. Justice Blackmun rejected the company's attempt to solve the very real problem of reproductive hazards by illegal discrimination rather than cleaning up the workplace. And even if it might cost more to employ women because of some increased risk of liability, increased cost was not a defense to intentional discrimination.

In concluding, Justice Blackmun, referring to the paternalism of *Muller v. Oregon*, wrote, "We do no more than hold that the Pregnancy Discrimination Act means what it says,"[207] and reiterated his previous argument about who decides.

> It is no more appropriate for the courts than it is for individual employers to decide whether a woman's reproductive role is more important to herself and her family than her economic role. Congress has left this choice to the woman as hers to make.[208]

The rights of the unconceived fetus do not trump all other rights, nor is the employer the one to balance competing concerns.

All nine members of the Court agreed that Johnson Controls's policy was disparate treatment and the company could only defend its policy by arguing that being unable to carry a child was a BFOQ for the job of manufacturing batteries. They also agreed that the lower courts were wrong to decide the case on summary judgment. Feminists, abortion activists, and Supreme Court watchers noted with interest that both Justice O'Connor and Justice Souter, the newest member of the Court, joined Justice Blackmun's opinion rather than siding with the more conservative members of the Court. Justices White and Scalia, however, wrote separate concurring opinions.

Justice White's concurrence was joined by Chief Justice Rehnquist and Justice Kennedy. He thought a significant threat of tort liability could justify a BFOQ, but the burden would be on the employer to prove that a serious threat exists. A more narrowly tailored policy might be lawful under Title VII. Justice White thought the BFOQ could include considerations of cost and safety, instead of merely whether women could perform the job. Justice Blackmun, he argued, had misrepresented the significance of *Manhart*. Fur-

---

207. 111 S.Ct. 1196, 1210 (1991).
208. Ibid.

thermore, concerns about the safety of third parties, such as customers, invitees, and even fetuses, was a proper business concern. He believed that the Court's opinion, presumably forbidding employers from excluding even pregnant women, went far beyond congressional intent or the wording of the statute.

He did, however, believe that Johnson Controls had overstated the risk, or at least it had not adequately measured what that risk was. Justice White demanded that Johnson Controls be consistent in its risk avoidance posture. If the risk of fetal injury was no higher than other levels of risk to employees' health or the safety of customers, then the company could not defend its policy. Finally, Justice White thought the company could have explored less discriminatory alternatives. Once the Court rejected consideration of the policy as neutral but instead determined that the employer's only defense was BFOQ, the employer had the burden of proof. Johnson Controls would have to convince the Court that the evidence on men was unpersuasive (a conclusion opposite to OSHA's) and that no alternatives were acceptable. Although Justices White, Kennedy, and Chief Justice Rehnquist would have permitted employers the opportunity to defend exclusionary policies under the BFOQ, they would have held them to a much higher standard of proof than had the circuit courts.

Justice Scalia's separate concurrence is particularly interesting. He dismissed the evidence on lead as irrelevant. Even if all women put their fetuses at risk, and men's exposure did not jeopardize the health of their offspring, Johnson Controls's policy is facially discriminatory because "Congress has unequivocally said so [in passing the Pregnancy Discrimination Act]."[209] Those who find that result unsatisfactory should appeal to Congress to amend the law. Although he agreed with Justice Blackmun that any action required by Title VII could not give rise to tort liability, Justice Scalia disagreed with Justice Blackmun's view that cost could not be a defense for explicit discrimination. A prohibitive expense, such as refitting a ship destined for a long journey to accommodate women sailors, might justify excluding women from certain jobs, but the employer would bear the burden of proof.

Justice Scalia's concurrence underlined the most surprising and significant part of the Court's holding. Justice Scalia argued that Title VII prohibits employers from excluding fertile women from hazardous work not because men face reproductive hazards from lead, too, but because the Pregnancy Discrimination Act states unambiguously that employers may not exclude women from jobs because of their capacity to become pregnant. Justice Blackmun, too, refers to the plain language of the Pregnancy Discrimination Act, but Justice Scalia explicitly mentions that a comparison is not required.

As feminist legal scholars have long maintained, pointing to decisions such as *General Electric v. Gilbert* and its British equivalents, the law incorporates a male standard. Women can have the right to work only if they are

---

209. Ibid., 1216.

just like men or can compare their circumstances to men. Pregnant women won some rights to protection under discrimination law because they could compare themselves to men with temporarily incapacitating disabilities. In *UAW v. Johnson Controls*, the Supreme Court says unequivocally that whether women can compare themselves to men or not, the law forbids employers punishing women because they can bear children.

Conclusion

Courts in the United States have changed the way they apply Title VII to exclusionary policies. In the cases the EEOC decided, as well as in *Zuniga*, the outcome hinged on whether the employer had considered alternatives short of dismissal. This focus reflected the Supreme Court's ambivalence about pregnancy discrimination, evidenced by its opinions in *Gilbert* and *Satty*—rulings Congress overturned through legislation.

Between *Zuniga* and the Supreme Court's ruling in *UAW v. Johnson Controls*, industry did not seek alternatives to excluding women but sought firmer scientific support for such policies—in *Olin*, for example, retroactively. Once the Pregnancy Discrimination Act defined sex discrimination to include pregnancy discrimination, courts moved beyond the question of whether the failure to consider alternatives had unduly burdened pregnant women, but clung to a disparate impact analysis. In *Olin*, the Fourth Circuit set out a legal framework for evaluating exclusionary policies, but continued to treat the policies as neutral. Fetal health was a legitimate business concern and policies that excluded fertile women, if carefully drafted and based on scientific evidence, were permissible under Title VII. Although the Eleventh Circuit appeared to challenge *Olin*'s reasoning in *Hayes*, it, too, permitted employers to justify exclusionary policies as a business necessity. Ruling that an exclusionary policy might be permissible under Title VII, the *Hayes* court carefully scrutinized the basis for the policy and how the hospital had carried it out, adopting a skeptical attitude to the policy and finding it unjustified. The Seventh Circuit lowered the standard of justification still further by making the burden of proof rest with the plaintiff at all times, modifying the *Olin* decision after *Wards Cove*.

By treating facially discriminatory policies as neutral and allowing employers to offer a business necessity defense, U.S. courts before 1991 were holding that employers could treat men and women differently as long as they were really different. Courts in the U.S. have occasionally distinguished between asserted differences resulting from stereotypes and prejudice and "real" differences between men and women. Sometimes, courts have exposed assertions of real differences to be the result of stereotypes, at other times they have permitted employers to treat men and women differently if they are really different. Even the concurring justices in *UAW v. Johnson Controls*, however, particularly Justice Scalia, rejected the proposition that treating men and women differently is not discrimination if men and women are really different. While not all justices agreed that asserted biological differences were merely the result of stereotypical thinking, they did agree that the statute did not permit employers to use such asserted differences to deny women employment opportunities.

Justice Scalia not only forcefully expressed the view that exclusionary policies were clearly facially discriminatory regardless of physical differences between men and women, but he also rejected the proposition that women must be just like men to win the right to work. Women's groups' briefs had self-consciously adopted the difference approach, hoping that judges would grasp that men and women were not really so different after all: either could damage their offspring as a result of exposure to hazardous substances. To pretend otherwise, to ignore men's role in reproduction, was another example of stereotypical thinking, the opponents of exclusionary policies argued. If men and women were not really so different, employers should not be able to treat women less favorably than men. While their briefs drew the comparison between men and women, they also argued that the plain language of the Pregnancy Discrimination Act dictated a finding that exclusionary policies were unlawful. Contrary to the dire predictions of employers, if the courts strictly interpreted the Pregnancy Discrimination Act they would not be jeopardizing future generations because as a practical matter toxins do not discriminate. "Protecting" only women by shutting them out of lucrative jobs would not guarantee healthy offspring. Once the ACLU and unions broadened the question beyond reproductive health to human health more generally, to reveal men's vulnerability to toxins, they escaped the limits of the comparative approach. If employers were subjecting large numbers of their workers to heart disease and other problems, the remote possibility of injury to future generations, and the question of whether substances are teratogenic and mutagenic at the same levels of exposure became less important. By broadening the question from discrimination and comparability to health and safety beyond mere reproductive health, feminist groups and unions strengthened their case. Because it is obvious that only women can bring the fetus into the workplace and that anything pregnant women are exposed to the fetus is also exposed to, judges must be persuaded to consider men's role in reproduction. The lower courts had dismissed the evidence on men, and continued to extol the significance of the differences between men's and women's reproductive capacities. The Supreme Court, however, overturned those rulings without arguing that it had been convinced by the evidence on men, that men and women are really alike. Instead, the Court held that whether men and women were different or not, Title VII outlawed Johnson Controls's policy.

The significance of *UAW v. Johnson Controls* for legal doctrine and feminist theory lies in these two points. Because the Court had upheld differential treatment based on assertions of biological difference in the past, its decision not to do so is particularly meaningful, and even more so because of the increasingly conservative disposition of the Court. In rejecting the claim that real differences should justify depriving women of employment opportunities and moving away from the comparative approach, the Supreme Court's interpretation of the law pleased feminists, who hailed the decision as a major Title VII victory.

Several other aspects of the decision were less revolutionary, but equally welcome. The Supreme Court rejected the lower courts' suggestion that good intentions could redeem facially discriminatory practices. The Court split over whether concerns about cost could ever be a defense to explicit discrimination, yet Justice Blackmun garnered five justices in support of his holding that it could not.

Many of the lower courts had skipped lightly over the question of whether it was reasonable to treat individual women as if they were members of a group: pregnant women or women likely to be pregnant. Johnson Controls said that it could not predict which women capable of bearing a child would do so. Furthermore, more was at stake than an individual woman's right to risk her own health. By exposing herself to hazardous substances, she might also be putting a fetus at risk. Precedents such as *Weeks* and *Manhart* militated against ascribing group characteristics, however accurate, to all individual members, but Johnson Controls and several judges moved quickly from the category woman worker to pregnant worker. This equation angered many women. The underlying yet perhaps unexamined assumptions are that women do not plan their pregnancies, do not know, or have any say over whether they conceive, and cannot be trusted with the welfare of future generations, who are unfortunately trapped in women's bodies and need others to protect them.

Cases on exclusionary policies go to the very heart of biological differences between the sexes: reproduction and sexuality. While feminists might argue that the construction of women as rapable and men not or of women's exposure to hazardous substances as more damaging to reproduction than men's are the result of social, not biological differences, judges and members of tribunals may see them as given biological facts. When cases raise questions about the relevance of sexual differences and involve a breakthrough for women into traditionally male jobs—high-risk and "unfeminine" jobs such as prison guards and lead battery workers—individual judges and members of tribunals' presuppositions about the biological differences between men and women may reinforce their views about women's role in society. The result may be that courts and tribunals choose to maintain the status quo, permitting segregation by sex in some occupations. Some judges have acted on their personal views of what is reasonable rather than critically examining the scientific basis for the claimed differences between the sexes. Judges also may be surprised or even shocked by women's desire to hold certain hazardous jobs or by some women's decision not to have children. The quips of judges about "the grandfather in me is opposed to the policies" or the preconception that "this case is about women who want to hurt their fetuses" reveal that many judges approach cases on exclusionary policies with horror at the women who want access to jobs, and operate under the assumption that the policies are reasonable and benign.

The Supreme Court did not explicitly debate the limitations of the comparative approach, nor challenge the dichotomy between sex and gender, thereby challenging justices' preconceptions about sexual difference. Instead, it appealed to the conventional interpretive strategies of a strict construction of the statute and a reliance on congressional intent. Before *UAW v. Johnson Controls*, judges and members of tribunals had used the difference approach in cases on exclusionary policies: once an employer shows that the sexes are different in a relevant way that is not the result of prejudice or stereotypes, it is not discrimination to treat the sexes differently. Those who adopt the difference approach may be quick to see the sexes as different with respect to whatever characteristic is at issue—sales aggressiveness, physical strength, or vulnerability to reproductive hazards, for example. The dominance approach takes a skeptical approach to the differences between men and women, finding them, if not illusory, often the result of societal discrimination. Yet under the dominance approach, even if the sexes are different, as they are with respect to reproduction, the employer is required to take extra steps to insure that these differences do not result in disadvantages. The dominance approach would require that an employer reduce the exposure to a level safe for a fetus or allow both men and women planning to become parents to remove themselves with full pay and benefits. Feminists committed to the dominance approach found an unlikely ally in Justice Scalia, who claimed merely to be following the law as written and avoided opining on the merits of the policy.

Some judges and members of tribunals in both Britain and the United States have upheld the legality of exclusionary policies and deemed the exclusion of women from hazardous work to be reasonable. As a consequence, they have been willing to disregard doctrine and classify the policies as neutral rather than facially discriminatory, holding that "justifiable" differential treatment is not discrimination at all. When British judges and members of tribunals substitute their own standards of what is reasonable for the law's definition of discrimination as less favorable treatment in cases on exclusionary policies, their behavior is consistent with their holdings in other discrimination cases at the time. Judges in the United States, however, were departing from settled practice. The Supreme Court's resounding rejection of exclusionary policies makes the two countries seem farther apart than if we carefully looked only at what the lower courts have done.

Until the Supreme Court ruled in *UAW v. Johnson Controls*, both U.S. and British judges and members of tribunals were willing to expand discrimination law to permit employers to justify exclusionary policies. In *Zuniga*, *Olin*, and *Hayes*, the U.S. appellate courts (including the dissenters in the Seventh Circuit in *UAW v. Johnson Controls*) were reluctant to find specific policies consistent with Title VII. Judges and members of tribunals in both countries, then, may have created exceptions to the law for exclusionary policies, but judges in the United States have been more suspicious of them, more willing to scrutinize employers' behavior, and more willing to hear evidence on complex scientific issues. British courts and tribunals have left employers free to determine policy, constrained only by health and safety standards. The circuit courts' decisions would have positioned U.S. judges as the arbiters of the lawfulness of exclusionary policies, weighing the scientific evidence and examining employment practices, but the Supreme Court implicitly rejected this role in *UAW v. Johnson Controls* in its sweeping ruling that requires companies to seek a gender-neutral way to protect employees' offspring.

Comparing cases on exclusionary policies illustrates many of the differences between the countries' legal systems. Judges in the United States are more comfortable scrutinizing scientific evidence, delving into employment practices, and making public policy. Lower courts in the United States defended their decision to manipulate doctrine to permit exclusionary policies on public policy grounds, yet, in declaring exclusionary policies to be unlawful, the Supreme Court claimed to be strictly interpreting the statute and referred those concerned about public policy to Congress. Consistent with the findings discussed in chapters 3 and 4, judges in the United States expressed more concern for the impact of exclusionary policies on women's employment opportunities.

A striking difference is the role of other groups in the process. The enforcement agencies are relatively disengaged from the issue in both countries. In Britain, the EOC intervened on appeal in *Page v. Freight Hire* and continued to press employers to adopt a narrow definition of women of reproductive capacity. The EEOC actively assisted plaintiffs in the early cases, ignored the issue in the late 1980s, then issued policy guidelines initially supporting exclusionary policies but finally declaring them to be facially discriminatory. The courts weighed the EEOC's interpretations more heavily than British tribunals did the EOC's, but it is hard to draw firm conclusions from so few cases.

Women's groups, the civil rights community, health and environmental activists, and trade unions formed a coalition in the United States to challenge exclusionary policies. These groups supported plaintiffs, litigated, lobbied Congress to put pressure on the EEOC, and submitted amicus curiae briefs. In these activities they had no British counterpart once the indefatigable Sheila McKechnie left ASTMS. Pinning down the influence of groups is difficult; the victory in *UAW v. Johnson Controls* vindicates their efforts. Courts at all levels referred to their arguments and evidence, they played a key role in helping to shape how judges and the public framed the issue, and they kept the issue on the public agenda. Without their activities, the issue would no doubt have been viewed as one that is as marginal and exceptional as it currently is in Britain.

CHAPTER 7

The American Cyanamid Case

Previous chapters examined sex discrimination law in both Britain and the United States and described what happened when each country's courts and tribunals applied that law to exclusionary policies. Pursuing a complaint of discrimination, however, is not the only legal alternative for aggrieved women workers. Statutes whose purpose is to promote health and safety in the workplace offer a secondary alternative. In fact, many activists working on this issue would prefer to frame the issue of reproductive hazards in the workplace as a matter of health and safety for all workers rather than as a problem of sex discrimination or as a "women's issue." They feel discussing the justification for excluding women distracts attention from the real issue: workers' vulnerability to toxins. As a result, activists might prefer to lobby state legislatures and Congress for stricter standards of exposure to hazardous substances, pressure administrative agencies to enforce existing regulations, or develop the right to refuse hazardous work. Both Britain and the United States have laws that oblige employers to protect the health and safety of workers,[1] and enforcement agencies in both countries have dealt with the problem of reproductive hazards in setting exposure levels for some hazardous substances.[2] Yet only in the United States have cases on exclusionary policies come before administrative agencies (and eventually the court of appeals) under health and safety law. This chapter shows that fighting exclusionary policies under health and safety law rather than discrimination law was short-lived because of the Occupational Safety and Health Review Commission's decision in 1979 in a case involving American Cyanamid Company.

This chapter examines OSHA's efforts to prohibit the exclusion of women whose infertility is not medically documented from toxic work environments, and, in particular, its attempts to fine companies that required women to undergo sterilization to keep jobs that exposed them to hazardous substances. The most notorious example of such a policy was the one devel-

---

1. The Health and Safety at Work Act of 1974, and the Occupational Safety and Health Act, 29 U.S.C. §650 et seq. (1970).

2. See Joan E. Bertin, "Occupational Hazards to Reproductive Health: Conflicts Redefine Issues and Solutions," *Labor Relations* (P-H) ¶40,056 (November 1, 1985). See U.K. Health and Safety Commission, *Control of Lead at Work Regulations* (1980).

oped by American Cyanamid. In addition to being an example of using the Occupational Safety and Health Act to fight exclusionary policies, the administrative action arising out of Cyanamid's policy publicized the many flaws in employers' solutions to the problem of reproductive hazards. The alleged connection between working with visual display terminals and miscarriage has come to epitomize, rightly or wrongly, the public's idea of a reproductive hazard;[3] similarly, the Cyanamid case dramatized the failure of certain industries to safeguard its workers and their future offspring in a nondiscriminatory way. If American Cyanamid had chosen to exclude all women rather than promote sterilization as a way to maintain employment, the case might not have generated as much interest. Sterilization as a job requirement was news.[4]

Although this chapter focuses on one company's policy and OSHA's response, Cyanamid's policy is not unique. Corporations such as B. F. Goodrich, Sun Oil, Union Carbide, Allied Chemical, DuPont, Dow, Monsanto, and General Motors have adopted similar exclusionary policies.[5] *Chemical and Engineering News* reported in 1980 that no chemical company it interviewed permitted women biologically capable of bearing children to work with fetotoxins,[6] companies believed that potential fetuses were at risk at levels of exposure that were safe for adult men and women,[7] and companies prefer the risk of lawsuits for discrimination to liability for malformed children.[8] Employers excluded women from an estimated 100,000 to 20 million jobs.[9] Thus, although this chapter examines only one case, the outcome has

---

3. Tamar Lewin, "Protecting the Baby: Work in Pregnancy Poses Legal Frontier," *New York Times*, August 2, 1988.

4. Randall and Short identify the importance of OSHA's media strategy as well as press coverage of this issue (Donna M. Randall and James F. Short, "Women in Toxic Work Environments: A Case Study of Social Problem Development," *Social Problems* 30 [April 1983]: 410–24). Also see Brenton R. Schlender, "Sterilization is main issue in OSHA suits," *Wall Street Journal*, December 9, 1980; "Company and Union in Dispute as Women Undergo Sterilization," *New York Times*, January 4, 1979; "Pigment Plant Wins Fertility-Risk Case," *New York Times*, September 8, 1980; Philip Shabecoff, "U.S. Appeals Ruling on Women in Hazardous Jobs," *New York Times*, September 9, 1980; Philip Shabecoff, "Job Threats to Workers' Fertility Emerging as Civil Liberties Issue," *New York Times*, January 15, 1979; "The Women at Cyanamid," *New York Times*, January 7, 1979; Gail Bronson, "Bitter Reaction, Issue of Fetal Damage Stirs Women Workers at Chemical Plants," *Wall Street Journal*, February 9, 1979.

5. Rebecca Rawls, "Reproductive Hazards in the Workplace," *Chemical and Engineering News* 58 (February 18, 1980): 35–37.

6. Rebecca Rawls, "Reproductive Hazards in the Workplace," *Chemical and Engineering News* 58 (February 11, 1980): 30.

7. Ibid., 29.

8. Rawls, February 18, 1980, 36.

9. Equal Employment Opportunities Commission and Office of Federal Contract Compliance Programs, "Interpretive Guidelines on Employment Discrimination and Reproductive Hazards," 45 *Fed. Reg.* 7514 (February 1, 1980).

an impact on many employers with exclusionary policies other than Cyanamid and Bunker Hill.

Although they have lobbied civil servants over setting standards of exposure, British women have not invoked health and safety law to challenge the legality of exclusionary policies. This chapter, thus, focuses almost exclusively on cases in the United States and on one case in particular. After examining this attempt to fight exclusionary policies under health and safety law, this chapter makes several points. First, the Occupational Safety and Health Review Commission (OSHRC) and the court of appeals concluded that the general provisions of the Occupational Safety and Health Act do not permit OSHA to cite employers for requiring women to undergo sterilization if they work with hazardous substances. Second, responding to the discriminatory potential of policies for reproductive hazards has "fallen between the cracks": OSHA cannot act under the general duty clause of the Occupational Safety and Health Act and the Equal Employment Opportunity Commission (EEOC) was slow to act under Title VII.[10] Although both the EEOC and OSHA moved to thwart exclusionary policies under the Carter administration, during the Reagan administration, neither agency made promoting nondiscriminatory policies to safeguard against reproductive hazards a priority. Third, an analysis of both the development and implementation of Cyanamid's policy reveals that a corporation pursuing a goal that finds wide public support—protecting the health of the unborn—may pursue it in such a botched and flawed way that the negative publicity brings all exclusionary policies into disrepute.

I will first analyze the requirements of health and safety law in the United States. Second, I discuss the role of administrative agencies and courts in the development and implementation of health and safety standards by looking at how OSHA handled reproductive hazards in setting standards of exposure to lead. Third, I trace the development and implementation of Cyanamid's policy and analyze the case from OSHA's citation to the court of appeals's decision. Fourth, I will compare and contrast OSHA's response to exclusionary policies to the EEOC's by reviewing the EEOC's proposed interpretive

---

10. If the two agencies fail to cooperate, the EEOC, acting without the scientific expertise of OSHA, may be too willing to defer to corporate experts rather than challenge the underlying assumptions and motivations for the policies. Or the EEOC may use the complexity of the issue as a reason not to act at all. Similarly, OSHA, while engrossed in the scientific evidence, may fail to sufficiently weigh the importance of nondiscrimination. The Oil, Chemical and Atomic Workers International Union addressed which agency should handle the issue of exclusionary policies in its comments on the EEOC's proposed interpretive guidelines on reproductive hazards: "We believe that the protection of workers from reproductive hazards should be left squarely in the hands of OSHA" (*Daily Labor Report* [BNA] 133 [July 9, 1980]: G-1).

guidelines on reproductive hazards. The responses of OSHA and the EEOC and the activities of interest groups invite comparison with the activities of policymakers and interest groups in Britain on health and safety.

Health and Safety Law

In 1970, Congress passed the Occupational Safety and Health Act "to assure so far as possible every working man and woman in the Nation safe and healthful working conditions and to preserve our human resources."[11] The Act created three bodies: the Occupational Safety and Health Administration (OSHA) in the Department of Labor, which sets and enforces standards; the National Institute of Occupational Safety and Health (NIOSH) in the Department of Health and Human Services, which conducts research; and the Occupational Safety and Health Review Commission (OSHRC), an independent, quasi-judicial body, which, among other things, reviews OSHA's citations to employers.[12] Because OSHA is part of the Department of Labor, the Secretary of Labor directs and is responsible for the agency, which is headed by an Assistant Secretary. The Occupational Safety and Health Act both imposed a general duty on employers to provide a safe workplace and authorized OSHA to set standards for exposure to hazardous substances. The wording of the statute guaranteed that the courts would be integrally involved in the process, not only to make sure that OSHA carried out the prescribed process of consultation, but also to review the substance of the standards. This section discusses, in turn, these three points: the general duty of employers to provide a safe workplace, OSHA's setting of standards, and the role of the courts.

The general duty clause is contained in section 5(a)(1) of the act.

> Each employer shall furnish to each of his employees employment and a place of employment which are free from recognized hazards that are causing or are likely to cause death or serious harm to his employees.[13]

This clause places primary responsibility for preventing workplace hazards on the employer. Congress included this provision to cover hazards for which OSHA has set no standard, and to prohibit hazardous conduct for which OSHA is setting standards or that occurs before the effective date of standards.[14] The general duty clause covers only recognized hazards—defined as hazards that are common knowledge in the industry or known by the em-

---

11. 29 U.S.C. §651(b) (1970).

12. The president appoints three members to the OSHRC, who are confirmed by the Senate, for staggered, six-year terms.

13. 29 U.S.C. §654(a)(1).

14. Congress, Office of Technology Assessment, *Reproductive Health Hazards in the Workplace* (Washington, D.C.: U.S. Government Printing Office, 1985), 189.

ployer. Only the federal government has enforcement powers: the statute provides no private right of action. In issuing a citation under the general duty clause, the Secretary of Labor must show not only that the employer did not provide a workplace free from recognized hazards but also that feasible alternative precautions could reduce or eliminate the hazard.[15]

Using the general duty clause to issue citations to employers who expose employees to reproductive hazards has two problems. First, OSHA has to prove that the hazard is recognized in the industry and scientific community. Little evidence is available on most reproductive hazards. Second, if the agency has already set a standard for a substance, even if that standard does not properly consider potential reproductive hazards, OSHA cannot claim that the general duty clause obliges employers to lower exposures below that standard.[16] For these reasons, as well as the limits placed on OSHA by the court of appeals's ruling in the Cyanamid case, OSHA's ability to use the general duty clause to prevent exposure to reproductive hazards is limited.

In addition to imposing a general duty on employers to provide safe working conditions, the Occupational Safety and Health Act gives OSHA the authority to set standards of exposure to hazardous substances in the workplace.

> The Secretary [of Labor], in promulgating standards dealing with toxic materials or harmful physical agents under this subsection, shall set the standard which most adequately assures, to the extent feasible, on the basis of the best available evidence, that no employee will suffer material impairment of health or functional capacity even if such employee has regular exposure to the hazard dealt with by such standard for the period of his working life.[17]

OSHA has interpreted "health or functional capacity" as granting it authority to protect the reproductive health of workers.[18] The requirements that the

---

15. National Realty and Construction Company, Inc. v. OSHRC, 489 F.2d 1257, 1265, 1266 (D.C. Cir. 1973), cited in Ray Marshall, Secretary of Labor v. American Cyanamid Company, OSHRC Docket no. 79-5762, Memorandum of the Secretary in Opposition to Respondent's Motion for Summary Judgment (June 30, 1980): 19 (hereinafter referred to as DOL Memo).

16. Office of Technology Assessment, 191. For example, if OSHA sets a standard for vinyl chloride that is above the level necessary to insure reproductive health, employers cannot be held responsible for failing to meet a lower standard. A case against General Dynamics may have called this principle into question; see "Supreme Court Supports OSHA 'General Duty' Clause," *Women's Occupational Health Resource Center News* 9 (December 1987): 1.

17. 29 U.S.C. §655(b)(5).

18. The Court of Appeals for the District of Columbia Circuit upheld OSHA's mandate to act to protect reproductive health in United Steelworkers of America v. Marshall, 647 F.2d 1189 (D.C. Cir. 1980), *cert. denied*, Lead Industries Association v. Donovan, 453 U.S. 913 (1981).

standards be based on the best medical evidence and that they be feasible, however, may circumscribe OSHA's ability to protect workers from reproductive hazards because so little medical evidence exists about what level would protect workers' reproductive capacities.

The act obliges OSHA to follow certain procedures in setting standards and obliges employers to meet those standards. It must give notice in the *Federal Register* that it is proposing to set standards for a substance and interested parties may then submit data or written comments. OSHA holds hearings to question witnesses and allow parties to present their points of view. This process is protracted, not only because OSHA is a governmental agency subject to the Administrative Procedures Act, but also because the agency must develop an evidentiary record to prove that a substance is hazardous and that reducing the level of exposure is feasible. Courts have set a high standard for what OSHA must do to meet these two requirements. "There is widespread agreement that the OSHA rule making process is slow, cumbersome, a drain on resources and extremely adversarial."[19] Unlike the British system of setting standards by tripartite committees, the OSHA hearings are not geared toward reaching a consensus among the parties, but toward persuading the OSHA staff who will set the standard, the validity of which will ultimately be decided by the courts.

The willingness of the courts to engage in policy-making, the disposition of industry and unions to take their disputes into the legal arena,[20] and the wording of the Occupational Safety and Health Act all contribute to making it inevitable that standards OSHA sets without a consensus among interested parties will result in protracted litigation. Industry will often claim standards are too strict, not justified on the basis of scientific evidence, and impossible to attain, while unions will claim that OSHA has not protected workers from all risks. Those who object to OSHA's standard may file a complaint with a federal court of appeals within sixty days.[21] Furthermore, the standard of judicial review for OSHA regulations is the more demanding test of "substantive evidence in the record considered as a whole"[22] that allows courts to set aside standards if the evidence does not support them, rather than merely if

---

19. Office of Technology Assessment, 193.

20. In *The Politics of Safety and Health: Occupational Safety and Health in the United States and Britain* ([Oxford: Clarendon, 1985], 30), Graham K. Wilson takes exception to the view that it is the political culture, in this case a propensity to litigate, that determines the nature of health and safety policy, but argues to the contrary that it is the result of decisions by political actors and the judiciary.

21. Complainants may file in the jurisdiction in which they have their businesses or in the Court of Appeals for the District of Columbia Circuit.

22. *"The determinations of the Secretary shall be conclusive if supported by substantial evidence in the record considered as a whole"* (29 U.S.C. §655(f); italics added).

OSHA has not followed designated procedures under the Administrative Procedures Act.[23] As Wilson concluded,

> The Courts have not shown themselves willing to be confined to purely procedural matters either. . . . Rarely, if ever, do Appeals Courts appear to act on any belief that OSHA is more competent to make difficult technological decisions than they are themselves.[24]

The provision for judicial review insures that judges will face the difficult task of assessing the scientific evidence for themselves, both on the extent of the hazard as well as on the standard's feasibility. OSHA now conducts hearings primarily to establish a record for future litigation rather than to gather data or to allow interested parties to participate. Instead of being the rule makers, OSHA regulators merely propose rules and build a record for the inevitable judicial proceedings.

The Lead Standard

The background of OSHA's standard on exposure to lead illustrates the role of the courts in the setting of health and safety standards. It is also one of the few examples of how OSHA tried to set a standard for a substance that is a reproductive hazard. Although the lead standard was not in force at the time of the Cyanamid case, it is nevertheless relevant because Cyanamid's policy focused on the reproductive hazards of lead. The conclusions OSHA drew about the evidence on the reproductive hazards of lead as well as its strategy for dealing with women's exposure (the court of appeals upheld both) stand in marked contrast to Cyanamid's findings and strategy.

"Lead is one of the oldest, most ubiquitous, most toxic and most studied substances,"[25] yet scientists disagree about how much exposure is harmful. Scientists monitor occupational exposure to lead in two ways: by measuring the amount of lead in the air and by measuring the amount of lead in a person's blood. One problem with setting very low standards of exposure to lead, besides being potentially economically infeasible, is that workers are exposed to lead outside the workplace and, thus, workers in cities with high levels of pollution or high concentrations of lead in the water may already have high levels of lead in their blood. While all scientists agree that very high

---

23. Wilson contends that establishing this standard of judicial review was a mistake, and Congress actually believed that it was setting a minimal, nonsubstantive standard (90).

24. Ibid., 96.

25. Cassandra Tate, "American Dilemma of Jobs, Health in an Idaho Town," *Smithsonian* 12 (1981): 77.

levels of exposure (blood levels of lead more than 80 μg/100g) cause serious health risks and that much higher exposure can cause death, they do not agree on what level of exposure is safe for a developing fetus,[26] at what level men's reproductive capacity is damaged,[27] and whether men's reproductive injury could lead to fetal malformations.

OSHA issued its standard for exposure to lead in 1978.[28] Despite industry claims that men's reproductive capacity was not at risk from exposure to lead while even low levels might damage a developing fetus, OSHA explicitly rejected demands to set a different standard of exposure to lead for men and women or to allow industry to exclude fertile women altogether. The standard set a permissible exposure limit of 50 μg/m^3 of air averaged over an eight-hour period with an action level of 30 μg/m^3.[29] The standard also contains a provision, phased in over five years, for the medical removal of workers.[30] In the fifth year, employers would have to remove workers from jobs exposing them to lead if the level of lead in their blood was at or above 50 μg/100g. Unlike other hazardous substances, lead is not retained in the bodies of most workers. Thus, once the worker is removed from exposure, the blood level of lead drops. While medical removal may be satisfactory for a worker seeking to reduce blood lead levels before conception, it is less satisfactory as a solution for women workers who discover that they are pregnant because they will have been exposed to lead during the first six to eight weeks of pregnancy. Some experts (by no means all) believe this is when the fetus is especially vulnerable to injury. The lead standard requires employers to test workers periodically and offer job security and retention of benefits for anyone removed for medical reasons. OSHA's justification for the standard states:

> Because of lead's ability to pass through the placental barrier and also because of the demonstrated adverse effects of lead on reproductive function in both the male and the female as well as the risk of genetic damage of lead on both the ovum and sperm, OSHA *recommends* a 30

---

26. Given new evidence about the developmental effect of lead exposure on small children, the pressure for estimates of a "safe" level for a fetus is downward.

27. There is evidence that exposure to lead decreases men's ability to father a child; see Ioana Lacranjan, Horia I. Popescu, Olimpia Gavenescu, Iulia Klepsch, and Maria Serbanescu, "Reproductive Ability of Workmen Occupationally Exposed to Lead," *Archives of Environmental Health* 30 (1975): 396–401. See also A. C. Fletcher, *Reproductive Hazards of Work* (Manchester, U.K.: Equal Opportunities Commission, 1985).

28. 29 C.F.R. §1910.1025 (1978).

29. Ibid. OSHA aimed to produce average blood levels of lead of 40 μg/100g. This was a substantial reduction, since the previous standard had been twice as high. Before the 1980 regulations, Britain, for example, had a standard of 80 μg/100g.

30. 43 *Fed. Reg.* 54,354 (1978); the effective date of the standard is February 1, 1979. Sections 54,451–52 outline the four-year process to incorporate the medical removal provisions.

μg/100g maximum permissible blood lead level in both males and females who wish to bear children.[31]

Both industry and trade unions challenged OSHA's lead standard before the Court of Appeals for the District of Columbia Circuit.[32] The Steelworkers argued that, after recognizing that some workers would suffer injury to their reproductive capacity at levels of lead in blood higher than 30 μg/100g, OSHA nevertheless set a standard that would allow an average level of lead in blood of 40 μg/100g. The court of appeals noted the provisions for medical removal and held that OSHA was justified in balancing the level of exposure that injures no one against the level of exposure that is feasible. The Lead Industry Association argued that any standard that protected the reproductive capacity of women workers and a developing fetus (30 μg/100g) would be infeasible, and, thus, OSHA should allow the lead industry to exclude all fertile women. It further disputed the evidence that lead harmed men's reproductive capacity. The court of appeals went into great detail in examining the work of one study on the effects of lead on men and concluded that OSHA correctly recognized the hazards to men as well as women and was justified in setting a single standard of exposure for men and women.

OSHA found evidence that lead-exposed males suffer serious harm to their spermatogenesis, including malformed sperm (teratospermia), decreased motility of sperm (asthenospermia), and decreased number of sperm (hypospermia). The chief study was that of the European neuroendocrinologist Dr. Lacranjan, whose work revealed adverse effects of spermatogenesis among lead-exposed workers with blood-lead levels as low as 41 μg/100g.[33]

The court did, however, conclude that OSHA had not proven that its standard was feasible for the lead pigments industry.

Both OSHA's proposed single standard of exposure for men and women and the court of appeals's decision to uphold this standard (except as it applied to certain parts of the lead pigments industry) are remarkable when compared to the British response to the same evidence on lead.[34] The British Health and

---

31. 29 C.F.R. §1910.1025 (July 1, 1987), Appendix C—Medical Surveillance Guidelines, CII(5); italics added.

32. United Steelworkers of America v. Marshall, 647 F.2d 1189 (D.C. Cir. 1980), *cert. denied*, Lead Industries Association v. Donovan, 453 U.S. 913 (1981).

33. "OSHA thus found abundant support for the view expressed by experts from NIOSH and the American Health Foundation that a lead standard must protect the reproductive capacities of males as well as females" (647 F.2d 1189, 1257 [D.C. Cir. 1980]).

34. The British Health and Safety Executive rejected Lacranjan's study of effects of lead on men (Dr. Carole Bishop, high-ranking medical officer for the Health and Safety Executive,

Safety Executive chose to set different standards of exposure for men and women, and to prohibit women altogether from certain jobs with exposure to lead. Since there was no consensus on the scientific evidence, both OSHA and the court of appeals had to make a judgment. In setting and upholding a single standard of exposure and rejecting exclusion as an option, the court of appeals and OSHA rejected the British path and reinforced the presumption that women and men are more alike than different. Both the court of appeals and OSHA preferred alternatives to excluding all women or fertile women, and both recognized men's role in reproduction and the seriousness of potential damage to men's reproductive capacity. Although the Steelworkers Union did not succeed in getting OSHA or the court to set an even lower standard, it did manage to get both bodies to set a single standard of exposure for men and women, overcoming strong opposition from the industry.

OSHA and the court of appeals could have concluded that certain types of reproductive injury were more serious than others. For example, they could have decided that it was more important to prevent a malformation, miscarriage, or stillbirth from occurring through damage to an existing fetus than to prevent damage to eggs, sperm, or chromosomes, although either might lead to an adverse reproductive outcome. They could have also concluded that damage to fertility, such as sterility or low sperm counts, is significantly different than damage to a developing fetus: one makes conception difficult or impossible while the other damages an existing fetus.

Industry has a special interest in making these distinctions. First, the evidence available to prove different injuries varies: more evidence exists on reproductive hazards from women's exposure than men's. A company may, therefore, conclude that the evidence warrants excluding women but not enough evidence exists to justify excluding men. If the company were to conclude that both were at risk, it would have to institute engineering controls, use protective clothing, or substitute another product—all of which cost more than excluding women. Second, different reproductive injuries may lead to different legal claims. A worker may find it difficult to receive payments under workers' compensation for reproductive injury, but the parents of a malformed child could sue for damages.[35] If OSHA or the court of appeals

---

interview with author, London, 1985). Dr. Bishop commented that, "Lacranjan's work was never repeated on males exposed to lead," concluding that there was not sufficient evidence that lead harmed men's reproductive capacity to require a single standard for men and women.

35. "Under the laws of most states, reproductive impairment cannot be compensated within the workers' compensation system; moreover, workers are at present barred from bringing tort claims against their employers" (Office of Technology Assessment, 4). "For developmental injuries, however, the offspring of exposed workers would not be covered by workers' compensation and therefore would have a right to sue the parent's employer" (17). For whatever reasons, industry seems far more concerned about liability from a malformed child than it does from sterility or miscarriages. One woman has sued in Canada and at least three in the United States,

had distinguished between different types of reproductive injury, it might have permitted a different posture toward the risks of different injuries. That is, it might have allowed any evidence to justify extreme caution or exclusion for fertile women (assuming they might be pregnant) but require solid evidence (both animal and human) before men's injury would be taken seriously. Ultimately, drawing a distinction between reproductive injuries that puts damage to an existing fetus in a category of its own would allow the exclusion of women,[36] particularly if evidence on men's ability to damage their offspring is not collected. Instead, in a victory for opponents of exclusionary policies, OSHA concluded that damage to men's reproductive capacity is also important, and that employers must take seriously all kinds of damage to reproductive capacity.

While OSHA's lead standard was not in effect when Cyanamid implemented its policy, the standard does influence how we should view that policy ex post facto. OSHA's standard is important both as a statement of its preferred strategy for dealing with reproductive hazards as well as for its conclusions about the medical evidence. Both should be kept in mind when considering Cyanamid's policy.

Cyanamid's Policy

The corporate medical director of American Cyanamid became concerned about reproductive hazards in 1975 when more women bid for jobs that exposed them to toxic substances.[37] He began to develop an exclusionary policy that prohibited women from any exposure to twenty-nine different substances, identified from a "quick review of computer sheets"[38]—presum-

---

alleging that they have given birth to malformed children because of occupational exposures (see Jarvis v. Providence Hospital, 444 N.W.2d 236 [Mich. Ct. App. 1989]; Security National Bank v. Chloride, 602 F.Supp. 294 [D. Kansas 1985]; and Dillon v. S.S. Kresge Co., 192 N.W.2d 661 [Mich. Ct. App. 1972]. For additional cases, see "Fetal Protection Issues Remain After Ruling in *Johnson Controls*," 17 *Daily Labor Report* [BNA] [January 27, 1992]: A-1). Men, too, have sued claiming a variety of reproductive injuries from exposure to DBCP and Agent Orange (see In re "Agent Orange" Product Liability Litigation, 506 F. Supp. 762 [E.D. N.Y. 1980]; Monaco v. United States, 661 F.2d 129 [9th Cir. 1981]; Coley v. Commonwealth Edison Co., 703 F. Supp. 748 [1989]). In light of the difficulties of proof, one might wonder why industry would be more worried about lawsuits from adverse reproductive outcomes more so than cancer, but surely in light of the history of such lawsuits, damage to men is as urgent a concern as damage to women.

36. This is precisely the approach taken in Britain. For example, the nuclear industry assumes that some of its male workers may be temporarily sterile or suffer mutagenic effects, while it excludes women from high exposure to radiation on the grounds that the exposure might harm a developing fetus.

37. The information for this discussion of the American Cyanamid policy is drawn from the Office of Technology Assessment's Report and DOL Memo.

38. Office of Technology Assessment, 253.

ably the printout from a computer search of journal articles.[39] Although evidence showed only one listed substance, lead, was a reproductive hazard, the medical director extrapolated that suspected carcinogens might be embryofetotoxic. Cyanamid conducted no animal studies to confirm the findings on its list nor did it conduct any epidemiological studies of men and women workers to see if they had experienced any reproductive problems. Nor did the company check how much exposure workers received (it would exclude women from jobs where there was *any* exposure). The director did not investigate the possibility of substituting another product, instituting engineering controls, job rotation, or using protective equipment. The Office of Technology Assessment concluded, "The chronology of events suggests that the company initiated its exclusionary policy with little scientific justification and little sensitivity to the needs of its workers."[40]

Although twenty-eight of the substances on the list were suspected carcinogens, Cyanamid did not eliminate all exposure. Instead, the company presumably attempted to insure that the exposures were as low as possible and workers assumed some risks. Although more evidence exists about the carcinogenicity of substances than for reproductive injury, the company banned women because of reproductive hazards but allowed workers to continue working with carcinogens. For some unexplained reason, the director decided to exempt all women lab workers from the policy.

Not only did the medical director fail to "protect" all women, but, because he decided early on that there was more evidence of embryofetotoxicity from maternal exposure than mutagenicity (affecting both men and women), he did not investigate the likelihood of reproductive injury resulting from men's exposure.

Although the medical director excluded fertile female production workers from exposure to the twenty-nine chemicals with virtually no data to support this policy, he stated that he was unwilling to exclude fertile men in the absence of "epidemiological studies indicating that the compound was indeed a human mutagen." He would not be persuaded by animal studies showing evidence of a chemical's mutagenic effect on sperm and claims that "the only meaningful information that [he] would accept is epidemiological information."[41]

39. As the Office of Technology Assessment reports: "He defined the reproductive health hazards problem as one of embryofetotoxicity (toxic effects on the embryo or fetus) due to the exposure of either parent to hazardous chemicals. He considered embryofetotoxicity to have four components: direct toxicity to the fetus, mutagenicity, teratogenicity, and transplacental carcinogenicity. Such a definition excludes negative reproductive outcomes such as infertility and sterility" (252).

40. Ibid., 251.

41. Ibid., 255.

He also concluded that women were unlikely to know they were pregnant early on and rejected the possibility of excluding only pregnant women or women planning to conceive. The proposed policy applied to women between the ages of sixteen and fifty-five. He circulated the policy in August, 1976.

In September, 1976, the company's executive committee considered the exclusionary policy. Despite findings that, in many instances, female exposure to the substances was slight, the company continued developing the policy. It did change the age from fifty-five to fifty, although it rejected a proposal to lower it to forty-five.[42] Before approving the policy, Cyanamid conducted no additional research—either experiments of its own, studies of its workforce, or reviews of the medical literature. The executive committee approved the policy in September, 1977. Soon after, the medical staff changed exposure prohibitions to exposure limitations. They set the permissible levels of exposure (PELs) so low, however, there was little practical difference. The medical director wrote that the PELs, "were arrived at quite arbitrarily and really constitute an educated professional guess rather than anything that we could document on the basis of clinical or laboratory experience."[43]

Cyanamid announced its policy in some plants in late 1977. At the plant in Willow Island, West Virginia, company officials told women workers that, beginning May 1, 1978, Cyanamid would exclude all women who were not sterilized from eight of the plant's ten departments. The company did not try to determine the exposure levels in the ten departments to see if they exceeded the policy's PELs. Managers told the women that they might transfer to the other two departments or to janitorial work subject to the availability of jobs and that most transfers would receive lower wages. The company extended the policy to include women laboratory workers, although for some unknown reason it never applied the policy to them. Perhaps the company thought that professional women were more likely to be aware of the hazards and could evaluate the risk for themselves or believed the company could more easily control exposure in a laboratory setting or believed individual laboratories could make arrangements on a case-by-case basis. A company official conducted meetings with women workers in January and February of 1978 and told them that hundreds of chemicals were harmful to fetuses and that the company would no longer allow women between the ages of sixteen and fifty to work with them.[44] "[Glen Mercer, Director of Industrial Relations, who

---

42. One in five thousand women between the ages of forty-five and forty-nine gives birth each year in the United States (ibid., 254). The corporate medical director admitted that he did not, in fact, know the birth rates for different ages.

43. Ibid., 255.

44. DOL Memo, 5. OSHA protested the fact that it was not allowed full discovery to investigate Cyanamid's fetal protection policy. Despite this limitation, the brief in opposition to the motion for summary judgment included an analysis of the policy as drawn from the accounts of a number of Cyanamid women, including the women who had been sterilized.

conducted meetings with groups of three to five employees in January and February of 1978] also represented that a similar sterilization policy was being implemented by a number of other chemical companies and he anticipated that in the near future no women of childbearing age would be able to work in any chemical company in the United States."[45] A company doctor and nurse at the meetings told the women that sterilization (described as "buttonhole surgery") was simple and could be obtained locally, that the company's medical insurance would pay for the procedure, and that the women would be entitled to sick leave for the surgery.[46] The company official also informed them that the plant would have only seven jobs for the thirty fertile women; it would dismiss all others.

Between February and July of 1978, five women in the lead pigments department opted for sterilization and two women transferred into other departments.[47] The women did not know that the company had decided to delay implementation of the policy pending further review.[48] The review resulted in a new policy covering only six substances and conferring the right to transfer to another job and to retain the same wages. In February, 1979, the company dropped another substance from the list. Although Cyanamid significantly changed its policy after announcing it to the women at Willow Island,[49] five women elected to have themselves sterilized on the basis of the initial announcement. Unfortunately, the sterilizations did not enable the women to keep their jobs because Cyanamid closed the lead pigment department in late 1979.[50]

In drafting its policy, Cyanamid made a number of assumptions that merit scrutiny. It assumed that men were not at risk from exposure to lead—or, rather, that while one should presume women were always endangering a

---

45. Mercer refused to give the women a copy of the policy and claimed that the EPA and OSHA supported the findings about the harmful effects to the fetus, although he refused to let the women see the letters from the EPA and OSHA (ibid.).

46. "When asked if the use of other forms of birth control would be acceptable as a means of abating the potential hazard, Mercer emphatically stated that only surgical sterilization would be acceptable, since women could not be relied upon to faithfully employ other methods of birth control" (ibid.).

47. After ninety days, their pay was lowered to correspond to the rate for their new jobs.

48. In April, 1978, Cyanamid delayed implementation in order to further assess scientific evidence. That reassessment may have resulted, in part, from a meeting company officials had with OSHA in November, 1977, at OSHA's request. Following a complaint filed by the Steelworkers about the policy, OSHA and NIOSH officials expressed a number of concerns.

49. Cyanamid announced that only lead was covered and that women would be transferred to a janitorial pool and would receive their rate of pay for ninety days only after five women had undergone sterilizations (DOL Memo, 10).

50. For the stories of the women, see Susan Faludi, "Your Womb or Your Job," *Mother Jones* 16 (November/December): 59, excerpted from *Backlash: the Undeclared War Against American Women* (New York: Crown, 1991).

fetus until conclusive evidence exists to the contrary, one need not presume men endanger their offspring until conclusive evidence exists. This presumption was made although scientists have focused almost exclusively on the hazards to the fetus posed by women's exposure and ignored the potential evidence on men, thus the evidence that existed was and is very one-sided.[51]

Further, Cyanamid took the position that no risk to the fetus is acceptable, however minimal, while the company would assume some risk to both men's reproductive capacity and to the fetus from men's exposure. This zero-risk posture led to the exclusion of all fertile women rather than all pregnant women. Cyanamid assumed that women do not know when they are pregnant or likely to conceive, and that all categories of fertile women, whether they are on the pill, or their husbands are sterile, or they are closer to fifty-five than fifteen, are likely to become pregnant. Furthermore, this refusal to accept any risk to the fetus from women's exposure did not weigh the risk to the fetus of having an unemployed mother who may lose access to health benefits as well as income.[52] The policy probably rested on the assumption that women's childbearing role takes priority over their role as breadwinner, or that it is only appropriate for women to hold certain kinds of jobs, or that women's place is in the home. Finally, Cyanamid assumed that no acceptable alternatives to exclusion such as lowering exposure, substituting another product, using protective clothing, removing those with high levels of lead in blood, or more carefully determining who is likely to conceive existed.

In early 1980, several women workers filed suit against American Cyanamid claiming that its exclusionary policy constituted discrimination on the basis of sex in violation of Title VII. "After 3 ½ years of pretrial proceedings and shortly before the trial was to begin, the case was resolved by an offer of $200,000 plus costs and attorneys' fees."[53] Because the case of

---

51. "Historically, research into reproductive hazards has focused on chemical and physical agents which result in birth defects in the newborn through maternal exposure. . . . The historical focus on teratogenesis has stemmed from the relative availability for many years of good laboratory techniques for assessing fetal damage following maternal exposures. . . . More recent research indicates that paternal reproductive toxicity is an important human health effect which requires significantly greater attention than it has previously received. . . . [T]here appears to be no scientific basis for the differential exclusion of fertile women from contact with vinyl chloride or lead" (Anthony Robbins, M.D., Director, National Institute for Occupational Safety and Health, letter to Eleanor Holmes Norton, Chair, Equal Employment Opportunity Commission, July 8, 1980).

52. This assumes that women lose their jobs rather than transfer to others. In many complaints to the EEOC about exclusionary policies, employers fired pregnant women who then lost their health benefits. Obtaining another job while pregnant is difficult, just as finding a well-paid blue-collar job in towns with few employment opportunities is difficult.

53. Office of Technology Assessment, 251. Cyanamid closed its lead pigments department in late 1979, one year after it announced its exclusionary policy (257).

discrimination against Cyanamid did not come to trial, we can only speculate what the outcome would have been based on the precedents discussed in chapter 6.

OSHA's Response to Cyanamid's Policy

After the Oil, Chemical and Atomic Workers filed a complaint, OSHA inspected Cyanamid's plant in Willow Island, West Virginia, between January 4, 1979, and April 13, 1979. On October 9, OSHA issued a citation charging that Cyanamid had violated the general duty clause—the first time it had cited an employer under this provision[54]—and fined the company $10,000.

> The employer did not furnish employment and a place of employment which were free from recognized hazards that were causing or were likely to cause death or serious physical harm to employees in that: the employer adopted and implemented a policy which required women employees to be sterilized in order to be eligible to work in those areas of the plant where they would be exposed to certain toxic substances.[55]

Cyanamid contested the fine and submitted a motion for summary judgment to vacate the order. OSHA urged the administrative law judge to uphold the citation because the case raised an important legal issue: "whether the recognized hazards of a policy requiring sterilization may be imposed upon employees as a means of abating another hazardous condition in the workplace."[56] OSHA argued four points: Cyanamid's requirement of sterilization was a hazard in violation of the general duty clause; the sterilizations were coerced by company officials as an employment policy rather than undertaken voluntarily by the five women; the company did not consider alternatives to sterilization, such as the ones OSHA's lead standard required; and the EEOC's proposed interpretive guidelines on employment discrimination and reproductive hazards did not preempt OSHA from acting.[57]

First, OSHA noted that the general duty clause requires an employer to provide a workplace free from recognized hazards. "The hazard in this case is a corporate policy requiring sterilization and respondent clearly failed to render its workplace free of that hazard."[58] In support of its argument that the general duty clause covered hazards that occurred outside the workplace but

---

54. Rawls, February 11, 1980, 31.
55. DOL Memo, 12.
56. Ibid., 16.
57. 45 *Fed. Reg.* 7514 (February 1, 1980).
58. DOL Memo, 19.

were within the power to the employer to control, OSHA cited decisions of the Review Commission.[59] The Review Commission had, for example, held that the general duty clause required employers to insure that trucks transporting workers be safe[60] and obliged employers to provide sanitary conditions in labor camps.[61] Furthermore, OSHA pointed to Review Commission statements that an employer must furnish employment free from hazards as well as a safe place of employment.[62] Finally, OSHA drew the Review Commission's attention to the new lead standard's prohibition against prophylactic chelation, a risky medical procedure workers employ to accelerate the excretion of lead from their bodies, concluding that: "OSHA has recognized its responsibility to deal with lead-related hazards that arise out of the employment relationship even though the locus of the violation is away from the physical worksite."[63] As these examples illustrate, OSHA claimed the power to protect workers from work-related injuries, even if that meant regulating behavior outside the workplace. In urging the Review Commission to continue to interpret the Occupational Safety and Health Act broadly to protect employees from work-related hazards, OSHA argued that the employer could not "shift its responsibility for maintaining a safe and healthful workplace to its employees."[64]

OSHA's second argument was to deny that the women voluntarily chose sterilization. "Complainant disputes the 'voluntariness' of a choice made under duress, as in this case, where women had to choose between their jobs and their fertility."[65] Based on testimony from several of Cyanamid's employees, OSHA argued that company officials presented the "option" of sterilization to women as if they had no choice—that is, if they wanted to keep their jobs. The sterilizations were a condition of employment, a policy of the company. According to established law on health and safety, "an employer may not defend against a general duty clause citation by claiming that an employee voluntarily submitted him/herself to the harm or consented to it."[66]

It was vital that OSHA prove that it cited Cyanamid for the policy of sterilization rather than because specific women had been sterilized. Section 9(c) of the Occupational Safety and Health Act limits OSHA's power to cite an employer for noncompliance to six months after the occurrence of a violation, and the date of the citation to Cyanamid was more than six months after

---

59. The Review Commission reviews OSHA citations.

60. DOL Memo, 21; see Sugar Cane Growers Cooperative of Florida, 4 O.S.H. Cas. (BNA) 1320 (1976).

61. DOL Memo, 25.

62. Ibid., 21.

63. Ibid., 23.

64. Ibid., 26.

65. Ibid., 17.

66. Ibid., 28.

the sterilizations. OSHA argued that the policy of requiring sterilization remained in effect in the six-month period preceding the citation and continued until Cyanamid closed down the lead pigments division in 1980.

Third, OSHA argued that Cyanamid had not considered possible alternatives. The agency referred to the decision of the Court of Appeals for the District of Columbia Circuit upholding the section of the lead standard that states that the hazards posed by lead provide no grounds for excluding women. Cyanamid should have considered monitoring and temporarily removing workers whose blood levels of lead were high—or allowed employees to move to other jobs if they were planning to become parents. The company also could have permitted women who practiced less irreversible but effective means of contraception to retain their jobs. OSHA pointed out that "millions of women in America effectively practice birth control without having to resort to radical sterilization procedures."[67]

Not only did Cyanamid fail to consider alternatives, OSHA pointed out, but the company's failure to follow OSHA's lead-in-air standards belied the company's supposed concern for fetal health. The lead-in-air levels at the plant at Willow Island were well above the permissible exposure levels of 200 $\mu g/m^3$. American Cyanamid would have had to institute engineering controls to reduce the exposure levels for all employees to comply with the law.[68] OSHA further criticized Cyanamid's inconsistent application of its policy among female workers (because Cyanamid did not enforce the policy for women lab workers) and its failure to recognize the potential reproductive hazards resulting from male workers' exposure to lead, concluding that "such selective protection based on the effects lead may have on fetuses demonstrates that the respondent's reason for instituting its sterilization policy was not related to its concerns for the well-being of the fetuses."[69]

Finally, OSHA argued that it was not preempted from acting by section 4(b)(1) of the act, which says:

Nothing in this Act shall apply to working conditions of employees with respect to which other Federal agencies . . . exercise statutory authority to prescribe or enforce standards or regulations affecting occupational safety or health.[70]

---

67. Ibid., 40.

68. "A separate citation arising out of the same inspection involving alleged employee exposure to excessive lead levels is docketed separately under OSHRC Docket No. 79-2438 and is currently pending before the Commission" (Secretary of Labor v. American Cyanamid Company, 9 O.S.H. Cas. [BNA] 1596, 1601 n.2 [April 27, 1981]).

69. DOL Memo, 40.

70. 29 U.S.C. §653(b)(1).

The EEOC proposed interpretive guidelines on reproductive hazards in 1980,[71] but it later withdrew them.[72] OSHA argued that the goal of the EEOC was to prevent discrimination, while the goal of OSHA was the promotion of occupational safety and health. Just because the EEOC was pursuing its goal of nondiscrimination did not mean that it was setting occupational health standards, thereby preempting OSHA from acting.

In a decision and order filed on July 15, 1980, Judge William E. Brennan, member of the Review Commission, granted Cyanamid's motion for summary judgment and vacated the citation and penalty. He was persuaded that the statute of limitations prevented OSHA from issuing a citation more than six months after the sterilizations occurred,[73] and that OSHA was preempted from acting because the EEOC had issued proposed interpretive guidelines. OSHA filed a petition with the Review Commission for discretionary review. Judge Timothy F. Cleary, chair of the Review Commission, granted the petition and the Review Commission heard the case.

In its brief, OSHA reiterated its three points in opposition to summary judgment. First, it argued that it was Cyanamid's policy requiring sterilizations that violated the general duty clause. Although no employee had been sterilized in the six months preceding the citation, the policy remained in effect after OSHA issued its citation in 1979. Thus, the administrative law judge had erred in concluding that the statute of limitations had run.[74] OSHA claimed that it had only emphasized the actual sterilizations rather than the policy because the judge refused to allow OSHA to conduct any discovery on the circumstances surrounding the adoption and implementation of Cyanamid's exclusionary policy.[75] Until Cyanamid closed the lead pigments division in 1980, the policy remained in effect for any woman who might have been assigned to or wanted to transfer into one of the jobs. OSHA argued that

> it should be noted that one of the women who declined to undergo sterilization (Mary Carpenter) and was subsequently transferred with resulting loss of pay and benefits was not working in the Inorganic Pigments Department. However, her job did involve walking through a lead pigment area in order to go to the rest room or lunchroom. Because of this lead exposure, Ms. Carpenter was given the choice of undergoing surgical sterilization or losing her job. It is therefore clear that the impact

---

71. 45 *Fed. Reg.* 23,7524 (February 1, 1980).

72. 46 *Fed. Reg.* 3916 (January 16, 1981).

73. Ray Marshall, Secretary of Labor v. American Cyanamid Company, OSHRC Docket No. 79-5762, brief of the Secretary of Labor, 6 (hereinafter referred to as DOL brief).

74. Ibid., 7.

75. Ibid., 9.

of Respondent's sterilization policy went far beyond the women who were working in the Inorganic Pigments Department.[76]

Second, OSHA denied that the existence of the proposed interpretive guidelines from the EEOC activated section 4(b)(1), preempting OSHA from acting against Cyanamid's policy. OSHA argued that Title VII does not have the safety or health of employees as its concern, and that the EEOC's guidelines were aimed at preventing discrimination, not at insuring occupational safety and health.[77] The EEOC was not like other agencies, such as the Mine Safety and Health Administration, whose primary concern was occupational health. Furthermore, the EEOC had only proposed guidelines, not implemented them; therefore the EEOC would be unlikely to act on the basis of them for some time.

Finally, OSHA referred to the lead standard's provisions that reflected concern for the reproductive health of both men and women workers and validated OSHA's authority to act in this area. If OSHA could institute a plan to remove those workers planning to conceive and prohibit risky medical procedures to accelerate the excretion of lead, it could protect reproductive health by prohibiting a policy of sterilization.

The Occupational Health and Safety Review Commission's Decision

Unlike Judge William E. Brennan, the Review Commission did not decide the case on the question of the statute of limitations or preemption. Instead, in a two to one decision, the commission addressed only the question of "whether a policy which excludes from employment women who have not been surgically sterilized constitutes a hazard within the meaning of the general duty clause."[78] The commission found that OSHA had not made a cognizable claim under the act, because the policy of sterilizations was not a hazard within the meaning of that clause.

The commission recognized that the act did not define the word *hazard* and turned to the legislative history to give the word meaning, ruling that "Congress conceived of occupational hazards in terms of processes and mate-

---

76. Ibid., 14 n.7.

77. OSHA cited the introduction to the EEOC guidelines, which states, "The proposed guidelines do not attempt to implement or enforce policies related to health and safety. . . .The task of assuring a workplace free of conditions that threaten the health and safety of employees remains with the federal agencies specifically granted that responsibility" (45 *Fed. Reg.* 7514 [February 1, 1980]; DOL brief, 18).

78. Secretary of Labor v. American Cyanamid Company, 9 O.S.H. Cas. (BNA) 1596, 1598 (April 27, 1981).

rials that cause injury or disease by operating directly upon employees as they engage in work or work-related activities."[79] The commission conceded that the sterilizations were the result of a policy on the part of Cyanamid and that sterilization was a condition of employment, but concluded that Congress did not intend the act to apply to every conceivable aspect of employer-employee relations. Hazard referred to materials and processes, not job requirements.

The commission further found that the women had undertaken the sterilizations voluntarily. Their decisions were the result of economic and social factors outside the workplace and beyond the employer's control.

> An employee's decision to undergo sterilization in order to gain or retain employment grows out of economic and social factors which operate primarily outside of the workplace. The employer neither controls nor creates these factors as he creates or controls work processes and materials.[80]

It mattered to the commission that the sterilizations occurred outside of the workplace "in a hospital not associated with Respondent."[81]

In a strongly worded dissent, Commissioner Bertram Robert Cottine argued that the issue was not merely whether OSHA had made a cognizable claim under the general duty clause. The primary issue was whether the judge had been correct in granting summary judgment. Cottine also asserted that the case raised issues of triable fact. He not only disagreed with the commission's finding that the policy of sterilizations was not a hazard under the general duty clause, but, unlike the commission, he went on to address Judge Brennan's other findings on the statute of limitations and preemption.

Cottine's sharpest words attacked the commission's conclusion that although sterilization was a condition of employment, it was not covered by the general duty clause.

> Corporate policy that offers employees a choice between jobs and surgical sterilization is comparable to a corporate policy that offers employees a choice between jobs and exposure to sterilizing chemicals. To say one is prohibited by the Act while the other is not is to repudiate the letter and spirit of the Act.[82]

Agreeing with OSHA, Cottine argued that it did not matter that the women were sterilized outside the workplace if they had undergone the pro-

---

79. Ibid., 1600.
80. Ibid.
81. Ibid., 1597.
82. Ibid., 1603.

cedure to keep their jobs. He cited commission statements saying: "the Act's remedial jurisdiction is not limited to locations where work is actually performed," but is based on "whether a particular condition bears a sufficient nexus to employment to permit enforcement of the Act."[83]

Cottine disagreed with the other commissioners' interpretation of the act. While the majority turned to the legislative history to define hazard, surmising that Congress only had in mind protecting employees from processes and materials, Cottine argued that the commission should interpret the act according to its purpose: protecting the health of workers. Rather than concluding that the legislative record showed that Congress did not envision that the general duty clause would prohibit such a policy, Cottine suggested there was no evidence that Congress intended to *exclude* such circumstances from coverage. A liberal interpretation of the act would have been consistent with the commission's prior constructions of general language in a statute "in favor of those it seeks to protect."[84]

Cottine pointed out that the commission's recognition that sterilization was a condition of employment confirmed that the sterilizations were a result of a policy, thereby ruling out the claim that OSHA issued the citation too late. He further warned of the consequences of upholding such a policy.

> The exclusion of fertile women from certain employment invites employers to exclude other highly susceptible groups from employment when the effect varies among the exposed classes of individuals. As a result, the burden for safety and health is borne by the employees.[85]

Cottine addressed the question of whether OSHA was preempted from acting to prohibit sterilizations, pointing out that section 4(b)(1) of the act prevents the agency from exercising authority to regulate the working conditions of employees only if: (1) a sister agency has statutory authority to regulate the health and safety of the affected employees, and (2) that agency has actually exercised its authority over the cited working conditions.[86] The EEOC has no statutory authority to regulate occupational safety and health and expressly disavowed any attempt to do so. Furthermore, the proposed guidelines would have had no substantive legal effect until adopted. Cottine's arguments carried no more weight with the Court of Appeals for the District of Columbia Circuit than they did with his colleagues on the commission.

---

83. Ibid., 1604.
84. Ibid., 1605.
85. Ibid.
86. Northwest Airlines, Inc., 8 O.S.H. Cas. (BNA) 1982 (1980).

The Court of Appeals's Decision

The Oil, Chemical and Atomic Workers Union (OCAW) appealed the decision of the Review Commission to the Court of Appeals for the District of Columbia Circuit, an appeal OSHA declined to join. Judge Robert H. Bork, in a unanimous decision of the three-judge panel, wrote the opinion for the court, an opinion that became an issue in his confirmation hearings for the Supreme Court. The only question on appeal was whether the policy of sterilizations constituted a hazard for purposes of the general duty clause.

Judge Bork conceded that one could arguably stretch the language of the act to cover Cyanamid's policy.

> There is no doubt that the words of the general duty clause can be read, albeit with some semantic distortion, to cover the sterilization exception contained in American Cyanamid's fetus protection policy.[87]

Yet he suggested "that conclusion is necessary, however, only if the words of the statute inescapably have the meaning petitioners find in them and are unaffected by precedent, usage, and congressional intent."[88] He observed that previous rulings held that the act covered "the environmental area in which an employee customarily goes about his daily duties" and Congress intended for it to cover "less than the employment relationship in its entirety."[89] He concluded that the general duty clause does not apply to a policy as contrasted with a physical condition of the workplace.[90]

Bork pointed out that the Court of Appeals for the District of Columbia Circuit had held OSHA's Lead Standard infeasible for the lead pigments industry.[91] He did not, however, mention that, in setting the single standard of exposure for men and women, OSHA explicitly rejected the option of excluding women, and concluded that men's reproductive capacity was also at risk from exposure to lead. Cyanamid's policy arguably became more justifiable if reducing the exposure level were impossible, and certainly Judge Bork thought

---

87. Oil, Chemical and Atomic Workers International Union v. American Cyanamid Company, 741 F.2d 444, 447 (D.C. Cir. 1984).

88. Ibid., 448.

89. Ibid., 448, quoting Southern Ry. v. OSHRC, 539 F.2d 335, *cert. denied*, 429 U.S. 999 (1976).

90. 741 F.2d 444, 448 (D.C. Cir. 1984).

91. United Steelworkers of America v. Marshall, 647 F.2d 1189, 1294 (D.C. Cir. 1980): "We find, however, that OSHA has not presented substantial evidence of the technological feasibility of the standard for this [pigment manufacture] industry." This does not mean that the court was persuaded that the standard was infeasible, but merely that OSHA had not proven its feasibility.

that it was. The company was not choosing whether to lower exposure to lead or expose workers to a reproductive hazard. Instead, it was choosing whether to let women have the option of becoming sterilized rather than banning them from this work.

Bork's opinion emphasized the voluntary nature of the choice facing the women. He found that whether an employer can offer women a choice of sterilization that they might later regret is a legislative and moral question, not one for a court. He discovered no evidence that Congress intended to prohibit employers from giving women such a choice. Arguing that the court's task was to interpret Congress's language and apply its policy, Judge Bork concluded that, even if the court's task were to determine what Congress would have done if it had conceived of such a scenario, it is not at all clear that Congress would have chosen to prohibit what Cyanamid did.

Because Bork agreed that the word *hazard* referred to materials and processes and because sterilizations were a choice taken for economic and social reasons, he explicitly rejected Cottine's analogy. "A chemical is not the same thing as a policy and a congressional decision to deal with one does not necessarily constitute a decision to deal with the other."[92] He concluded that the sterilizations were a policy, a condition of employment, different than something that workers are exposed to every day at work. Barring a generic OSHA standard on reproductive hazards or guidance from Congress, both the Review Commission and the court of appeals were unwilling to extend the general duty clause to cover policies such as Cyanamid's.

In the September 18 session of the Senate Judiciary Committee's hearings to confirm Robert Bork to the Supreme Court, Senator Metzenbaum stated that the Cyanamid women were faced with a "horrible choice" and called Bork's opinion "shocking." Bork explained:

> The basic decision was based on Congress' intent. In the 1970 Occupational Safety and Health Act, Congress had been concerned with physical conditions in the workplace, not policy. This is not an anti-women decision. . . . The company was offering women a choice. That's all it was about.

"You can't tell me that any member of Congress thought that a safer workplace could be achieved by sterilization," Metzenbaum retorted. "That's a distortion of the statute beyond recognition. It's also unfair and inhumane." "This was not a forced sterilization opinion," Bork replied. Cyanamid may have given the women a "distressing choice," but "I suppose the five women who chose sterilization were glad to have the choice the company gave them." In a telegram to Senator Metzenbaum, Betty Riggs, one of the women

---

92. 741 F.2d 444, 449 (D.C. Cir. 1984).

who was sterilized informed the committee that she was not glad to have the choice. "Only a judge who knows nothing about women" could believe that some welcomed the option of sterilization. "I was only twenty-six years old, but I had to work so I had no choice. . . . This was the most awful thing that happened to me." Because of the Cyanamid case, the American Public Health Association opposed Bork's confirmation.[93]

The EEOC's Response to Exclusionary Policies

Up to this point in exploring the events surrounding the Cyanamid case, the only governmental agency's actions this chapter considered have been OSHA's. Because the Review Commission ruled the EEOC's proposed interpretive guidelines on reproductive hazards preempted OSHA from fighting exclusionary policies, it is worth considering what those guidelines said about the legality of exclusionary policies under Title VII. Although many interest groups may have preferred OSHA to have responsibility for setting guidelines for exclusionary policies because of its scientific expertise, *Cyanamid* forced them to concentrate their efforts on the EEOC.

Both the EEOC and OSHA became aware of reproductive hazards before *Cyanamid*. The EEOC had received complaints on exclusionary policies as early as 1976. The Bunker Hill Company of Kellogg, Idaho, operated a lead smelter and zinc plant.[94] In 1972, in response to pressure from the EEOC,[95] Bunker Hill hired forty-five women to work in high-paying production jobs.[96] Three years later, the company instituted an exclusionary policy, requiring all fertile women exposed to lead to undergo sterilization or lose their jobs. At least three women had themselves sterilized solely to keep their jobs. The local affiliate of the United Steelworkers of America lacked the resources and expertise to help the women make a claim, and the national union worried that if it protested the policy, Bunker Hill, the only lead smelter that employed women, would refuse to hire women altogether.[97] The union also doubted that a lawsuit challenging an exclusionary policy would succeed.

On their own, the women filed complaints with the Idaho Human Rights Commission (IHRC) and the EEOC. Because of a power-sharing agreement, the EEOC could only intervene once the IHRC had finished with the case. The IHRC sought to permit exclusion, but retain the wage rates for women who

---

93. Quotations reported in "Bork's Opinion in Sterilization Case at Issue in Senate Hearing," *Workplace Health* (BPI), September 23, 1987, 156–57.

94. Lead smelting is a job with very high exposure to lead and, except for a brief period during World War II, women had been excluded from such jobs in the United States. In Britain, women are banned from working in lead smelters.

95. Randall and Short, 414.

96. Ibid.

97. Ibid., 415.

transferred. The company rejected that proposal. Bunker Hill had already stated publicly that they would prefer a lawsuit claiming discrimination to a lawsuit claiming that occupational exposure had resulted in the birth of malformed children.

> From Bunker Hill's perspective, an employment discrimination charge was preferable to a possible damages lawsuit. Dennis Brendel, the company's vice president of environmental affairs, explained: "Bunker Hill is willing to be criticized for not employing some women—but not for causing birth defects."[98]

After the IHRC failed to negotiate a settlement, the EEOC began its investigation. Without a policy on exclusionary policies or a ruling from the courts on their legality, the EEOC would have had difficulty improving upon the IHRC's proposal.

Despite these limitations, the EEOC reached an agreement but left the women completely out of the negotiations.[99] Bunker Hill would give the women other jobs and they would retain the same pay and benefits, but they could not hold jobs that exposed them to lead. Moreover, the company made its offer on the condition that all of the women accept. The company succeeded in its plan to divide and conquer because women who most feared losing their jobs pressured women who wanted to fight the exclusion from production work to accept.

> One woman explained, 'The question was settled when $1,000 bills were flashed in the faces of the women.' However, a couple of the women did not want to accept the settlement and resisted doing so for some time.[100]

The EEOC's handling of the case left many women less than satisfied.[101]

> Without an official position on exclusionary policies, the EEOC could not institutionalize and routinize the handling of the complaint. Similar complaints in the future would have to be negotiated on a case-by-case basis. The complainants wanted a clear-cut policy decision by the EEOC on exclusionary policies, but they didn't get it. The women felt that the

---

98. Ibid., 417, quoting Steven Anderson, "Bunker Hill: Sterilization Not Required," *Idaho Statesman*, September 17, 1980.

99. Randall and Short, 417.

100. Ibid.

101. "The resolution of their claim left many of the women extremely cynical about the EEOC's and the federal government's interests in exclusionary policies" (ibid., 418).

EEOC did not want to get involved with the issue of exclusionary policies and was only making a symbolic response to their complaints.[102]

Four years after the EEOC had "resolved" the dispute over Bunker Hill's policy, OSHA simultaneously issued citations to Bunker Hill and American Cyanamid. OSHA had known about Bunker Hill's policy for several years, but the agency had promulgated a new lead standard in 1978. Furthermore, Bunker Hill had a long history of failure to comply with OSHA's and EPA's standards,[103] and OSHA may have seen the exclusionary policy as an opportunity "to exert regulatory control over the agency."[104] OSHA used the media effectively to publicize the issue while Bunker Hill was under a "gag order" from another lawsuit and could not respond to the unfavorable publicity about its policy.[105] Because of the sterilizations, "OSHA was able to supply a sensational story to the press,"[106] and both the *Wall Street Journal* and the *New York Times* ran stories. The Review Commission's decision for Cyanamid, holding that a policy of requiring sterilization was not a hazard under the general duty clause, also applied to Bunker Hill. Despite the publicity OSHA generated against exclusionary policies, the Review Commission and the court of appeals's decisions prevented OSHA from using the general duty clause to fight exclusionary policies such as Bunker Hill's and Cyanamid's.[107]

---

102. Ibid., 417.

103. "The Occupational Safety and Health Administration (OSHA), the federal agency that sets and enforces standards for workplace health and safety, has measured lead levels up to 7.37 milligrams—7,370 micrograms—per cubic meter of air in areas of the smelter. (The current OSHA standard for lead in occupational environments is a maximum average of 50 micrograms per cubic meter of air over eight hours.)" (Tate, 78).

104. Randall and Short, 418.

105. Ibid., 419.

106. Ibid.

107. Although rulings from the District of Columbia Circuit Court of Appeals are binding only on that circuit, in practice, the court's ruling in *Cyanamid* eliminated the general duty clause as an avenue for OSHA to fight exclusionary policies. Section 11(a) of the Occupational Safety and Health Act provides: "Any person adversely affected or aggrieved by an order of the Commission issued under subsection (c) of section 10 may obtain a review of such order in any United States court of appeals for the circuit in which the violation is alleged to have occurred or where the employer has its principal office, or in the Court of Appeals for the District of Columbia Circuit, by filing in such court within sixty days following the issuance of such order a written petition praying that the order be modified or set aside" (29 U.S.C. §660(a)). If OSHA were to issue another citation under the general duty clause, an employer would first request review by the Occupational Safety and Health Review Commission, and, if the OSHRC were to follow its ruling in the Cyanamid case, it would set aside the citation. Should the OSHRC decide to abandon its precedent and uphold the citation, the employer would then be able to choose whether to appeal to the District of Columbia Circuit or in the circuit where its business is located. Since the Court of Appeals for the District of Columbia Circuit had already interpreted the general duty clause to foreclose such an action on the part of OSHA, the employer would most easily have the

Cyanamid was a catalyst for the 1979 formation of the Coalition for the Reproductive Rights of Workers (CRROW) to fight exclusionary policies.[108] The coalition was composed of labor unions, women's groups, and health and environmental organizations. Two very active organizations that focused on legal reform and litigation in the coalition were the Women's Rights Project of the American Civil Liberties Union and the Women's Legal Defense Fund. CRROW publicized and criticized such company policies as American Cyanamid's, issued a newsletter to report on new regulatory and scientific developments, coordinated legal challenges to exclusionary policies,[109] and lobbied regulatory agencies. Not only did several groups join to form a coalition to fight exclusionary policies, but the case spawned protests in the wider legal community. *Cyanamid* spawned several law review articles that analyzed the legality of exclusionary policies and questioned their justification.[110] *Page v. Freight Hire*, in contrast, generated little interest in the British legal community.

The EEOC received complaints about exclusionary policies like the complaint against Bunker Hill, but lacked any clear guidance from Congress or the courts on how to approach the issue. The Coalition for the Reproductive Rights of Workers (CRROW) reported that, in 1981, the EEOC had a backlog of forty unresolved complaints related to reproductive hazards.[111] Members

---

chance of having the citation set aside by appealing to that circuit. Thus, unless the District of Columbia Circuit reverses itself, the Supreme Court overturns the ruling, or an employer is foolish enough to file in another circuit, the opinion of the Court of Appeals for the District of Columbia Circuit guarantees that OSHA will be unsuccessful in sustaining the citation. Because OSHA is capable of this very calculation, it will not likely issue another citation under the general duty clause.

108. *Coalition for the Reproductive Rights of Workers Newsletter* 1 (Spring 1981): 2.

109. The Occupational Safety and Health Review Commission allowed CRROW to participate as a nonparty intervenor in the Cyanamid case. In addition, the Women's Rights Project of the ACLU has filed an amicus brief or represented the women for every case on exclusionary policies.

110. Wendy Williams, "Firing the Woman to Protect the Fetus: The Reconciliation of Fetal Protection with Employment Opportunity Goals under Title VII," *Georgetown Law Journal* 69 (1981): 641–704; Hannah Arterian Furnish, "Prenatal Exposure to Fetally Toxic Work Environments: The Dilemma of the 1978 Pregnancy Amendments to Title VII of the Civil Rights Act of 1964," *Iowa Law Review* 66 (1980): 63–129; Mary E. Becker, "From *Muller v. Oregon* to Fetal Vulnerability Policies," *University of Chicago Law Review* 53 (1986): 1219–73; Donald R. Crowell and David A. Copus, "Safety and Equality at Odds: OSHA and Title VII Clash over Health Hazards in the Workplace," *Industrial Relations Law Journal* 2 (1978): 567–95; Joan I. Samuelson, "Employment Rights of Women in the Toxic Workplace," *California Law Review* 65 (1977): 1113–42; Patricia A. Timko, "Exploring the Limits of Legal Duty: A Union's Responsibilities with Respect to Fetal Protection Policies," *Harvard Journal on Legislation* 23 (1986): 159–210; Lois Vanderwaerdt, "Resolving the Conflict Between Hazardous Substances in the Workplace and Equal Employment Opportunity," *American Business Law Journal* 21 (1983): 157–84.

111. *Coalition for the Reproductive Rights of Workers Newsletter* 1 (Spring 1981): 5.

of CRROW met with Eleanor Holmes Norton and other top officials at the EEOC and urged the agency to propose guidelines instructing the courts, employers, and its own staff on how they should apply Title VII and Executive Order 11246 to exclusionary policies.

The EEOC responded with proposed interpretive guidelines that insisted that the agency was enforcing Title VII and not the Occupational Safety and Health Act.[112] The guidelines distinguished the goal of insuring equal employment opportunity from the goal of insuring the safety and health of workers, yet assumed the two statutes not to be in conflict. The EEOC defined OSHA's role as one of consultation "particularly with reference to scientific data."[113] The introduction to the guidelines stated that the EEOC and Office of Federal Contract Compliance Programs had received complaints and that both the EEOC and OSHA had previously recognized problems with exclusionary policies. The EEOC had earlier issued a policy statement,[114] and Eula Bingham had written a letter to all major corporate medical directors expressing OSHA's reservations about the policies.[115]

The explanatory note to the guidelines commented that employers often instituted exclusionary policies without adequate regard for whether men's exposure could result in harm to an unborn child, concluding that "if the hazard is known to affect the fetus through either parent, an exclusionary policy directed only at women would be unlawful under Title VII and E.O. 11246."[116] The guidelines warned that the law prohibited overinclusive as well as underinclusive policies. If an employer could prove that a hazard affected the fetus through women only, the guidelines permitted employers to exclude only pregnant women rather than all fertile women.

After creating a strong presumption against the scientific justification for exclusionary policies, the guidelines explained how Title VII applied to them. Any policy that excluded workers from jobs because of sex would be a *per se* violation of Title VII. The EEOC pointed out that the Pregnancy Discrimination Act made differential treatment on the basis of pregnancy, childbirth, or related conditions discrimination on the basis of sex. The BFOQ exception applied only when all or substantially all members of a group were unable to perform the duties of the job. Thus, an employer would not be able to defend an exclusionary policy under the rubric of disparate treatment. If, however, an employer instituted a neutral policy that was not a pretext for discrimination, it could invoke the business necessity defense.

The EEOC identified the following factors as relevant in determining whether an employer's policy was discriminatory: whether the policy had

112. 45 *Fed. Reg.* 7514 (February 1, 1980).
113. Ibid.
114. Mentioned in 45 *Fed. Reg.* 7514 (February 1, 1980), as dated April 21, 1978.
115. Mentioned in 45 *Fed. Reg.* 7514 (February 1, 1980), as dated May 31, 1978.
116. 45 *Fed. Reg.* 7514, 7515 (February 1, 1980).

been applied consistently to both sexes, whether the employer had complied with health and safety laws, whether the employer had investigated all reproductive hazards for all employees, whether the evidence suggested that one group is more at risk than another, whether the employer had a pattern of discrimination against the excluded group, whether the policy was narrowly tailored to the type of hazard posed, whether evidence suggested the substance that employers excluded some workers from because of reproductive hazards posed other hazards to health, whether there were alternatives to exclusion, and whether the employer was monitoring scientific developments.[117]

To exclude a group because of medical evidence, an employer had to prove the relevance of the evidence by monitoring the actual level of exposure in each workplace. In situations where evidence existed for one sex only, the guidelines permitted employers to exclude those affected while carrying out additional research, with such research to be completed within one year. The EEOC provided for assistance or special consideration for small employers and asked corporations to comment on the expected effect on small businesses.

In developing its guidelines, the EEOC responded sympathetically to CRROW, perhaps because of the good relationship the chair of the EEOC had with the civil rights community. The EEOC was headed by Eleanor Holmes Norton, "a politically savvy New York civil-rights lawyer."[118] While feminist groups may have had access to Norton, she did have reservations about the guidelines, especially after she received industry's comments. She was particularly wary of women being exposed to substances that would lead to malformations.[119]

> This is a frontier area for us and is something that I'm not all that comfortable with. There are a lot of uncertainties. The only certainty is that a blanket exclusion won't stand up, at least in the absence of supporting medical evidence.[120]

The head of OSHA, Dr. Eula Bingham, was even more sympathetic than Norton to CRROW's position. Bingham, who had a deep commitment to occupational safety and health and was particularly concerned about the health of employed women, had already taken a stand against exclusionary

---

117. Ibid.

118. Joann Lublin, "Guideline-Happy at the EEOC," *Wall Street Journal*, August 28, 1980.

119. "We're very concerned about this issue. I have not been very impressed with the reliability of pregnancy tests during the early stages of pregnancy. We're going to review the guidelines very carefully in this area" (James W. Singer, "Should Equal Opportunity for Women Apply to Toxic Chemical Exposure?" *National Journal* 12 [October 18, 1980]: 1755, quoting Eleanor Holmes Norton).

120. Ibid., 1753, quoting Eleanor Holmes Norton.

policies. She was not only President Carter's personal choice for the job but enjoyed the strong support of unions.[121] In response to industry's claims that potential fetuses were endangered by women's occupational exposure, she replied:

> So clean up! Clean up the workplace! This business of having people go out and be sterilized—and I would feel the same way if it were men—to me it's like saying you're going to work on this machine and you might get your hand cut, so to prevent our liability, you'd better go out and have your hand amputated.[122]

Bingham pressed the EEOC for guidelines on reproductive hazards because she discovered, "companies were using OSHA standards as a bogus reason for excluding women" from certain jobs.[123]

Although members of CRROW had pushed for guidelines from the EEOC, many were unhappy with the result. The Cyanamid women's representative, Anthony Mazzocchi, director of health and safety for the Oil, Chemical and Atomic Workers Union, stated, "I've never seen anything as bad as this. It's a step backwards; we were better off before, with just Title VII."[124] Unions and feminists did not want to establish the principle that companies could exclude women or other susceptible groups on the basis of industry-sponsored research,[125] and they feared that the guidelines legitimated exclusion as an option. Some members of CRROW took the position that exclusionary policies could never be justified under Title VII.[126] Others feared that, "without governmental action, some courts may abandon traditional equal employment principles out of a paternalistic concern for women's health without considering the risk to men."[127] The UAW refused to support the guidelines unless OSHA simultaneously issued a generic standard on reproductive hazards.[128] CRROW criticized the guidelines while lobbying for improvements favorable to its interests. Industry vigorously attacked

---

121. Wilson, 62–63.

122. Tate, 80.

123. Lublin, quoting Eula Bingham.

124. Marlene Cimons, "Protection of Women or Sex Bias: Unions, Feminists Protest Guidelines," *Los Angeles Times*, April 10, 1980.

125. "Selected Comments Relating to EEOC Proposed Guidelines on Employment and Reproductive Hazards," *Daily Labor Report* (BNA) 133 (July 9, 1980). See Comment by Oil, Chemical and Atomic Workers International Union, G-1; Comments by Coalition for the Reproductive Rights of Workers, G-2; Comment by U.S. Chamber of Commerce, G-9.

126. Donna Lenhoff, attorney, Women's Legal Defense Fund, interview with author, Washington, D.C., 1986.

127. Singer, 1753, quoting Donna Lenhoff.

128. The UAW, a member of CRROW, wanted OSHA guidelines to include a presumption that all substances that were a fetal hazard from women's exposure were also a hazard from men's

the proposed guidelines, claiming that they were vague, costly, and, if they prohibited the exclusion of women, would make the fetus a "sacrificial lamb."[129]

> With the corporate world demanding their withdrawal because they went too far, and feminists and trade union groups demanding that they be amended and strengthened, the proposed regulations were extremely vulnerable and would have faced an uncertain future in any event. The election of a conservative national administration hostile to the direction OSHA policy had taken under Eula Bingham, sympathetic to business interests, and committed to an antiregulatory posture guaranteed that the EEOC and OFCCP effort would fare badly.[130]

After Ronald Reagan's election, the guidelines were quickly withdrawn.

> Upon reviewing the comments, the agencies have concluded that the most appropriate method of eliminating employment discrimination in the workplace where there is potential exposure to reproductive hazards is through investigation and enforcement of the law on a *case by case basis*, rather than by the issuance of interpretive guidelines.[131]

Although the EEOC's litigation department continued to participate as amicus in *Olin*, filing its brief in December, 1981, and in *Hayes*, filing its brief in June, 1983, once Clarence Thomas replaced Eleanor Holmes Norton as chair of the EEOC the agency stopped challenging exclusionary policies. The proposed guidelines were not revived or amended. By 1983, the EEOC had a backlog of approximately forty cases on discrimination resulting from fetal protection policies. The compliance manual stated that such cases were "non-commission decision precedent." Section 624.1 stated,

> Such charges [Title VII challenges to fetal protection policies] are non-CDP [Commission Decision Precedent]. After investigating the charge according to the following subsections, the EOS [Equal Opportunity

---

exposure until proven otherwise: "The Memorandum of Understanding between the EEOC and DOL-OSHA must also establish the presumption, based on scientific data to date, that a substance harmful to the reproductive health of one sex is more likely than not, absent reputable scientific evidence to the contrary, harmful to the health of the other sex" (Comments by the International Union, United Automobile, Aerospace and Agricultural Implement Workers of America [UAW] on Interpretive Guidelines on Employment Discrimination and Reproductive Hazards, 3).

129. Cimons, 12.

130. Ronald Bayer, "Women, Work, and Reproductive Hazards," *Hastings Center Report* 12 (October, 1982): 18.

131. 46 *Fed. Reg.* 3916 (January 16, 1981); italics added.

Specialist] should contact the Guidance Division of the Office of Legal Counsel for further instructions.[132]

Attempts to make the guidance to investigators more clear on this matter were blocked.

The EEOC completely halted any resolution of cases on exclusionary policies. Equal Opportunity Specialists investigated complaints, sent them to the head office, and nothing happened. The EEOC treated all the cases as if their resolution hinged on expertise in complex scientific and medical questions that the agency did not have. Yet some of the questions involved firing pregnant X-ray technicians, an issue the commission had already ruled on in the complaint filed by Rita Zuniga. Other cases involved exposure to lead, and the 1978 OSHA Lead Standard had explicitly rejected excluding all fertile women from exposure. Still others were obvious pretexts for pregnancy discrimination. One employer told an EOS that he did not have to cite any medical evidence that the substances employees worked with were hazardous to a developing fetus because pregnant women should not work with this stuff. Another employer refused to hire a typist at a bank when the bank's polygraph operator discovered in the course of questioning her that she was pregnant. The House Education and Labor Committee staff report charged that the agency had "entombed" and "warehoused" complaints.[133]

Staff from the House Education and Labor Committee, in the course of fulfilling its responsibility for overseeing the EEOC, began questioning the agency about its handling of cases on exclusionary policies in 1986.[134] After congressional staff accelerated the investigation in the summer of 1988, the commission "found cause" in the case of an X-ray technician who had been fired when she became pregnant.[135] She had filed a complaint in 1980 and EEOC staff joked that her child would go to law school and litigate the complaint himself before the agency resolved the case.

The agency issued an interpretive guidance directive in 1988, seven-and-one-half years after it had withdrawn its proposed guidelines.[136] Calling it "too little, too late," the congressional report vehemently criticized the guid-

132. *EEOC Compliance Manual* (Washington D.C.: Bureau of National Affairs, 1983), Sec. 624, "Reproductive and Fetal Hazards."

133. House Education and Labor Committee, *A Report on the EEOC, Title VII and Workplace Fetal Protection Policies in the 1980s*, 101st Cong., 2d sess., April 1990.

134. See Edmund D. Cooke, Jr., and Sally J. Kenney, "The View from Capitol Hill," in *Reproductive Laws for the 1990s*, ed. by Sherrill Cohen and Nadine Taub (Clifton, N.J.: Humana Press, 1989), 331–40.

135. "Hospital Fails to Justify 'Fetal Protection' Policy," *Toxic Substances and Right-to-Know* (BPI), November 2, 1988.

136. "EEOC's Policy Guidance on Reproductive and Fetal Hazards," *Daily Labor Reports* (BNA) 193 (October 5, 1988): D-1–4.

ance.[137] After the Seventh Circuit Court of Appeals issued its ruling in *UAW v. Johnson Controls*, the EEOC altered its policy guidance to agree with the dissenting judges,[138] and amended that guidance to reflect the Supreme Court's ruling.[139] It remains to be seen whether the agency will aggressively apply the policy in support of complainants' challenges to exclusionary policies in the future. In any case, the EEOC not only abdicated its responsibility to guide courts and employers in interpreting Title VII, but failed to do justice in cases where women asked the agency to perform its statutory duty of adjudicating their claims. Few of the charging parties had hired lawyers or asked for a right-to-sue letter. It is unlikely that many who filed complaints with the EEOC in the past will benefit from the ruling, since the EEOC can "administratively close" any case in which it cannot reach the charging party.

Conclusions

The first conclusion resulting from an examination of *Cyanamid* is that OSHA cannot use the general duty clause to cite employers for exclusionary policies. Even if there were a change in the opinion of the Review Commission or the court of appeals on whether requiring sterilizations as a condition of employment constituted a hazard for purposes of the general duty clause, both bodies might choose to follow Judge William E. Brennan's finding that OSHA was preempted from acting because the EEOC had asserted its jurisdiction over reproductive hazards by issuing proposed interpretive guidelines. OSHA could issue regulations on substances that are reproductive hazards in the same way that it issues standards for exposure to hazardous substances, but the current political climate makes that possibility unlikely. Business groups favored exclusionary policies,[140] and their concerns received a sympathetic hearing from the leadership of both OSHA and the EEOC.

Both OSHA's issuance of citations and the EEOC's proposed interpretive guidelines show the significance of the choice of political appointees. The Carter administration might have appointed Democrats who were similarly sympathetic to labor interests but who would not have taken the same action as Eula Bingham and Eleanor Holmes Norton. They were strong advocates of working women, had particular interests in reproductive hazards, and made challenging exclusionary policies a priority in their administrations. CRROW

---

137. House Education and Labor Committee, *Report on Fetal Protection Policies*, 22–26.

138. "EEOC Policy Guidance on Seventh Circuit Decision in *United Auto Workers v. Johnson Controls, Inc.*," *Daily Labor Report* (BNA) 18 (January 26, 1990): D-1–5.

139. "EEOC Issues Guidance to Staffers on Biased Fetal Protection Policies," *Daily Labor Report* (BNA) 132 (July 10, 1991): A-1.

140. "Selected Comments Relating to EEOC Proposed Guidelines on Employment Discrimination and Reproductive Hazards, Comment by U.S. Chamber of Commerce," *Daily Labor Report* 133 (July 9, 1980): G-9–12.

lobbyists not only had access to Bingham and Norton, but both were sympathetic and Bingham, especially, had a sophisticated understanding of the issue. Progress toward guidelines on reproductive hazards, slowed by industry objections and disagreement among unions and feminist groups, ground to a halt when the Reagan administration took office.

Although I have focused on the United States in this chapter, it is worth noting that British and U.S. laws and standard-setting processes for health and safety differ. In Britain, judges have not been central actors in applying health and safety law to policies on reproductive hazards or any other health and safety matter. The U.S. Court of Appeals for the District of Columbia Circuit, on the other hand, not only upheld the provision of the OSHA lead standard but gave its explicit approval to OSHA's interpretation of the medical evidence. The same court, however, determined that OSHA could not cite employers under the general duty clause for making sterilization a condition of employment for women. Because health and safety statutes provide for different standards of judicial review, because the personnel of the courts differ (British courts are notoriously unsympathetic to workers and unions under industrial relations law), and because interest groups pursue different strategies, British courts are not important in setting or altering the course of health and safety law, generally, and are important only for their absence in the debate over exclusionary policies.

I have touched only tangentially on administrative agencies' policies on reproductive hazards, but they differ substantially. A broader array of interest groups are represented in the United States. While the British tripartite system of having Health and Safety Executive committees set health and safety standards by consensus includes the views of trade union groups and industry and coopts them in support of the result, feminist groups are not included in the process. In contrast, in the United States, feminist groups, unions, and coalitions such as CRROW were active in litigation, in submitting evidence on the lead standard, and in lobbying for the EEOC's guidelines on reproductive hazards.

Although my focus has been primarily on litigation rather than administrative action, administrative agencies' actions have a significant impact on litigation. Exclusionary policies have "fallen between the cracks" of the EEOC and OSHA. The Review Commission's decision in *Cyanamid* prevented OSHA from using the general duty clause to fight exclusionary policies. After 1980, the EEOC, on the other hand, chose to ignore the issue. After 1980, the ACLU and unions had no governmental ally in their legal battles. Those challenging exclusionary policies, however, have been helped by OSHA's determination to set a single standard for men and women exposed to lead, by its provisions for medical removal, and by its medical findings on reproductive hazards to men. If OSHA had determined that employers could exclude all fertile women from exposure to lead, feminist groups would have had an even harder time fighting exclusionary policies in court. Conversely, if the EEOC had promulgated interpretive guidelines like those it proposed in 1980, judges would probably have given them deference and would have been more likely to find that exclusionary policies violated Title VII. These guidelines would have been important, not only for aiding courts in interpreting Title VII, but in helping them determine what factors are relevant in evaluating a firm's behavior and what presumptions they should make about scientific evidence.

The EEOC could have affected the behavior of both industry and the courts by assisting complainants in bringing cases or by filing amicus curiae briefs. Instead, it chose to do virtually nothing about exclusionary policies during the Reagan administration. Although the EEOC has not assisted claimants challenging exclusionary policies or advised courts how to interpret Title VII in the last few years, Title VII rather than the Occupational Safety and Health Act is the only real legal avenue left for challenging employers' policies. Unless administrative agencies change their positions, groups or individuals cannot use health and safety law to fight exclusionary policies.

Although we can draw few conclusions from examining the litigation surrounding one policy, the shortcomings of Cyanamid's policy are often evident in other exclusionary policies. The development and implementation of Cyanamid's policy were so problematic that the fears of the EEOC, expressed in its preamble to its proposed interpretive guidelines, warning that companies often ignore the reproductive hazards to men and are not justified in excluding all fertile women rather than just pregnant women, as well as the fears of commentators in law reviews, that exclusionary policies unfairly deny women employment opportunities and leave men unprotected, are well founded. The Office of Technology Assessment, OSHA, the EEOC, legal scholars, trade unions, national newspapers, and CRROW's scrutiny of Cyanamid's policy seriously questioned the company's pursuit of a seemingly progressive corporate goal: enhancing the health of future generations. Feminists and trade unionists will carry over their justified doubts, questions, and suspicions about Cyanamid's policy to other exclusionary policies. Just as the vigilance of probing lawyers and amici curiae produced a more favorable result for the challengers of exclusionary policies in the United States in comparison to Britain, the focus of interest groups and governmental agencies in the United States influenced public perception of this issue as a result of the controversy surrounding one case, even though those opposed to exclusionary policies neither persuaded the EEOC to issue guidance (until 1988) nor succeeded in sustaining OSHA's citations.

Conclusion

Analyzing and comparing cases on exclusionary policies in the United States and Britain serves three purposes. First, the book assesses the soundness of exclusionary policies from a public policy perspective. In the abstract, exclusionary policies may draw widespread support. Yet, studying the assumptions underlying them, the motivations of those proposing them, the scientific evidence underpinning them, and the way companies have implemented them, calls into question the value of what some may have initially seen as a desirable policy option. The information and analysis in this book contribute to the debate on an important public policy question: how to insure the reproductive health of workers without sacrificing equal employment opportunity.

Second, comparing litigation on exclusionary policies allows me to explore differences between the British and U.S. legal systems and political institutions. By demonstrating how the different histories of protective legislation, feminist movements, discrimination laws, performances of enforcement agencies, and roles of the courts in the political systems contribute to different outcomes in cases, broader comparisons are grounded in concrete examples. Whether or not the legislature has passed a specific act forbidding pregnancy discrimination, the degree of politicization of the civil service, how the government selects judges, the relationship of the women's movement to the labor movement, and the legal culture of litigation all affect cases on exclusionary policies. The findings of this case study reinforce previous comparisons of British and U.S. legal and political institutions by exploring an area of law and set of questions that has been less well traveled: sex discrimination.

Third, by examining how judges and members of tribunals have dealt with what they have considered hard cases for discrimination doctrine, comparing litigation on exclusionary policies provides an opportunity for scrutinizing and critiquing the concept of discrimination and the underlying assumptions about the nature of equality. Although the differences in outcomes are striking, particularly if we compare *Page v. Freight Hire* to *UAW v. Johnson Controls*, if we momentarily put all of the legal opinions on an equal footing and examine the reasoning in the cases rather than merely compare the final holding—when we, for example, consider the industrial tribunal's holding in Johnston. Highland Regional Council and the district court's opinion in *Wright v. Olin*—the similarities between the reasoning in cases are as revealing as the differences in final outcome. Some judges and members of tribunals have seen discrimination to be only that conduct that strikes them as unreasonable, regardless of any statutory definition of the term. They may act on stereotyped assumptions about the nature of sex differences and the proper social roles of men and women. A close reading of legal opinions on exclusionary policies, when placed in the context of the law and politics of discrimination, exposes the male norm in discrimination law and illustrates how the law legitimates the disadvantaging of those who are different. Finally, it illustrates the importance of life experience for deciding legal cases and highlights the significance of who the judges and members of tribunals are.

Exclusionary Policies as Public Policy

Analyzing and comparing exclusionary policies in Britain and the United States exposes many questionable assumptions that underlie exclusionary policies. The first assumption is that the fetus is at risk from women's exposure, even nonpregnant women's exposure, but not at risk from men's exposure.[1] Some employers have approached the scientific evidence differently depending on whether it revealed that maternal exposure or paternal exposure is risky—adopting a gendered posture toward risk. American Cyanamid maintained that exposing men to lead did not endanger their offspring but exposing women to lead did. They presumed that women were always endangering a fetus until conclusive evidence emerged to the contrary, but presumed that men were not similarly endangering a fetus until conclusive evidence showed otherwise. Several prominent scientists, whose research Johnson Controls relied on to support its exclusionary policy, argued strongly that the scientific evidence on lead did not justify "protecting" fetuses by preventing only women's exposure.

A double standard on the evidence of risk is even more problematic when one considers the lopsided nature of scientific evidence on reproductive hazards. Scientists have focused largely on the risk to offspring from women's exposure, despite the National Institute for Occupational Safety and Health's acknowledgement that, in situations of scientific uncertainty, the only safe assumption is that men are also at risk. Johnson Controls argued that without hard evidence about the effect of lead on the fetus at different levels of maternal exposure, one could extrapolate from evidence about children's ex-

---

1. As Wendy Williams concludes, "the presumption should be that all workers may be subject to the reproductive hazards that could result in birth defects and the exclusion solely of women workers is unwarranted unless the contrary is shown" (Wendy Williams, "Firing the Woman to Protect the Fetus: The Reconciliation of Fetal Protection with Employment Opportunity Goals Under Title VII," *Georgetown Law Journal* 69 (1981): 665).

posure to lead. Yet the company vociferously denounced attempts to speculate about the risk of lead exposure to men, denying such a risk existed. The company assumed a different posture toward scientific evidence according to whether the evidence supported or undermined its policy of excluding women.

The second assumption is that no risk to the fetus is acceptable, however minimal. After firing a pregnant X-ray technician, Shelby Memorial Hospital's administrator said that a pregnant woman's sunbathing in a bikini posed an unacceptable risk to the fetus. Yet the hospital let male X-ray technicians assume a low-level risk that their exposure to radiation would affect their fertility or cause mutations in their genes. When *UAW v. Johnson Controls* reached the court of appeals, the dissenting judges questioned the "zero-risk" strategy for pregnant or even nonsterilized women.[2] Judge Easterbrook preferred to think of the risks to the fetus in the context of women's lives, questioning whether the fetus was more at risk from low-level exposure to lead or from having an unemployed mother who may lose not only her ability to secure such health benefits as prenatal care, but even the ability to maintain proper nutrition. Judge Easterbrook recognized that no life choices for pregnant women, or anyone else, are without effect. Pregnant women drive cars, drink coffee and alcohol, smoke, and eat sugar. Those who live in Los Angeles breathe; those who live in New York take the subway. The differences between the magnitude of risk to which Johnson Controls would refuse to subject fetuses and that women assume outside of the workplace become more stark when one considers that many of the women working in the plant would not become pregnant. Judge Easterbrook demanded that Johnson Controls quantify the net risk, concluding that "surely Title VII does not allow an employer to adopt a policy that makes both women and their children worse off."[3]

The third assumption underlying exclusionary policies is that reproductive hazards affecting women are different and more serious than other occupational hazards. Exclusionary policies remove reproductive hazards from the context of sound health and safety policies. Some men who have high blood levels of lead will develop high blood pressure and heart disease and die prematurely. These men "choose" to assume additional risks by exposing themselves to lead. Yet employers instituting exclusionary policies would deny a forty-five-year-old single woman the right to assume some risk to a fetus she is determined to avoid bringing into existence. The danger is that by focusing on the risks of reproductive hazards—hazards that attract a lot of media attention, such as the alleged higher incidence of miscarriage among workers using video display terminals—other occupational health issues will

---

2. 886 F.2d 871, 907, 913–20 (7th Cir. 1989).
3. Ibid., 918.

be eclipsed. Focusing on VDTs and miscarriages may deflect public attention from the other serious health hazards of VDTs and the dramatic changes in office work that their introduction has brought about.

Many workers are exposed to carcinogens and assume an increased risk of developing cancer. When these carcinogens are essential to a manufacturing process, or for a health treatment, the policy is to reduce exposure as much as possible. Is an increased risk of miscarriage, particularly for a woman who is not and does not want to be pregnant, more serious than an increased risk of developing cancer? To compare these risks is not to suggest that, because our society permits workers to expose themselves to substances that give them cancer, it is acceptable for them to "choose" to poison their offspring. Women should not have to work with substances that damage them or their offspring. Neither should men. Neither should men or women have to face a serious risk of occupational illness. But the reality is, we all assume some risk, and we should not put reproductive hazards in a class by themselves and treat them more seriously than the risks of heart disease or cancer. We must embed any policy on reproductive hazards in a sound health and safety policy. Removing women workers is a simpler and less expensive alternative to lowering exposures to all hazardous substances, but it should not be employers' chief way of minimizing reproductive hazards or, more likely, insulating themselves from an exaggerated risk of tort liability.

The fourth assumption underlying exclusionary policies is that women are always pregnant. By adopting exclusionary policies, employers treat women as if they are incapable of making choices about or controlling their reproductive capacities. Most women, however, plan their pregnancies. Very few are pregnant for their entire working lives. All women are not equally likely to get pregnant because they are biologically capable of doing so—or more accurately, because they have not been sterilized or reached menopause. It is ludicrous to assume that the only safe policy is to treat a woman whose husband has had a vasectomy, a forty-five-year-old single mother, a lesbian, or a woman who is celibate as if she were pregnant. The policies lump all women together as vessels always filled with babies.

The fifth assumption the policies rest on is that women's childbearing role takes priority over their role as a breadwinner. A corollary assumption is that it is only appropriate for women to hold certain kinds of jobs (usually low-paid, dead-end jobs). Some employers, judges, and members of industrial tribunals continue to act on the unconscious assumption that women's place is in the home. Employers and policymakers may still see women as "out of place" in traditionally male jobs.[4] Women work for the same reasons

---

4. "Women and their children are 'protected' by fetal vulnerability policies only when women are perceived as marginal members of the workforce" (Mary Becker, "From *Muller v. Oregon* to Fetal Vulnerability Policies," *University of Chicago Law Review* 53 (1986): 1237).

men do—to earn money to feed themselves and their families, to maintain their standard of living, and to enjoy personal satisfaction and self-esteem. Companies' concern about reproductive hazards only in male-dominated, well-paid jobs, when they lack concern for reproductive hazards in job categories dominated by women, raises questions about the partiality of the "protection" of women workers. In the past, these same inconsistencies led many to question protective legislation that, for example, banned women from tending bar but not from serving as cocktail waitresses.

Sixth, some employers have assumed that excluding women should be the first option considered rather than the last. The policies in this study reveal that employers have been too hasty in excluding women rather than exploring such alternatives as lowering exposure, substituting another product, using protective clothing, removing workers registering high levels of the substance in their bodies, or more carefully determining who is likely to conceive. Although practicing good industrial hygiene can often minimize exposure, employers assume that women, or pregnant women, cannot be relied upon to act in their own interests and in the interests of their offspring.

Seventh, employers have assumed that the threat of tort liability from a malformed child whose mother was exposed to occupational hazards threatens the financial viability of business. Experts in civil liability have shown, for example in the thalidomide case, how difficult it is to prove causation for any malformation, even when one knows that the mother took a specific dosage of a drug on a specific day. Proving causation for an occupational injury presents greater obstacles. While one can show a pattern of increased miscarriages or malformations, it is difficult to prove that a specific occupational exposure caused any particular adverse pregnancy outcome. Instead, it could have been one of the high number of unexplained miscarriages or malformations that occur spontaneously. Such suits are nearly impossible to win. Companies are rightly concerned about having to bear the cost of litigating, even if they might win. Furthermore, charges of causing miscarriages or malformations damage the public image of the company. However companies assess their vulnerability to lawsuits for offspring damaged as a result of occupational exposure, they would be wrong to assume that only women whose children are allegedly injured would sue. In fact, men may be more likely to sue, as the examples of the cases over Agent Orange and the pesticide DBCP (which made male workers sterile) show. Since both men and women can damage their offspring as a result of an occupational exposure and both men and women can sue, companies who adopt exclusionary policies are trying to shield themselves from the risk of lawsuits from half, or less than half, of their workforce while ignoring the possibility of lawsuits from the other half. Employers should not be able to shield themselves from tort liability by making stereotyped assumptions that are untrue: that only women reproduce, that only women may damage their offspring, and that only women bring lawsuits.

Exposing the underlying assumptions makes exclusionary policies seem less desirable as a public policy option, regardless of whether or not they are permissible under sex discrimination law. Looking at specific cases and company policies also casts them in an unfavorable light. When ICI ordered Freight Hire to ban women from merely driving trucks filled with hazardous substances, when Shelby Memorial fired a pregnant X-ray technician without reference to the medical literature or the level of exposure, when Johnson Controls refused to transfer a man wanting to start a family, when American Cyanamid required women to be sterilized on the basis of "an educated guess," we begin to have serious questions about exclusionary policies. *Cyanamid* brought all exclusionary policies into question. Women were sterilized but lost their jobs anyway. Cyanamid's policy, like Olin's and Shelby Memorial Hospital's, arose in a male-dominated workplace. In all three examples, the hazard posed potential reproductive risks to men as well as women. Freight Hire did not consider the possibility of doing something to lessen exposure or even to determine the level of exposure. Although the company considered the risk to be to fetuses, not adult men and women, and Jacky Page was not and did not plan to be pregnant, she could not drive a truck because the company treated her as if she were pregnant. The company ignored the potential health risks, reproductive and nonreproductive, to men. Feminist methodology invites us to look at issues by focusing on the concrete experiences of women's lives. The narratives of women's work experiences, as revealed through litigation, call into question the value of policies that may seem more defensible in the abstract.

Comparing U.S. and British Political and Legal Systems

In addition to assessing a public policy, comparing cases on exclusionary policies widens our understanding of similarities and differences between legal and political systems in Britain and the United States. A premise of this study is not only that cases on exclusionary policies cannot be understood unless they are placed in a political and legal context of how institutions function, but also that such policies have a history. Chapter 1 places contemporary exclusionary policies in the context of legislative efforts to treat men and women workers differently over the last 150 years—the history of protective legislation. Both the history of protective legislation and the accounts of litigation over exclusionary policies show that the important battles took place in different arenas in Britain and the United States. In the United States, the courts determined whether state protective legislation conflicted with federal discrimination law after both Congress and the Equal Employment Opportunity Commission failed to decide that question. In Britain, Parliament initially avoided determining whether protective legislation was discriminatory and asked the Equal Opportunities Commission to make recommendations—recommendations Parliament then ignored. In 1986, Parliament adopted Prime Minister Thatcher's proposals to reduce burdens on industry and rescinded the protective laws over the objections of feminists and trade unionists. In the United States, the courts settled this public policy question; in Britain, Parliament implemented the Government's proposals. It is not surprising, then, that the conflict over exclusionary policies in the United States also would take place in the courts. Applying British sex discrimination law to the case of exclusionary policies was left to industrial tribunals. The differences in arenas become more apparent when comparing the development of regulations on lead and radiation. The courts were a key decision maker in the United States but were nonparticipants in Britain, confirming the more important role of U.S. courts in setting public policy.

The arena in which the battles take place has significant consequences. Courts and tribunals are less likely than health and safety agencies to have the ability to assess complex scientific questions and may be more likely to be guided by legal principles and doctrine than scientific conclusions. They may feel less competent to determine employment policies. Governmental agencies, on the other hand, may place less emphasis on legal norms such as formal equality. The arena not only determines which rules will apply to making the decision, but who gets to participate and what arguments they may make.

The comparison reveals interest groups to have been more active participants on the issue of exclusionary policies in all arenas in the United States. Working with unions such as the United Auto Workers, feminist litigators, especially the American Civil Liberties Union's Women's Rights Project, made challenging exclusionary policies a priority. Their consultations with the enforcement agencies, the Equal Employment Opportunity Commission and the Occupational Health and Safety Administration, ended with the new Republican administration in 1981. Since that time, they have fought exclusionary policies through arbitration and in the courts. Counsel for feminist groups as well as the EEOC argued as amicus curiae about the scientific and legal issues exclusionary policies raise. Some state occupational health agencies and activist groups have also championed the issue. The strategy reflects the importance courts play in deciding public policy questions, the contingencies of which party controlled the White House, executive agencies, and Congress, and the opportunity presented when different parties control the legislative and executive branches.

The writings of feminist activists and scientists in the United States influenced the few British feminist trade union safety representatives who have challenged the Health and Safety Executive's practice of setting different standards of exposure to substances such as lead and radiation for men and women. Although several articulate health and safety representatives and a committed staffer in the Equal Opportunities Commission addressed the discriminatory consequences of exclusionary policies, neither their organizations nor feminist pressure groups made the issue a priority in litigation or lobbying for legislation. This reflects the low priority health and safety issues command in general in trade unions, as well as the low importance many unions attach to furthering equality. Even if the EOC had aggressively pursued its compromise position, it did not have the power to exert its will on the Health and Safety Executive, trade unions, or employers. The one legal challenge to exclusionary policies in Britain was assisted by the Equal Opportunities Commission on appeal, but was not part of a long-term legal strategy on the part of the EOC, feminist groups, or trade unions to challenge exclusionary policies.

The history of feminists' different approaches to protective legislation in Britain and the United States partially explains differences in reactions to exclusionary policies. During the second wave of feminism, feminists in the United States came to believe that protection led to discrimination, while British feminists continued to believe that it shielded women from exploitation. The so-called equal treatment wing was stronger in the United States, while the so-called special treatment wing was stronger in Britain. The finding that feminists in the United States are more likely than those in Britain to see any legal recognition of difference as discriminatory helps explain their response to exclusionary policies. Given the history of protective legislation, it is not surprising to find that feminists in the United States denounced exclusionary policies as a return to protective legislation and that several judges drew the analogy between the paternalism of *Muller v. Oregon* and exclusionary policies. The discovery that feminists in Britain have not focused on this issue and written about it with the same foreboding is consistent with their greater toleration of legal recognition of difference, as well as their preference for advancing their claims in arenas other than the courts.

When British feminists have taken up the issue of exclusionary policies, however, their positions are closer to their U.S. counterparts than on protective legislation more generally. An important systemic difference that the comparison of litigation on exclusionary policies points out is the closed nature of the British political system and the consequences of this for mobilizing a mass movement women's organization. Unless they work within trade unions, feminists are denied participation in the setting of health and safety standards by a tripartite bureaucracy largely closed to outside groups. Unless they work within political parties, they have little access to Parliament or parliamentary committees. Different legal rules make it harder for British activists to shape how courts and tribunals perceive the issue.

Nor have British feminists had a close working relationship with the Equal Opportunities Commission. The ethos of the British civil service and the low level of politicization of the British bureaucracy means that individuals do not move between interest groups and government. As a result, the EOC is not staffed by leaders in the feminist movement. Its tripartite structure, the failure of the Home Office to appoint dynamic, committed leaders, and restrictions on litigation have limited its effectiveness. Policy and funding limitations of the government of the day also constrain the agency. The EOC intervened in *Page* only on appeal, making legal arguments rather than presenting scientific evidence. The EOC argued that employers may treat women of childbearing capacity differently than other employees in some situations, but urged that the definition of women of childbearing age be flexible.

In contrast, the U.S. Equal Employment Opportunity Commission is more responsive to changes in administrations. In the late 1970s, both the EEOC and OSHA took up the issue of the discriminatory nature of exclusionary policies. The EEOC also proposed interpretive guidelines in 1980 that would have made it difficult for an employer to justify an exclusionary policy under Title VII. The EEOC withdrew its draft guidelines on reproductive hazards shortly before Reagan took office. The agency challenged exclusionary policies as part of broad litigation against sex and race discrimination in *Wright v. Olin*. In *Hayes v. Shelby Memorial Hospital*, the EEOC as amicus again presented both scientific and legal arguments and advocated that the court of appeals declare the hospital's policy to be a violation of Title VII. The agency later prevented the Justice Department from submitting a brief in support of Johnson Controls. Yet under the Reagan and Bush administrations, the EEOC let sit more than forty complaints on discrimination resulting from exclusionary policies, effectively keeping the issue off the public agenda until Congress addressed the issue and the Supreme Court heard *UAW v. Johnson Controls*. While comparisons of the two enforcement agencies in the late 1970s shows that the EEOC was more active in opposing exclusionary policies, the differences narrow when one compares the EEOC under Reagan to the EOC under Thatcher. The lesson to be drawn from comparing the two enforcement agencies in general, as well as on the issue of exclusionary policies, is that the U.S. agency has greater power to either hinder or advance certain sex discrimination policy goals than does its British counterpart.

Comparing the role of courts and industrial tribunals in cases on exclusionary policies in the two countries highlights differences between the judiciaries, the roles of the courts in the political systems, and roles of litigation in promoting social change. British feminists are understandably cautious about pinning their hopes on courts and industrial tribunals. Close inspection of the behavior of industrial tribunals in cases involving discrimination leads to the conclusion that the system will need overhauling to meet its aims. Not only has the tribunal system failed to be informal and inquisitorial, but members made frequent errors in applying the law, made comments in conflict with the purposes of the act, and were reluctant to find that discrimination occurred. Women have not found it easy to make their case; skilled representation, available to few complainants, increased the likelihood of success. The meager awards neither remedied the harm of discrimination nor deterred employers.

Many judges and members of industrial tribunals have been unsympathetic to the purpose of the Sex Discrimination Act. Furthermore, they are less likely than their U.S. counterparts to see their role as upholding individual rights and restraining the government. They lack a feminist perspective on cases before them, not only because the bench and bar are male dominated, but because feminists bring few test cases and rarely participate as amicus curiae. Trade unions and feminist groups are just beginning to coordinate assisting complainants and have yet to lobby effectively for more supportive panel members. While feminists in the United States have placed more emphasis on the legal arena, British feminists are now beginning not only to develop a coordinated legal strategy but also to use European Community law to bolster their cases.

Exploring the British case of *Page v. Freight Hire* in detail confirms findings about British sex discrimination law. The opinion reveals considerable confusion over which party has the burden of proof. The EAT effectively held that Jackie Page, to prove discrimination, must prove that DMF was harmful to men, or that she was not exposed to dangerous levels, or that alternatives to exclusion existed, or that she would not become pregnant. In *Page*, as in the cases Leonard studied, the industrial tribunal seemed reluctant to conclude that discrimination had occurred, although it agreed that Freight Hire had treated Page less favorably on the grounds of sex. The industrial tribunal did not feel compelled to demand additional evidence. Nor did the EAT require the tribunal to rehear the case and hear evidence on the hazards of DMF to men. The EAT's interpretation of section 51 of the Sex Discrimination Act of 1975 confirms the finding that members of tribunals do not interpret the act in a way that gives it maximum force. They appear unsympathetic to the harm of discrimination and fail to scrutinize employers' accounts of their behavior. In short, they are not very suspicious of differential treatment on the basis of sex. Finally, *Page* highlights the importance of specialized representation, knowledgeable about both industrial tribunals' performance in sex discrimination cases and the necessary scientific evidence.

The lack of help Page received from feminist groups and her trade union contrasts with the assistance available to women in the United States.

Johnston highlights the differences between the problems of reproductive hazards in female- and male-dominated workplaces. The industrial tribunal required the employer to at least try to accommodate a pregnant woman worker's concerns about the safety of working on a video display unit. The tribunal found firing her for refusing to work on a VDU to be unlawful sex discrimination. Johnston is one example of Leonard's finding that Scottish tribunals were more inquisitorial and more likely to scrutinize carefully employers' behavior than their English counterparts. Johnston raised questions that will be important in the future. How do employers and tribunals respond to limited or even contradictory evidence about reproductive hazards? What alternatives and accommodation must employers provide to male and female workers planning to become parents? How does the fact that most of the workers in a given job are men or women affect what course of action employers choose?

Although their record is mixed, U.S. courts have been more likely to declare exclusionary policies unlawful. Some judges in the United States have, in the past, been supportive of Title VII, expanding its scope, scrutinizing employers' policies, and ordering significant remedies.[5] In *Zuniga v. Kleberg County Hospital*, the Court of Appeals for the Fifth Circuit, applying Title VII prior to the passage of the Pregnancy Discrimination Act, held that employers must consider alternatives short of firing pregnant women whose fetuses may be at risk from exposure to hazardous substances at work—the same result as in a case the EEOC decided in 1975. In *Doerr v. B. F. Goodrich*, the District Court for the Northern District of Ohio declined to issue a temporary injunction prohibiting an exclusionary policy; instead, the court directed Doerr to file a complaint and allow the EEOC to try conciliation as prescribed by Title VII. The court did, however, suggest in its opinion that such exclusionary policies were not inconsistent with Title VII.

Although judges in the United States departed from precedent on Title VII, allowing employers to justify exclusionary policies under an expanded business necessity defense, the arguments of plaintiffs and amici in *Zuniga*, *Olin*, and *Hayes* led judges to set high standards for justifying an exclusionary policy. In *Olin*, the Court of Appeals for the Fourth Circuit allowed Olin Corporation to offer a business necessity defense, but established guidelines that an exclusionary policy must meet to be lawful under Title VII. In *Hayes v. Shelby Memorial Hospital*, the Court of Appeals for the Eleventh Circuit

---

5. To suggest that there is a difference between the two groups, however, is not to suggest that the U.S. judiciary has been exemplary. Many legal scholars commenting on U.S. judges' handling of exclusionary policies decried the sex bias of the judiciary; see, as one example, Becker, 1260–61.

quibbled with the analysis of *Olin* but reached the same conclusion. In *Hayes*, the court held that the employer did not meet the first step of the *Olin* guidelines because it had not proven that pregnant X-ray technicians put their fetuses at risk.

Before the Seventh Circuit's ruling in *UAW v. Johnson Controls*, courts placed the burden of proof squarely on an employer who wanted to justify an exclusionary policy. No specific policy was finally upheld to be lawful. The Seventh Circuit's reversal of that standard in *UAW v. Johnson Controls*, in effect placing the burden of proof on an employee to prove an exclusionary policy unjustified, was overturned by the Supreme Court. The Court of Appeals for the Sixth Circuit in *Grant* and the Supreme Court in *UAW v. Johnson Controls* switched the rubric from disparate impact to disparate treatment making it impossible for an employer to justify an exclusionary policy under Title VII. With radical changes in the composition of the U.S. judiciary, the two systems may be becoming more alike. Feminists in the United States, faced with a federal judiciary of Reagan and Bush appointees, may also be more likely to diversify their efforts to other arenas. The Supreme Court's decision in *UAW v. Johnson Controls*, however, illustrates how complex the relationship is between the conservatism of the judges and their views on exclusionary policies.

Differences in the wording of the two countries' sex discrimination laws also have affected the outcomes of cases on exclusionary policies. Although a comparison reveals the statutes to be similar (the British Sex Discrimination Act was modeled on Title VII), there are two significant differences. First, Title VII, as amended by the Pregnancy Discrimination Act, contains an explicit prohibition against pregnancy discrimination. Second, the British Sex Discrimination Act contains loopholes, most important, section 51, which (even as amended) permits discrimination if treating men and women differently is necessary to comply with another law. The wording of the statutes alone is not enough to determine what judges and industrial tribunals will do in specific cases, but the differences in the wording of the statutes do matter. While lower courts in the United States chose to ignore or reinterpret the Pregnancy Discrimination Act, in *UAW v. Johnson Controls* the Supreme Court declared its mandate to be unambiguous and restored prior doctrine.

The responses of judges and members of tribunals, administrative agencies, pressure groups, and legislators to exclusionary policies are best understood in the context of their efforts and positions surrounding issues of sex discrimination. Only by grounding the analysis of specific cases in the broader context of sex discrimination doctrine and the operation of political and legal institutions do the cases make sense. Looking only at the cases on exclusionary policies without viewing the two countries' sex discrimination laws might lead to overstating the differences. Part of the British industrial tribunal's failure to scrutinize an employer's exclusionary policy may well stem from a more general reluctance to interfere with business practices, a desire to avoid delving into evaluations of scientific evidence, and a reluctance to engage in policy-making. Differences in outcomes also may reflect the relative newness of the British legislation. Other, more general features of the law and legal culture distinguish the two countries. In the United States, a constitutional guarantee of equal protection in governmental actions, contract compliance, and affirmative action supplement Title VII and create a more favorable climate for the promotion of equal employment opportunity. Furthermore, the possibility of class action suits and the widespread participation of interest groups as amicus curiae have aided the cause. The ability to take cases on a contingency fee basis, the support provided for legal aid, and the amount of money trade unions and governmental agencies have for litigation all make it easier for complainants to bring cases in the United States.

In the United States, but not in Britain, the agency whose duty it is to enforce health and safety regulations, OSHA, has been a party to litigation. The case resulting from an OSHA citation to American Cyanamid, in which OSHA fined the company for requiring women who were exposed to lead to be sterilized, is important because Cyanamid's policy came to symbolize exclusionary policies and the case was a catalyst for the mobilization of feminists, trade unionists, and health and safety specialists against exclusionary policies. The result of the Cyanamid case is that, unless OSHA issues a generic policy on reproductive hazards or incorporates concern for reproductive injury in standards of exposure for specific substances, the agency is powerless to stop exclusionary policies. *Cyanamid* foreclosed the possibility of using the general duty clause of the Occupational Safety and Health Act to prevent employers from excluding women workers or requiring proof of sterilization.

The Concept of Discrimination

Judges in the United States may have been more willing to examine the scientific evidence, more suspicious of sex-based categories, and more likely to require employers to pursue less-discriminatory alternatives than judges and members of tribunals in Britain. The outcomes in cases on exclusionary policies ultimately reflect these differences. If, however, we compare the reasoning in the opinions rather than the holdings, and if we analyze all the opinions rather than merely the final opinion in each case, striking similarities emerge. British tribunals ignored the law's definition of discrimination in cases on exclusionary policies. They substituted their own standard of reasonableness for the law's definition of less favorable treatment on the basis of sex. Their behavior is consistent with their behavior in other sex discrimination cases.

In the United States, where judges are less likely to view differential treatment as reasonable, some judges abandoned traditional Title VII doctrine. Although exclusionary policies are facially discriminatory, some judges treated them as neutral policies and allowed employers to try to justify them under a modified business necessity defense. The judges who permitted this maneuver (the Supreme Court eventually rejected it) varied on how high a standard of justification they required of employers. While analyzing exclusionary policies under the rubric of disparate impact was a surprising departure from traditional Title VII analysis, it was not without precedent in equal protection doctrine. In cases such as *Michael M.* and *Rostker*, U.S. courts have concluded that differential treatment on the basis of sex was not discriminatory when based on "real" differences between the sexes. While judges in the United States, like their British counterparts, may hold that treating men and women differently when they are not "similarly situated" does not constitute discrimination, judges in the United States are more likely to be suspicious of claims that differences between men and women are relevant. While this skepticism is very much evident at the court of appeals in the appeals of *Hayes* and *Olin* and with the Supreme Court in *UAW v. Johnson Controls*, it did not guarantee that all U.S. judges found differential treatment to be unjustified.

A close reading of the legal opinions in cases on exclusionary policies thus provides an opportunity to analyze and critique the concept of discrimination embedded in the law in both Britain and the United States. When combined with an analysis of other sex discrimination cases, opinions in cases on exclusionary policies show that judges and members of tribunals tend to distinguish between "real" and stereotypical differences between men and women. Only acting on the latter constitutes discrimination. Underpinning this dichotomy is a belief in a rigid distinction between sex and gender as well as an empiricist belief that sex differences are knowable. In *Page*, for example, the tribunal saw men and women as different in relevant respects and allowed employers to treat women differently, accepting the assertion that men and women differed in relevant respects without substantiation. Analyzing exclusionary policies demonstrates, however, that the scientific "facts" about sex differences are contested terrain. Are men and women similar in their ability to damage their offspring through exposure to hazardous substances? Is the fetus more susceptible than adults? Are women more subject to reproductive injury than men? Do the answers to these questions vary depending on the substance in question? Given present scientific technique, how much certainty can we have about our answers to these questions?

At best, cases on exclusionary policies show that the science of reproductive hazards has been biased against studying male effects. At worst, an exploration of the scientific evidence shows it to reflect our cultural norms about the attributes and relative value of males and females. Regardless of one's degree of skepticism about what we can know about reproductive hazards from scientific inquiry, regardless of whether one takes an empiricist or more postmodern view, analyzing cases on exclusionary policies lends support to Michel Foucault's proposition that the mechanisms of power are not merely repressive, but constitutive. That is, giving judges and members of tribunals the power to define sex differences and then to construct their findings as givens, truths, or discovered facts is an immense power when one considers that employers are acting lawfully when they base their policies on the judges' ideas about "real" sex differences. The power of British judges and members of tribunals to determine what the "real" differences are between the sexes that employers may recognize is even more immense when one considers how few participants in the process are in a position to challenge or disrupt judges' and tribunal members' unexamined views about what those differences are. In the United States, specialist lawyers and amici presented strong scientific evidence that persuaded some judges that men and women were not sufficiently different that employers could exclude women from hazardous work.

Cases on exclusionary policies also illuminate the concept of discrimination by illustrating that many judges and members of tribunals think of discrimination as intentional acts motivated by prejudice, a characteristic of bad people, or a disease, rather than the result of unexamined and changeable institutional practices. Since the employers do not seem like bad guys but as people who want to protect babies, how can judges and members of tribunals find them "guilty" of discrimination? The perception of some U.S. judges that employers were not intentionally excluding women but sincerely trying to protect their offspring may have caused them to treat exclusionary policies as neutral, thereby altering the burden of proof.

Cases on exclusionary policies also offer an excellent example of how discrimination law employs a male standard. Employers discriminate when they fail to treat likes alike but do not discriminate if they treat people who are different differently. Under this approach, once employers have established a relevant difference between the sexes—a "real" rather than stereotypical difference—treating men and women differently does not constitute discrimination. Not only does this comparative standard rest on the assumption that we can separate stereotypes from true differences—it fails to recognize that sex differences are socially constructed—but the comparative approach fails to ask, different than whom? Men and women are different than each other; but when you employ a male standard, the difference lies within the woman—

something is different about *her*. Adopting a comparative standard freezes the status quo that employs rules that work to women's disadvantage. By adopting exclusionary policies, employers were taking the position that the male worker must be the standard for all health and safety standards. If women and their offspring need a different level to protect them, the employer can refuse to hire them.

Justice Scalia's concurrence in *UAW v. Johnson Controls* inadvertently challenges the view that, once judges discover a real difference, it is all right to treat men and women differently, even if it leads to women's continued subordination, although he would probably assert that he was merely strictly interpreting the statute. Justice Scalia argued that Title VII prohibits employers from excluding fertile women from hazardous work, not because men face reproductive hazards from lead, too, but because the Pregnancy Discrimination Act states unambiguously that employers may not exclude women from jobs because of their capacity to become pregnant. Justice Blackmun, too, refers to the plain language of the Pregnancy Discrimination Act, but Justice Scalia explicitly mentions that a comparison is not necessary. In *UAW v. Johnson Controls*, the Supreme Court says unequivocally that whether women can compare themselves to men or not, the law forbids employers punishing women because they can bear children—the statute says that though men and women may have different reproductive capacities, it is discriminatory to treat them differently.

Judges and members of industrial tribunals' substitution of their standard of reasonableness for the law's definition of discrimination, while more pronounced in Britain than the United States, highlights the importance of the composition of the judiciary. What individuals take to be the facts of sex differences, what importance they attach to women's equal employment opportunity, whether they see women's primary role as childbearer, how they assess risk, and how they conceptualize discrimination all affect the outcome of cases on exclusionary policies. In his dissenting opinion for the Seventh Circuit Court of Appeals in *UAW v. Johnson Controls*, Judge Cudahy eloquently noted that all the judges deciding cases on exclusionary policies in the United States (before Justice O'Connor heard *UAW v. Johnson Controls*) had been men. Judge Cudahy acknowledged that one's life experiences determined how one approached the case. Examining cases on exclusionary policies thus helps to debunk the idea that legal cases are decided through the use of disembodied reason and the objective application of legal rules. The Senate Judiciary Committee's grappling with the question of what was "reasonable" behavior for a victim of sexual harassment during the confirmation hearings of Judge Clarence Thomas recently proved the importance of one's life experiences to understanding certain issues. Similarly, analyzing cases on exclusionary policies shows the consequences of the distance between the experiences of those deciding cases on exclusionary policies and working-class women.

Finally, exploring the cases on exclusionary policies continues the debate within the women's movement and feminist theory about difference and equality. Grounding this debate historically and comparing their positions over time offers a context for understanding why British and U.S. feminists took different positions on protective legislation in the 1970s and 1980s. Learning about protective legislation in the United States during this time taught me that the one "true" feminist position opposed such legal distinctions. Learning why British feminists might think differently led me to reconsider the history of protective legislation in both countries and to conclude there were always feminists and working-class women on both sides of the debate. True to my origins, I still find protective legislation problematic, and my study of exclusionary policies has further reinforced this view. But my exploration of contrasting views has left me with an appreciation of how complex it is to formulate a legal strategy on questions of equality and difference and the drawbacks of each of the choices. However much I have rethought protective legislation in general, I am unmoved in my conviction that, while sound workplace policies that protect the health and safety of all workers have yet to be negotiated, getting rid of exclusionary policies is a step in the right direction.

Conclusions

What does the future hold for "the occupational health issue of the 1980s"?[6] In the United States, the Supreme Court's decision in *UAW v. Johnson Controls* resolved one issue raised by exclusionary policies. It interpreted Title VII and the Pregnancy Discrimination Act as outlawing all such policies. Congress could legislatively overturn this decision, but such a prospect is unlikely. Although *UAW v. Johnson Controls* put women's exclusion from hazardous work back on the public agenda and eliminated one "solution" employers have offered to the problem of protecting workers from reproductive hazards, finding an alternative solution has yet to be accomplished.

The decision of the Court of Appeals for the District of Columbia Circuit that American Cyanamid's exclusionary policy was not a violation of health and safety law, combined with OSHA's failure to address the problem in the 1980s, shifted the legal debate from the terrain of health and safety to a debate over equality. Now that the Supreme Court has declared exclusionary policies to be discriminatory, the impediment to discussions about protecting the re-

---

6. M. Donald Whorton, "Adverse Reproductive Outcomes: The Occupational Health Issue of the 1980s," *American Journal of Public Health* 73 (January 1983): 15–16.

productive health of all workers and the effects of toxins on workers more generally is gone. Because feminists did not seek equal rights for men and women to poison their offspring, but sought equal access to a workplace free from hazards, reproductive or nonreproductive, for all workers, the battle has only begun. *UAW v. Johnson Controls* removed the obstacle to focusing on the workplace by displacing attention from the sex of the worker. The debate now returns to health and safety rather than equality and difference. Yet it remains to be seen how employers will fashion gender-neutral policies that protect the reproductive health of their employees.

How will British feminists, trade unionists, judges, policymakers, enforcement agency officials, and employers react to the outcome in *UAW v. Johnson Controls*? Given high levels of unemployment, few women in Britain are entering hazardous jobs traditionally held by men. With few exceptions, feminists and trade unionists have not devoted energy to this issue. Although companies are increasingly aware of the problem,[7] few will discuss their policies and practices, even with sympathetic journalists.[8] The issue has not been a high priority in Britain, nor is it likely to be soon. One possible force for change would be if the European Commission took up the issue or if a woman successfully pursued a discrimination claim before the European Court of Justice. Will the Supreme Court's ruling make any difference in how these groups regard the issue of exclusionary policies? Will the attention focused on this issue in the United States affect discussions in Britain and the European Community? Will more working women come forward to challenge such policies? Will those engaged in health and safety policy-making be less likely to sanction policies that exclude all women from hazardous work? Will feminist litigators seek additional test cases or campaign on the issue in other arenas? Will the revival of the issue in the United States have any impact at all on how the United Kingdom and European Community address the issue? How the "resolution" of the issue in the United States affects policy, thinking about discrimination, and interest-group opinion and strategy in Britain will be an interesting area to watch in the future.

7. Chemical Industries Association, *Employment and Reproductive Health* (London: Chemical Industries Association, 1984).

8. The *Health and Safety Information Bulletin* wrote to a number of companies asking them to confidentially discuss their policies with me. All but two declined. Their letters revealed deep concern that the discrimination issue not become part of public discussion in Britain.

Abbreviations

ACLU   American Civil Liberties Union (U.S.)

ASTMS   Association of Scientific, Technical, and Managerial Staffs (U.K.)

CBI   Confederation of British Industry (U.K.)

CRROW   Coalition for the Reproductive Rights of Workers (U.S.)

EAT   Employment Appeal Tribunal (U.K.)

EEOC   Equal Employment Opportunity Commission (U.S.)

EOC   Equal Opportunities Commission (U.K.)

EPA   Environmental Protection Agency (U.S.)

HSE   Health and Safety Executive (U.K.)

NCCL   National Council for Civil Liberties (U.K.)

NOW   National Organization for Women (U.S.)

OSHA   Occupational Safety and Health Administration (U.S.)

PDA   Pregnancy Discrimination Act (U.S.)

Quango Quasiautonomous nongovernmental organization (U.K.)

SDA   Sex Discrimination Act (U.K.)

T&G   Transport and General Workers Union (U.K.)

TUC   Trades Union Congress (U.K.)

UAW   International Union, United Automobile, Aerospace and Agricultural Implement Workers of America (U.S.)

WLDF   Women's Legal Defense Fund (U.S. and U.K.)

Selected Bibliography

Alexander, Sally. *Women's Work in Nineteenth-Century London: A Study of the Years 1820–50*. London: Journeyman Press, 1983.

"All Pregnancy Dismissals Breach EEC Law." *Industrial Relations Legal Information Bulletin* 414 (December 7, 1990): 11–12.

Angell, Ernest. "The Amicus Curiae: American Development of English Institutions." *International and Comparative Law Quarterly* 16 (October 1967): 1017–44.

Appelby, George, and Evelyn Ellis. "Formal Investigations: The Commission for Racial Equality and the Equal Opportunities Commission as Law Enforcement Agencies." *Public Law*, Summer 1984, 236–76.

Arnull, Anthony. "The Direct Effect of Directives: Grasping the Nettle." *International and Comparative Law Quarterly* 35 (October 1986): 939–46.

Ashford, Nicholas A. "Legal Mechanisms for Controlling Reproductive Hazards in the Workplace." *Occupational Health and Safety* 52 (February 1983): 10.

———, and Charles C. Caldart. "The Control of Reproductive Hazards in the Workplace: A Prescription for Prevention." *Industrial Relations Law Journal* 5 (1983): 523–63.

Atkins, Susan, and Brenda Hoggett. *Women and the Law*. Oxford: Basil Blackwell, 1984.

Babcock, Barbara Allen, Ann E. Freedman, Eleanor Holmes Norton, and Susan C. Ross. *Sex Discrimination and the Law: Causes and Remedies*. Boston: Little, Brown, 1975.

Baer, Judith A. *The Chains of Protection: The Judicial Response to Women's Labor Legislation*. Westport, Conn.: Greenwood, 1978.

———. "Equality and Protection in the Twentieth Century." Paper presented at the annual meeting of the Midwest Political Science Association, Chicago, April 1984.

———. "Nasty Law or Nice Ladies?: Jurisprudence, Feminism, and Gender Difference." *Women and Politics* 11 (1991): 1–31.

Bailey, Suzanne. "Maternity Rights." *Industrial Law Journal* 17 (September 1985): 191–95.

"Ban On Woman Transporting DMF Not Unlawful Discrimination." *Health and Safety Information Bulletin* 62 (February 1981): 18–19.

Banks, Olive. *Faces of Feminism: A Study of Feminism as a Social Movement*. Oxford: Martin Robertson, 1981.

Barlow, Susan M., and Frank M. Sullivan. *Reproductive Hazards of Industrial Chemicals*. London: Academic Press, 1982.

Bayer, Ronald. "Women, Work, and Reproductive Hazards." *Hastings Center Report* 12 (October 1982): 14–19.

Beard, Jane, and Marcia D. Greenberger. "Women and the Law." In *Women in Washington: Advocates for Public Policy*, edited by Irene Tinker, 165–76. Beverly Hills: Sage, 1983.

Becker, Mary E. "From *Muller v. Oregon* to Fetal Vulnerability Policies." *University of Chicago Law Review* 53 (Fall 1986): 1219–73.

Bell, Carolyn. "Implementing Safety and Health Regulations for Women in the Workplace." *Feminist Studies* 5 (1979): 286–301.

Belloni, Frank. "Politics and the Law: Industrial Conflict in Britain." Paper presented at the annual meeting of the American Political Science Association, Washington, D.C., August 1986.

Benn, Melissa, Anna Coote, and Tess Gill. *The Rape Controversy*. London: National Council for Civil Liberties Rights for Women Unit, 1983.

Berg, Richard K. "Title VII: A Three Years' View." *Notre Dame Lawyer* 44 (February 1969): 311–44.

Berger, Margaret A. *Litigation on Behalf of Women: A Review for the Ford Foundation*. New York: Ford Foundation, 1980.

Bertin, Joan E. "Occupational Hazards to Reproductive Health: Conflicts Redefine Issues and Solutions." *Labor Relations* (P–H) ¶40,219 (November 1, 1985).

———. Review of *Double Exposure: Women's Health Hazards on the Job and at Home*, edited by Wendy Chavkin. *Women's Rights Law Reporter* 9 (Winter 1986): 89–93.

———. "Workplace Bias Takes the Form of 'Fetal Protectionism.' " *Legal Times* 6 (August 1, 1983): 18.

Bird, Carolyn. *Born Female: The High Cost of Keeping Women Down*. New York: David McKay, 1968.

Blakesee, Sandra. "Father Figures: The Male Link to Birth Defects." *American Health* 10 (April 1991): 54–57.

———. "Research on Birth Defects Turns to Flaws in Sperm." *New York Times*, January 1, 1991.

Blanco, Alan Carlos. "Fetal Protection Programs Under Title VII—Rebutting the Procreation Presumption." *University of Pittsburgh Law Review* 46 (1985): 755–94.

Blank, Robert H. "Fetal Protection Policies in the Workplace." Paper presented at the annual meeting of the Midwest Political Science Association, Chicago, April 1991.

Boffey, Chris. "I Got the Sack for Being a Girl—Jackie." *Daily Star*, March 27, 1980.

Bor, Victoria L. "Exclusionary Employment Practices in Hazardous Industries: Protection or Discrimination?" *Columbia Journal of Environmental Law* 5 (1978): 97–155.

Bordo, Susan R. "The Body and the Reproduction of Femininity: A Feminist Appropriation of Foucault." In *Gender/Body/Knowledge: Feminist Reconstructions of Being and Knowing*, edited by Alison Jaggar and Susan R. Bordo, 13–33. New Brunswick, N.J.: Rutgers University Press, 1989.

"Bork's Opinion in Sterilization Case at Issue in Senate Hearing." *Workplace Health* (BPI), September 23, 1987, 156–57.

Bourn, Colin. "The Defense of Justifiability." *Industrial Law Journal* 18 (1989): 170–73.

———, and John Whitmore. *The Law of Discrimination and Equal Pay.* London: Sweet and Maxwell, 1989.

Braybon, Gail. *Women Workers in the First World War: The British Experience.* London: Croom Helm, 1981.

Bridge, John. "American Analogues in the Law of the European Community." *Anglo-American Law Review* 11 (April-June 1982): 130–54.

"Bring Out the Stilettos." *Economist*, July 11, 1987.

"Britain: There's Plenty Still to Do." *Economist*, June 27, 1987.

"British EEO Agency Warns Employers that Discharge for Pregnancy is Illegal." *Daily Labor Report* (BNA) 175 (September 11, 1987): A5.

Bronson, Gail. "Bitter Reaction: Issue of Fetal Damage Stirs Women Workers at Chemical Plants." *Wall Street Journal*, February 9, 1979.

Brown, Lionel Neville. *The Court of Justice of the European Communities.* 3d ed. London: Sweet and Maxwell, 1989.

Buckley, Mary, and Malcolm Anderson, eds. *Women, Equality and Europe.* London: Macmillan, 1988.

Bureau of National Affairs. *Pregnancy and Employment: The Complete Handbook on Discrimination, Maternity Leave, and Health and Safety.* Washington, D.C.: Bureau of National Affairs, 1987.

Burstein, Paul. *Discrimination, Jobs, and Politics: The Struggle for Equal Employment Opportunity in the United States since the New Deal.* Chicago: University of Chicago Press, 1985.

Buss, Emily. "Getting Beyond Discrimination: A Regulatory Solution to the Problem of Fetal Hazards in the Workplace." *Yale Law Journal* 95 (1986): 577–98.

Byre, Angela. *Indirect Discrimination.* Manchester: Equal Opportunities Commission, 1987.

Byrne, Paul, and Joni Lovenduski. "The Equal Opportunities Commission." *Women's Studies International Quarterly* 1 (1978): 131–47.

Cairncross, Francis. "Is the EOC Worth £3 Million of Public Money?" *Guardian*, December 7, 1983.

Campbell, A. "The Single European Act and the Implications." *International and Comparative Law Quarterly* 35 (October 1986): 932–39.

Carter, April. *The Politics of Women's Rights.* London: Longman, 1988.

Carty, Hazel. "The Sex Discrimination Act 1986: Equality or Employment Deregulation?" *Journal of Social Welfare Law*, 1987, 175–79.

Chafe, William H. *The American Woman: Her Changing Social, Economic, and Political Roles, 1920–1970.* London: Oxford University Press, 1972.

Chamallas, Martha. "Evolving Conceptions of Equality Under Title VII: Disparate Impact Theory and the Demise of the Bottom Line Principle." *UCLA Law Review* 31 (December 1983): 305–83.

———. "Listening to Dr. Fiske: The Easy Case of *Price Waterhouse v. Hopkins.*" *Vermont Law Review* 15 (Summer 1990): 89–124.

Chamberlain, Geoffrey, ed. *Pregnant Women at Work*. London: The Royal Society of Medicine and Macmillan, 1984.

Chapman, Fern Schumer. "A No-win Dilemma for All Sides." *USA Today*, October 11, 1990.

Chavkin, Wendy, ed. *Double Exposure: Women's Health Hazards on the Job and at Home*. New York: Monthly Review Press, 1984.

———. "Hazards to Reproduction: A Review Essay and Annotated Bibliography." *Feminist Studies* 5 (1979): 310–29.

———. Response to Joan Bertin's Review of *Double Exposure: Women's Health Hazards on the Job and at Home*. *Women's Rights Law Reporter* 9 (Spring 1986): 179–80.

"Chemical Ban on Woman Driver Upheld." *Evening Gazette*, May 28, 1980.

Chemical Industries Association. *Employment and Reproductive Health*. London: Chemical Industries Association, 1984.

"Chemical May Draw Sperm to Egg." *New York Times*, April 2, 1991.

Chenier, Nancy Miller. *Reproductive Hazards at Work: Men, Women, and the Fertility Gamble*. Ottawa: Canadian Advisory Council on the Status of Women, 1982.

Cimons, Marlene. "Protection of Women or Sex Bias: Unions, Feminists Protest Guidelines." *Los Angeles Times*, April 10, 1980.

Coalition for the Reproductive Rights of Workers Newsletter 1 (Spring 1981).

Cohen, Sherrill, and Nadine Taub, eds. *Reproductive Laws for the 1990s*. Clifton, N.J.: Humana Press, 1989.

Colker, Ruth. "Privacy or Sex Discrimination Doctrine: Must There Be a Choice?" *Harvard Women's Law Journal* 4 (1981): ix–xiv.

"Comments Oppose EEOC Hazardous Job Guides." *Daily Labor Report* (BNA) 133 (July 9, 1980): A-5, G-1.

"Company and Union in Dispute as Women Undergo Sterilization." *New York Times*, January 4, 1979.

Conaghan, Joanne. "Statutory Maternity Pay Under the Social Security Act 1986." *Industrial Law Journal* 16 (June 1987): 125–29.

———, and Louise Chudleigh. "Women in Confinement: Can Labour Law Deliver the Goods?" *Journal of Law and Society* 14 (Spring 1987): 133–47.

Cook, Blanche Wiesen, ed. *Crystal Eastman on Women and Revolution*. New York: Oxford University Press, 1978.

Cooke, Edmund D., Jr., and Sally J. Kenney. "Commentary: The View from Capitol Hill." In *Reproductive Laws for the 1990s*, edited by Sherrill Cohen and Nadine Taub, 331–40. Clifton, N.J.: Humana Press, 1988.

Cooper, Sandi E. "Introduction to the Documents." *Signs* 4 (Summer 1986): 753–79.

———. "Women's Work on Trial." *New Directions for Women* 14 (November/December 1985): 1–2.

Coote, Anna. *Women Factory Workers: The Case Against Repealing the Protective Laws*. London: National Council for Civil Liberties, 1975.

———, and Beatrix Campbell. *Sweet Freedom: The Struggle for Women's Liberation*. London: Picador, 1982.

Corcoran, Jennifer. "Enforcement Procedures for Individual Complaints: Equal Pay and Equal Treatment." In *Women, Equality and Europe*, edited by Mary Buckley and Malcolm Anderson, 56–70. London: Macmillan, 1988.

Cott, Nancy F. *The Grounding of Modern Feminism.* New Haven: Yale University Press, 1987.

Coussins, Jean. *Maternity Rights for Working Women.* 2d ed. London: National Council for Civil Liberties Rights for Women Unit, 1980.

_____. *The Shift Work Swindle . . . Or How the EOC's Proposals to Repeal Protective Legislation Would Really Affect Women Workers.* London: National Council for Civil Liberties Rights for Women Unit, 1979.

Coyle, Angela. "The Protection Racket?" *Feminist Review* 4 (1980): 1–12.

Creighton, William B. *Working Women and the Law.* London: Mansell, 1979.

Crowell, Donald R., and David A. Copus. "Safety and Equality at Odds: OSHA and Title VII Clash over Health Hazards in the Workplace." *Industrial Relations Law Journal* 2 (1978): 567–95.

Curtin, Deirdre. *Irish Employment Equality Law.* Blackrock, County Dublin: Round Hall Press, 1989.

_____. "The Province of Government: Delimiting the Direct Effect of Directives in the Common Law Context." *European Law Review* 15 (June 1990): 195–223.

_____. "Scalping the Community Legislator: Occupational Pensions and *Barber.*" *Common Market Law Review* 27 (1990): 475–506.

"Cyanamid Closes Plant Cited in Sterilization Case." *New York Times,* January 16, 1980.

Dahlerup, Drude, ed. *The New Women's Movement: Feminism and Political Power in Europe and the USA.* London: Sage, 1986.

Dalton, Alan J. P. *Health and Safety at Work.* London: Cassell, 1982.

Daniel, W. W. *Maternity Rights: The Experience of Women.* London: Policy Studies Institute, June 1980.

Daniels, Lee. "Five Makers of Agent Orange Charge U.S. Misused Chemical in Vietnam: Companies Replying to Suit, Say Federal Negligence Is Responsible For Any Harm to Veterans and Kin." *New York Times,* January 7, 1980.

Darcy, Lynne. "Birth Defects Caused by Parental Exposure to Workplace Hazards: The Interface of Title VII with OSHA and Tort Law." *Journal of Law Reform* 12 (1979): 237–60.

Davis, Anne. "Patronage and Quasi-Government: Some Proposals for Reform." In *Quangos in Britain: Government and the Networks of Public Policy-Making,* edited by Anthony Barker, 167–80. London: Macmillan, 1982.

Davis, Devra Lee. "Fathers and Fetuses." *New York Times,* January 1, 1991.

Deakin, Simon. "Equality Under a Market Order: The Employment Act of 1989." *International Law Journal* 19 (1980): 1–19.

Dickens, Linda. "Justice in the Industrial Tribunal System." *Industrial Law Journal* 17 (March 1988): 58–61.

Dingwall, Helen. "Protective Legislation for Women: A Case of Legal Discrimination?" B.Sc. diss., University of Bath, 1983.

Docksey, Christopher. "The European Community and the Promotion of Equality." In *Women, Employment and European Equality Law,* edited by Christopher Mc-Crudden, 1–22. London: Eclipse, 1987.

Downing, Paul M. *The Equal Employment Opportunity Act of 1972: Legislative History.* Washington, D.C.: Congressional Research Service, 1972.

_____. *Federal Protection of Equal Employment Opportunity for Racial and Ethnic*

Minorities and for Women in the Private Sector. Washington, D.C.: Congressional Research Service, 1983.

Doyal, Lesley, Ken Green, Alan Irwin, Dougie Russell, Fred Steward, Robin Williams, David Gee, and Samuel Epstein. *Cancer in Britain: The Politics of Prevention.* London: Pluto Press, 1983.

Drake, Charles D., and Frank B. Wright. *Law of Health and Safety at Work: The New Approach.* London: Sweet and Maxwell, 1983.

Durward, Lyn. "Changes in Maternity Payments." *Legal Action*, April 1987, 9–11.

————. "Maternity Rights in Crisis." *Rights of Women Bulletin*, December 1986, 21.

————. "More Legislation, Fewer Rights—A New Sex Discrimination Bill." *Rights of Women Bulletin*, December 1986, 20–21.

Dworkin, Ronald. *Taking Rights Seriously.* Cambridge, Mass.: Harvard University Press, 1977.

Dye, Nancy Schrom. *As Equals and As Sisters: Feminism, the Labor Movement, and the Women's Trade Union League of New York.* Columbia: University of Missouri Press, 1980.

Edwards, Susan. *Female Sexuality and the Law: A Study of Constructs of Female Sexuality as they Inform Statute and Legal Procedure.* Oxford: Martin Robertson, 1981.

"EEC Law Does Not Override SDA Compensation Limit." *Equal Opportunities Review Discrimination Case Law Digest* 5 (Autumn 1990): 1.

Eisenstein, Hester. *Contemporary Feminist Thought.* London: Unwin, 1984.

Eisenstein, Zillah R. *The Female Body and the Law.* Berkeley: University of California Press, 1988.

Ellis, Evelyn. *Sex Discrimination Law.* Brookfield, Vt.: Gower, 1988.

————, and Philip Morrell. "Sex Discrimination in Pension Schemes: Has Community Law Changed the Rules?" *Industrial Law Journal* 11 (March 1982): 16–28.

"The Employment Act of 1989." *Industrial Relations Legal Information Bulletin* 391 (December 19, 1989): 2–8.

Epstein, Samuel S. *The Politics of Cancer.* Rev. ed. Garden City, N.Y.: Anchor Press, 1979.

Erickson, Nancy S. "*Muller v. Oregon* Reconsidered: The Origins of a Sex-Based Doctrine of Liberty of Contract." Paper presented at the annual meeting of the Association of Social and Legal Historians, Baltimore, Md., October, 1983.

Equal Opportunities Review. *Discrimination Case Law Digest* 1 (Autumn 1989).

————. *Discrimination Case Law Digest* 6 (Winter 1990).

Evans, Richard J. *The Feminists: Women's Emancipation Movements in Europe, America and Australia, 1840–1920.* Totowa, N.J.: Barnes and Noble, 1977.

Faludi, Susan. "Your Womb or Your Job." *Mother Jones* 16 (November/December 1991): 59.

Fawkes, Johanna. *Maternity Rights and Industrial Tribunals.* Manchester: Equal Opportunities Commission, 1983.

"Fetal Protection Issues Remain After Ruling in *Johnson Controls*." 17 *Daily Labor Report* (BNA) (January 27, 1992): A-1.

Finneran, Hugh M. "Title VII and Restrictions on Employment of Fertile Women." *Labor Law Journal* 31 (1980): 223–31.

Fitzpatrick, Barry. "The Sex Discrimination Act 1986." *Modern Law Review* 50 (1987): 934–51.

Fletcher, A. C. *Reproductive Hazards of Work*. Manchester: Equal Opportunities Commission, 1985.

"Four Women Assert Jobs Were Linked to Sterilization." *New York Times*, January 5, 1979.

Frankel, Maurice. *Chemical Risk*. London: Pluto, 1982.

Freeman, Jo. *The Politics of Women's Liberation: A Case Study of an Emerging Social Movement and its Relation to the Policy Process*. New York: McKay, 1975.

Freidan, Betty. "How to Get the Women's Movement Moving Again." *Des Moines Sunday Register*, December 1, 1985.

Furnish, Hannah Arterian. "Prenatal Exposure to Fetally Toxic Work Environments: The Dilemma of the 1978 Pregnancy Amendments to Title VII of the Civil Rights Act of 1964." *Iowa Law Review* 66 (1980): 63–129.

Gallagher, Janet. "Prenatal Invasions and Interventions: What's Wrong with Fetal Rights." *Harvard Women's Law Journal* 10 (Spring 1987): 9–58.

Gay, Vivienne. "Sex Discrimination and Sexual Harassment." *Industrial Law Journal* 19 (March 1990): 35–39.

Gelb, Joyce. *Feminism and Politics: A Comparative Perspective*. Berkeley: University of California Press, 1989.

———. "Feminism in Britain: Politics Without Power?" In *The New Women's Movement: Feminism and Political Power in Europe and the USA*, edited by Drude Dahlerup, 103–39. London: Sage, 1986.

———. "Social Movement 'Success': A Comparative Analysis of Feminism in the U.S. and U.K." In *The Women's Movements of the United States and Western Europe: Consciousness, Political Opportunity and Public Policy*, edited by Mary Fainsod Katzenstein and Carol McClurg Mueller, 267–89. Philadelphia: Temple University Press, 1987.

Genn, Hazel. "The Myth of Informality." *Legal Action*, September, 1989, 9.

———, and Yvette Genn. *The Effectiveness of Representation at Tribunals: Report to the Lord Chancellor*. London: Lord Chancellor's Department, 1989.

Gill, Tess, and Larry Whitty. *Women's Rights in the Workplace*. Harmondsworth, England: Penguin, 1983.

Gilligan, Carol. *In a Different Voice: Psychological Theory and Women's Development*. Cambridge, Mass.: Harvard University Press, 1982.

Gold, Rachel Benson. "Women Entering Labor Force Draw Attention to Reproductive Hazards for Both Sexes." *Family Planning/Population Reporter* 10 (February 1981): 10–14.

Goldhaber, Marilyn, Michael R. Polen, and Robert A. Hiatt. "The Risk of Miscarriage and Birth Defects Among Women Who Use Video Display Terminals During Pregnancy." *American Journal of Industrial Medicine* 13 (1988): 695–706.

Goodman, Ellen. "Women's Rights, Fetal Risks." *Iowa City Press Citizen*, October 16, 1990.

Goodman, Michael J. *Industrial Tribunals: Practice and Procedure*. 4th ed. London: Sweet and Maxwell, 1987.

Grant, Jane W. *Sisters Across the Atlantic: A Guide to Networking in the U.S.* London: National Council for Voluntary Organisations, 1988.

Greenhouse, Linda. "Court Backs Right of Women to Jobs with Health Risks." *New York Times*, March 21, 1991.

————. "Justices Hear Arguments in Fetal Protection Case." *New York Times*, October 11, 1990.

Gregory, Jeanne. *Formal or Substantive Legality: The Future of Protective Legislation.* Middlesex Polytechnic Occasional Paper no. 3, November 1981.

————. "Sex Discrimination Bill: Update." *National Council for Civil Liberties Women's Rights Unit Newsletter* 1 (October 1986): 2.

————. *Sex, Race and the Law: Legislating for Equality.* London: Sage, 1987.

————. *Trial by Ordeal: A Study of People Who Lost Equal Pay and Sex Discrimination Cases in the Industrial Tribunals During 1985 and 1986.* London: HMSO, 1989.

Griffith, John A. G. *The Politics of the Judiciary.* 3d ed. Glasgow: Fontana, 1985.

Grosskurth, Anne. "Industrial Justice." *Legal Action*, September 1988, 6–7.

Guerrier, Charles E. "State Protective Legislation: Good Faith Compliance or Convenient Discrimination?" *Employee Relations Law Journal* 1 (1975/1976): 452–73.

Hall-Smith, Vanessa, Catherine Hoskyns, Judy Keiner, and Erika Szyszczak. *Women's Rights and the EEC: A Guide for Women in the UK.* London: Rights of Women Europe, 1983.

Hallstein, Walter. *Europe in the Making.* New York: Norton, 1972.

Hatch, Maureen. "Mother, Father, Worker: Men and Women and the Reproductive Risks of Work." In *Double Exposure: Women's Health Hazards on the Job and at Home*, edited by Wendy Chavkin, 161–79. New York: Monthly Review Press, 1984.

Hawkesworth, Mary E. "Knowers, Knowing, Known: Feminist Theory and Claims of Truth." *Signs* 14 (1989): 533–57.

"Health Hazards for Women Working in Chemicals and Pharmaceuticals." *Health and Safety Information Bulletin* 46 (1979): 1–11.

Hepple, Bob. "Judging Equal Rights." *Current Legal Problems* 36 (1983): 71–90.

————. "The Judicial Process in Claims for Equal Pay and Equal Treatment in the United Kingdom." In *Women, Employment and European Equality Law*, edited by Christopher McCrudden, 143–60. London: Eclipse, 1987.

Hill, Ann Corinne. "Women Workers and the Courts: A Legal Case History." *Feminist Studies* 5 (Summer 1979): 247–73.

Hill, Herbert. "The Equal Employment Opportunity Acts of 1964 and 1972: A Critical Analysis of the Legislative History and Administration of the Law." *Industrial Relations Law Journal* 2 (1977): 1–96.

————. "The Equal Employment Opportunity Commission: Twenty Years Later." *Journal of Intergroup Relations* 11 (Winter 1983): 45–72.

"Hospital Fails to Justify 'Fetal Protection' Policy." *Workplace Health and Safety Liability* (BPI), November 2, 1988.

Howard, Linda G. "Hazardous Substances in the Workplace: Implications for the Employment Rights of Women." *University of Pennsylvania Law Review* 129 (1981): 798–855.

Hubbard, Ruth. "The Political Nature of 'Human Nature.'" In *Theoretical Perspectives on Sexual Difference*, edited by Deborah L. Rhode, 63–73. New Haven: Yale University Press, 1990.

Huckle, Patricia. "The Womb Factor: Pregnancy Policies and Employment of Women." In *Women, Power and Policy*, edited by Ellen Boneparth, 144–61. New York: Pergamon Press, 1982.

Hughes, Sally. "Pressure Group Litigation in the U.S." *Legal Action*, May 1988, 8.

Humphries, Jane. "Protective Legislation, the Capitalist State, and Working Class Men: The Case of the 1842 Mines Regulation Act." *Feminist Review* 7 (Spring 1981): 1–33.

Hunt, Vilma. *Work and the Health of Women*. Boca Raton, Fla.: CRC Press, 1979.

Hutchins, B. L., and A. Harrison. *A History of Factory Legislation*. 3d ed. London: P. S. King and Son, 1926.

Hutton, John. "How the SDA Has Failed." *Legal Action*, April 1984, 10–11.

"Idaho Company Denies Requiring Sterilization of Female Workers." *New York Times*, September 18, 1980.

"Implementing the Social Charter." *Industrial Relations Legal Information Bulletin* 413 (November 23, 1990): 2–11.

"In Brief." *Centre for Research on European Women Reports* 6 (May 1986): 9.

"In Brief." *Health and Safety Information Bulletin* 62 (March 1981): 3.

Jaggar, Alison M. *Feminist Politics and Human Nature*. Totowa, N.J.: Rowman and Littlefield, 1988.

Jones, Rose. "The Politics of Reproductive Biology: Exclusionary Policies in the United States." In *Births and Power: Social Change and the Politics of Reproduction*, edited by W. Penn Handwerker, 39–51. Boulder, Colo.: Westview Press, 1990.

Josefowitz, Natasha. *Paths to Power: A Woman's Guide from First Job to Top Executive*. Reading, Mass.: Addison-Wesley, 1983.

Justice. *Industrial Tribunals*. London: Justice, 1987.

Kaminer, Wendy. "The Fetal Protection Charade." *New York Times*, April 29, 1990.

Kanter, Rosabeth Moss. *Men and Women of the Corporation*. New York: Basic Books, 1977.

Kaplan, David A. "Equal Rights, Equal Risks." *Newsweek*, April 1, 1991, 56.

Katzenstein, Mary Fainsod, and Carol McClurg Mueller, eds. *The Women's Movements of the United States and Western Europe: Consciousness, Political Opportunity and Public Policy*. Philadelphia: Temple University Press, 1987.

Kay, Herma Hill. "Equality and Difference: The Case of Pregnancy." *Berkeley Women's Law Journal* 1 (1985): 1–38.

———. *Sex-Based Discrimination*. 2d ed. St. Paul: West, 1981.

"Keeping a Fairly Straight, Middle Course." *Equality Now* 2 (Winter 1984): 9.

Kenen, Regina. "Fetal Protection Policies: An Update." *The National Women's Health Network News*, January/February 1987, 1.

Kennedy, Joseph P. "Sex Discrimination: State Protective Laws Since Title VII." *Notre Dame Lawyer* 47 (1972): 514–49.

Kenney, Sally J. "Reproductive Hazards in the Workplace: The Law and Sexual Difference." *International Journal of the Sociology of Law* 14 (1987): 393–414.

———. "Reproductive Hazards in the Workplace: 1." *Health and Safety Information Bulletin* 122 (1986): 2–5.

———. "Reproductive Hazards in the Workplace: 2." *Health and Safety Information Bulletin* 123 (1986): 6–9.

Kerber, Linda K., and Jane De Hart Mathews, eds. *Women's America: Refocusing the Past*. New York: Oxford University Press, 1982.

Kessler-Harris, Alice. "Protection for Women: Trade Unions and Labor Laws." In *Double Exposure: Women's Health Hazards on the Job and at Home*, edited by Wendy Chavkin, 139–54. New York: Monthly Review Press, 1984.

———. "Where are the Organized Women Workers?" *Feminist Studies* 3 (1975): 92–110.

Kilborn, Peter T. "Employers Left with Many Decisions." *New York Times*, March 21, 1991.

Kingdom, Elizabeth. Review of *Sexism and the Law* by Albie Sachs and Joan Hoff Wilson. *m/f* 4 (1980): 71–88.

Kirp, David L. "The Next Right-to-Life Battleground." *Christian Science Monitor*, December 13, 1989.

———. "The Pitfalls of 'Fetal Protection.'" *Society* 28 (March/April 1991): 70–76.

———. 1990. "Toxic Choices." University of California, Berkeley, Graduate School of Public Policy Working Paper no. 172.

Krislov, Samuel. "The Amicus Curiae Brief: From Friendship to Advocacy." *Yale Law Journal* 72 (1963): 694–721.

Lacey, Nicola. "Dismissal by Reason of Pregnancy." *Industrial Law Journal* 15 (1986): 43–46.

———. "Legislation Against Sex Discrimination: Questions from a Feminist Perspective." *Journal of Law and Society* 14 (1987): 411–21.

Lacranjan, Iona, Horia I. Popescu, Olimpia Gavenescu, Iulia Klepsch, and Maria Serbanescu. "Reproductive Ability of Workmen Occupationally Exposed to Lead." *Archives of Environmental Health* 30 (1975): 396–401.

Lamson, Peggy. "Eleanor Holmes Norton Reforms the Equal Employment Opportunities Commission." In *Women Leaders in American Politics*, edited by James David Barber and Barbara Kellerman, 340–44. Englewood Cliffs, N.J.: Prentice-Hall, 1986.

Landau, Eve C. *The Rights of Working Women in the European Community*. Brussels: Commission of the European Communities, 1985.

Landes, Elisabeth M. "The Effect of State Maximum-Hours Laws on the Employment of Women in 1920." *Journal of Political Economy* 88 (1980): 476–94.

Law, Sylvia A. "Rethinking Sex and the Constitution." *University of Pennsylvania Law Review* 132 (1984): 955–1040.

Lee, Simon. *Judging Judges*. London: Faber and Faber, 1988.

Lehrer, Susan. "A Living Wage Is for Men Only: Minimum Wage Legislation for Women, 1910–1925." In *Hidden Aspects of Women's Work*, edited by Christine Bose, Roslyn Feldberg, and Natalie Sokoloff, 201–21. New York: Praeger, 1987.

Leonard, Alice M. *The First Eight Years: A Profile of Applicants to the Industrial Tribunals under the Sex Discrimination Act 1975 and the Equal Pay Act 1970*. Manchester: Equal Opportunities Commission, 1986.

———. *Judging Inequality: The Effectiveness of the Industrial Tribunal System in Sex Discrimination and Equal Pay Cases*. London: Cobden Trust, 1987.

———. *Pyrrhic Victories: Winning Sex Discrimination and Equal Pay Cases in the Industrial Tribunals, 1980–1984*. London: HMSO, 1987.

Lewenhak, Sheila. *Women and Trade Unions: An Outline History of Women in the British Trade Union Movement*. New York: St. Martin's, 1977.

Lewin, Tamar. "Protecting the Baby: Work in Pregnancy Poses Legal Frontier." *New York Times*, August 2, 1988.

———. "Women of Childbearing Age Win a Court Round on Jobs." *New York Times*, March 4, 1990.

Lewis, Richard. "*OCAW v. American Cyanamid*: The Shrinking of the Occupational Safety and Health Act." *University of Pennsylvania Law Review* 133 (1985): 1167–91.

Lindgren, J. Ralph, and Nadine Taub. *The Law of Sex Discrimination*. St. Paul: West, 1988.

Lipschultz, Sybil. "Social Feminism and Legal Discourse, 1908–1923." In *At the Boundaries of Law: Feminism and Legal Theory*, edited by Martha Albertson Fineman and Nancy Sweet Thomadsen, 209–26. New York: Routledge, 1991.

Littleton, Christine A. "Reconstructing Sexual Equality." *California Law Review* 75 (1987): 1279–1337.

Lock, David. "Unfair Dismissal and the Right to Return to Work After Maternity Leave." *Legal Action*, March 1989, 11–13.

Logan, Shelley Reed. "Adapting Fetal Vulnerability Programs to Title VII: *Wright v. Olin*." *Employee Relations Law Journal* 9 (Spring 1984): 605–28.

"Lorry Driver Jackie Loses Out." *Northern Echo*, March 27, 1980.

Lovenduski, Joni. *Women and European Politics: Contemporary Feminism and Public Policy*. Amherst: University of Massachusetts Press, 1986.

———. "The Women's Movement and Public Policy in Western Europe: Theory, Strategy, Practice and Politics." In *Women, Equality and Europe*, edited by Mary Buckley and Malcolm Anderson, 107–25. London: Macmillan, 1988.

Lublin, Joann. "Guideline-Happy at the EEOC?" *Wall Street Journal*, August 28, 1980.

Lucas-Wallace, Kathleen. "Legal Considerations Bearing on the Health and Employment of Women Workers." In *Work and the Health of Women*, edited by Vilma R. Hunt, 181–99. Boca Raton, Fla.: CRC Press, 1979.

Lustgarten, Laurence. *Legal Control of Racial Discrimination*. London: Macmillan, 1980.

———. "Race Inequality and the Limits of the Law." *Modern Law Review* 49 (1986): 68–85.

McCrudden, Christopher. "Discrimination Against Minority Groups in Employment: A Comparison of Legal Remedies in the U.K. and the U.S." D.Phil. Thesis, Oxford University, 1981.

———. "Equal Pay for Work of Equal Value: The Equal Pay (Amendment) Regulations 1983." *Industrial Law Journal* 12 (December 1983): 197–219.

———. "Institutional Discrimination." *Oxford Journal of Legal Studies* 2 (1982): 303–67.

———. "Rethinking Positive Action." *Industrial Law Journal* 15 (December 1986): 219–43.

———, ed. *Women, Employment, and European Equality Law*. London: Eclipse Publications, 1987.

McGarity, Thomas O., and Elinor P. Schroeder. "Risk-Oriented Employment Screening." *Texas Law Review* 59 (August 1981): 999–1076.

McGhee, Dorothy. "Workplace Hazards: No Women Need Apply." *Progressive* 41 (October 1977): 20–25.

McIlroy, John. *Industrial Tribunals*. London: Pluto, 1983.

McKechnie, Shelia. "Comments on EOC Report, *Health and Safety: Should We Distinguish Between Men and Women?*" Association of Scientific, Technical and Managerial Staffs, Bishops Stortford, U.K., May, 11, 1983. Photocopy.

Mackie, Lindsay, and Polly Patullo. *Women at Work*. London: Tavistock, 1977.

MacKinnon, Catharine A. "Feminism, Marxism, Method and the State: Toward Feminist Jurisprudence." *Signs* 8 (Summer 1983): 635–58.

———. *Feminism Unmodified: Discourses on Life and Law*. Cambridge, Mass.: Harvard University Press, 1987.

———. *Sexual Harassment of Working Women: A Case of Sex Discrimination*. New Haven: Yale University Press, 1979.

———. "Toward Feminist Jurisprudence." Review of *Women Who Kill* by Ann Jones. *Stanford Law Review* 34 (1982): 703–37.

———. *Toward a Feminist Theory of the State*. Cambridge, Mass.: Harvard University Press, 1989.

McLean, Sheila, and Noreen Burrows, eds. *The Legal Relevance of Gender: Some Aspects of Sex-Based Discrimination*. London: Macmillan, 1988.

Malone, Michael. *A Practical Guide to Discrimination Law*. London: Grant McIntyre, 1980.

Mansbridge, Jane J. *Why We Lost the ERA*. Chicago: University of Chicago Press, 1986.

Marshall, Carolyn. "Fetal Protection Policies: An Excuse for Workplace Hazard." *Nation* 244 (April 25, 1987): 532–34.

Martin, Emily. "The Egg and the Sperm: How Science has Constructed a Romance Based on Stereotypical Male-Female Roles." *Signs* 16 (1991): 485–501.

———. *The Woman in the Body: A Cultural Analysis of Reproduction*. Boston: Beacon Press, 1987.

Maschke, Karen J. "The Ideology and Practice of Fetal Protection." Paper presented at the annual meeting of the Midwest Political Science Association, Chicago, April 1991.

Masters, Kim. "EEOC's Reproductive Hazards Guidelines Criticized." *Legal Times*, July 14, 1980.

Mathews, Jane De Hart. "The New Feminism and the Dynamics of Social Change." In *Women's America: Refocusing the Past*, edited by Linda K. Kerber and Jane De Hart Mathews, 397–425. New York: Oxford University Press, 1982.

Mayhew, Judith. "Pregnancy and Employment Law." In *Gender, Sex and the Law*, edited by Susan Edwards, 102–11. London: Croom Helm, 1985.

Meehan, Elizabeth M. "British Feminism from the 1960s to the 1980s." In *British Feminism in the Twentieth Century*, edited by Harold L. Smith, 189–204. Aldershot, England: Edward Elgar, 1990.

———. "Equal Opportunity Policies: Some Implications for Women of Contrasts Between Enforcement Bodies in Britain and the U.S.A." In *Women's Welfare: Women's Rights*, edited by Jane E. Lewis, 170–92. London: Croom Helm, 1983.

_____. "Implementing Equal Opportunity Policies: Some British-American Comparisons." *Politics* 2 (April 1982): 14–20.

_____. "The Priorities of the Equal Opportunities Commission." *Political Quarterly* 54 (January/March 1983): 69–76.

_____. *Women's Rights at Work: Campaigns and Policy in Britain and the United States.* London: Macmillan, 1985.

Messing, Karen. "Do Men and Women Have Different Jobs Because of Their Biological Differences?" *International Journal of Health Services* 12 (1982): 43–51.

Mezey, Susan Gluck. "When Should Differences Make a Difference: A New Approach to the Constitutionality of Gender-Based Laws." *Women and Politics* 10 (1990): 105–19.

Milkman, Ruth. "Women's History and the Sears Case." *Feminist Studies* 12 (1986): 375–400.

Miller, Robert Stevens, Jr. "Sex Discrimination and Title VII of the Civil Rights Act of 1964." *Minnesota Law Review* 51 (1967): 877–97.

Minow, Martha. "Justice Engendered." *Harvard Law Review* 101 (1987): 10–95.

Moelis, Laurence S. "Fetal Protection and Potential Liability: Judicial Application of the Pregnancy Discrimination Act and the Disparate Impact Theory." *American Journal of Law and Medicine* 11 (1985): 369–90.

Monteith, Maggie. "More Legislation, Fewer Rights—A New Sex Discrimination Bill." *Rights of Women Bulletin*, December 1986, 20–21.

_____. "Movement News." *Rights of Women Bulletin*, Winter 1988, 11.

_____. "Tackling the Problems of the Equality Legislation: The EOC Review A Decade of Legislation." *Rights of Women Bulletin*, May 1987, 8–9.

_____. "Women's Legal Defense Fund: A New Fund to Fight for Women's Rights." *Rights of Women Bulletin*, May 1987, 12–13.

Mullen, Tom. "Representation at Tribunals." *Modern Law Review* 53 (March 1990): 230–36.

Mullins, Hattie-Jo P. "Women and the Law: Will Real Life Catch Up to TV?" *Ms.*, June 1987, 64–66.

Murphy, Walter F., James E. Fleming, and William F. Harris II. *American Constitutional Interpretation.* Mineola, N.Y.: Foundation Press, 1986.

Nelkin, Dorothy, and Michael S. Brown. *Workers at Risk: Voices from the Workplace.* Chicago: University of Chicago Press, 1984.

Newcastle-upon-Tyne Trades Council. *Laws with Claws: Government Attacks on Women.* Newcastle-upon-Tyne, U.K., 1980.

"The New Employment Bill." *Industrial Relations Legal Information Bulletin* 368 (1989): 14–15.

"No Discrimination Against Woman Lorry Driver." *Times*, November 5, 1980.

Norris, Pippa. "Cultural Attitudes Toward Sexual Equality." In *Politics and Sexual Equality: The Comparative Position of Women in Western Democracies*, edited by Pippa Norris, 132–41. Boulder, Colo.: Rienner, 1987.

_____. *Politics and Sexual Equality: The Comparative Position of Women in Western Democracies.* Boulder, Colo.: Rienner, 1987.

Nothstein, G. Z. *Toxic Torts: Litigation of Hazardous Substances Cases.* Colorado Springs, Colo.: McGraw-Hill, 1984.

_____, and Jeffrey P. Ayres. "Sex-Based Considerations of Differentiation in the

Workplace: Exploring the Biomedical Interface Between OSHA and Title VII." *Villanova Law Review* 26 (1981): 239–321.

O'Connor, Karen. *Women's Organizations' Use of the Courts.* Lexington, Mass: Lexington Books, 1980.

————, and Lee Epstein. "Court Rules and Workload: A Case Study of Rules Governing Amicus Curiae Participation." *Justice System Journal* 8 (1983): 35–45.

O'Donovan, Katherine. "Protection and Paternalism." In *The State, the Law and the Family*, edited by Michael D. A. Freeman, 79–90. London: Tavistock, 1984.

————. *Sexual Divisions in Law.* London: Weidenfeld and Nicolson, 1985.

————, and Erika Szyszczak. *Equality and Sex Discrimination Law.* Oxford: Basil Blackwell, 1988.

————. "Indirect Discrimination—Taking a Concept to Market—I." *New Law Journal*, January 4, 1985, 15–18.

————. "Indirect Discrimination—Taking a Concept to Market—II." *New Law Journal*, January 11, 1985, 42–44.

Oldham, James. "Sex Discrimination and State Protective Laws." *Denver Law Journal* 44 (1967): 344–76.

Olsen, Frances. "Statutory Rape: A Feminist Critique of Rights Analysis." *Texas Law Review* 63 (November 1984): 387–432.

O'Neill, William L. *Everyone Was Brave: The Rise and Fall of Feminism in America.* Chicago: Quadrangle, 1969.

Opheim, Teresa. "Potential Papas Beware: Your Work May Be Hazardous to Your Child's Health." *Utne Reader* 46 (July/August 1991): 26–27.

"Our Sheila." *Hazards* 11 (1986): 11.

Palmer, Camilla, and Kate Poulton. *Sex and Race Discrimination in Employment.* London: Legal Action Group, 1987.

Pannick, David. *Sex Discrimination Law.* Oxford: Clarendon Press, 1985.

Paoli, Chantal. "Women Workers and Maternity: Some Examples from Western Europe." *International Labor Review* 121 (January/February 1982): 1–16.

Patner, Andrew. "Court Upholds 'Fetal Protection Policy' Barring Most Women from Certain Jobs." *Wall Street Journal*, September 28, 1989.

Patullo, Polly. *Judging Women: A Study of Attitudes that Rule Our System.* London: National Council for Civil Liberties Rights for Women Unit, 1983.

Paul, Maureen, Cynthia Daniels, and Robert Rosofsky. "Corporate Response to Reproductive Hazards in the Workplace: Results of the Family, Work, and Health Survey." *American Journal Of Industrial Medicine* 16 (1986): 267–80.

Peake, Diane Sanders. "Employment Discrimination—*Wright v. Olin Corp.*: Title VII and the Exclusion of Women from the Fetally Toxic Workplace." *North Carolina Law Review* 62 (June 1984): 1068–90.

Pescatore, Pierre. "The Doctrine of 'Direct Effect': An Infant Disease of Community Law." *European Law Review* 2 (1983): 155–77.

Petchesky, Rosalind. *Abortion and Woman's Choice: The State, Sexuality and Reproductive Freedom.* Rev. ed. Boston: Northeastern University Press, 1990.

————. "Fetal Images: The Power of Visual Culture in the Politics of Reproduction." *Feminist Studies* 13 (Summer 1987): 263–92.

————. "Workers, Reproductive Hazards, and the Politics of Protection: An Introduction." *Feminist Studies* 5 (Summer 1979): 233–45.

Peterson, Sophia. "Public Opinion and Policy Implementation: The Sex Discrimination Act in Great Britain, 1976–82." Paper presented at the annual meeting of the American Political Science Association, Washington, D.C., September, 1987.

"Pigment Plant Wins Fertility-Risk Case." *New York Times*, September 8, 1980.

Pollitt, Katha. " 'Fetal Rights': A New Assault on Feminism." *Nation* 12 (March 26, 1990): 409–48.

Powell, Thomas Reed. "The Judiciality of Minimum Wage Legislation." *Harvard Law Review* 37 (March 1924): 545–73.

"Pregnancy and Maternity: 1." *Industrial Relations Legal Information Bulletin* 376 (May 10, 1989): 2–9.

"Pregnancy and Maternity: 2." *Industrial Relations Legal Information Bulletin* 377 (May 23, 1989): 2–7.

"Pregnancy Discrimination is Sex Discrimination." *Equal Opportunities Review* 35 (January/February 1991): 40–44.

"Pregnancy Dismissal Not Automatically Discriminatory." *Industrial Relations Legal Information Bulletin* 399 (April 19, 1990): 10–11.

"Pregnant Women Banned From AT&T Chip Lines." *Washington Post*, January 14, 1987.

"Protecting the Unborn Child: A Precautionary Policy at Ciba-Geigy." *Health and Safety Information Bulletin* 66 (1981): 3.

"Protective Restrictions on Women's Employment: a HSIB Guide." *Health and Safety Information Bulletin* 14 (1977): 1–5.

"Proving Pregnancy Discrimination." *Discrimination Case Law Digest* 1 (Autumn 1989): 2.

Purvis, Andrew. "The Sins of the Fathers: Both Parents May be Vulnerable to Toxins that Cause Birth Defects." *Time*, November 26, 1990.

"The Qualified Majority Vote." *Industrial Relations Legal Information Bulletin* 399 (April 19, 1990): 4.

Randall, Donna M., and James F. Short, Jr. "Women in Toxic Work Environments: A Case Study of Social Problem Development." *Social Problems* 30 (April 1983): 410–24.

Randall, Vicky. *Women and Politics*. London: Macmillan, 1982.

———. *Women and Politics: An International Perspective*. 2d ed. Chicago: University of Chicago Press, 1987.

Rawls, John. *A Theory of Justice*. Cambridge, Mass.: Belknap Press, 1971.

Rawls, Rebecca. "Reproductive Hazards in the Workplace." *Chemical and Engineering News* 58 (February 11, 1980): 28–31.

———. "Reproductive Hazards in the Workplace." *Chemical and Engineering News* 58 (February 18, 1980): 35–37.

"Review of 1988." *Industrial Relations Legal Information Bulletin* 368 (January 10, 1989): 5–16.

Rhode, Deborah L. "Gender Difference and Gender Disadvantage." *Women and Politics* 10 (1990): 121–35.

———, ed. *Theoretical Perspectives on Sexual Difference*. New Haven: Yale University Press, 1990.

Rideout, R. W. "The Industrial Tribunals." *Current Legal Problems* 21 (1968): 178–94.

Rifkin, Janet. "Toward a Theory of Law and Patriarchy." *Harvard Women's Law Journal* 3 (1980): 83–95.

Robertshaw, Paul. "Semantic and Linguistic Aspects of Sex Discrimination Decisions: Dichotomised Woman." In *Semiotics, Law and Social Science*, edited by Domenico Carzo and Bernard S. Jackson, 203–27. Liverpool: Liverpool Law Review, 1984.

Robinson, Donald Allen. "Two Movements in Pursuit of Equal Employment Opportunity." *Signs* 4 (1979): 413–33.

Robinson, Gail. "Environmental Hazards: A New Form of Discrimination." *Spokeswoman* 9 (April 1979): 12–13.

Rosen, Ruth. "What Feminist Victory in the Court?" *New York Times*, April 1, 1991.

Ross, Susan Deller, and Ann Barcher. *The Rights of Women*. New York: Bantam, 1983.

Rothstein, Mark A. "Employee Selection Based on Susceptibility to Occupational Illness." *Michigan Law Review* 81 (May 1983): 1379–1495.

Rubenstein, Michael. "Beyond the Whinge." *Oxford Journal of Legal Studies* 2 (1991): 254–63.

―――――. *The Dignity of Women at Work: A Report on the Problem of Sexual Harassment in the Member States of the European Communities*. Luxembourg: EC Publications, 1987.

―――――. *Discrimination: A Guide to Relevant Case Law on Race and Sex Discrimination and Equal Pay*. 3d ed. London: Eclipse, 1990.

―――――. "Educating the Judges." *Equal Opportunities Review* 1 (May/June 1985): 48.

―――――. "The Law of Sexual Harassment at Work." *Industrial Law Journal* 12 (1983): 1–16.

Rubery, Jill. Review of *Pyrrhic Victories: Winning Sex Discrimination and Equal Pay Cases in the Industrial Tribunals, 1980–1984* by Alice Leonard. *Industrial Law Journal* 17 (March 1988): 61–62.

Rudden, Bernard. *Basic Community Cases*. Oxford: Clarendon Press, 1987.

Ruhemann, Clare. "Hazards of Reproduction." *Health and Safety at Work*, May 1982, 23–25.

Ruggie, Mary. *The State and Working Women: A Comparative Study of Britain and Sweden*. Princeton, N.J.: Princeton University Press, 1984.

Sachs, Albie. "Barristers and Gentlemen: The Roots and Structure of Sexism in the Legal Profession." Feminist Library, London, 1977. Photocopy.

―――――, and Joan Hoff Wilson. *Sexism and the Law: A Study of Male Beliefs and Legal Bias in Britain and the United States*. Oxford: Martin Robertson, 1978.

"Sacked Mum in Screen Victory." *Daily Record*, September 20, 1984.

Sacks, Vera. "The Equal Opportunities Commission—Ten Years On." *Modern Law Review* 49 (1986): 560–92.

Samuelson, Joan I. "Employment Rights of Women in the Toxic Workplace." *California Law Review* 65 (1977): 1113–42.

Sandalow, Terrance, and Eric Stein, eds. *Courts and Free Markets: Perspectives from the United States and Europe*. Oxford: Clarendon Press, 1982.

Sayrs, Janet. *Biological Politics: Feminist and Anti-feminist Perspectives*. London: Tavistock, 1982.

Scales, Ann C. "Towards a Feminist Jurisprudence." *Indiana Law Journal* 56 (1980–81): 375–444.

Schlei, Barbara Lindemann, and Paul Grossman. *Employment Discrimination Law*. 2d ed. Washington, D.C.: Bureau of National Affairs, 1983.

Schlender, Brenton R. "Sterilization is Main Issue in OSHA Suits." *Wall Street Journal*, December 9, 1980.

Schwartz, Herman. *Packing the Courts: The Conservative Campaign to Rewrite the Constitution*. New York: Scribner, 1988.

Scott, Joan W. "Deconstructing Equality-versus-Difference: Or, the Uses of Poststructuralist Theory for Feminism." *Feminist Studies* 14 (Spring 1988): 33–50.

Scott, Judith A. "Keeping Women in Their Place: Exclusionary Politics and Reproduction." In *Double Exposure: Women's Health Hazards on the Job and at Home*, edited by Wendy Chavkin, 180–95. New York: Monthly Review Press, 1984.

Sedley, Anne. "Equal Opportunities in the U.S.A." *Rights: The Journal of the National Council for Civil Liberties* 8 (Autumn 1984): 5.

Selwyn, Norman. *Law of Health and Safety at Work*. London: Butterworth, 1982.

Sevenhuijsen, Selma. "Justice, Moral Reasoning and the Politics of Child Custody." In *Equality, Politics, and Gender*, edited by Elizabeth Meehan and Selma Sevenhuijsen, 88–103. London: Sage, 1991.

"Sex Discrimination Tribunals . . . Extracts from a Real Experience." *National Council for Civil Liberties Rights for Women Unit Newsletter*, January 1984, 3–4.

Shabecoff, Philip. "Job Threats to Workers' Fertility Emerging as Civil Liberties Issue." *New York Times*, January 15, 1979.

———. "Union, Citing Birth Defects, Asks Ban On a Herbicide." *New York Times*, November 9, 1979.

———. "U.S. Appeals Ruling on Women in Hazardous Jobs." *New York Times*, September 9, 1980.

Shapiro, Martin. *Courts: A Comparative and Political Analysis*. Chicago: University of Chicago Press, 1981.

Shaw, Josephine. "The Burden of Proof and the Legality of Supplementary Payments in Equal Pay Cases." *European Law Review* 15 (June 1990): 260–66.

Shrubsall, Vivien. "Recent Cases." *Industrial Law Journal* 16 (June 1987): 118–21.

Siegel, Reva. Review of *Origins of Protective Labor Legislation for Women, 1905–1925* by Susan Lehrer. *Berkeley Women's Law Journal* 3 (1987–88): 171–87.

Sim, Raymond S., and D. M. M. Scott. *A-Level English Law*. 5th ed. London: Butterworth, 1978.

Singer, James W. "Should Equal Opportunity for Women Apply to Toxic Chemical Exposure?" *National Journal* 12 (October 18, 1980): 1753–55.

Smart, Carol. *Feminism and the Power of Law*. London: Routledge, 1989.

———. *The Ties that Bind: Law, Marriage, and the Reproduction of Patriarchal Relations*. London: Routledge, 1984.

———. "The Woman in Legal Discourse." Women's Studies Paper Series, University of Utrecht, May 16, 1991.

Smith, Harold L., ed. *British Feminism in the Twentieth Century*. Aldershot, England: Elgar, 1990.

Smith, Roger. "Five Years of Tribunals." *Legal Action*, September 1989, 7–8.

Soldon, Norbert C. *Women in British Trade Unions, 1874–1976.* Totowa, N.J.: Rowman and Littlefield, 1978.

Stamp, Paddy. "Working Women Better Off?" *Civil Liberty* 3 (February, 1987): 2.

————, and Sadie Robarts. *Positive Action for Women: The Next Step in Education, Training and Employment.* London: National Council for Civil Liberties, 1980.

Steiner, J. M. "Sex Discrimination under U.K. and EEC Law: Two Plus Four Equals One." *International and Comparative Law Quarterly* 32 (April 1983): 399–423.

Stellman, Jeanne Mager. "Protective Legislation, Ionizing Radiation and Health: A New Appraisal and International Survey." *Women and Health* 12 (1987): 105–25.

————. *Women's Work, Women's Health: Myths and Realities.* New York: Pantheon, 1977.

————, and Joan E. Bertin. "Science's Anti-Female Bias." *New York Times*, June 4, 1990.

————, and Mary Sue Henifin. "No Fertile Women Need Apply: Employment Discrimination and Reproductive Hazards in the Workplace." In *Biological Woman— The Convenient Myth: A Collection of Feminist Essays and a Comprehensive Bibliography*, edited by Ruth Hubbard, Mary Sue Henifen, and Barbara Fried, 117–45. Cambridge, Mass.: Schenkman, 1982.

Stillman, Nina G. "The Law in Conflict: Accommodating Equal Employment and Occupational Health Obligations." *Journal of Occupational Medicine* 21 (1979): 599–606.

Strachey, Ray. *"The Cause": A Short History of the Women's Movement in Great Britain.* London: Bell & Sons, 1928.

Sullivan, Charles A., Michael J. Zimmer, and Richard F. Richards. *Federal Statutory Law of Employment Discrimination.* Indianapolis: Michie, 1980.

"Supreme Court Supports OSHA 'General Duty' Clause." *Women's Occupational Health Resource Center News* 9 (December 1987): 1.

Swinton, Katherine. "Regulating Reproductive Hazards in the Workplace: Balancing Equality and Health." *University of Toronto Law Journal* 33 (1983): 45–73.

Tate, Cassandra. "American Dilemma of Jobs, Health in an Idaho Town." *Smithsonian* 12 (1981): 74–83.

"A Test for Women's Job Rights." *Chemical Week*, March 12, 1980.

"TGWU Action." *Hazards* 11 (1986): 10.

"Thalidomide 20 Years On." *Lancet* 2 (1981): 510–11.

Thane, Pat. "Late Victorian Women." In *Later Victorian Britain, 1867–1900*, edited by T. R. Gourvish and Alan O'Day, 175–208. London: Macmillan, 1988.

Timko, Patricia A. "Exploring the Limits of Legal Duty: A Union's Responsibilities with Respect to Fetal Protection Policies." *Harvard Journal on Legislation* 23 (1986): 159–210.

Tobias, Sheila, and Lisa Anderson. "What Really Happened to Rosie the Riveter? Demobilization and the Female Labor Force, 1944–47." In *Women's America: Refocusing the Past*, edited by Linda K. Kerber and Jane De Hart Mathews, 354–73. New York: Oxford University Press, 1982.

Tong, Rosemarie. *Feminist Thought: A Comprehensive Introduction.* Boulder, Colo.: Westview Press, 1989.

Townshend-Smith, Richard. "The Impact of European Law on Equal Pay for Women." In *The Effect on English Domestic Law of Membership of the European Com-*

munities and of Ratification of the European Convention on Human Rights, edited by M. P. Furmston, R. Kerridge, and B. E. Sufrin, 69–107. The Hague: Martinus Nijhoff, 1983.

————. *Sex Discrimination in Employment: Law, Practice and Policy*. London: Sweet and Maxwell, 1989.

Trebilcock, Anne M. "OSHA and Equal Employment Opportunity Laws for Women." *Preventative Medicine* 7 (1978): 372–84.

"Unborn Children: the New Workforce." *Health and Safety Information Bulletin* 9 (1976): 1–5.

"Unborn Children: the New Workforce (Part 2)." *Health and Safety Information Bulletin* 11 (1976): 1–4.

Vaas, Francis J. "Title VII: Legislative History." *Boston College Industrial and Commercial Law Review* 7 (1965–66): 431–58.

Valentine, Jeannette M., and Alonzo L. Plough. "Protecting the Reproductive Health of Workers: Problems in Science and Public Policy." *Journal of Health Politics, Policy and Law* 8 (Spring 1983): 144–63.

Vanderwaerdt, Lois. "Resolving the Conflict Between Hazardous Substances in the Workplace and Equal Employment Opportunity." *American Business Law Journal* 21 (1983): 157–84.

Vogel, Lise. "Debating Difference: Feminism, Pregnancy, and the Workplace." *Feminist Studies* 16 (1990): 9–32.

Vose, Clement E. "The National Consumers' League and the Brandeis Brief." *Midwest Journal of Political Science* 1 (1957): 267–90.

Wade, Emlyn C. S., and A. W. Bradley. *Constitutional and Administrative Law*. 10th ed. London: Longman, 1985.

Weiler, Joseph. "The Community System: the Dual Character of Supranationalism." In *The Yearbook of European Law*, edited by F. G. Jacobs, 267–306. Oxford: Clarendon Press, 1981.

Weitzman, Lenore J. "Beneath the Surface: The Truth about Divorce, Custody, and Support." *Ms.*, February 1986, 67–70.

————. *The Divorce Revolution: The Unexpected Social and Economic Consequences for Women and Children in America*. New York: Free Press, 1986.

West, Robin. "Jurisprudence and Gender." *University of Chicago Law Review* 55 (1988): 1–72.

Whorton, Donald M. "Adverse Reproductive Outcomes: The Occupational Health Issue of the 1980s." *American Journal of Public Health* 73 (January 1983): 15–16.

Whitesides, Keith, and Geoffrey Hawker. *Industrial Tribunals*. London: Sweet and Maxwell, 1975.

Willborn, Steven L. *A Secretary and a Cook: Challenging Women's Wages in the Courts of the United States and Great Britain*. Ithaca, N.Y.: ILR Press, 1989.

————. "Theories of Employment Discrimination in the United Kingdom and the United States." *Boston College International and Comparative Law Review* 9 (1986): 243–56.

Williams, Donald B., and Denis J. Walker. *Industrial Tribunals—Practice and Procedure*. London: Butterworth, 1980.

Williams, Glanville. *Learning the Law*. 11th ed. London: Stevens, 1982.

Williams, Heather. "Case Note: Direct Discrimination Against Pregnant Woman." *Legal Action*, January 1989, 24.

Williams, Wendy W. "The Equality Crisis: Some Reflections on Culture, Courts and Feminism." *Women's Rights Law Reporter* 7 (1982): 175–200.

———. "Equality's Riddle: Pregnancy and the Equal Treatment/Special Treatment Debate." *New York University Review of Law and Social Change* 13 (1984–85): 325–80.

———. "Firing the Woman to Protect the Fetus: The Reconciliation of Fetal Protection with Employment Opportunity Goals Under Title VII." *Georgetown Law Journal* 69 (1981): 641–704.

———. "Notes From a First Generation." *University of Chicago Legal Forum*, 1989, 99–113.

Wilson, Graham K. *The Politics of Safety and Health: Occupational Safety and Health in the United States and Britain*. Oxford: Clarendon Press, 1985.

Wiseman, Stephen. "Sex Discrimination: Some Recent Decisions of the European Court of Justice." *Columbia Journal of Transnational Law* 21 (1983): 621–40.

"The Women at Cyanamid." *New York Times*, January 7, 1979.

Women's Health and Information Centre. Broadsheet no. 11. *VDUs and Pregnant Women*. London: WHIC, 1985.

"Women's Legal Defense Fund." *Civil Liberty* 3 (April 1987): 4.

Wood, B. Dan. "Does Politics Make a Difference at the EEOC?" *American Journal of Political Science* 34 (May 1990): 503–30.

Woodall, Jean, Anne Showstack, Bridget Towers, and Carolyn McNally. "Don't Tell Me the Old Boys' Story." *Guardian*, September 10, 1985.

Woollam, D. H. M. "Principles of Teratogenesis: Mode of Action of Thalidomide." *Proceedings of the Royal Society of Medicine* 58 (July 1965): 497–501.

Wright, Michael J. "Reproductive Hazards and 'Protective' Discrimination." *Feminist Studies* 5 (Summer 1979): 302–9.

Zander, Michael. *A Matter of Justice: The Legal System in Ferment*. Rev. ed. Oxford: Oxford University Press, 1989.

Zener, Robert V. "Women in the Workplace: Toxic Substances and Sex Discrimination." *Toxic Substances Journal* 1 (1979): 226–36.

U.S. Government Documents

General Accounting Office. Report to Congressional Requesters. *Equal Employment Opportunity: EEOC Birmingham Office Closed Discrimination Charges Without Full Investigation*. Washington, D.C.: Government Printing Office, 1987.

U.S. Commission on Civil Rights. *Federal Enforcement of Equal Employment Requirements: The Equal Employment Opportunities Commission*. Washington, D.C.: U.S. Government Printing Office, 1987.

U.S. Congress. House. Committee on Education and Labor. Subcommittee on Employment Opportunities. *Oversight Hearings on the OFCCP's Proposed Affirmative Action Regulations*. 98th Cong., 1st sess., 1983.

U.S. Congress. House. Committee on Education and Labor. Subcommittee on Employment Opportunities. *Oversight Hearings on the Federal Enforcement of Equal Employment Opportunity Laws.* 98th Cong., 1st sess., 1983.

U.S. Congress. House. Committee on Education and Labor. Subcommittee on Employment Opportunities. *Oversight Review of the Department of Labor's Office of Federal Contract Compliance Programs and Affirmative Action Programs.* 99th Cong., 1st sess., 1985.

U.S. Congress. House. Committee on Education and Labor. Subcommittee on Employment Opportunities. *Oversight Hearing on EEOC's Proposed Modification of Enforcement Regulations, Including Uniform Guidelines on Employee Selection Procedures.* 99th Cong., 1st sess., 1985.

U.S. Congress. House. Committee on Education and Labor. Subcommittee on Employment Opportunities. *Hearings on Equal Employment Opportunity Commission Policies Regarding Goals and Timetables in Litigation Remedies.* 99th Cong., 2d sess., 1986.

U.S. Congress. House. Committee on Education and Labor. *Staff Report on the Investigation of Civil Rights Enforcement by the Equal Employment Opportunity Commission.* 99th Cong., 2d sess., 1986.

U.S. Congress. House. Committee on Education and Labor. Subcommittee on Employment Opportunities. *A Report by the Majority Staff on the Investigation of the Civil Rights Enforcement Activities of the Office of Federal Contract Compliance Programs.* 100th Cong., 1st sess., 1987.

U.S. Congress. House. Committee on Education and Labor. *A Report by the Majority Staff on the EEOC, Title VII and Workplace Fetal Protection Policies in the 1980s.* 101st Cong., 2d sess., 1990.

U.S. Congress. Office of Technology Assessment. *Reproductive Health Hazards in the Workplace.* Washington, D.C.: U.S. Government Printing Office, 1985.

U.S. Congress. Senate. Committee on Labor and Human Resources. Subcommittee on Labor. *Discrimination on the Basis of Pregnancy: Hearings on S. 995.* 95th Cong., 1st sess., 1977.

U.S. Congress. Senate. Committee on Labor and Human Resources. Staff Report. *Committee Analysis of Executive Order 11246.* 97th Cong., 2d sess., 1982.

U.S. Congress. Senate. Committee on the Judiciary. *Hearings on the Nomination of Robert H. Bork to be Associate Justice of the Supreme Court of the United States.* 100th Cong., 1st sess., 1987.

U.S. Congress. Senate. Committee on the Judiciary. *Report on the Nomination of Clarence Thomas to be an Associate Justice of the United States Supreme Court.* 102d Cong., 1st sess., 1991.

U.S. Congress. Senate. Committee on the Judiciary. *Hearings on the Nomination of Clarence Thomas to be an Associate Justice of the United States Supreme Court.* 102d Cong., 1st sess. 1991.

U.S. Department of Labor. Office of Inspector General. *OFCCP Can Do More Enforcement and Have Greater Impact Using Fewer Dollars?* Washington, D.C.: U.S. Government Printing Office, 1985.

U.S. Equal Employment Opportunity Commission. *Compliance Manual.* Washington, D.C.: Bureau of National Affairs, 1983.

British Government Documents

Equal Opportunities Commission. *Women in the Legal Services: Evidence Submitted by the EOC to the Royal Commission on Legal Services*. Manchester: Equal Opportunities Commission, 1978.

————. *Health and Safety Legislation: Should We Distinguish Between Men and Women?* Manchester: Equal Opportunities Commission, 1979.

————. *Eighth Annual Report*. London: HMSO, 1984.

————. *Equality Now* 3 (Manchester: EOC, 1984).

————. *Ninth Annual Report*. London: HMSO, 1985.

————. *Twelfth Annual Report*. London: HMSO, 1988.

————. *United Kingdom Report Under the UN Convention on the Elimination of All Forms of Discrimination Against Women: Views of the Equal Opportunities Commission*. Manchester: EOC, 1987.

————. *Equal Treatment for Men and Women: Strengthening the Acts*. London: HMSO, 1988.

————. *Pregnancy and the Sex Discrimination Act: A Guide for Advisers*. Manchester: EOC, 1989.

————. *Pregnant and Lost Your Job?* Manchester: EOC, 1989.

————. *Towards Equality: A Casebook of Decisions on Sex Discrimination and Equal Pay, 1976–88*. London: HMSO, 1989.

————. *Thirteenth Annual Report*. London: HMSO, 1989.

————. *1989 Annual Report*. London: HMSO, 1990.

Health and Safety Commission. *Control of Lead at Work Regulations: Approved Code of Practice*. London: HMSO, 1980.

Health and Safety Executive. *Visual Display Units*. London: HMSO, 1983.

————. *Working With VDUs*. London: HMSO, 1986.

U.K. Parliament. *Lifting the Burden*. Cmnd 9571 (London: HMSO, 1985).

————. *Report of the Royal Commission on Civil Liability and Compensation for Personal Injury*. Cmnd 7054 (London: HMSO, 1978).

European Community Documents

"Protective Legislation for Women in the Member States of the European Community." Com. (87) 105 final.

U.S. Cases

Adkins v. Children's Hospital, 261 U.S. 525 (1923).

In re "Agent Orange" Product Liability Litigation, 506 F.Supp. 762 (E.D. N.Y. 1980).

Air Line Pilots Association et al. v. Western Air Lines, Inc., 22 Empl. Prac. Dec. (CCH) ¶30,636 (N.D. Cal. 1979), 722 F.2d 744 (9th Cir. 1983), *cert. denied*, 465 U.S. 1101 (1984).

Albermarle Paper Co. v. Moody, 422 U.S. 405 (1975).

Bailey v. Delta Air Lines, Inc., 722 F.2d 942 (1st Cir. 1983).

Bowe v. Colgate-Palmolive Co., 416 F.2d 711 (7th Cir. 1969).

Brown v. Foley, 29 So.2d 870 (Fla. 1947).

Burwell v. Eastern Air Lines, Inc., 458 F. Supp. 474 (E.D. Va. 1978), 633 F.2d 361 (4th Cir. 1980), *cert. denied*, 450 U.S. 965 (1981).

California Federal Savings and Loan Association v. Guerra, 479 U.S. 272 (1987).

Chambers v. Omaha Girls Club, Inc., 834 F.2d 697 (8th Cir. 1987).

Cheatwood v. South Central Bell Telephone and Telegraph, 303 F. Supp. 754 (M.D. Ala. 1969).

In re Cities Services Co., 87 Lab. Arb. (BNA) 1209 (1986).

City of Los Angeles Department of Water and Power v. Manhart, 435 U.S. 702 (1977).

City of Richmond v. Croson Company, 488 U.S. 469 (1989).

Cleveland Board of Education v. LaFleur, 414 U.S. 632 (1974).

Coley v. Commonwealth Edison Co., 703 F. Supp. 748 (1989).

Condit v. United Airlines, Inc., 12 Empl. Prac. Dec. (CCH) ¶11,195 (E.D. Va. 1976), 558 F.2d 1176 (4th Cir. 1977), *cert. denied*, 435 U.S. 934 (1978).

Craig v. Boren, 429 U.S. 190 (1976).

Diaz v. Pan American World Airways, Inc., 311 F. Supp 559 (S.D. Fla. 1970), 442 F.2d 385 (5th Cir. 1971), *cert. denied*, 404 U.S. 950 (1971).

Dillon v. S. S. Kresge Co., 192 N.W. 2d 661 (1971).

Doerr v. B. F. Goodrich Co., 22 Fair Empl. Prac. Cas. (BNA) 345 (N.D. Ohio 1979).

Dothard v. Rawlinson, 433 U.S. 321 (1977).

EEOC v. Associated Dry Goods Corp., 449 U.S. 590 (1981).

EEOC v. Container Corp. of America, 352 F. Supp. 262 (M.D. Fla. 1972).

EEOC v. Delta Air Lines, Inc., 441 F. Supp. 626 (S.D. Tex. 1977), 619 F.2d 81 (5th Cir. 1980), *cert. denied*, 465 U.S. 1101 (1984).

EEOC v. Sears, Roebuck and Co., 628 F.Supp. 1264 (N.D. Ill. 1986), *aff'd.* 839 F.2d 302 (7th Cir. 1988).

EEOC v. Service News Company, 898 F.2d 958 (4th Cir. 1990).

Fancher v. Nimmo, 549 F. Supp. 1324 (E.D. Ark. 1982).

Frontiero v. Richardson, 411 U.S. 677 (1973).

Geduldig v. Aiello, 417 U.S. 484 (1974).

General Electric Co. v. Gilbert, 429 U.S. 125 (1976).

General Electric Co. v. Hughes, 454 F.2d 730 (6th Cir. 1972).

General Telephone Co. of the Northwest, Inc. v. EEOC, 446 U.S. 318 (1980).

Goesaert v. Cleary, 335 U.S. 464 (1948).

Grant v. General Motors Corp., 743 F.Supp. 1260 (N.D. Ohio 1989), *vacated and remanded*, 908 F.2d 1303 (6th Cir. 1990).

Griggs v. Duke Power Co., 401 U.S. 424 (1971).

Griswold v. Connecticut, 381 U.S. 479 (1965).

Harper v. Thiokol Chemical Corp., 619 F.2d 489 (5th Cir. 1980).

Harriss v. Pan American World Airways, Inc., 437 F. Supp. 413 (N.D. Cal. 1977), 649 F.2d 670 (9th Cir. 1980).

Hayes v. Shelby Memorial Hospital, 546 F. Supp. 259 (N.D. Ala. 1982), 726 F.2d 1543 (11th Cir. 1984), *rehearing denied*, 732 F.2d 944 (11th Cir. 1984).

Holden v. Hardy, 169 U.S. 366 (1898).

Hughson v. St. Francis Hospital of Port Jervis, 459 N.Y.S.2d 814 (N.Y. App. Div. 1983).

International Union, United Automobile, Aerospace and Agricultural Implement Workers of America, UAW v. Johnson Controls, Inc., 680 F. Supp. 309 (E.D. Wis. 1988), aff'd, en banc, 886 F.2d 871 (7th Cir. 1989), 111 S.Ct. 1196 (1991).

Jarvis v. Providence Hospital, 444 N.W.2d 236 (Mich. Ct. App. 1989).

Johnson v. Transportation Agency, Santa Clara County, 480 U.S. 616 (1987).

Langley v. State Farm Fire and Casualty Co., 644 F.2d 1124 (5th Cir. 1981).

LeBlanc v. Southern Bell Tel. & Tel. Co., 333 F. Supp. 602 (E.D. La. 1971), aff'd, 460 F.2d 1228 (5th Cir.), cert. denied, 409 U.S. 990 (1972).

Levin v. Delta Airlines, 730 F.2d 994 (5th Cir. 1984).

Lochner v. New York, 198 U.S. 45 (1905).

McDonnell Douglas v. Green, 411 U.S. 792 (1973).

Maclennan v. American Airlines, Inc., 440 F. Supp. 466 (E.D. Va. 1977).

Meyer v. Brown and Root Construction Co., 661 F.2d 369 (5th Cir. 1981).

Michael M. v. Superior Court of Sonoma County, 450 U.S. 464 (1981).

Monaco v. United States, 661 F.2d 129 (9th Cir. 1981).

Muller v. Oregon, 208 U.S. 412 (1908).

Nashville Gas Co. v. Satty, 434 U.S. 136 (1977).

In re National Airlines, 434 F. Supp. 249 (S.D. Fla. 1977).

National Realty and Construction Co., Inc. v. OSHRC, 489 F.2d 1257 (D.C. Cir. 1973).

Newport News Shipbuilding and Dry Dock Co. v. EEOC, 462 U.S. 669 (1983).

New York City Transit Authority v. Beazer, 440 U.S. 568 (1979).

Northwest Airlines, Inc., 8 O.S.H. Cas. (BNA) 1982 (1980).

Oil, Chemical and Atomic Workers, International Union v. American Cyanamid Co., 741 F.2d 444 (D.C. Cir. 1984).

In re Olin Corporation and International Association of Machinists and Aerospace Workers, 73 Lab. Arb. (BNA) 291 (August 7, 1979).

Personnel Administrator of Massachusetts v. Feeney, 442 U.S. 256 (1979).

Phillips v. Martin Marietta Corp., 416 F.2d 1257 (5th Cir. 1969), 400 U.S. 542 (1971).

Price Waterhouse v. Hopkins, 490 U.S. 228 (1989).

Radice v. New York, 264 U.S. 292 (1923).

Reed v. Reed, 404 U.S. 71 (1971).

Richards v. Griffith Rubber Mills, 300 F. Supp. 338 (D. Ore. 1969).

Robinson v. Lorillard Corporation, 444 F.2d 791 (4th Cir. 1971).

Roe v. Wade, 410 U.S. 113 (1973).

Rosenfeld v. Southern Pacific Co., 283 F. Supp. 1219 (C.D. Ca. 1968), 444 F.2d 1219 (9th Cir. 1971).

Rostker v. Goldberg, 453 U.S. 57 (1981).

Sail'er Inn, Inc. v. Kirby, 95 Cal.Rptr. 329 (1971).

Scherr v. Woodland School Community Consolidated District no. 50, 867 F.2d 974 (7th Cir. 1988).

Secretary of Labor v. American Cyanamid Co., 9 O.S.H. Cas. (BNA) 1596 (1981).

Security National Bank v. Chloride, Inc., 602 F.Supp. 294 (D. Kansas, 1985).

Sprogis v. United Airlines, Inc., 444 F.2d 1194 (7th Cir. 1971).

In re Stauffer Chemical Co., 78 Lab. Arb. (BNA) 1276 (1982).

Sugar Cane Growers Cooperative of Florida, 4 O.S.H. Cas. (BNA) 1320 (1976).

Texas Department of Community Affairs v. Burdine, 450 U.S. 248 (1981).

United Automobile, Aerospace and Agricultural Implement Workers of America, Local 674 and General Motors Corporation GMAD-Norwood, Umpire Decision Q-6, Appeal Case Q-160, Grievance nos. 843841 and 993833, filed June 11, 1976, and September 9, 1976.

United States v. Paradise, 480 U.S. 149 (1987).

United Steelworkers of America v. Marshall, 647 F.2d 1189 (D.C. Cir. 1980), *cert. denied*, Lead Industries Association v. Donovan, 453 U.S. 913 (1981).

United Steelworkers of America v. Weber, 443 U.S. 193 (1979).

University of California Board of Regents v. Bakke, 438 U.S. 265 (1978).

Wagner v. Taylor, 836 F.2d 566 (D.C. Cir. 1987).

Washington v. Davis, 426 U.S. 229 (1976).

Weeks v. Southern Bell Telephone and Telegraph Co., 277 F. Supp. 117 (S.D. Ga. 1967), 408 F.2d 228 (5th Cir. 1969).

Wright v. Olin, 24 Fair Empl. Prac. Cas. (BNA) 1646 (W.D. N.C. 1980), 697 F.2d 1172 (4th Cir. 1982), *on remand*, 585 F. Supp. 1447 (W.D. N.C. 1984), *vacated without opinion*, 767 F.2d 915 (4th Cir. 1984).

Wygant v. Jackson Board of Education, 476 U.S. 267 (1986).

Zuniga v. Kleberg County Hospital, 78 E.E.O.C. Dec. (CCH) 4180 ¶6642 (November 14, 1974), C.A. no. 77-C-62 (S.D. Texas January 23, 1981), 692 F.2d 986 (5th Cir. 1982).

Canadian Case

General Motors of Canada Ltd. v. the International Union, United Automobile, Aerospace and Agricultural Implement Workers of America, UAW and its Local 222, Arbitration Case no. 00-6 (December 5, 1979).

British Cases

Alexander v. Home Office, [1988] IRLR 190 (CA).

Almeida v. Cabeldu, Case no. 6344/81/LS (March 16, 1982).

Automotive Products Ltd. v. Peake, [1977] IRLR 365 (CA).

Barber v. Guardian Royal Exchange Assurance Group, 262/88 [1990] IRLR 240 (ECJ).

Berrisford v. Woodard Schools (Midland Division) Ltd., [1991] IRLR 247 (EAT).

Boyd v. Franklins Solicitors, Case no. 8909/89 (August 16, 1989).

Bracebridge Engineering Limited v. Darby, [1990] IRLR 3 (EAT).

Brear v. Wright Hudson Ltd., [1977] IRLR 287.

Brown v. Stockton-on-Tees Bourough Council, [1988] IRLR 263 (HL).

Bryan v. Wolsey, Case no. 4681/89 (May 26, 1989).

Bullock v. Alice Ottley School, [1991] IRLR 324 (EAT).

Burton v. British Railways Board, 19/81 [1982] IRLR 116 (ECJ), [1983] ICR 544 (EAT).

Callan v. Majid, Case no. S/1829/89 (November 2, 1989).

Commission of the European Communities v. United Kingdom of Great Britain and Northern Ireland, 61/81, [1982] ICR 578.

Commission of the European Communities v. United Kingdom of Great Britain and Northern Ireland, 165/82, [1984] ICR 192.

CRE v. Amari Plastics Ltd., [1982] ICR 304 (CA).

Community Task Force v. Rimmer, [1986] IRLR 203 (EAT).

E. Coomes (Holdings) Ltd. v. Shields, [1978] ICR 1159 (CA).

Coyne v. Exports Credits Guarantee Department, [1981] IRLR 51.

Crilly v. Durham Area Health Authority, June 17, 1981, unreported.

Deignan v. Lambeth, Southwark and Lewisham Area Health Authority, Case no. 22152/79/D (December 21, 1979).

Del Monte Ltd. v. Mundaon, [1980] ICR 694 (EAT).

Donley v. Gallaher Limited No. 1, Case no. 66/86 (Northern Ireland) (November 6, 1987).

Drake v. Chief Adjudication Officer, 150/85, [1986] 3 All ER 65 (ECJ).

Duke v. GEC Reliance, [1988] IRLR 118 (HL).

Elegbede v. The Wellcome Foundation Ltd., [1977] IRLR 383.

Enderby v. Frenchay Health Authority, [1991] ICR 382 (EAT).

The Financial Times Ltd. v. Byrne, Case no. 701/91, (January 7, 1992) (EAT).

Foster v. British Gas PLC., 188/89, [1990] IRLR 354 (ECJ).

Garland v. British Rail Engineering Ltd., 12/81 [1982] IRLR 111 (ECJ), [1982] IRLR 257 (HL).

George v. Beecham Group, [1977] IRLR 43.

Gill and Coote v. El Vinos Co. Ltd., [1983] IRLR 206 (CA).

Gloucester Working Men's Club and Institute v. James, [1986] ICR 603 (EAT).

Greater London Council v. Farrar, [1980] ICR 266 (EAT).

Grimsby Carpet Co. v. Bedford, [1987] ICR 975 (EAT).

Hayes v. Malleable Working Men's Club and Institute, [1985] ICR 703 (EAT).

Hugh-Jones v. St. John's College, Cambridge, [1979] ICR 848 (EAT).

Hurley v. Mustoe, [1981] ICR 490 (EAT), [1983] ICR 422 (EAT).

James v. Eastleigh Borough Council, [1990] IRLR 288 (HL).

Jenkins v. Kingsgate (Clothing Productions) Ltd., 96/80, [1981] ICR 592 (ECJ), [1981] ICR 715 (EAT).

Jeremiah v. Ministry of Defence, [1979] IRLR 436 (CA).

Johnston v. The Chief Constable of the Royal Ulster Constabulary, 222/84, [1987] ICR 83 (ECJ).

Johnston v. F. L. Walker and Co., Case no. S/2584/89 (February 20, 1990).

Johnston v. Highland Regional Council, Case no. S/1480/84 (July 31, 1984).

Jordan v. Northern Ireland Electricity, Case no. 28/83 (Northern Ireland) (July 3, 1984).

Kelley v. Liverpool Maritime Terminals Ltd., [1988] IRLR 310 (CA).

Kidd v. DRG (UK) Ltd., [1985] IRLR 190 (EAT).

Lloyds Bank, Ltd. v. Worringham and Another, 69/80, [1981] ICR 558 (ECJ).

Lyttle v. The Board of Governors of St. Colmcille's Nursery School, Case no. 1649/87 (Northern Ireland) (November 17, 1988).

Macarthys Ltd. v. Smith, 129/79, [1980] ICR 672 (ECJ).

Mandla v. Dowell Lee, [1983] ICR 385 (HL).

Marshall v. Southampton and Southwest Hampshire Area Health Authority, 152/84, [1986] ICR 335 (ECJ).

Marshall v. Southampton and Southwest Hampshire Area Health Authority (no. 2), [1988] IRLR 325.

Martin v. McConkey, Case no. 1577/89 (Northern Ireland) (March 8, 1990).

Maughan v. Northeast London Magistrates Court Committee, [1985] ICR 703.

McCullough v. Geralidine and Corr, Case no. 1769/87 (Northern Ireland) (June 8, 1988).

McQuade v. Dabernig, Case no. 427/89 (Northern Ireland) (August 31, 1989).

Munday v. Standard Telephones and Cables Ltd., Case no. 28579/81/LN (February 18, 1982).

Nasse v. Science Research Council, [1979] IRLR 465 (HL).

Nelson and Another v. Tyne and Wear Passenger Transport Executive, [1978] ICR 1183 (EAT).

Newstead v. Department of Transport and H. M. Treasury, 192/85, [1988] ICR 332 (ECJ).

Noone v. Northwest Thames Regional Health Authority, [1988] IRLR 195 (CA).

Page v. Freight Hire (Tank Haulage) Ltd., Case no. 1381/80 (March 26, 1980), [1981] IRLR 13 (EAT).

Pickstone v. Freemans plc, [1988] IRLR 357 (HL).

Pinder v. Friends Provident Life Office, unreported, County Court, 1985.

Prestcold Ltd. v. Irvine, [1981] ICR 777 (CA).

In re Prestige Group plc, [1984] 1 WLR 335 (HL).

R v. CRE ex parte Cottrell and Rothon, [1980] 3 All ER 265 (QBD).

R. v. CRE ex parte Hillingdon LBC, [1982] AC 779 (HL).

Reaney v. Kanda Jean Products Ltd., [1978] IRLR 427.

Roberts v. Tate and Lyle Industries Ltd., 151/84, [1986] IRLR 150 (ECJ).

Robinson v. Tees Components, Case no. 9/129/79 (February 1, 1980).

Selvarajan v. Race Relations Board, [1976] 1 All ER 12 (CA).

Skyrail Oceanic Ltd. v. Coleman, [1981] ICR 864 (CA).

Stevenson v. The Governors of The Grammar School Stockport, Case no. 7966/89 (August 18, 1989).

Taylor v. Harry Yearsley Ltd., Case no. 25716/88 (May 22, and June 29, 1989).

Todd v. Eastern Health and Social Services Board, Case no. 1149/88 (May 2, 1990).

Turley v. Allders Department Stores Ltd., [1980] IRLR 4 (EAT).

Webb v. EMO Air Cargo (U.K.) Ltd., [1989] IRLR 124 (EAT).

Winston v. Oldham Crompton Batteries Ltd., Case no. 23237 (January 23, 1990).

Wednesbury Corp. v. Ministry of Housing (no.2), [1965] 3 All ER 571 (CA).

European Court of Justice Cases

Amministrazione delle Finanzo dello Stato v. Simmenthal s.p.A., 106/77, [1978] ECR 629.

Bilka-Kaufhaus GmbH V. Karin Weber von Hartz, 170/84, [1986] 2 CMLR 701.

Commission v. France, 312/86, [1989] 1 CMLR 408.

Commission v. Italy, 163/82, [1984] CMLR 169.

Costa v. ENEL, 6/64, [1964] ECR 585.

Defrenne v. Sabena, 43/75, [1976] ECR 455.

Dekker v. Stichting Vormingcentrum voor Jonge Volwassenen (VJV-Centrum), 177/ 88, [1991] IRLR 27.

Handels-og Kontorfunktionaerernes Forbund i Danmark (acting for Hertz) v. Dansk Arbeidsgiverforening (acting for Aldi Marked k/s), 179/88, [1991] IRLR 31.

Handels-og Kontorfunktionaerenes Forbund I Danmark v. Dansk Arbeidsgiverforening ex parte Danfoss, 109/88, [1991] CMLR 8.

Hofmann v. Barmer Ersatzkasse, 184/83, [1984] ECR 3047.

Rinner-Kuhn v. FWW Spezial-Gebawdereinigung GmbH, 171/88, [1989] IRLR 493.

Van Gend en Loos v. Nederlands Administratie der Belastingen, 26/62, [1973] ECR 1.

von Colson and Kamann v. Land Nordrhein-Westfalen, 14/83, [1984] ECR 1891.

Index

AAUW, 51

Abortion, 166, 194

Administrative Procedures Act, 284, 285

Affirmative action, 61, 67, 74, 90, 172, 176–79; EC recommendation on, 81

AFL-CIO, 44, 53

Airlines, 147, 157–62

Alison, Michael, MP, 32

American Civil Liberties Union (ACLU), 38, 183, 198, 252, 256, 306, 313, 321; *Grant*, 244; *Hayes*, 235, 238–39, 241; *Olin*, 224; *Zuniga*, 215–17

American Cyanamid. *See* Cyanamid

American Public Health Association, 256, 303

Amicus curiae, 45, 156, 172, 181, 197, 201, 208, 215, 306, 310, 314, 321, 323, 324, 325, 327, 329; EEOC, 52, 53, 54, 224, 238; EOC, 97, 98, 192; feminist groups, 273, 277; *Olin*, 224, 229; *UAW v. Johnson Controls*, 256; *Webb*, 130

Arbitration, 212, 245

Aristotle's view of equality, 68

Article 177, 103

Assimilationist approach, 68, 85, 182

ASTMS, 39, 277

AT&T, 170

Babcock, Barbara, 13, 42

Banks, Olive, 43

Barcher, Ann, 165

Bingham, Eula, 307–10, 312

Blackmun, Justice, 165, 262, 268, 269, 270, 271, 274, 330

Bona fide occupational qualification (BFOQ), 54, 143–48, 164, 307; in airline cases, 158–61; in California law, 265; and EEOC guidelines on exclusionary policies, 307; EEOC's guidelines for, 145, 161; *Grant*, 244; *Hayes*, 234, 235, 237–239; *Olin*, 224; and protective legislation, 51, 52; and state protective laws, 53; and stereotyped assumptions, 145, 146; *UAW v. Johnson Controls*, 252, 255–57, 259, 261–63, 267–71

Bordo, Susan, 11

Bork, Judge, 301–3

Brandeis, Louis, 45

Brandeis brief, 45

Brandon, Lord Justice, 123

Brennan, Judge, 297–99, 312

Brennan, Justice, 152, 168

Brewer, Justice, 46

Brightman, Lord Justice, 123

British civil service, 93, 99, 102, 174, 323

British feminism, 37, 100–102, 175–76; and EOC, 92–93, 98; and protective legislation, 322

British judiciary, 110–24, 207; appointments, 180; canons of interpretation of, 115; effect of EC law on, 123; effect of EC membership on, 78, 116; and exclusionary policies 275; and health and safety, 312; hostility toward SDA of, 118; hostility toward women of, 111; and Labour Party, 117; reluctance to interfere with business, 116; views of, 113

Broadhurst, Henry, 24

Case Index

373